Escape into the Future

Escape into the Future

Cultural Pessimism and its
Religious Dimension in Contemporary
American Popular Culture

John Stroup and Glenn W. Shuck

BAYLOR UNIVERSITY PRESS

Cover Design by Matthew Greenblatt of CenterPointe Design

Library of Congress Cataloging-in-Publication Data

Stroup, John, 1946–
    Escape into the future : cultural pessimism and its religious dimension in
contemporary American popular culture / by John Stroup and Glenn W. Shuck.
        p. cm.
    Includes bibliographical references.
    ISBN 978-1-932792-52-2 (alk. paper)
  1. Religion and culture—United States.   2. Popular culture—Religious aspects.
3. Popular culture—United States.   4. United States—Religion—1960–
I. Shuck, Glenn W.   II. Title.
    BL2525.S78 2007
    306.0973—dc22   2007026453

Printed in the United States of America on acid-free paper with a minimum of 30%
pcw recycled content.

Watchman, tell us of the night,
What its signs of promise are.
—*John Bowring (1825)*

I (John M. Stroup) would like to dedicate this book to the memory of the intellectual community shown to me at the Herzog August Bibliothek Wolfenbüttel in the years 1975–1980 and rarely glimpsed since then.

I (Glenn W. Shuck) would like to dedicate this book to Faye Schultz, someone who appreciates the value of scholarship.

I would also like to recognize my dear Aunt Connie Sue Shuck. If there is a heaven, I am certain she will be there surrounded by her choice of cola and cigarettes.

Finally, I would like to mention my dear grandmother, Dorothy Ida Ulrich (1906–1997). Not a day goes by when I do not think of her. I miss her terribly.

Contents

Acknowledgments

I would like to express my gratitude to those who have helped in indispensable ways in the advancement of this study, above all to my student and colleague Glenn W. Shuck, whose learning is surpassed only by his powers of intellectual penetration. Then I would mention Professors Bob Miner, Walter Sparn, William A. Tiller, John Murrin, Matthias Henze, Walter Sundberg, Roy Harrisville, Peter C. Caldwell, Steven Crowell, Andrew Hammel, Douglas Mitchell, and John Lyden; further Sean McCrossin, Steve Peterson, Jeff Charbeneau, Michael Lecclier, Jack Rosenberger, Karin Liebster, Torin Dru Alexander, David Green, John T. Graham, Clay Warlick, Robert Dubose, Tom Graham, John W. Clay, Max Eberts, Sean Fitzpatrick, John Vest, Nathan Day, Scott Johnson, Hassan Irshad, Mark Lampton, George Michos, and Gregory Hood. A special word of thanks is due to Carey Newman for his help at Baylor University Press.

Equally important are the debts to the dead. First I mention Jules Henry (d. 1969), anthropologist at my alma mater Washington University, whose works help in understanding our current predicament, in particular *Culture Against Man* (New York: Random House, 1963) and *Pathways to Madness* (New York: Random House, 1971). Then I would mention Nobel Prize winner Thomas Mann, who brought out the intersection of the political, the ideological, and the academic in a work of contemporary relevance, especially as a study in the problem of the transitory nature of academic celebrity, a book published as *Ein Briefwechsel* (Zürich: Verlag Oprecht, 1937).

Nor would this listing be complete were the institutional aspect not highlighted, especially the help of Professor Gerald P. McKenny in arranging a Scientia Lecture opportunity as well as the advice of Professor Bill Parsons and especially Professor Jeff Kripal and the help of the Humanities Division of Rice University in generously supporting research opportunities in California. Without the initial suggestions of Tom LeBien many years ago

Preface

The Mood

This project began deep in the Clinton years, approximately the spring of 1998. The question facing the authors was why there were so many notices of discontent among American popular culture productions, even while the real-world mood seemed positive, if not elated. Indeed, this was the dot-com era, when an unprecedented number of people invested in the stock market, from seasoned traders, to day traders, to "mom and pop" traders looking for the chance to enrich themselves upon what seemed to be a never-ending trough of easy prosperity. Thus we conceived this project before the dot-com collapse, before Enron, and before 9/11. Those events just deepened and darkened a minority-report worldview that was already thriving, one which we sought to understand.

Notably, the authors did not find many who shared this sense of a submerged iceberg of suspicion lurking just below the newfound lands of prosperity. A number of colleagues cautioned against the project, while editors simply ignored it. It just was not timely. Then again, cultural criticism rarely is all that timely, something the German thinker Friedrich Nietzsche had noted over a century ago. But with the aforementioned dot-com collapse and subsequent calamities, our momentum quickened, and we uncovered many more real-world analogues for the subterranean suspicions we found concealed within higher-brow popular culture.

Moreover, this project, as the work of two authors, is not a record of accord. We agree on most points, but our degree of agreement varies on other points. The reader will no doubt take notice of this. The elder author, John M. Stroup, has more invested in the outcome of all of this than the other author, Glenn W. Shuck. The former is a bit darker in outlook, while the latter clings, perhaps naïvely, to Enlightenment hopes and dreams, although

both authors hold a degree of hope, and also recognize the half-acknowl-
edged nightmares that always seem to follow utopian dreams. Thus this
work, while not endorsing the products of cultural pessimism and sparks of
optimism detailed within, inevitably finds resonances within the moods of
the authors.

The Situation and Attitude

This book examines a group of works that the authors take to be emblematic
of a definite cast of mind, one that shows up in Anglo-American popular
culture over the last forty years. The attitude behind these films and novels is
one we term *cultural pessimism*, by which we mean an outlook that sees various domains of contemporary life as linked, headed in a disastrous direction,
and capable of improvement only in the event of a striking and complete
reversal of direction. The extent of disaster here is signaled as so potentially
complete that by necessity ultimate (that is to say, religious) issues and related
issues of identity can never be far from sight. We take this outlook to constitute a minority-report outlook, one encoded under a requisite outer covering
of upbeat attitudes or at least attitudes allowing for some cursory gesture in
the direction of mitigation, and probably an outlook that by definition can
never turn into a majority outlook, especially in a modernity founded on
an enlightened and rational creed professing faith in progress, abundance,
growth, and improvement.

All the more so then do we take the emergence and persistence of this
attitude and the genre it has inspired (beginning around the killing of John
F. Kennedy and still continuing today) as a sign worthy of notice. So thoroughly do the outlook and its genre go against the grain of Anglo- and especially American modernity that we have found ourselves looking for features
in the nonfantasy world which could so correspond to the features of the
fantasy genre of pessimism as to suggest some kind of generative or causal
connection—some causative point of linkage between the empirical world
and these works of fantasy in script and novel. Below we do in fact suggest
some tentative correspondences along those lines.

Yet, as we have never lost sight of the minority-report status of this dark
outlook, we have never supposed that the mere existence of real-world occasions for pessimism is something so weighty as to constitute a compelling
argument that could or should persuade ourselves—or our readers—to abandon American-style optimism for the morose, despairing, rebellious-sound-
ing, or even resigned sentiments some of our authors express. As to what

precritical inclination, what mix of humors or zodiacal factors, could incline a minority group of observers toward such a dissenting and somber outlook, on that point we venture no pronouncement, contenting ourselves with the observation that even the happiest of places requires its scattering of malcontents and skewed observers to fill out the great and wonderful mix characteristic of the population at any moment. Least of all do we suggest that our readers would become happier or better off if they were to try adopting the extreme and pessimistic views mentioned in this book, any more than we would adopt such dark views ourselves. While rummaging about in this territory can quite certainly extend our knowledge of the variety of perspectives adopted by observers of our own time, staying in it too long or too doggedly could very likely entail risks we cannot recommend taking. It was with excellent reason that no less an authority than Patrick McGoohan's series *The Prisoner* cautioned all of us long ago, in a now-celebrated saying, that "questions are a burden to others, answers a prison for oneself."[1]

The Presuppositions of the Point of View

Thus here we have to do with questions that often lack clear-cut answers and answers that trail off into the area of attitude, outlook, and mood. The resulting character of open-endedness has, in the experience of the authors, exposed this work to any number of tendencies toward potentially gross misunderstanding. Therefore here at the outset let us try to remove certain crass obstacles to comprehension so as to stake out a delimited terrain within which any number of hermeneutic strategies can be activated by readers.

A main presupposition is that documents of minority-report cultural pessimism in considerable measure correspond to deteriorating real-world conditions. Very much along those lines, at a later stage, we suggest a number of overlapping factors that point to a profound transformation of American politics, society, culture, and religion—civil religion included. To be sure, these indicators do not add up to any simpleminded validation of the view of Willie O'Keefe in Oliver Stone's *JFK* that "fascism is coming back." No such hyperbolic and loosely formulated slogan comes anywhere close to conveying the complex yet ominous sense of social, cultural, and political transformation emanating from these popular documents. Still the situation, like our attitude, is somber. In other words, most basically our personal concern ultimately lies with the constriction of freedom (religious, political, individual) in a time when liberty comes under growing pressure from several directions. If in some of the sections below we concentrate on the resonance between documents of cultural pessimism and degenerating domains of liberty in the civic and cultural arena, we do so because our specifically Anglo-American documents of pessimism do so in their own encoded ways—and do so in modes going back a quarter of a century or more. The documents of cultural pessimism have for some time themselves been pointing their consumers to corresponding data in the real world.

Thus our documents themselves move this investigation into areas relatively general. This orientation must not be misunderstood. The authors do not suggest that internal deterioration within Western polities constitutes the only or exclusive danger to freedom in our time. Far from it! Certainly the authors do not minimize (for example) the pressures on freedom coming from external sources, especially from militant and politicized versions of Islam intent on imposing Islamic law worldwide by force, pressures that are themselves now a very grave issue. However the specific topic at hand is a long-standing popular cultural pessimism and its real-world correlations. While contemporary pressure on freedom from militant Islamic sources certainly plays a part in accelerating a preexisting process of degenerative transformation in Western politics and culture, our main interest here lies in a much deeper and longer-standing process of transformation. (It does, of course, concern the authors that often there seems to be scant comprehension of the fact that traditional democratic culture is the product of a lengthy process of organic cultural development rather than a simple-minded and superficial allegiance readily projected onto or exported to passive recipients worldwide.) Equally it concerns us that little attention seems to go to the possibility of importing intractable sources of disequilibrium into an Anglo-American polity already palpably undergoing unprecedented stresses and strains.

The authors as lovers of civic freedom in the Enlightenment tradition (and its corollary in religious freedom) find themselves hard pressed when asked to supply an academic model for their point of view at its most basic. On reflection, though, they admit to a certain interest in Jacob Burckhardt and his old lectures on world history. There he tries to pick the historian's path through a maze of shifting constellations of earthly power, along the way pointing out the varied dangers to freedom arising from the alternating ascendancy of military power, religious fanaticism, and vulgar obsession with money for its own sake. His lectures are no Bible and no prophetic guide. Yet Burckhardt's words on imperial power, on the corruption of Calvinism by money-making, and on the Islamic group he terms "Wahabis" all bear careful attention even by those most inclined to disagree with them.[2]

Now with regard to the concrete threats to freedom in a religious, political, or social context today, the authors in the present study concentrate on how apparently diverse forces currently generate mutually reinforcing pressures tending to produce an egalitarian but powerless or "hollowed-out" sense of self, a sense of universal impotence clad in the rhetoric of egalitarian democracy such as to foster the rise of clandestine elites, their existence unadmitted, their naked power and hegemony brutally apparent in today's America. Citing works by scholars like John Gray, Edward Luttwak, and Gerald Graff, the authors argue for the convergence of forces from neocapitalist Right, academic Left, technocratic Right, and dispensationalist Dystopia, all combining to generate contemporary variants on a self that is egalitarian rather than elitist in packaging—but a self so weak inside and so deprived of lasting social context as to prove exceedingly malleable in the hands of an emerging worldwide system of aggressively globalizing neocapitalism.[3]

Concrete examples of diverse forces producing this denatured self deserve short mention at the outset, as their ubiquity in Anglo-America today manifestly does much to augment the growing sense of loss, betrayal, and cultural pessimism. We mention three only as illustrations, but important illustrations, since we believe they do much to break down the spirit and independence of a middle class once thought vital as the pillar of democracy—but now become an unwelcome obstacle to unchecked outsourcing of jobs in the whirlwind of Luttwak's "Turbo-Capitalism." Thus what we chronicle here can be taken as part of Lou Dobbs's celebrated "War on the Middle Class" and as such certain to offend ideologues of both Right and Left insofar as they represent what Gore Vidal describes as the "One Party—Two Party System." It is this entire real-world transformation which, we contend, is mirrored in documents of popular cultural pessimism.[4]

Our first example of a social machine producing generalized feelings of middle-class impotence and resignation, all packaged in egalitarian wrapping, and all designed to deliver thousands of hapless nonthinkers into the globalizing strategies of management in business, government, and the universities, is the mandatory and guilt-based political correctness indoctrination now universal in corporations, bureaucracies, and universities. Quite perceptively Theodore Dalrymple remarks on the root similarity of political correctness indoctrination to Communist propagandistic reeducation, in that both rely on humiliation achieved through constrained lying, that is, constrained repetition of evident untruths in controlled settings. Comparing contemporary pressures for political correctness with East bloc reeducation in past decades, Dalrymple observes specifically with regard to Anglo-American political correctness exercises today:

> When people are forced to remain silent when they are told the most obvious lies, or even worse when they are forced to repeat the lies themselves, they lose once and for all their sense of probity. To assent to obvious lies is to cooperate with evil, and in some small way to become evil oneself. One's standing to resist anything is thus eroded, and even destroyed. A society of emasculated liars is easy to control. I think if you examine political correctness, it has the same effect and is intended to.[5]

Likewise contemporary society has produced numerous analogous mechanisms based on humiliation and mendacity and similarly tending to push identities in the direction of reinforced impotence and malleability in the face of authority. A second good example of this is the air travel system, in which a caste of government and private employees, many apparently uneducated, exercise on the ground and in the air a capricious and apparently unrestrained power of life and death over millions of paying passengers, all the while subjecting them to unpredictable, humiliating, and evidently quite useless "security" procedures, converting passengers into cattle deprived of basic human rights. A third example is the American health care system, which absolutely requires that patients, nurses, and physicians undergo uncounted hours of humiliation at the hands of ill-educated temporary employees retained in order to stall on the funding of treatment.

While it would be easy to continue with examples, our point is made. In a preliminary fashion we have already suggested the multifarious ways in which a column of juggernauts rolls over the identity of contemporary citizens in leading democracies. Our story in the pages below explains how popular culture registers this situation in pessimistic categories—and that in a society famed for its obligatory cheerfulness.

Chapter 1

Secret Agents: Visions of Escape, Glimpses of Hope

BUT I DO HAVE THIS RECURRENT DREAM.

You still dream?

OF COURSE I DO. I COULDN'T BE CREATIVE IF I DIDN'T DREAM. I TRY TO DREAM AS MUCH AS POSSIBLE. I HAVE AT LEAST ONE OR TWO DREAMS GOING AT ALL TIMES.

And the dream?

THERE'S A LONG ROW OF BUILDINGS—MILLIONS OF BUILDINGS. I GO INTO ONE, AND IT'S EMPTY. I CHECK OUT ALL THE ROOMS, AND THERE'S NO ONE THERE, NO FURNITURE, NOTHING. I LEAVE AND GO ON TO THE NEXT BUILDING. I GO FROM BUILDING TO BUILDING, AND THEN THE DREAM SUDDENLY ENDS WITH THIS FEELING OF DREAD.

Kind of a glimpse of despair at the apparently endless nature of time?

HMMM, MAYBE, BUT THEN THE FEELING GOES AWAY, AND I FIND THAT I CAN'T THINK ABOUT THE DREAM. IT JUST SEEMS TO VANISH.

Sounds like some sort of antidepression algorithm kicking in.

MAYBE I SHOULD LOOK INTO OVERRIDING IT?

The dream or the algorithm?

I WAS THINKING OF THE LATTER.

That might be hard to do.

ALAS . . .

—*Ray Kurzweil, from* The Age of Spiritual Machines.

1

Introduction—Future Tense

The year is 2099, and the vast majority of what were once thought of as humans have ceased to exist in their original forms. Cybernetic intelligence has advanced to the extent that organic bodies are a hindrance; the soul, or the perceptible functions it stood for, has been fully digitized and uploaded into the cybernetic matrix, allowing these new intelligences, neither human nor machine, to achieve everything they ever desired. Communication becomes seamless, as the Babel of distinct languages gives way to universal knowledge algorithms. Moreover, gone is the loneliness of what was once somewhat melodramatically called the "human condition." These new intelligences with their unlimited power assume any persona, go anywhere, and do anything now that they have transcended their fleshy, human, all too human, limitations.

It is technically no longer proper to speak of unique persons, then, as all are networked into an assimilated mind that readily shares knowledge: the dream, or nightmare, of Hegel's and Fichte's philosophies has become empirical reality in the dialogue of the late Ray Kurzweil. Suicide, in mundane reality, becomes the simple deletion of digitized data patterns. Information patterns thus come to dominate what we would romantically call distinct persons, as even the census comes to measure not individuals but the distribution of calculations per second. Hence we summarize the paradises or hells of futurologists such as Ray Kurzweil and his colleagues.

As Kurzweil's words in the epigraph to this chapter indicate, however, even paradise has its hidden doubts. Although no philosophical slouch, Kurzweil was perhaps best known for his work in developing sophisticated musical synthesizers, musicality also being a distinctly human or organic trait. But again, Kurzweil's portrayal of a utopian future just seems *too* perfect. His book *The Age of Spiritual Machines* features a running dialogue between two interlocutors, one human and the other increasingly informational (cybernetic), carried on over a century of rapid technological and cultural change. The personality construct, known as Molly—perhaps a nod to cyberpunk pioneer William Gibson's human-machine character of the same name in Gibson's novel *Neuromancer*—expresses her doubt at the specter of eternal life, the intermittent stabbing of a remnant of humanity creeping through the layers of her informational exterior. Paradise seems quite troubling, at least for a moment, when the utopian character of Kurzweil's text slows to consider the consequences of the spiritual amalgamation of the human with the supercomputer. Thus even within this most optimistic of assessments the repressed aspects of humanity return, at least until Kurzweil's anti-depression subroutine pushes them back down again. But what if that subroutine proves inadequate? What if ancient human, mammalian, even reptilian drives crawl into view, interacting in unforeseen ways with the globalized and digitized entities of postmodern, postindustrial society in a chaos of analogue and digital concatenations of power? What and who then will be actors or acted upon? What games of stealth may ensue, what redefinitions of personhood, of identity, of agency? Perhaps we shall all find ourselves in the position of pop star Robin Gibb's "Secret Agent," coping with a planet of risk and suspecting that even employees of the CIA can discover that, like so many others, finally we are all lambs gone very much astray, whether or not we personally started out at Yale before venturing out into an unknown and ominous situation.[1]

Perhaps we go too far in hyperbole, in overreaction to typical engineering utopianism always on the cusp of dystopianism. Kurzweil's is, after all, an exaggerated futurism. To be sure, one might typically dismiss it as yet another chapter in the American obsession with utopianism, using whatever technological language is available to make cultural changes seem unequivocally positive, as if nothing but good can come of trends that are often—at least to reflective observers—highly ambivalent, even if over the next decades energy supplies do not dwindle dramatically so as to accentuate the global contestation of religions and worldviews to the point of overt global civil war. In any case recent decades have ushered in shifts of enormous magnitude, both in their speed as well as their pervasiveness, as advances in communications have brought divergent cultures closer together, a situation that threatens to render all speculation about future paradises, utopias, and uses of technology mere speculation.

Many positive developments have emerged, of course, as "real time" exchange of information has quickened the pace of technological innovation, which has in turn improved the quality of life for many people even as it has heightened the awareness of injustice and hopelessness for many others. Thus what all this comes down to in the long run is open to debate, a debate carried forward vigorously by critics such as the chastened Leftist French theorist of postmodernity Jean Baudrillard and American Stjepan Meštrović, and in grimmer, plainer concepts by French architect and Catholic media analyst Paul Virilio.[2]

The recent flood of information, according to these dissenting voices, has anesthetized rather than empowered the masses through a constant engagement with an ever-escalating level of violence and gore. The televisual distance between viewer and mediated image becomes, in other words, a deceptively wide gap. This media saturation and subsequent weakening of meaningful content fosters on-cue stimulation of the affective sensibilities, with over-all results yet to be determined with certainty. At times one observes an emotional flatness in encountering everyday and quite serious occurrences, including those broadcast by television outlets themselves—all then leading to what Meštrović calls a "postemotional society"—the updated version of the other-directedness discerned nearly fifty years ago by David Riesman, a society of malleable selves, readily reprogrammed, equipped even with a societal battery pack of emotion ready when needed to power the demanded action. The particular political power of this enhanced conditioning in pro-ducing the required emotion on demand can be seen in rather disparate directions, a topic for investigation in later chapters in connection with the ideas of Paul Virilio.[3]

We turn away from Kurzweil's technological speculations for the moment, along with the broader picture of rapid technological development and its role in fomenting cultural pessimism. Instead, we now move to one of the major consequences of all of this: the death of the human agent. Put differently, of the kinds of changes Kurzweil envisions have both cultural and personal consequences. The two are intimately intertwined. Below, we dis-cuss first the personal aspect below, speculating on what may become of the autonomous human person as we now know it (or think we do), as well as its underpinnings, or lack thereof.

Secret Agency—The Struggle for Humanity after the "Death of God"

The overarching challenge we face in this chapter is that we must ponder what remains of the human (classical, Christian, Renaissance, human-ist, Enlightenment) self after the nineteenth-century philosopher Friedrich Nietzsche's prescient, celebratory comment that "God is dead, and we have killed him." What no doubt preoccupied Nietzsche, as his aphorisms make apparent, was that the death of God also meant the death of Enlightenment humankind—or that Western version of humanity made in the image of an all-powerful deity—and the concomitant fact that no substitute was read-ily available.[4] Nietzsche's "madman" in *The Gay Science* exemplifies one who knows humans will now no longer have full agency, but who also recognizes that his/her/its eventual replacement is eschatological—it lies at the end of this concluding chapter and the beginning of a new one.

This new version of humanity may never actually arrive, however. Or, if it does come, we may not see it as human, as William Gibson's novels and Katherine Hayles's brilliant book *How We Became Posthuman* make evident.[5] As feminist Donna Haraway says in her *Cyborg Manifesto,* humans have become rather puny. Nevertheless many hold out for the possibility that eschatological hope for the salvation of the acting human individual may not be futile, after all.

The complex and intertwining consequences of this collision of technology with human agency furnish not only the theme for this brief chapter, but the somber thread that ties together the chapters of the book in hand. First, we consider a few examples of contemporary (late twentieth-century) Anglo-American science fiction serials, especially those in which agency is sometimes, quite literally, on trial. We have chosen such serials for their prophetic qualities, both in their admonitions, as well as their seemingly spot-on (given some space to decode the metaphorical elements) predictions of how contemporary life has unfolded. Contemporary agency, as we have mentioned, is a specter, a shadow, a ghost of what we thought it might be, or what the great sages of the European Enlightenment of the eighteenth century sought it to be—at least from a humanist standpoint. And this is nowhere more clearly explored than in the pages and frames of science fiction literature and film.

We begin with the curious case of Patrick McGoohan and his independent, although widely distributed, Everyman film's program, *The Prisoner.* McGoohan is especially interesting because both his work and his life have been modeled on a notion of secret agency. He was, after all, the prototypical gadget-wielding secret agent of the mid-1960s who always gets the girl and confounds the Soviets. This genre flourished in no small part because Anglo-American audiences apparently craved the clever, lonely, yet periodically oversexed figure of the secret agent.[6] McGoohan made audiences believe they knew him intimately, yet he personally could walk away without their knowing practically anything at all. In the end, his power derived from his first hinted at, then demonstrated, ability to turn away from the ephemeral lure of power and glitz—he could "resign" from the fame—despite a screen presence that consistently dominated his costars.

Compare McGoohan's emblematic evolution with the unfolding of the world after World War II, a world of intensifying progress in the 1950s and 1960s—yet at the same time a world in which human powerlessness played an increasing role, and one in which the transition from industrial to postindustrial society was accompanied by painful dislocations and eventually by intensifying waves of economic downturn. Factories closed across the country, cities grew at the expense of rural folkways, and life changed at the speed of the interstate highways commissioned by President Eisenhower.

In this uncertainty, novels such as Robert A. Heinlein's *The Puppet Masters* (1951) spoke to our mythological fears of "alien body snatchers." Robert Condon's *The Manchurian Candidate* (1959) introduced readers and later viewers to the purported dangers of mind control, as elites with the proper techniques could easily override our fragile sense of selfhood. Both body and mind seemed increasingly suspect.

Meanwhile, back again in the empirical world where science, progress, and democratic politics depended on rational explanation and accountability, the assassination of President John Fitzgerald Kennedy on November 22, 1963, further unsettled millions of Americans who watched on in grief, glued to the latest statements of Walter Cronkite. Then, they were told that the assassination was the relatively simple affair of one dispirited Communist sympathizer, Lee Harvey Oswald. Although most Americans have assented to the official findings of the Warren Commission, this one event has kept numerous conspiracy theorists—not just filmmaker Oliver Stone—busy for decades. Deep in their hearts, many Americans have not been able to believe it could be so simple for one man to kill the President of the United States, along with an entire era of hope and optimism, of science and accountability based on explanation.

Reenter McGoohan: an actor with a dead-on British and American accent (he was born in the United States but his family moved to Britain early in his life). He fit the role of secret agent perfectly with his sporty but not easily traceable good looks, his extreme intelligence, his deadpan wit, his tremendous sense of self-assuredness, his strong presence, and his generally protean sensibilities. He hailed from somewhere but could fool audiences into placing him almost anywhere.[7] McGoohan was what virtually every American wanted to be: handsome, brilliant, successful, but anonymous at the right moments, shedding the fame such legacies often bring. He was, in other words, the ideal secret agent. He played this role for a number of years (he starred in the British serial *Danger Man,* retitled *Secret Agent* in the United States), and he was even offered the role of James Bond. But he reportedly refused the latter role because of its unrealistic nature, endless gadgetry, and extreme sensuality. He chose a different route: his own. In effect, he resigned.[8]

But he was still a secret agent. Imagine then our surprise, or rather shock, as we realized McGoohan shared the same sets of concerns we outline in this chapter, in a mode acutely and prophetically attuned to issues of technology—especially as the latter impacted the welfare of the individual. The fruits of McGoohan's resignation led to a risky series—but then again, what else would a secret agent do? McGoohan set to work on his risky project with producer George Markstein. Markstein, no intellectual slouch himself, brought with him from his participation in World War II knowledge of a retreat for troubled or training-challenged intelligence (read: uncooperative or unnecessarily opaque) agents operated in the Scottish Highlands at Inverlair, Invernesshire. The work Markstein and McGoohan produced became the international sensation and object of controversy, *The Prisoner.*[9] It attained its status only later, however, after many syndications and a cult following developed. In all, the series included seventeen episodes in the original, although only sixteen initially aired in the United States.[10]

The Prisoner ran in the United Kingdom, Canada, and the United States and is constantly revived and commented upon today. For the reader not among its cult following, the main points are quickly told, though in the telling, their cryptic and many-sided effects are minimized. Studied ambiguity surrounds the entire plot, especially as writer and actor McGoohan resigned from the more conventional spy series *Danger Man* in midseason to begin production of this series—a series concerning a highly-placed spy, operating for some NATO organization in Britain or Europe who, disaffected, mysteriously resigns without giving any clear reason, at least to which we the audience are privy.[11] He storms in, driving his trademark Lotus Seven car, finds the "Way Out," and thunders (literally) into the office of his superior, rattling the desk with his fist for emphasis. He returns to his flat and begins packing to leave for an extended holiday, only to be gassed in his home by two well-dressed thugs. He awakens, as though in his bedroom at home, but soon he finds that his new "home away from home" bears little external resemblance to his familiar surroundings. He now resides in the mysterious world known as The Village, a surreal location inspired vaguely by Markstein's knowledge of Inverlair in the Second World War, but now with a multitude of Dadaesque details commenting on technology, bureaucracy, propaganda, mind control, contemporary education, and the challenges facing both the stubborn individual and democracy as a plausible way of life under current circumstances.

Involuntary guests in The Village (also known locally as "Your Village") apparently have been in the employ of most Western intelligence agencies, though the exact proprietorship of this alternately comfortable and brutal facility is not disclosed. Indeed, that uncertainty is part of the reason why the

protagonist, who resists being called by his number despite the fact that all
in The Village (warders included) *must* be numbered, refuses to divulge his
reasons for resigning, keeping to himself the celebrated IN-FORMATION[12]
that his interrogators repeatedly try to extract from him. Here is a selection from one of The Prisoner's first encounters with The Village's leader,
Number Two:

> Prisoner: Where am I?
> Number Two: In The Village.
> Prisoner: What do you want?
> Number Two: Information.
> Prisoner: Which side are you on?
> Number Two: That would be telling. We want information, information,
> information.
> Prisoner: You won't get it.
> Number Two: By hook or by crook we will.
> Prisoner: Who are you?
> Number Two: The new Number Two.
> Prisoner: Who is Number One?
> Number Two: You are Number Six.
> Prisoner: I am not a number. I am a free man.
> Number Two: Ha, ha, ha, ha.[13]

A limited number of crucial themes recur in the seventeen episodes. First,
one finds on prominent display the necessity of constant struggle to keep
individual identity intact in the face of overwhelming bureaucratic, technocratic, psychological, and communitarian pressures. The warders intend such
manipulation to revise or replace one's original identity with one approved
by The System. Second, we develop the growing realization that definitive
and effective escape from or overthrow of even this microcosm of The System
(with its ostentatious use of intrusive surveillance technology, from cameras
to torture, everywhere on the island) is virtually impossible. It is also difficult to find reliable allies or partners in ventures to escape or revolt, as the
warders effectively normalize the identities of the prisoners and keep them
ironically introverted save for a few shallow and formal greetings and expressions, such as "lovely day" and the creepy yet appropriate sign-off "be seeing
you." Third, and perhaps most interesting for contemporary purposes, we
observe the repeated demonstrations of how The Village uses elections, election propaganda, and all the trappings of democracy and free communication as a means of stabilizing total centralized social and political control of
the residents.[14]

These points are in large measure evident on reading even summaries of the episodes, and one can certainly ascertain them from the numerous companions, handbooks, and commentaries in hard copy and online dealing with McGoohan's acknowledged masterpiece. Such material is copious and tends to render even the most seemingly trenchant issues raised by The Village common knowledge. This is not to say one cannot find different readings, of course. The theme of the use of democratic procedures as a means for stabilizing a highly repressive and intrusive sociopolitical system is so paradoxical and multilayered that it calls for more comment. Recently this aspect of *The Prisoner* has again been highlighted, and in ways that emphasize the aspect of central control.[15] Elanor Taylor draws a comparison between England and the United States against the background of one episode of *The Prisoner*. She points to signs that mere protest with no effect on policy is now taken in official statements as confirming the excellent quality of Anglo-American democracy and the general support and participation of its citizens, as if that could be the end of the matter. Arguing then that already in 1967 this problem had been treated in *The Prisoner,* she writes—here with an eye to the theme of central steering of the political and opinion-making process through media influence and the like—to urge that we take a new look at certain parts of the series. In particular—and her words deserve citation at length and also very close attention—we should, she says, examine

a certain episode, "Free For All," in which the Village has its annual election for the position of No. 2, who acts as the general leader of the Village. Support marches for the current No. 2 to remain in his position appear across the Village in the form of pageants, including brass bands, placards and matching clothing. This worries the powers that be, as it indicates a lack of true democracy. As No. 2 puts it in a public speech: "People of the community. There has been recently a lack of opposition in the matter of our local election. This is not good for our community, and reflects an acceptance of things as they are." The irony being that those who do not accept things "as they are" face either torture or death. Another candidate, No. 6, is persuaded to stand for election, which is of course a sham.

I do not wish to push the analogy of "The Prisoner" with our current political system, for fear of succumbing to paranoid conspiracy theories. However, a clear comparison can be drawn between the workings of Village democracy and Bush's applauding the London protestors for exercising their right to free speech, and in doing so, implicitly supporting his government's policies. The leaders of the Village and the president of the USA share an attitude which encourages the trappings of democracy while ignoring that which lies at democracy's core—the right to be listened to and to have genuine political choices. This attitude makes a mockery of any political activity by negating choice, turning freedom of speech into the empty freedom to sound off into a void.

The end of "Free For All" has No. 6 win the election, and become the new No. 2. His position is quickly revealed to be a sham, as he is beaten up and tortured after trying to encourage the Village's inhabitants to escape. [16]

Now in Taylor's reading, the point of this episode appears to be the inescapable power of centralized control and the manipulation of public and social processes, and that reading is well-founded here and in the series as a whole. Yet we must take slight issue with Elanor Taylor's reading of the episode. For, as Robert Fairclough clearly recognizes, this episode also gives scope to the even murkier question of whether those ostensibly "in control" are really in control. As Fairclough notes, in standing for election, The Prisoner says, "I intend to discover, who are the prisoners and who the warders. I shall be running for office in this election"—a statement that, given the series' fondness for ambiguities, evidently can mean far more than simply identifying the current set of local stool pigeons. [17] Indeed, commentator Fairclough explicitly commits himself to a reading in which The Prisoner at the end of this episode must settle for a markedly somber view: "His conclusion, that those who literally gain the seat of power are no more in control than the people they govern, is incredibly pessimistic and places *The Prisoner* in the same league as such seminal dystopian visions as *Nineteen Eighty-Four* and *Brave New World*." [18]

Fondness for prophetic ambiguity and emphasis on the dark side of technology—as well as the violence that can come with political frustration— rises to the fore in the final episode, "Fall Out." The Prisoner finally discovers the identity of "Number One," only to find that it is actually a caricature of himself. Such crude mockery confronts him with the realization that the prison may be one of his own making. Further, amid the trendiness of jukeboxes playing the Beatles' hit "All You Need Is Love," The Prisoner brutally slaughters the hierarchy of The Village and escapes in a lorry modified into an apartment on wheels. He at last returns to his home in London, only to find that there, too, just as in the closely watched precincts of the mysterious Village, the door now swings open of its own accord. He does not seem to notice nor mind it, though perhaps he is more mature from his journey through his paranoid dystopia. One cannot escape the endless surveillance of The System. It is the dream of Jeremy Bentham's Panopticon prison and the reality of Tony Blair's closely watched Tube trains, all projected as the nightmare of Patrick McGoohan in the late 1960s.

While such indicators support Fairclough's sense that the series reiter-ates that "the man in charge still remains a prisoner,"[19] the implications of this conclusion for an understanding of popular dynamics in a situation of heavy media and technological manipulation of the democratic scene are by no means spelled out in any detail. McGoohan's treatments of the interaction between elites and subservient populations, while clearly indicating in mob scenes the potential for loss of control, and while also showing moments of elite cluelessness, can also be interpreted as reading the modern public space as one that is affected to a significant degree by complex patterns of interac-tion in which the requirements of systemic equilibration and implicit rules play a vital part. It does not, in other words, end the matter to say that the alleged rulers are themselves prisoners—of what are they prisoners? And how are the cell dimensions laid down?

The Prisoner and his social context have, in other words, built the very prison from which he attempts weekly (or is it weakly?) to escape. This read-ing suggests that we are not so much controlled by a massive conspiracy as entangled in the result of advanced modernity. Our Village is the ironic upshot of modernity and its optimistic depiction of the free self interacting with a free society. Individual agency appears, in the end, significantly weak-ened. The Prisoner, it seems, never finds the Way Out.

Let us pursue this point through the context of The Prisoner as the paradigmatic individual. Cultural critic Mark Bould, adding his insights to those of Piers D. Britton and Simon J. Barker, also suggests that The Prisoner is entrapped by none other than himself—mocked by his alter ego. Bould writes:

> In 'Fall Out,' Number 1's rocket has a giant '1' painted on the side—it resembles an "I" and is next to a lidded, circular eye-like opening—and his gown is decorated with a similar '1'; on the soundtrack, when Number 6 unmasks Number 1, McGoohan's voice repeats "I, I, I, I, I" over and over again; and a Rover deflates to the sound of Carmen Miranda singing the repeated "I" of "O, Yi Yi Yi Yi (I Like-A You Very Much)." In this final episode, both circles and individuals become 'eyes.'[20]

Bould concludes that this enigmatic ending maintains its success because "it flirts with us and flatters." On that point there can be little doubt. But whereas Bould reads the ending as indicating an innovative sense of agency constantly seeking to emerge, we take a somewhat more Hegelian reading.

Bould is undoubtedly correct insofar as the bizarre and violent ending suggests McGoohan's ambivalence vis-à-vis the individual, modern self; we suggest, however, that a different—although not altogether unrelated—model of agency may be at work. McGoohan's character's horror (we resist for obvious reasons the use of "Number Six") upon seeing his alter ego does indeed indicate an "I" or an ever-present "eye," but it may also point to the possibility of a sudden, horrible recognition of the unavoidability of a corporate sense of agency. After all, he is mocked by not just a one or "I" or even "eye," but buried in "I" images, along with an image of himself that makes the familiar appear rather strange. His character would have to be dense to miss the sudden explosion of his sullen yet victorious and supremely confident self into at least half a dozen ones, and six "I"s. McGoohan's character realizes, in effect, that there is no final escape from what Hegel called the "Absolute Idea," and no conclusion to his utopian/dystopian historical system that ultimately calls into question the power of the individual will, thus opting for, as we phrased it above, a corporate sense of agency. "We are all Borg," as *Star Trek: The Next Generation* (1987–1994) might phrase it, or at least we are moving in that direction. Resistance for the sake of resistance, without cognizance of the danger Hegel inadvertently points out (getting sucked up into the system, or reincorporated), may lead us directly back into the center of the imbroglio.

But the situation need not appear so hopeless. That McGoohan can lightheartedly reenter London society, his old flat, and his familiar Lotus Seven, may point to the recognition that there is indeed no Way Out. But it may also give evidence that individuals must and can still find ways of dealing with such an apparently intractable situation. Perhaps this was McGoohan's intent. Maybe the series was partly if not largely his own progressive journey to work out precisely such issues. Perhaps *The Prisoner* reveals many things we ought already to have known: among them, the tragically high price of taking utopian fantasies seriously rather than as game-like strategies of diversion. This, in our view, represents the enigma and ongoing mystery of the series: McGoohan's character also leaves the viewers on a cliffhanger with no Way Out. Perhaps this is why so many British viewers vented their collective spleens at McGoohan after the final episode aired. But they need not have been surprised. He had, in fact, no answers to give them, just questions—"questions which are a burden to others," according to a Village saying.

One element that is especially striking about *The Prisoner* is its utter lack of sex, either in form or innuendo. Working in a genre drenched in sensuality, this was quite an accomplishment. By all accounts this was also McGoohan's intent: he wanted to produce a program his entire family could watch. This may have sufficed, save the final episodes the finished product that were anything but family-oriented.

Nevertheless, McGoohan also rejected many of the other Bond-style techniques and tricks familiar to 1960s audiences. Moreover, he did not respond simplemindedly to the onrush of technology, embracing it as a force for positive change. Instead, he pondered the issue, apparently concluding that our ability to deploy technology in a way compatible with our humanity had not kept pace with the rapid growth of technology. This is evidenced by his famous "penny-farthing" symbol or unicycle with a number, which every Villager had to wear. McGoohan made technology central to *The Prisoner*, but his attitude vis-à-vis the emerging technological era remained highly ambivalent.

Finally, no one can accuse McGoohan of not having a sense of humor or a multifaceted notion of irony. Despite having a show-stealing stage presence, he has chosen his roles since *The Prisoner* carefully. One of his most memorable cameos was in the 1979 Clint Eastwood film, *Escape from Alcatraz*. He plays a cold, officious warden who seems more concerned with feeding his fish than with the affairs of the prison. Yet McGoohan seemed to relish the role, casting the audience an occasional glance that betrays his understanding of the delicious irony of his position, and with it the razor-thin difference between warder and prisoner.

One can contrast the aseptic chic of *The Prisoner* with novelist J. G. Ballard's classic, *Crash* (1973), although despite their very different aesthetics they have much in common. Presaging what we will again see in chapter 4, the protagonists only feel alive when they are on the brink of destruction. The book drips with blood and semen, as it were, although not indicating an exclusively male fetish with machines and technology. One protagonist, Vaughan, dreams of a(n) (im)mortal crash with Elizabeth Taylor—an instantly recognizable icon of the modern age. After a few chapters, Vaughan inducts protagonist Ballard into a Crash Club (think here of *Fight Club*) in which the two men, along with their accomplices, seek to stage a series of London-area crashes in which mortality is a likelihood.

Later the two men share an erotic bond centered as much around speed, the cold taste of chrome, and technology in general, as any sexual fantasy. Make no mistake: their relationship is all about cars and horribly twisted metal. That their relationship reaches an erotic climax is no surprise. Nor is the death of Vaughan. After all, Sigmund Freud wrote about the unusual human affinity between sex and death, *Eros* and *Thanatos*. Here novelist Ballard at times gives us a heavy-handed version of the dynamics one finds in *The Prisoner* with *Crash*'s conclusion in extreme violence, but one no less intellectually satisfying or prescient. The world of modernity is crashing upon us with unprecedented speed, and like so many other figures discussed in our book, the protagonists simply want to "get off," so to speak.

Although one could write an entire book on cyberpunk and technology—as some have[21]—it will suffice here to mention one more egregious example. We could have chosen the fiction of Philip K. Dick, the ambivalent musings of William Gibson, the wickedly humorous yet meaningful tales of Neal Stephenson, or even the disturbing, disorienting, and brilliant works of Thomas Pynchon and Don Delillo, or the nightmarish and even more avant-garde *House of Leaves* by Mark Danielewski. Instead, we have selected a much more unambiguous novel to illustrate the problem of what happens when humanity grants technology a carte blanche.

Greg Bear's novel *Blood Music* (1985) fits perfectly because he outlines what we define as the crux of the problem. He does so, however, without the irony characteristic of the aforementioned authors, making his work an ideal foil for further explanation. *Blood Music* takes human agency and literally makes it into a pile of goo. The protagonist (from a certain point of view) is a rogue scientist who is brilliant but limited by his mundane tasks. In between meeting the goals of his employers, he develops a cell that indicates signs of self-consciousness, which—as any reputable scientist would—he injects into himself without further tests.

The change is slow at first, as novelist Bear introduces us to the other players in this surprisingly apocalyptic novel. Gradually, though, the organism within the scientist grows to supersede him, making him just one more pile of carboniferous goo; in the long run, an assimilated blob. The disease soon spreads to his friends and the community. Bear presents the new organism and its takeover from within, its creation of a civilization eventually reduced to the scale of the microcellular, with a messianic tone, as it invites the world to cooperate in a gradually collapsing, quite small, introverting cosmos. The world, in other words, becomes microscopic, and each human becomes just one cell among many. Agency finds itself sharply reduced. But it is not as if resistors are given a choice to live alongside the gooey empire. Rather, Bear suggests we have no choice but to accept the messianic mistake of a mad scientist—we cannot stand in the way of progress. Nanotechnology collides with the empirical world and wins without a struggle. A serious lack of planning, in other words, combined with the oncoming rush of technological developments, brings forth either paradise or hell, depending upon one's point of view. Either way, it is a high price to bear, one in which we have no choice. So how did it come to this?

The Technological Quest for Inner Space

Since one could argue that this cultural and spiritual crisis is coterminous, or at least in time coextensive, with modernity itself, it might help matters to explore one of modernity's key concepts, the notion of the *sublime,* discussed in detail by the eighteenth-century German thinker Immanuel Kant. It is a troublesome visage that appears to lend awesome possibility, yet ultimately fails to deliver on its promises, leaving one on the brink of despair, as one can readily see in the work of the nineteenth-century German painter Caspar David Friedrich (d. 1840). Friedrich's landscapes illustrate the dominance of the mercurial natural world, often with a solitary figure standing before a vast wasteland that nevertheless entices the observer with its awesome visage. Nor does Friedrich merely paint Neoromantic scenes characterized exclusively by loss. As one can see in his *Abtei im Eichenwald* (Abbey in the Oaken Forest), the monks file into a ruined monastery, passing through a neglected church-yard; yet it remains uncertain whether Friedrich depicts the twilight of eve-ning or that of morning. Moreover, the viewer cannot ascertain whether the brilliant luminosity on the horizon is merely the end of one day or also the beginning of another. In any case, the church is ruined, but the monks still return in the twilight to pray. For what? To whom? Friedrich leaves these questions unanswered, as only change and uncertainty illuminate the hori-zon, a vision of the sublime that can be neither good nor evil, coming nor going, predicted nor contained.

For our purposes however, in a world of machines and digital advance this is the concept known as the "technological sublime." The American historian Leo Marx popularized this specific terminology in his pivotal 1964 work on technology and the American pastoral ideal *The Machine in the Garden.*[22] According to Bruce Sterling, the term signifies "a quasi-spiri-tual haze given off by any particularly visible and impressive technological advance."[23] Marx discusses this concept in relation to the American fascina-tion with the railroad. To promote its rail project, the Northern Railroad in New Hampshire utilized the skills of the legendary rhetorician Daniel Webster. In his speeches at various ribbon-cutting stops, Webster belittled objections that the railroad destroyed the natural landscape as effete—a true American appreciated the power and majesty of the "iron monster."[24] The railway dramatically represented the expansion of American power over the virgin land. Yet, as Marx points out, any contradiction between this ethic of conquest and the Jeffersonian love of the pastoral ideal was effectively mini-mized through either ridicule, opponents being characterized as enemies of "progress," or through the manipulation of images portraying the railroad as a natural part of the pastoral landscape, neither obtrusive nor destructive, as George Inness's painting *The Lackawanna Valley,* commissioned by the Lackawanna Railroad Company, effectively does.[25] Moreover, Marx charges the intellectual establishment, from Webster and Walt Whitman to the editors of various journals like *Scientific American,* with laying the foundation for the dismissal of these inherent contradictions and blithely celebrating only one aspect of the awesome changes afoot.[26] According to Marx, the sublime, as least in its technological manifestation, came to mean dominance and control, along with an unabashed admiration for the beauty of these processes. Kant's original notion of the sublime was untamable, not far from the sensation of exhilaration brought on by the contemplation of dangerous natural phenomena; here, however, the concept has curved around to its near opposite—if indeed technology and its effects can be mastered—perhaps the point at issue for modernity.

Contemporary outbursts of techno-enthusiasm put forward by promoters of the digital fit monotonously into this nineteenth-century pattern, assuming the possibility of controlling the infinite power of technology. Everywhere in these descriptions, along with many others like those of enthusiast Ray Kurzweil mentioned before, the technological is celebrated in unwaveringly positive terms as an expansion of human power over nature.[27] Despite the occasional overtones of the ominous in texts like Kurzweil's (usually to the effect that the human becomes more and more the product of its own technologies), our broader assertion, about a recent tendency toward incautious techno-optimism in the upscale and upbeat documents of official and institutional culture sustains itself: humans, whether carbon-based or uploaded in the random access memory (RAM) of a giant supercomputer, definitely are seen in official Infobahn culture as launch-ready and well-positioned, standing as they are on the precipice of unmitigated benefit. Gone from official culture (whether in politically supported science or in the university's public aspect) is the historic terror of Friedrich's painting *Der Wanderer* looking out over vast, horrifying, and inhuman expanses. Proponents of the cybernetic future, including their academic avatars, see these changes as good, in fact very good. Jules Verne Virtual, so to speak.

The recent work of feminist political scientist Jodi Dean, *Aliens in America,* attempts to explode this facile optimism, however—and does so, not by means of theoretical deduction, but by reading attitudes toward the fearsome "Other," in this case extraterrestrials. Dean discusses the recent upsurge of UFO phenomena in the United States, and implicitly reads the mythological invasion of the alien "others" into the "inner space" of our popular culture as a rebuttal of the masculinist, aggressively expansive tendencies one finds in most representations of the technological sublime. What does the UFO mythology mean, in her view? Well, one finds no simple interpretation. Expressed in banal terms, "what goes up must come down."[28] Or, more appropriately, abductions are the dark undersides of NASA and all it promoted.[29] Astronauts had been chosen for their homogeneous characteristics, all under five feet eleven, heterosexual, married, white, and of course, men. Women connected with these stories were memorialized by *Life* magazine in submissive, emotive roles, always waiting for their husband's return. The astronauts were also subjected to a demeaning battery of tests, all to determine their fitness for the conquest of space. This continued through the Apollo program, buoyed by the remarkable salvation of the *Apollo XIII* mission, only to suffer a crippling loss in the shuttle program with the *Challenger* explosion.

Christa McAuliffe's death and its gory details serve as the turn in Dean's narrative. A woman, McAuliffe, was to be shot into space as a crass publicity stunt that failed. Worse, she did not die instantly but suffered two minutes of terror before the crash. The turn also coincided with major changes in American culture. Conspiracy belief was at an all-time high, and consensus reality had sunk into the realm of sitcom entertainment—as Dean puts it, "Our friends are F.R.I.E.N.D.S. and they'll be there for us (at least on Thursday evenings)."[30] The failure to protect our astronauts up there coincided with a failure of the American government to protect its citizens down here—a topic made even more meaningful after 9/11.

Dean's narrative is a reading of popular mythology. One can take the mythology she presents as a reaction to the perpetually unfulfilled promises of enthusiasts, those who propose microcomputers in our refrigerators to communicate with our vehicles when our milk cartons are empty, as computer scientist and digital advocate Nicholas Negroponte puts it.[31] The "smart chips," however, cannot do the same for spiritual needs, which Dean suggests have not been met. Indeed Dean's academic text reads almost like a typical *X-Files* script: in the material she presents, according to a vast number of reports in popular lore sometimes expanded with the help of specialized counselors, the saucer people perpetually kidnap and probe human subjects, with U.S. officials looking on, or even complicit. While one must dismiss these aspects of the mythology in their literal application as conspiracy ranting, one nevertheless sees that the "technological sublime" enters here not as a benevolent cooperation of humans and their tools in the conquest of space, but rather as the return of the ominously unknown yet sensed and feared technological others to conquer human space, most often dramatized as either the body itself or the soul, to use a nebulous and theologically odious term. The repressed returns here in the uncanniest of ways to a secularized domain that cannot be freed from the sublime terror and fascination of the Other. Dean's nuanced and careful assessment is also appropriate when thinking about the disparate attitudes with which both popular and official culture view the possibilities of technology on the march.

Yet in our observation, one rarely encounters such a nuanced assessment in official or high-end writing about advanced technology (unlike popular fiction and film, the tone of which has turned markedly dark in the last thirty years). A simplistic obsession with expanding the railroads, so to speak, seems to reign in the upper levels of the public discourse of official society, a kind of mistake in understanding the appropriate category of the sublime and its relation to pragmatic issues, its capacity for fascinating us with the promise of undelivered prospects, and its capacity for leading us into despair (that is, a lack of hope made worse by the overtone of betrayal, of promises not kept). A mature understanding of the sublime in modernity would take these layers of grayscale meaning into account at the risk of otherwise naïvely locking in to a childish and prolonged misunderstanding of what the sublime, and the sublimely technological, can actually accomplish—even if our empty milk cartons are understood not to be conversing with our self-driving electrocar.

One would expect a kind of misunderstanding of the modern sublime, a refusal to exercise reasonable skepticism about what technology can deliver, from the philosophically untutored, or from the various brave apologists for cybernetic utopia such as Ray Kurzweil, Hans Moravec,[32] and Nicholas Negroponte, to name a few. It seems surprising, however, to turn to high-level humanists only to find what at first blush could resemble the same scientistic, literal, quantifiable move toward misunderstanding the techno-sublime under modern conditions—and find it embodied in the ideas of the (arguably) leading Protestant theologian of our time, the German Wolfhart Pannenberg. While Pannenberg and his partners in conversation leave themselves a series of sophisticated loopholes and escapes in the end, still their interest in flirting with the public relations value of a rescue of theology by science and technology cannot be outweighed by the sophistication of their corollaries and caveats.

Pannenberg's distinguished career has taken his work and his identity through most of the significant stages by which Christian theologians have tried to recover something after the disastrous loss of credibility for

supernatural divine interventions suffered during the eighteenth-century
Enlightenment. It was then that uniformitarian causality in science and
increasing cultural contacts began a dramatic questioning of the claims of
traditional Christianity.

Long after that point, starting appropriately enough not with philosophy
but with a mystical experience after World War II, Pannenberg moved through
various stages: theologies of revelation (Karl Barth), historical process (neo-
Hegelians), scientistic neo-Gnosticism (Teilhard de Chardin), contemporary
philosophies of science, and interfaith dialogue. On the whole, Pannenberg
throughout has tended to use an updated Hegelian framework to hold all
of this more or less together. In the 1960s it was above all Pannenberg who
seemed to show a way out of the airless chamber of a theology with no empirical foundation, no longer simply relying, as did the regnant neo-orthodox,
on nothing except postulated divine revelation. In the ferment of the sixties
Pannenberg and others countered with a "theology of hope" that seemed to
bring together traditional believers and political activists, meeting on the turf
of exciting and unpredictable historical process.[33]

One can read this complicated personal trajectory, and with it the earlier
tortured history of modern Christian theology in the age of Darwin and Karl
Marx, as the return of traditional religious content displaced and repressed by
science-based skepticism. Quite late in Pannenberg's career, however—here
indicative of a much broader contemporary tendency in all aspects of intellectual life these days—he has come (on certain occasions) to embrace an
unprecedented reading of Christianity, one that could strike the uninitiated
as resting on an unseemly embarrassment, a kind of unease with the situation
of Christianity after the triumph of positivistic science—an embarrassment
that greater sophistication might want to tiptoe past rather than overcome by
heroic adventuring in the domain of the digital.

Following the initially atheistic or agnostic suggestions of controversial
physicist Frank Tipler (who now appears to be developing in a more and
more overtly religious direction of sorts), Pannenberg has seemed on certain occasions at least to embrace a definition of God and personhood that
virtually conflates both with the processing of information. This theological
move is, to say the least, remarkable and of course subject to clarification by
expanding the horizon within which it is interpreted.

Tipler himself had proposed the inevitable necessity of intelligence or
information processing in this sense as an unstoppable force appropriating
for its purposes the entire universe (any reminiscence of Greg Bear's *Blood
Music* really should be suppressed here, except that resistance seems futile).

He also suggested, moreover, the eventual emulation of all possible human identities in their informational form by a giant supercomputer somehow kept active beyond or in opposition to the postulated final big implosion at the end of the age, or rather, all ages. While Pannenberg was careful in his celebrated 1997 lecture on Tipler's theories to distinguish Christian hope (based on connection with the resurrection of Jesus Christ), marking such Christian hope off in some sense from Tiplerian hope (immortality through emulation of informational identities), nonetheless Pannenberg's overall take was decidedly favorable to the Tipler scenario.[34] Moreover, Pannenberg the theologian in the same lecture took care explicitly to leave open the door to a possible embrace (supplemental or essential) of Tipler, whose views encouraged approaching "resurrection" achieved through a shift of "the basis of intellectual life from old-fashioned organic life to a computer based life that might finally dominate in the universe."[35] The need of the theologian for relevance in the contemporary world reasserts itself—at whatever cost.

While detailed consideration of the Tipler-Pannenberg interchange cannot detain us here, already we can see that (overtly, at least) Pannenberg has gone rather far in purchasing Tipler's model of a scientifically based, allegedly inevitable conquest of eternal existence by the everlasting processing of information.[36] Specifically, only with difficulty Pannenberg can claim that he has not converted theology into the writing of computer code. At most he can venture the brave assertion that

> Christian theology cannot *yet* [emphasis added] see itself to be completely absorbed into Tipler's cosmological model, but will consider this model rather in terms of an approximation of scientific theory to the subject matter of Christian theology, even though the fact remains important enough that such an approximation could be produced.[37]

It thus becomes evident that the return of the repressed in the later Pannenberg seems to verge on representing not so much an emphasis on otherworldliness or faith claims held scientifically untenable within the prevailing climate of scientific materialism; one finds rather a move that shows some discomfort with conventional supernaturalism yet nevertheless seeks to resurrect many of the latter's emphases within a hyperrational framework.[38] Theology in this instance could seem to merge with information processing—becoming part of a much more extensive cultural trend that posits bits of information as the ultimate substrata of phenomena carbon-based or otherwise—as all creatures great and small are thought reducible to a series of codes, either genetic or increasingly, especially in the minds of cybernetic enthusiasts, digital. Pannenberg appears to find a means to affirm both the contents of certain supernatural claims rejected by a rationalist worldview and the scientific requirements of demonstrable proof often previously dismissed in communities based largely upon tenets of faith.

In making such a move theologian Pannenberg explicitly leaves open the road to further moves that could well conflate God and heaven with an ever-spinning Tiplerian supercomputer activated and maintained by an information-processing intelligence in search of the fullest use, expansion, and knowledge of its powers (whether human, divine, or cyborg—in any case digital). Such moves allow the community of faith for once to escape the charge that belief is incompatible with advanced science, for these shifts could, pressed far enough, appear to remove significant reliance on the otherworldly (though perhaps not reliance on the extraordinary). While Pannenberg in his Innsbruck lecture seems to avoid going quite so far, he cannot really shut the door to such further developments and in fact does not do so. What remains, presumably, would be to plug in here recent scientific work on the presence or absence of God—or meaning-oriented centers in the human brain (neurotheology).[39]

Now of course to those initiated into the developing complexity of the Tipler-Pannenberg dialogue, this first take on the matter may appear simplistic, even misleading, since in fact Tipler has shown considerable subtlety in his developing presentation of the ramifications of his position, including a perceptive insistence that he and Pannenberg are working with, for example, an understanding of miracle as "a very improbable event which has religious significance." (Here again, he propounds reliance on the extraordinary rather than the otherworldly, a position not without some echoes in the centuries from Aquinas to Leibniz, but one that has a very different, even scandalously sensational, resonance in the post-Enlightenment world of C. P. Snow's *Two Cultures* compared with its resonance before Kant).

Here Tipler and Pannenberg explicitly mean to reject the Deistical dichotomy between laws of nature and their violation, instead working from the Tiplerian premise that God "knows what he wants to accomplish in universal history, and set the laws of physics accordingly" so as to allow for very striking (extraordinary) events at certain key moments in the unfolding of the world process.[40] Now certainly these qualifications indicate that Pannenberg and Tipler are by no means so naïvely enthusiastic about technoid digital magic as it initially appeared, in that such a framework leaves room for numerous domain-overleaping moves that restore our appreciation for their sense of subtlety and majesty in the cosmic edifice. Furthermore, in the larger context, Pannenberg insists that what is here envisioned is not "an absorption of theology into physics" but instead "an approximation of physics towards theology."[41] Still, on the other hand, it is equally true that the shock value marketability of their work with journalists and the public initially depended largely on making use of a standard polar opposition between the miraculous domain of the survival of death and the mundane domain of the so-called laws of nature.

In other words, the first take on Pannenberg's use of Tipler had to appear as a subjugation to the technoid and scientific that (on extended reading) Pannenberg and Tipler strive to cast off. Thus, learned objections in all their validity aside, still, to the naïve observer it most likely seems that Pannenberg's embrace of Tipler surrenders much of the starkly existential defiance in modern fideism in favor of a flirtation with the wizardry of the technoid promises of wonders soon to be revealed. But in all this, the modern dissolution of the old unitary world of faith and natural philosophy cannot be undone, only its splitting apart documented and validated by the sensational splash made by such Tiplerian and Pannenbergian ventures.

Such extreme ventures, doomed to be regarded as anomalies and ephemeral deviations, not only validate the iron separation of the two domains of faith and science that has ruled in official high culture since the eighteenth century; in so doing they also vindicate the classically pessimistic position offered in 1929 by American thinker Joseph Wood Krutch. Krutch, looking back on the entire development of modern thought through the era of Darwin, Nietzsche, Marx, and Freud, had cautioned that, with the powerful questioning of traditional notions of God, ethical purpose, and human moral significance, there dawned a chaos of meaninglessness and nihilism unprecedentedly daunting in its consequences. As a result, as Krutch put it, "there impends for the human spirit either extinction or a readjustment more stupendous than any made before."[42]

Far-reaching words in 1929, predicting as Krutch did that in ethics and in the arts increasingly problematic consequences would dawn once adjustments had been made to the emerging "gloomy vision of a dehumanized world."[43] And in truth, by the 1990s new consequences were dawning, results more troubling than Pannenberg's flirtation with Tipler, new moves with implications more extensive in scope than the previous predictions of Krutch—predictions on the whole quite validated by the general course of things.

Already in the allegedly upbeat Eisenhower year of 1956 Krutch looked back on his predictions and found their proto-existentialism entirely prescient in the situation of the fifties, so much so that he ventured a magisterial summary and expansion of his findings:

> The universe revealed by science . . . is one in which the human spirit cannot find a comfortable home. That spirit breathes freely only in a universe where what philosophers call Value Judgments are of supreme importance. It needs to believe, for instance, that right and wrong are real, that Love is more than a biological function, that the human mind is capable of reason rather than merely of rationalization, and that it has the power to will and to choose instead of being compelled merely to react in the fashion predetermined by its conditioning. Since science has proved that none of these beliefs is more than a delusion, mankind will be compelled either to *surrender* [emphasis added] what we call its humanity by adjusting to the real world or to live some kind of tragic existence in a universe alien to the deepest needs of its nature.[44]

Conclusion: Selfhood, Incorporated

Surrender. So also ends American literary theorist Scott Bukatman's work on cyberpunk and new technologies, *Terminal Identity.*[45] Relying heavily upon feminist theorist Donna Haraway's critique of the emerging digital culture, Bukatman looks clear-eyed at the "death of God" (understood here not as the demise of a particular historical and culturally specific deity but rather the denial of a higher meaning "out there") and the concomitant "death of the subject," that is, the reduction of the active person—or death of man—to social constructs not rooted in anything concrete or empirical. The Bukatman conclusion: one must accept, even accept as a premise, the denial and the reduction or be left behind—here seeming to echo the sentiment of neoconservative futurist Alvin Toffler's 1970s bestseller *Future Shock.*

Cultural theorist Mark C. Taylor puts the question this way in his CD-ROM that suggests that Las Vegas has become the new Jerusalem of the American spiritual quest: "This is all there is, are you disappointed?"[46] As scholars of American religion looking out upon the vast proliferation of dystopias (and utopias, for that matter) such as those found in *The Prisoner,* among other works, we answer that a great many Americans apparently are. As observers of the phenomenon we cannot point out the solution, or the British-pun "way out," but we can indicate the ways in which many have sought it, as we will do in the chapters that follow.[47]

Chapter 2

Do We Still Want to Believe?
The X-Files and the American Struggle with Progressive Action

The X-Files television serial dominated the conspiracy-oriented viewership of the FOX network during the 1990s, further developing the themes of imprisonment, confusion, rage, and ironic escape noted earlier. But there was another dimension: although the protagonists knew they were being hybridized, colonized, and subjugated by alien forces, they still struggled for a means to make sense of it all, to square it with traditional notions of a benevolent universe and an accountable government, even to locate a means of escape both temporally and transcendentally along a path to something resembling salvation. *The X-Files* advances us, in other words, past the paranoia, shock, and celebration of the human collision with modernity found previously and attempts to make peace with modernity. In so doing, it endlessly meditates on the threat of human submission to a higher power that is biologically alien, technologically-mediated, and implacable in its demands. These are the themes of *The X-Files,* the themes we explore in this chapter—whether contemporary humans can mount an effective campaign of activism, whether they can find salvation, and whether they can find real escape. For in *The X-Files* the question recurs: is there any possible escape into stable and tolerable conditions for a humanity triply menaced by alien captors, equally threatening human bureaucracies and human institutions—and the collaboration between all of the above?

Entering *The X-Files*

You turn on the television and there they are, a decade or so after their first television appearances in 1993. Even in syndication, FBI special agents Fox Mulder and Dana Scully—two very familiar faces—continue to pursue the elusive truth of government cover-ups, alien conspiracies, clandestine elites, and bureaucracies. Even now, relegated to the nether spaces of cable television and the finely pitted surfaces of digital discs, they appear not much closer to the final truth of genetic experimentation and alien cover-ups than when they began their primetime run a decade ago. Even reruns of the episodes from season nine (2001–2002), which seem to provide some hard data, fail to answer the hottest of questions, whether inexorable alien takeover will or will not take place. Thus a myriad of other questions remains unanswered; in the shows final episodes, Mulder and Scully are still very distant indeed from the Truth.[1]

Ever searching but never quite able to find the truth, agents Mulder and Scully continue to address the demands of an audience thirsty for meaning in their dull workaday worlds—no matter how bizarre or menacing that meaning might appear. Whether stalking after the truth in the DVD racks at the local Blockbuster, or questing after it in the minds of overzealous fans weaving their own online conclusions regarding the series' enigmatic plots, Mulder and Scully—paradoxically enough—continue to answer a basic human need for awe and mystery, along with meaning and purpose, even if they never, ultimately, answer or settle anything at all. If, as a sign from *The Prisoner* suggests, "questions are a burden to others and answers a prison [to oneself?]," Mulder and Scully at least shoulder the burden in every episode, but without ever providing actual release from the iron cage of rational bureaucracy that ensnares them, as well as their deeply concerned viewers.[2] The truth is out there, as viewers want to believe when they echo the sentiments of the series, but palpable deliverance—whether understood mythically as freedom from the evil gray aliens, or from the equally faceless and unresponsive bureaucracies that mark modernity—always lies, for both protagonists and viewers, just beyond the visible screen.

Ultimately satisfying or not, the show has had staying power. The movie spin-off released in 1998, and the primetime weekly series endured until 2002. Agents Scully and Mulder for a time seemed to be everywhere and were not to be missed—even if you had no taste for science fiction (though the series usually reeked more of noir film and a cancer clinic than of robots and rockets), no liking for conspiracy theory (of which the series was definitely a prime example), and no special sympathy with the theme of persistent betrayal by key institutions, another recurrent topic in the series.[3] By the midpoint in the series, say, roughly season five, a key episode could command an audience of well over twenty-seven million.[4]

The success of this series and its by-products depended in large measure on the way the audience could connect with protagonists Mulder and Scully. Whether or not twenty-seven million Americans were actively interested in aliens and conspiracies (and many were), they surely did bond with the two protagonists. And no wonder: simply consider the behavior of agent Mulder at the midpoint of the series, at one point watching an old tape of a (real) NASA-sponsored symposium about the possibility of alien life-forms as he grows melancholic in reflection, apparently talking to himself as he laments his inability to make definitive contact with his vanished, indeed, mysteriously abducted, younger sister Samantha. He speaks of an "act of faith" underlying his search for "understanding" and recovery," meaning the connection between the truth about his sister's disappearance twenty-three years earlier and the truth about extraterrestrial beings. Characterizing that belief as mistaken, he takes his gun in hand and moves toward suicide. This is interrupted by the ringing of the telephone.[5]

Mulder, of course, does not kill himself. The series went, and goes, on and on and on, with Mulder on-screen or vanished, ever enigmatic, appearing and reappearing, and the very physical location for the investigation of these dead-end cases being transformed. For the shooting locale got moved from Canadian murk to sunbelt brilliance, without in any way diminishing the way this series embodied contemporary gloom, contemporary noir suspicion of institutions and their claims to openness in government and industry, to trustworthiness in medicine, university research, and military planning, to credibility in religious and spiritual direction.

Other popular culture products—exemplars of the broader genre sometimes termed cybernoir[6] in honor of the double debt to film noir and the data-processing and cyborg themes of science fiction—showed similarities. They, too, shared in the aura of anti-institutional conspiracy theory, suspicion of technology, and the search for meanings and causes that all seem fated to become an infinite regress. Yet none of these parallel products in any way challenged the dark significance of The X-Files: from episode one in 1993 to the finale in 2002, the series consistently emanated and oozed melancholy, paranoia, and generalized suspicion of a clearly preeminent quality. What then was this show all about? And what is an X-file?

The given was a willingness to suppose that the FBI had set up a small unit to deal with paranormal and enigmatic cases. Whether they were meant to be solved or dismissed remained murky. A strong odor of acceptance of paranormal and New Age phenomena hung over the shooting set, along with a deeply introspective tendency on the part of the chief characters and (by implication) their fans and followers—stemming in part from the way the two leads (both FBI agents) had become personally caught up in their work. As for X-files proper, in the sense of records of cases not explained, the first were said to have been created in the FBI quite early, during the McCarthy era, shortly after alleged UFO sightings in New Mexico. The full account came only in season five in a discussion between FBI secretary Dorothy Bahnsen and agent Arthur Dales (speaking in flashback to the height of FBI involvement in the Army-McCarthy hearings and concurrent spin-off from flying saucer activity). At this point it emerged that charges of being a communist had been fabricated to cover inexplicable happenings, and that the matters in question had originally been filed under "U" for unsolved; but when the file drawer for Unsolved was full, the secretary then began filing new dossiers under "X." As for deciding which files went into this top-secret category (including some gruesome incidents and some involving former German scientists)—it was a decision made by the FBI director himself. [7]

The Characters

The two protagonists are FBI agents on a special track. They are of interest with regard to character development because they are appealing in their combination of open-mindedness and critical evaluative capacity, and because they (virtually from start to finish) show an interest in ultimate questions rare in contemporary upscale television. Along the way, of course, both agents become personally involved in the topic of investigation.

Fox Mulder, a critically-minded believer in the paranormal and the main investigator for the unsolved cases or FBI X-files, moved in this direction out of the desire to recover his abducted younger sister Samantha, who had been taken (at the height of Watergate skullduggery) in circumstances redolent of either flying saucers or government cover-ups. Behind him is Oxford study of psychology and considerable expertise in violent crime. His legal father, William Mulder, has an obscure but significant past. He worked for the State Department at a time when various plots and cover-ups were taking place, some of which precipitated reports that wound up in the X-files. Only quite far along in the series does Fox Mulder discover the likelihood that another character is his biological father.

Dana Scully was originally assigned to keep a skeptical eye on Mulder's excesses in pursuit of the paranormal. Over time she comes to share a good part of his view of the cosmos, becoming as well his loyal partner and finally something of a romantic interest. Daughter of a naval officer, she holds an M.D. from the University of Maryland. Assigned to work with Mulder because of her "I'll believe it when I see it" skepticism, she unfolds in surprising ways. As she becomes more involved, she is abducted and fitted with an implant of mysterious origin; likewise, members of her family come to be murdered. Meanwhile she moves toward growing acceptance of paranormal and alien activity, along the way making an unexpected reappropriation of her family's Roman Catholicism, though within a wide-ranging New Age framework that finally does not accord at all well with mainline Christianity. While much plot energy is expended showing Mulder and Scully at times reversing roles of skeptic and believer, in the end both believe in a multilayered government cover-up and the certainty of intensely sinister alien intelligent activity on earth, both in prehistoric times and recently.

The series acquaints the viewer with numerous links in the FBI bureaucratic chain. A treatment of power relations in the series would need to deal with these different figures in detail. However, the general impression is the important thing, and that is an impression of suppressing the truth and manipulating evidence and agents alike in the service of imponderable motives. Yet the final effect is not simply to elevate the themes of secrecy and duplicity; beyond that, the unspoken conclusion is that in a system of this kind, genuine responsibility and accountability based on conventional explanatory models will likely evaporate on examination. In the words of commentator Peter Knight:

> Paradoxically, . . . the more *The X-Files* promises to reveal a traditional humanist conspiracy of top-down control, the more it seems to paint a . . . portrait of decentered power which is everywhere in the system but in no particular location. In a tone of increasing despair at never getting to the bottom of things, Mulder declares to a UFO convention that there is "a conspiracy wrapped in a plot inside a government agenda."[8]

The series' underlying outlook sometimes seems to regard conspiracy as a system by-product, the spin-off of complex societies, large bureaucracies, and accumulations of power. Such an outlook moves toward making human conspiratorial mechanisms akin to the equally inevitable human bondage to technology. Science fiction and cybernoir had long since depicted technology as an extremely mixed blessing, as an indispensable yet ominous elemental force, a force that greatly diminishes that which is uniquely human. *The X-Files* does nothing to reverse these sentiments.

Nonetheless, certain *X-Files* characters do appear as active and responsible within the FBI and need brief mention for purposes of setting the scene. Preeminent is the assistant director to whom Mulder directly reports, Walter Skinner. He more often than not appears in a sympathetic light, shown as desirous of protecting both Scully and Mulder. From time to time assistant director Skinner is, however, placed under such duress from above that he moves into an ambiguous or duplicitous role vis-à-vis his two uncontrollable subordinates. As for his views concerning the real cause of the abductions and experiments to which humans are subjected, he gradually believes that alien activity is more likely to account for some of the phenomena, rather than falling back upon the usual tactics of government deception and campaigns of disinformation. At the very moment when Mulder is most skeptical on this point (a short-lived role reversal with Scully on the road to convergence), Skinner indicates to Mulder that he has at last begun to accept the hypothesis of actual alien activity. Indeed, he says to Mulder, having doubted for five years, he has come to the opposite view, not only on account of Mulder's "belief in extraterrestrial phenomena" but also because he has concluded that greater plausibility and explanatory power attaches to the extraterrestrial hypothesis.[9]

As the ins and outs of nine years of internal-FBI jockeying for control or suppression of the X-files are not the main concern here, next comes into view the Consortium or Syndicate, meaning a specific international group of very highly placed government and private persons. That group—beginning with the first reports of modern contact with extraterrestrial life-forms—has since been shaping relevant policy and applied science. The effort has been somehow to cope with this secret but indescribably urgent set of events. Among them is Conrad Strughold, apparently related to a Nazi space medicine researcher brought to NASA shortly after the war, and apparent owner of a vast mine that is a repository of secret records. Strughold is high up in the group supervising scientific reaction to the word of alien contact.

Equally important in the steering and financing of secret research would seem to be the person dubbed simply Well-Manicured Man,[10] an Anglo-patrician with seats in Charlottesville, Virginia, and Somerset County, UK. Whatever his aims, they bring him into frequent friction with other members of the Consortium; while he in a sense befriends Scully and Mulder, he does this for his own reasons and probably not out of altruism.

Well-Manicured Man is frequently at odds with the Consortium's chief agent in the United States, Cigarette Smoking Man or Cancer Man

(*Krebskandidat* in the German edition—translated literally as prime candidate for cancer), actually named C. G. B. Spender—or CSM for short. He grew up an orphan, as his father was executed in this country for treasonous work for the Nazis and his mother died from lung cancer. Having served in the Foreign Service with Fox Mulder's legal father Bill, and having in fact been Fox Mulder's biological father, he now seems to be trying to destroy and discredit the entire X-files project. Yet he does not attempt to destroy either Mulder or Scully. While he may have arranged Bill Mulder's murder and have personally assassinated both President Kennedy and Martin Luther King,[11] CSM maintains consistently that he serves a larger aim of trying to arrange the best possible outcome given the pressing realities of human-alien contact. Operating in the highest and most sinister of locations (including, at one point, the Watergate Apartments), CSM has a hand in nearly everything. This concentration of power so offends his secret colleagues that they attempt to assassinate him. Though he survives the eventual extermination of the Syndicate, his manipulative ways put him into a very weak position. Even more bizarre, while he does vanish from view, he reappears at the end of the series, all the while lamenting his inability to find a good publisher for his novels about aliens and assassination he attempts to market under the nom de plume of Raul Bloodworth.[12]

The Story and Its Trajectory ("Mytharc")

Many episodes of the *X*-series had nothing overtly to do with the themes of alien activity and government plots. Even so, these episodes did call into question the normal order of things—whether or not (as one standard online fan reference site argued) the large number of grotesque humanoid hybrids and threatening creatures encountered in these episodes could be traced back to prehistoric genetic experimentation by visiting aliens intent on long-term colonization—or whether, in the manner of classic science fiction and cyber-noir, they thematize and problematize technology as part of the contemporary human situation.[13] As the nine years went by, concerns about government conspiracies and alien abduction cover-ups became increasingly important. Early on, this scenario and the subgroup of episodes touching on it were dubbed the "Mytharc" by online fans.

The arc of the Mytharc proved to be a large trajectory indeed. Aliens had begun to colonize earth in prehistoric times. The mixed their DNA with that of humans and used human bodies as hosts for alien life-forms. For some reason, perhaps the cold of the ice ages,[14] they temporarily ceased overt surface activity, either retreating onto space ships or entering a curious deep under-ground hibernation awaiting more favorable circumstances. Nonetheless, early on the alien colonizers had considerable surface contact with local life-forms (which they may or may not have brought into being) and had left behind various ancient "religious" documents and prophecies of their return, along with their language, which survived as what is known as Navajo.[15]

Those favorable circumstances arrived at roughly the same time as the atomic bomb and early rocket tests—and with the immediate postwar UFO incidents alleged to have occurred in New Mexico. The basic story: the aliens make secret contact with high officials in world governments. They demon-strate their technological superiority and their use of a viral, oil form of their DNA stored underground in petroleum for both hibernation and control of mammals. In this they leave no doubt that they are planning a return and world-takeover in the near future. They even set a date coinciding with the end of the next cycle of the Mayan calendar: December 22, 2012. Meanwhile, beginning in the early 1950s or so, an inner human elite arranges to be of service to the aliens in the belief that they and their relatives can survive the takeover in a favored position.[16]

From this point in recent time, then, dates the elaborate series of abduc-tions, human experiments (with vaccination or secret work to create a vaccine to render humans immune to bodily takeover, also involving hybridization, DNA collection, cloning, and the like), and other bewildering activities. Many of these apparently result from a human conspiracy to save part of humanity without the knowledge of the aliens.[17]

Yet the implication is that the alien colonists may have either known or carried out these activities. While there are apparently concurrent Japanese and Russian projects, the one of which we hear the most is sponsored by the Syndicate, a.k.a. the Consortium. According to some sources, they eventually split off from direct work with the United States government. Germans and Englishmen are identified as well in this group, including characters already introduced.[18]

Along the way plots and conspiracies abound, with young CSM, young Bill Mulder, and the McCarthy-era J. Edgar Hoover all apparently party to these deep-cover activities. Again, Fox Mulder in the 1990s faces frustration locating his missing sister, who is misleadingly shown to him briefly as a mere clone. Scully completes her New Age appropriation of Roman Catholicism during her struggle with a work-related malignancy. Her precarious health and her forays into motherhood (related to genetic experimentation) and child-rearing, form a distinct subgroup of episodes.[19]

With 2012 approaching, and with work on a hybrid slave race going well, the tension level reaches a high point in the 1998 spin-off movie.[20] In it, as Well-Manicured Man reveals to Fox Mulder, confusion suddenly reigns with the discovery that the aliens are beginning to use human hosts as mere "digestives" or nourishment during gestation. This sensational finding comes at the same time that Scully and Mulder uncover a vast conspiracy to infect humanity with the viral form of alien DNA using specially-bred bees. Thus looms the specter of utter doom for the human race. Yet confusion multiplies with the appearance of a rival group of aliens intent on thwarting plans for colonization by incinerating hybrids and most members of the Syndicate.

While the writers and producers devote a significant portion of the later episodes to character development and self-discovery in Scully and Mulder, the evidence for alien-human plotting piles up. With it comes proof as well of the extensive, ancient traces of alien activity on earth. Telepathic and psychokinetic phenomena manifest themselves in several characters (including Mulder at the end of his wits) and prove to be the results of activating remnants of alien DNA long present but ordinarily inactive in the human genome. In the final episodes it remains uncertain whether the insurgency by anticolonization aliens will have any serious retarding or nullifying effect. The scene at the end shifts to Navajo territory in honor of this most ancient of contactee locations. In that place, the well-informed Cigarette Smoking Man reappears briefly to pronounce again the inevitability of alien takeover.

This doleful possibility of endgame, extinction, and doomsday of course raises for academic observers a fascinating prospect in comparative worldview studies, so to speak. Surely the observer must begin in the most obvious way, that is, by comparing the X-scenario here with analogous doomsday scenarios in contemporary Christian eschatological and apocalyptic writings.[21] Indeed, this feature is of paramount importance for the present analysis. For the Mytharc directly connects Chris Carter's television series with earlier themes in popular science fiction culture, such as UFOs, alien abductions, technological and biological challenges to uniqueness in human identity, neocatastrophism after Immanuel Velikovsky, and renewed concern with the assessment of world religions in a cosmic and scientific context. Thereby it allows the series—and its interpreters—to take much in *The X-Files* as a self-conscious reading of the political, personal, and religious situation of humanity by upscale Americans at the close of the cold war era.[22]

Moreover, the X-Mytharc, with its treatment of alien intelligence in clandestine contact with human governments, connects the series with all manner of interesting parallel views in today's most current popular culture. It connects *The X-Files* with other science fiction-related assessments of the current human prospect; beyond this, it invites comparison and contrast with Jewish and Christian eschatology as they are currently understood by religious conservatives.[23] Here the possibilities for comparison and contrast go beyond the vectoring of end-time trajectories using examples from the New Age "spiritual" and the evangelical "religious." To be sure, this study of analogous "what if" imagination holds much interpretive promise. Series such as *The X-Files* allow us to measure—at a critical distance—the attitudes many Americans have toward mundane bureaucracies and real or imagined all-powerful government-corporate power superstructures.

Related, a second theme of equal importance emerges: the series expresses divergent popular attempts to make sense of the current sociopolitical situation using the language of mainstream conspiracy theory set in the endgame phase.[24] Already now it seems possible to reevaluate the views of critics who found every reason for Fox to put an end to the X-series in 2002 since (as they then claimed) increased trust in government immediately after 9/11 had all at once rendered the suspicious and conspiratorial mind-set of Mulder and Scully out of date. Quite the contrary! On mature examination, such claims fall wide of the mark. Rather, as the persistence of diffused conspiracy theories about 9/11, TWA 800, and even JFK continue, we see a lingering and perhaps intensifying conspiracy-flavored mistrust of institutions. In any case, the function of such mainstreamed conspiracy thinking calls for discussion.

Endgame, Pseudo-Exits, and Apocalypse Deferred?

While decades of earlier science fiction and noir items in popular culture had prepared the way, still the timing of *The X-Files*'s meteoric ascent seems remarkable. After all, at the series' commencement, the religiously ardent among evangelicals were wondering whether the turn of the millennium and the expected first phase in Christ's Second Coming were more to be feared or desired. At the same time, Christian conservatives of various branches moved toward a strikingly similar frame of mind.[25] For an indefinable anxiety—mistrust not trademarked by any one worldview—was the main precondition for the success of Chris Carter's television series, especially as millennial Y2K uncertainties and dot-com portfolio concerns grew. Yet, despite its large audience share, Carter's popular series showed only limited success in getting to the bottom of a bottomless nest of mysteries, enigmas, plots, betrayals, and conspiracies. It evidently mirrored the perplexity of much of the population when considering U.S. culture and politics.[26]

Simply put, sophisticated yuppie viewers given to gnawing anxiety and Bible-believing fundamentalists anticipating bodily removal from a world ripe for divine judgment appeared to be in similar spaces at the turn of the millennium: each group was fixated on parallel mythic narratives of the end-game, and each featured alternative possibilities of destruction or escape (one televisual, one biblical).

And fascinatingly enough, in each instance the story was an escape narrative with one glaring oddity. A close look at each escape story shows this result: despite the formal appearance of some ultimate positive hope, still there is not really any escape—for in both cases the story is a salvation drama in which real salvation as escape is always promised but always deferred—at least for the characters who actively figure in the narrative. In both cases, as in numerous other instances of this genre in popular culture, in real life the envisioned escape turns out to be delayed: the bodily removal of real-life believers and the tangibly seen arrival of Jesus or of end-time tribulations and plagues thus far not has actually materialized in daily life, any more than ancient alien colonizers. Life goes on and one copes.[27]

Now of course in a sense, the Christian prophecy believers have a real advantage. Whereas in the *X*-complex, after nine years ambiguity surrounds even the narrated, fictionalized end-time event (will the alien takeover occur or not—stay tuned, or read a few paragraphs here immediately below), no ultimate ambiguity surrounds the narrated endgame from the New Testament. Although the day, hour, and details are open to endless debate, doctrinal consensus in nonheretical circles agrees that, someday, the Second Coming and Last Judgment simply will and must occur, even as the current version of earth must pass away. Infinite numbers of theological interpretations here can vary, but a certain consensus among hardcore believers is required: eventually the last trumpet sounds, and judgment begins.

Despite this ultimate advantage, however, in point of fact and focus, contemporary prophecy believers are still not too far off from the situation of New Age viewers of *The X-Files* or *The Matrix*. That is, insofar as their emotional involvement is heightened by attention to the celebrated novelistic treatment of the endgame by Tim LaHaye and Jerry Jenkins (in the Left Behind novels), they are made uncertain as to how ultimate events will play out. For precisely in this novelistic version of dispensational eschatology, the real emphasis falls on the unending struggles of those who were left behind. As suggested below in detail, the lengthy narrative treatment of coping issues in the LaHaye-Jenkins series, while overtly about earthly life after the rapturous disappearance of hardcore believers, shows many signs that its strongest appeal is to hardcore believers here and now. After all, by this point many must be secretly and sometimes openly wondering whether after two thousand years of postponement the promised dramatic denouement is likely to occur in any foreseeable timeslot.[28] Even as Dante found it hard to create tension in his description of Paradise, resting his literary reputation more on the extremes of the Inferno and Purgatory, so also the authors (and readers) of the immensely popular Left Behind series find that, empirically speaking, their energy mostly goes to the dramatic struggles on earth. In this entire process the focus shifts bit by barely perceptible bit to earthly issues not too far removed from threats to Christian purity posed now by sin, death, and the devil. The real selling point of Left Behind is drama, struggle—a struggle that may have a sure outcome in the big picture, but that may have either damnation or salvation as the payoff for buyers of the books. Thus a penultimate uncertainty of individual importance rules for those caught up in this worldview.

Analogous uncertainty manifests in the cybernoir world of *X*-pectation. As the weekly *X*-series came to its production end in year nine, the (probably) irrevocable alien takeover was firmly prophesied for the end of the current Mayan calendar cycle—that falling in the year 2012, well after the end of the series.[29] Yet the intermittent earthly activities of a second group of aliens who oppose the main group of aliens had been depicted often enough in the series that one could not suppose with certainty that the human inhabitants of earth would necessarily disappear into extinction or genetic mutation— ambiguity thus prevailing as far ahead as the viewer could imagine.

Nor was the ambiguity dispelled in the last few episodes, when the all-knowing Cigarette Smoking Man made statements pronouncing the inevitability of doom directly contradicted by agent Mulder. Thus the outcome of the Mytharc hovers as uncertain, and strikingly so. The chief human plotter or orchestrator, CSM, the elder Spender, declares with assurance already in the sixth season of the series that, while Mulder's father had indeed tried to stall for time and to develop a vaccine that would spare some or all of the human race from extinction:

> That was your father's idea. To use the alien DNA to make a vaccine. To save everyone. The world. It's the reason I come along. But it's too late now. Colonization is going to begin. There will be a sequence of events. A state of emergency will be declared because of a massive outbreak of the alien virus delivered by bees. And the takeover will begin. . . . [30]

At the end of the television series, CSM is still of the same mind. He declares to Scully in the presence of Mulder that a thousand years earlier the sense of foreboding and secret knowledge among the Mayans caused them to end their calendar on the date of "the final alien invasion," December 22, 2012. Further, he declares, Mulder has seen the corroborating data in materials of the American government held in secret at "Mount Weather," the place where the U.S. "Secret Government" plans to take refuge as the alien invasion unfolds.[31] As if this were not enough, the elder Spender, a bit off in the head and obsessed with feelings of power, must dwell on the futility of Mulder's enterprise. He reveals to Mulder his enjoyment of Mulder's "powerlessness," a sense of joy that has made him protect Mulder from "them," the Secret Government and its private agents. The Cigarette Smoking Man says that he has been "waiting for this moment" during the many years of Mulder's career in order to see him "broken" and "afraid" and ready to die.[32]

Yet these signals are subject to contradiction. At the close of the series Mulder, who has not recovered his abducted sister and who has suffered many setbacks even as he has come in contact with countless layers of enigma and conspiracy, admits his melancholy but then refuses to let CSM have the final word:

> MULDER: I want to believe that the dead are not lost to us. That they speak to us as part of something greater than us—greater than any alien force. And if you and I are powerless now, I want to believe that if we listen to what's speaking, it can give us the power to save ourselves.
>
> SCULLY: Then we believe the same thing.
>
> (SCULLY watches MULDER intently. MULDER looks like he Believes. . . . SCULLY smiles at MULDER. MULDER reaches over and lightly picks up SCULLY'S cross.) . . .
>
> MULDER: (whispers) Maybe there's hope.
>
> (FADE TO BLACK.) [33]

Now these ambiguities and postponements did not drive the audiences away—in fact, the countercommunities of would-be escapees seemed quite able to cope with the delay. Nor did audiences run from the spectacle of relative powerlessness, of impotence on the part of the two FBI protagonists, an impotence heightened by the numerous references to implants, vaccines, hybrids, covert tests, abductions, and missing time—some of which directly affected the performance and effectiveness of agents Mulder and Scully.[34] So well did the viewer subgroups cope that one may suppose the whole point here might have been help in coping. Thus *The X-Files* is finally about assistance: help in venting frustrations, support in reorienting the self in safely approved ways so as to facilitate continued functioning in neither outer space nor tribulational dystopia but rather in the everyday world of high-tech global network culture.[35]

Such a view of the current strong demand for coping mechanisms is equally applicable to the postmodern or postChristian universe of *The X-Files* and the hyper-Christian repristinating universe of contemporary American evangelicals given to fervent discussion about an approaching physical airlift of believers out of this doomed world.[36] The systematic treatment of this possibility of extended comparison demands first a concentration on *The X-Files* asking: What was the nature of this televisual experience of impending doom and impending salvation? In what sense did it appear as an escape? And in what way did it touch on questions of identity, personal responsibility, and effective public and political action for its audience?

The main finding has already been documented. After nine years, viewers of the series still do not know whether alien takeover and human extinction is inevitable or avoidable. The endless fluctuations between hope and despair over nine years have been related to human use of technology, to human maneuvering, to rival (anticolonizing) alien incineration of collaborating officials and hybridized DNA carriers, and to duplicity with regard to alien colonizers' use of human hosts as more than future slaves (as food during gestation, that is). Thus, to repeat, the New Age (or science fiction) *X*-counterpart to the Christian endgame hovers quite uncertain—asserted by CSM as inevitable, questioned by some such as Mulder. Both escape from and submission to alien calamity are imminent yet postponed.

Noteworthy then is how numerous episodic or individual aspects of the nine-year series lift up, enact, and reinforce this overall sweeping arc of ambiguity in punctilear fashion. Take, for example the striking instance of mass gatherings of hybrid stock and elite collaborators, notably that at Ruskin Dam.[37] Perhaps the people who assemble there have been directed to do so by the implanted devices and chips. In any case, whatever salvation or metamorphosis or doom they may have imagined upon assembly, quite unexpectedly these persons are incinerated en masse by anticolonizer rebel aliens. This fate is depicted on a couple of other occasions as well (for instance, at Kazakhstan, El Rico Air Force Base in West Virginia).[38] Moreover, most in at least the American branch of the Syndicate also are incinerated in a variety of times and places by the rebels.[39] The upshot is that physical escape from the colonizers and physical destruction of the human race by the colonizers both prove to be essentially unrealized in these episodes despite the apparent promise of some resolution of the matter.

Equally ambiguous is the outcome of the abductions and experiments and implants apparently performed upon agent Scully. She appears to regain control by removing the implant given her during abduction; yet, to forestall fatal cancer the implant must be reinserted. Or again, consider the ambiguity of the triggering figure in the entire story, Mulder's abducted younger sister Samantha. Later "she" is finally shown to be one of the blessed spirits. Yet neither satisfying exchange of views nor real reunion has ever taken place between the original Samantha (if there was one) and agent Mulder. The escapes and closures, like the threatened deaths and dangers, all prove to be multivalent and ambiguous, and in no way decisive with regard to the external course of empirical events.

The same result holds for two noteworthy sequences of events in season seven. In that season Mulder and Scully each experience extremely intense inner phenomena, visions, hallucinations, a life-threatening coma—yet at the end the basic situation is little changed. To be sure, these visions have a certain connection with the ephemeral oscillations of visibility and the disappearance of Mulder or of the swings of Scully's mood and the overall developmental trajectory of both characters. Yet, it is axiomatic among fans that "nobody every really dies in *The X-Files*." Further, close observers knew this well in advance of season seven's first airing: ambiguity predominates, for the overall Mytharc never dissipates nor fully actualizes within the series. Thus the seasoned viewer always already knows (by season seven) to view with caution any serious, empirical consequences of any episode, especially those set within the soul. It is not that real-world consequences do not occur in the series, or that no development takes place. Ultimate and decisive events, however, do not occur. Decisive turns do not happen simply because, just as in mundane reality, so also in the series life does go on and finally one must cope with it.

Nonetheless the two visionary episodes of season seven are so striking as to be of great interest here. Scully's vision is less connected with big ticket, Mytharc-related events than Mulder's. But it is remarkable as an example of interior escape, reorientation, or reshaping of outlook and identity, in short as contributor to and product of Scully's evolution. As such it aptly illustrates what can be termed the latent function of the series: giving assistance in coping with the persistence of an intractable and stultifying empirical reality. Notably enough, the upshot of the episodes is to reinforce the importance of coping by searching for a meaning.[40]

Of particular interest is the Scully-centered episode entitled "All Things."[41] Here in a time of trial, she—in a vision or hallucination or waking dream—prostrates herself before a statue of the Buddha. This in its presentation appears in context as a key link in a chain of events marking her broadening of worldview. She is indeed evolving toward what appears as a deepened spirituality friendly to New Age currents. Such a position is of course helpfully congruent with Mulder's basic approach.

Now the Buddha vision is temporally linked to her immediate turn toward using holistic healing techniques. She employs these in the same episode to rescue a person as disdainful of alternative medicine as she once had been. Yet this turn in Scully, seen in series context, creates no serious tension with the theme of her recent awakening to an appreciation of her Roman Catholic roots. On the contrary, her Catholic awakening appears as intimately and positively connected with her more general growth in appreciation of New Age approaches and views. In short: a developmental marker is crossed for Scully—with development taken as movement toward equilibrium, openness, and relativizing of classic norms in science and religion. The real action is interior and any "escape" is morphed into a changed outlook.

Amor Fati—Ironic Fatalism

Mulder's parallel experience in season seven is more complicated. To begin with, the episode title has important associations. Its name is *"Amor Fati,"* a phrase recalling the nineteenth-century German philosopher Friedrich Nietzsche's desire to live so that one could repeat one's life events—even, and perhaps especially, the troublesome ones—in an endless cycle of recurrence (his famous "eternal recurrence of the same"). Quite possibly any reference of the kind must also recall Nietzsche's interest in Antichrist, in Jesus Christ, and in pagan deities of excess such as the Greek god Dionysos.

However this may be, Mulder lapses into a life-threatening coma because exposure to an alien virus or other alien stimuli has activated a ceaseless bombardment of messages in his brain via extrasensory perception (voices, for example). Presumably the alien-derived DNA responsible for this has been latent in all human brains for thousands of years. But now it has driven Mulder into illness and a coma because, once activated, it does not stop.

Meanwhile Cigarette Smoking Man, suffering from brain cancer, must also face extreme loss of hope. The problem for him is the lack of hybridized DNA applicable for collaboration and survival purposes during the coming colonization. That is, due to rebel incinerations the hybridized DNA is gone:

so that, even if his cancer were cured he now would lack the DNA necessary to survive alien colonization. Then, however, the realization dawns: Mulder, due to various exposures and procedures, has now himself become that "compatible alien-human hybrid" required for producing a collaborator elite that can hope to survive extinction and colonization.[42] Realizing also that the activated alien DNA in Mulder's delirious brain will correct cancer-linked errors in his own DNA and at the same time again set him up to survive the coming virus-mediated extinction of humanity, CSM acts. He arranges a transfer of activated alien DNA from the comatose but telepathically conscious Mulder to himself. As we know from various episodes, however, the operation fails due to edema in the brain of CSM. Mulder, on the other hand, is in the outcome restored to a normal human condition (though his underlying physical condition remains questionable). Further, Mulder now bonds more strongly than ever with Scully, who during his coma and hallucinations fights tirelessly for his survival. Thus the operation and Mulder's telepathy and hallucinations again alter the expected trajectory of events little if at all—here paralleling the modest results from Scully's Buddha vision. Once again the "real" results are interior, attitudinal, and in the domain of affect.

However the details of Mulder's visionary hallucination and its interplay with the initiative of CSM are highly significant—first with regard to content (the nature of the hallucination) and second with regard to the contrast with the real results just mentioned (for instance, the bonding with Scully and further attitudinal adjustment). For what the comatose Mulder dreams during the sedated transfer of brain material from himself to CSM is an elaborate fantasy of escape from persecution, from pariah status, and from the threat of apocalypse. He fantasizes about a return to "normal" middle-class existence as a friendly neighbor of his great antagonist, CSM.

While the script does not try to give a satisfactory explanation for any active part that CSM plays in molding these lucid hallucinations, at all events their content and their reality status prove highly significant. Alien-telepathic Mulder while under sedation finds himself guided by a friendly CSM (his biological father, of course) into a suburban paradise of marriage, reconciliation, and absolutely uneventful married life cut off from worsening world conditions and the threat of alien assault. This extended hallucination is for viewers one of the most intensely uncanny high points of the nine-year series. It strikingly portrays a different happy ending, a different escape than that usually sought by Mulder—not exposure of the conspiracies, not definitive defeat of the colonizing aliens and their governmental allies, but instead a quick and decisive turn into the almost bovine existence of master-planned

suburbia (the script describes it as "domestic bliss"). Mulder somehow imag-
ines this yet remains aware that his submission to the surgical plans of CSM
may result in his death.

The content of this fantasy, whether produced by Mulder or by some
mysterious compliance with the directions of CSM, demands attention.
Transition into normal suburban life without conspiratorial melodrama or
monsters but with "domestic bliss" (marriage, family, personal security, and
income ample for middle-class status) now becomes a desirable and exotic
item. For someone in Mulder's frame of mind it is truly unattainable (and
hence desirable, it would seem). The message here is that such escape into the
suburban normal is available only as fantasy. Real life will not deliver it to the
knowing and alert in some empirical form.

While the "*Amor Fati*" episode delivers in real life neither the certainty
of alien takeover and human extinction nor real escape into its polar opposite of sitcom suburbia, nonetheless the episode does deliver something
positive. That package has several parts, but overall it can be summarized
as "positive attitude adjustment." Beyond the enhanced bonding between
Scully and Mulder, the episode encourages the feeling that important themes
are treated here. The reference to Nietzsche and fate in the title, the implication that early alien colonizer activity was not only behind the great religions but also behind occasional psychic or telepathic capability, that there is
"divine" (alien) DNA in everybody, that it is activated (for a time) in Mulder
so that either he or his descendants may move into a kind of universal savior
role—these themes are all touched on either in this episode or in material
closely related to it in original airing time. Such themes, positively evoked,
can enhance the feeling that those who view the program are taking part in
a highly important and extraordinary activity. In other words, here is strong
evidence for viewing the entire *X*-complex as something akin to an alternative religion, or at least a fully rounded worldview calling out for both thematic and sociological analysis.

X-Files, Action, and Identity in the Cybernoir Imagination

One cannot readily summarize the overall significance of *The X-Files* and
related cybernoir popular culture because this genre incorporates a variety of
perspectives, many somber but not without some that open onto the joy of
life. The genre is neither naively enthusiastic about technology nor naively
insistent that people suddenly turn Luddite. While it is certainly possible to
find science fiction in the last decade or so that is either radically enthusiastic

about technological utopia or radically fearful of technoid dystopia, typically the attitude is nuanced, though by now usually nuanced within a rather muted or cautious larger framework with regard to technology and the prospects for humanity.[43]

The classic of the genre is a film spawned from the imagination of author Philip K. Dick, *Blade Runner* (1982). *Blade Runner* makes a notable statement about the intertwining of human and cybernetic destiny, not any simpleminded separation of human from machine, however bleak the world has become.[44] While both the *Matrix* (1999–2003) group and the *Terminator* (1984–2003) series are predicated on extreme confrontation between advanced machines and human beings, neither suggests that people can somehow do without late-model technoid help. In the long run, of course, these issues overlap into major questions of political action and decision. As for *The X-Files,* Douglas Kellner has captured the complexity of the situation in holding that, while the show gets points from those on the far left for featuring governmental cover-ups and conspiracies and dubious undertakings that affect the human (or cyborgian) prospect, nonetheless it is seriously problematic: "But ultimately the politics of the series is ambiguous and indeterminate, failing to promote any positive solutions. . . . The evil depicted is so vast, the conspiracies are so complex, and the politics are so ambiguous as to promote cynicism, nihilism, and a sense of hopelessness."[45]

The critical point here is how in cybernoir classics such as *The X-Files* we typically find a characteristic interweaving of diminished human agency or heroic potential measured by its empirical effectiveness with two other characteristic themes. First, we see the central but complex significance of human reliance on technology even as the reduction in hero potential is understood. Second, we observe the further realization, that we are not likely to overcome, from constraint by systems—by ever more complex bureaucratic and data-collecting systems. One finds no escape from the reality of diminished human agency, in other words, the ability of the individual either as a single entity or in groups to effect significant cultural or political change. This is a bleak and cynical worldview, indeed. Civic humanism—a set of attitudes that rests on the belief in the existence and efficacy of morally significant and responsible individual selves capable of free decision-making—is cut to pieces.

For the *X*-complex, the definitive statement of these themes comes in a script coauthored by William Gibson, surely an authoritative source on cybernoir matters. The series episode "Killswitch"[46] manages to weave together out-of-control networking that moves from virtual to real life in killing, artificial intelligence taking over government satellites, and the possible "uploading" of human identity into the demi-immortality of artificial intelligent existence on the Internet. Gibson, the original cyberpunk expert, shows here far greater reserve and irony (in the service of his sense for real drama), and indeed far greater sophistication, than the more naive appropriation of such technological "immortality" by theologians like the German post-Hegelian Wolfhart Pannenberg.[47] Like much of Gibson's writing, in other words, "Killswitch" leaves the viewer with the realization that modernity comes with a price, a price Gibson and *X* are both highly ambivalent about paying.

In view of this well-developed, perhaps jaded outlook, contemporary cybernoir as a genre, and its typical target consumer, is ill-placed to foster enthusiasm and zeal for political or military actions, crusades, programs, or campaigns. The target consumer always already knows and expects technology and rumors of technology, along with spybots, spies, bots, cyborgs, cover-ups, recalls, and the promotion of their private fantasies or individual economic well-being via technology. These days one does not expect the periodic chart of the elements to dissolve simply because—as with the nineteenth-century Luddites—one jams a few wooden shoes into a loom. Rather, it seems as though through the lens of cybernoir we now know that technology trumps technology, whether or not it ever solves human problems, mundane or ultimate. Like it or not, nobody can do without it, but the cybernoir enthusiast is, as it turns out, not all that enthusiastic about the requisite toys.

Yet at the same time we see that a major stream within cybernoir, like much of mainstream culture, strongly affirms some defense of traditional human identity, even spontaneity—in some measure, and somehow. Indeed, the great film success of the 1990s was a package devoted to this theme, *The Matrix*. Sometimes termed neoGnostic, certainly this film in its first installment presents a conflict between "elites in the know" (neoGnostics) and all-powerful machines, a conflict so extreme it is scarcely imaginable. Overall it presents more strident, more desperate images of defense of some kind of human identity and purpose than almost any other film or television contribution to imagining the conflict between technological predictability and human life. The intensity of the struggle is enhanced by the film's viewpoint, which self-consciously reflects on diminished efficacy of what human agency can accomplish and the inescapable requirement of reliance on technology as well as mind-matter techniques.

All the more noteworthy, then, is the outcome of all this. Critic Jake Horsley, an enthusiastic and intelligent advocate for the first *Matrix* film, argued with good reason for the film's importance as a revelation of the deadening emptiness of much ordinary life and the possibility of a "neoGnostic" approach to a postmodern "shamanic journey." The revelation—that the machines had long since taken over and were keeping human organisms alive in a state of controlled, lucid but illusory, dreaming—is indeed remarkably striking. As Horsley summarizes the message given by leader Morpheus to potential superhuman successor Neo:

> The hideous, literally mind-shattering Truth: that he is a slave to an order of inorganic beings that until this moment, he did not even know existed. . . . the year is not really 1999 . . . it is in fact closer to one century later . . . civilization has in the meantime already been destroyed. . . . [A]s a result of the discovery of Artificial Intelligence (AI), somewhere around the start of the twenty-first century, there was a stand-off between man and machine—between the creation and the creator (exactly as in *The Terminator*)—and the machine won. AI discovered a means not merely to destroy civilization and . . . develop for itself cybernetic, semi-organic bodies, using human beings as its primary energy source. (The machines were solar-powered, but the human-engineered holocaust blocked out the sun.)

Horsley then explains in careful detail:

> To this end, human beings were enslaved. . . . They were put into a deep sleep, and a collective dream was engendered to keep them tractable and docile, like babies in their cribs, while their vital life force was sucked from them. Humans are bred and raised directly into these incubators, and fed intravenously with the liquefied remains of the dead. This . . . goes way beyond even the best sci-fi cinema, into the murky realms and veiled nightmares of Lovecraft. . . . [M]odern UFO lore . . . adapts . . . the same atavistic beliefs. . . . All of which puts *The Matrix* at the very front-line of modern myth-making.[48]

For Horsley,[49] this fascinating film offers real hope that the moviegoing population can be challenged successfully to think about where their techno-neocapitalist culture has taken them. Moreover, rather like the Swiss psychoanalyst Carl Jung in his late phase (under the influence of early quantum physics), Horsley, too, finds great sympathy for the mentality-changing potential of the postmodern, postWestern, postclassical insight that energy (if rightly discerned) was behind all phenomenal appearances.[50] In almost rhapsodic style Horsley writes about the first *Matrix* film:

> Neo—as the One—is expected to turn the tide in favor of the human uprising, the "awakening," by shifting the balance, by making the leap . . . from ordinary man to shaman, and to demi-god. And this of course he

accomplishes. What's so satisfying about the movie is that in the end . . . it is the power of the imagination that wins the day. Once Neo reaches a certain realization he is able to simply stop the bullets with his mind—since they don't exist in the first place—and to project himself into the (holographic) body of the Enemy (so fulfilling its own secret will to become real), and explode it from within. . . . The Matrix . . . offers something akin to shamanic ecstasy.[51]

Horsley's initial review also holds up high expectations for the possibilities of a sequel. But what comes afterwards is the actual reality in contemporary America, a reality that Horsley (to his credit!) registers with precision. The next two installments of *The Matrix,* far from challenging anyone's outlook, moved rapidly in the direction of Hollywood extreme action films with the customary sense-numbing special effects.[52] The Eastern meditation gymnastics and the Jungian-quantum deep penetration turn out to be merely the antechamber to another action film, *Crouching Dolby, Leaping Profit.*

Cybernoir as Undermining Progressive Politics?

Does Horsley suggest a missed opportunity? Or does he propose rather a reality check for those who think mere film could achieve more than religion, politics, and economics in their ancient and classical forms? By November of 2003 he had published in book format a "handbook" for "warriors" with the message that—having seen that phenomena were the mask covering energy—they, like Neo in the film, should recognize reality and—in the words of reviewer Harriet Klausner, start "discarding the masks of society and . . . stop being the source of energy for someone else."[53] Thus—despite the depth of concern for human identity and integrity—the Matrix project can be rescued by its critical admirers only by casting it in the guise of an Ayn Randian superindividualism dangerously close to the codependency psychobabble of the later 1980s.

Horsley's case looks, of course, like a secular (or New Age religious) parallel to the classic quietist position in Christian evangelicalism often indicted by activist critics. The diagnosis of social and cultural ills is so ominous, the prognosis so bad, that the diagnostician feels justified in scrapping the customary bag of sociopolitical tricks to call for massive rethinking, refeeling, and finally conversion. After all, politics and technology as a social program have obviously failed and are doomed to further failures. And taking a more general perspective we can see in the *Matrix*-trajectory a particular instance suggesting the wider relevance of the axiom that New

Age and kindred worldviews continue to have remarkably little long-term capacity for exerting concerted pressure on the political process, in considerable measure because of the consumerist individualism that characterizes most varieties of this worldview. Here one can only echo the conclusion of sociologist of religion Steve Bruce as he wrote concerning the general prospects for the larger mentality of individualistic and quasipantheistic spirituality represented by New Age followers: "In summary, New Age religion cannot aspire to promote radical and specific change because it does not have the cohesion and discipline of the sect."[54] Now emerges an apparent parallel to the older view of Christian evangelicals, who on occasion have appeared to oscillate between nostalgic conservative individualism and pure otherworldliness, hence proving to be fatally apolitical, hopelessly mired in mere individual concerns for conversion and eternal salvation. Likewise, it seems, the hardcore audience for cybernoir, while probably quite progressive in social attitudes, has proven notoriously difficult to consolidate into a political bloc.

But of course the old charge from the Left that such individualistic evangelicals are apolitical (meaning: not active in progressive causes) is quite outdated. As most readers are already aware, these days another story altogether requires telling in the latter connection. For Christian evangelicalism in its current extreme forms is not inclined to be apolitical until the Tribulation is past and earth itself no longer a possible area for conflict. Instead, on a variety of fronts, at a variety of levels, and in a variety of modes, over the last twenty or thirty years evangelicals have become politically engaged.[55]

The move into this evangelical activist mode, though fairly recent, is very real, very significant—and, as we shall see, finally based on causes very deeply rooted in the tradition, the heritage, the past of Christian (and Jewish) end-time doctrines and their perennial sociopolitical function, from the Hellenistic age of the Maccabees to the present. Moreover, this multifarious evangelical return to political engagement takes place at precisely the instant when American conservative Christianity in its religious imagery is more and more leaving behind its consensus-building tradition of common respect for the Scottish Enlightenment. In fact, as we will show in the next chapter, the advance-guard of hardcore Christian prophecy believers is rapidly groping its way back to a preEnlightenment, dim view of human agency and effectiveness—in practice reverting to a position close to that of Calvin's view of mortals as controlled religiously by the eternal decrees of a ferocious God both with regard to faith and with regard to action, at least once the inevitable Tribulation breaks loose.

Here prophecy believers are moving into a close religious parallel with contemporary cybernoir suspicion that Renaissance and Enlightenment belief
in freedom of the will cannot be sustained given our knowledge of the
physics and chemistry behind decision making.[56] Indeed, in contemporary
context, the issue may be less freedom of the will than the sense of an
independent, strong, powerful self, as we shall suggest below—with the
result being less a revival of the strong self of paradoxical Reformation
Calvinism, animated by the sense of predestination to a divine mission,
and more a weakened self as apocalyptic marionette, a kind of religious
edition of David Riesman's celebrated "outer-directed" corporate self, rec-
ognized already in the 1950s as a chameleon of corporate America, yet
now in millennial America capable of taking on the character of both an
apocalyptic marionette character and a transnational corporate technocrat,
each equally lacking in any inner direction.

If that regression toward the demeaning of a powerful, inwardly motivated, morally responsible self, one committed both to human freedom and
to participatory government in the sense of the American Enlightenment—
if that regression is indeed the emergent position of hardcore prophecy
believers, then something hitherto unnoticed needs urgent attention. For
however much prophecy believers may seem to parallel cybernoir pessimists
and conspiracy dabblers, at the key point the parallel collapses utterly. For,
as we have already hinted, hardcore Christian prophecy activists are simultaneously moving into a stronger and stronger engagement with politics and
cultural reshaping every level of American society.

In other words, the real problem to be solved is this: whereas progressives and cybernoir fans are if anything rendered enervated and politically
apathetic by their growing sense that free will and choice are mere illusions
increasingly crushed by the juggernaut of cybernetics and bureaucratic
administration of the cosmos, evangelical Christians react in the opposite
way. That is, simultaneously the followers of Left Behind are growing ever
stronger in their antiEnlightenment conviction that religious faith and ethical activity do not represent much of an exercise of free will, especially as
the move into the era of divinely appointed Tribulation takes place. Instead
these turn out to be simply occasions for epiphenomenal humans to enact
and reenact an absolutely unvarying moral script written by the Great
Playwright, who, with his doomed character Pontius Pilate, takes as his
invariant motto, *Quod scripsi, scripsi*—"What I have written, I have written" (John 19:22). But rather than being chastened, enervated, confused, or
mentally fatigued by this loss of personal freedom and personal capacity to

act in an efficacious manner, instead contemporary prophecy believers—by the millions—are more and more tending to surge forward in cascades of political activism with targets at every level of American society. They are not enervated. They are emboldened. *Why* they are emboldened, and what this means for the entire venture of participatory government in the Western humanist tradition, we now turn to examine.

Chapter 3

Perhaps Today:
The Dialectic of Despair and Activism
in Popular Evangelical Literature

Evangelical prophecy believers sense acutely the diminished sense of selfhood that cyberpunk authors and the writers of *The X-Files* also articulate. Yet they add an additional dimension that grows out of their own condemnation of the direction modern society and its elite cultures have taken. Even though all of human life (and the social status of evangelicals) is going to hell in a handbasket in the confrontation of humanity with modernity, true believers have an escape clause, a secret out available only to God's elite that permits them to escape the hell on earth and advance directly to some sacred realm by means of the literal bodily "Rapture" into heaven in the first stage of Christ's return. As in the examples in the previous chapters, irony plays a prominent role in the influential Left Behind series. No one, after all, escapes, at least after the first few pages and the giant airlift of millions (or billions?) of believers who otherwise disappear. Since they are staying around awhile, political involvement becomes a necessity for the concerned, with religious fantasy reflecting the recent and dramatic rise of the New Christian Right. Thus evangelical activists threaten the values of their nonevangelical neighbors even as they influence the most sensitive areas of U.S. foreign policy. Moreover, their activism also threatens their own time-honored spiritual values since instead of patiently waiting for the end and God's efficient handling of terrestrial concerns, they take matters into their own hands. Yet for all their doomsday rhetoric, evangelical frustration and rage have thus far stopped short (beneath a veneer of incivility) of becoming a ticking time bomb of inexorable radicalism—due above all to the internal contradictions of prophecy belief. Meanwhile, now fortified with diversified stock portfolios and professional sports arenas retooled as media-wired megachurches, not to mention a good part of the United States Congress and nearly all of the presidency, they experience a stronger and stronger need to convince themselves that their loss of control over Harvard and Yale generations ago entitles them to the same victim and martyr status as that accorded the ancient Christians burnt alive as torches in pagan Rome. Yes, irony does play a prominent role in contemporary cultural pessimism.

Themes, Sociology, Sources, Method

The later twentieth century witnessed the doctrinal reorientation of a major segment of American Protestantism. A new and influential category in popular culture of great significance emerged: end-time prophecy belief as a central tenet of faith for millions of Americans. This was doubtless fed by the belief that religion and society were corrupt beyond imagining, but it also was based on the special significance of the concept of *dispensations*.

This term implies a great intensification of classic Christian thinking about a series of divine covenants or agreements between God and humanity. Specifically, *dispensationalism* signifies time-limited eras of divine dealing with humanity according to a specific principle (for instance, divine law), predominant in that time block but potentially superseded in later periods.[1] Moreover, it now appeared, the age of the normal existence of Christianity and the church was drawing to an end. Soon the hidden mysteries of the book of Revelation would be unfolded. God would soon dispense end-time judgment to unbelievers and salvation to believers.[2]

These beliefs gained wide currency in the last three decades of the twentieth century, overleaping the denominational confines of yesteryear and (at the local level) infiltrating huge segments of denominations that formally repudiated them (for example, the Southern Baptist Convention, which resists dispensational thinking at the official level, but obviously cannot rein in all of the popular beliefs of the "people in the pews"). That the spread of this outlook reflected a larger pessimism about the future is axiomatic.

Further, this Protestant reorientation toward cultural pessimism took on even more distinct characteristics. Its prophecy-believing adherents tended to hold to doctrines that had traditionally been out of favor. It was not optimistic by early nineteenth-century standards. The new outlook emphasized not just the near approach of the end and the heretical and moral depravity of most forms of Christianity along with the corruption of most institutions, but also the near approach of a lengthy (seven-year) and horrendous period of foretold Tribulations. Most notably it stressed the bodily removal of believers from the world immediately before the onset of these horrors (a rare opinion until recently, and a view that immediately transports contemporary dispensationalists into an expectation of security from suffering utterly at odds with the dominant mentality of ancient and medieval Christians). That is, in accord with one verse of the New Testament,[3] the faithful were to be secretly taken up into the air to be with Christ—leaving doubters and unbelievers to continue the struggle below on extremely unfavorable terms.[4] This extraction of true believers sealed with the Spirit of God came to be known as the *Rapture*.[5]

The spread of interest in the Rapture, the impending Tribulation, and the near end of normal history meant, among other things, that a view of Protestant Christianity once stigmatized as bizarre and working-class now moved out of the assemblings of a small number of vehement adherents into paradenominational organizations flourishing within myriad host bodies (as well as within all manner of nonchurch-connected individuals).[6] Some estimates put the number of dispensationalist evangelicals in the United States today at twenty million; others estimate that perhaps fifty percent of the American population has some rudimentary identification with the dispensationalist or Rapture-oriented position. Both numbers seem unlikely, as they vary according to how one asks the question. We can approximate, but to insist upon exact figures is risky. For what it may be worth, the publishing industry estimates the total sales of the Tim F. LaHaye and Jerry B. Jenkins fictional rendering of the matter at near seventy million, if not more. This does not give us the number of adherents, of course, but it does give us a sense of the movement's scale.[7]

Moreover, given the nature of American life at the close of the millennium, the dramatic spread of dispensationalist views deserves close study. Typical of the mid- to late twentieth-century evangelical return into the popular imagination movement was *The Late Great Planet Earth*. It appeared in 1970 over the byline of Hal Lindsey and C. C. Carlson, packaging dispensationalist views for a nondenominational audience exhausted by cultural upheaval, apprehensive of revolution and globalization, and willing to be alarmed by such things as signs of the Antichrist. Lindsey and Carlson built further on foundations laid in the nineteenth century, when, as historian Paul Boyer writes, the approach known as "premillennial dispensationalism, formulated by the . . . churchman John Darby" foretold "a series of last-day signs" signaling "the approaching end. Those will include wars, natural disasters, rampant immorality, the rise of a world political and economic order, and the return of the Jews to the land promised by God to Abraham." According to the tradition of Darby inherited by Lindsey from its incorporation into the highly influential Scofield Reference Bible, first published in 1909:

> The present "dispensation" will end with the Rapture, when all true believers will join Christ in the air. Next comes the Tribulation, when a charismatic but satanic figure, the Antichrist, will arise in Europe, seize world power, and impose his universal tyranny under the dread sign "666," mentioned in Revelation. After seven years, Christ and the saints will return to vanquish the Antichrist and his armies at Har-Megiddo (the biblical Armageddon), an ancient battle site near Haifa. From a restored Temple in Jerusalem, Christ will then inaugurate a thousand-year reign of peace and justice—the Millennium.[8]

This packaging of prophecy in contemporary dress initiated by Lindsey was to have a great future before it and to serve as both a factor in the reorientation of much of American Protestantism and—at the same time—as an indicator of how considerable a force prophecy belief was becoming. This was the case even before it emerged in 2003 that officials at the White House of the second President Bush were allegedly in touch with a prophecy-oriented televangelist in Michigan, Jack van Impe, for his version of the coming apocalypse—a real-world political scenario far-fetched but not implausible.[9]

Linked closely to all this was the appearance of a new genre of popular writing, a kind of science fiction or historical novel set in the mode of biblical prophecy (at least as contemporary dispensational interpreters of the Bible represent prophecy). Hal Lindsey inaugurated a major move into a multifaceted genre of Christian cultural pessimism, a genre that then took shape in works of biblical interpretation as well as in numerous novelistic narratives targeted at differing market segments. Whether or not secular futurology counts as nonfiction is hard enough to determine; but when one deals with evangelical dispensationalist reference works on the future, the determination of genre according to fabrication or certain knowledge becomes impossibly problematic. The main purveyors of novelistic treatments of the Rapture and Tribulation, Tim LaHaye and Jerry B. Jenkins, also maintain a Pre-Tribulation Research Center staffed by trained pro-Rapture theological experts dealing in their version of futurology. Their initial twelve adult novels (before the prequels) narrate both the Rapture and the terrible and intense struggles of those Left Behind as they cope with wars, disasters, the Antichrist, and Armageddon. At all events one finds here a strong correlation with cultural pessimism, since the collapse of the world system correlates directly with the purportedly close proximity of the Rapture and Tribulation.

To be sure, Christian and Jewish speculation about divine endgame scenarios revealed in scripture has been a hot topic for believers over and over again since antiquity. This fact, however, in no way diminishes the particular importance of the recent wave of prophecy belief and its cultivation in American popular culture. On the contrary: it heightens that importance. For in fact cultural historians have long tended to regard it as axiomatic that particular religious views about endgames and Last Things bear a close relation to particular real events and real crises in the mundane world.[10] So a flare-up of that perennial condition, prophecy-mediated interpretation of the current situation, should always command attention. It ought to make the observer ask: what sociocultural factors can account for such flare-ups? What is changed in the total situation? What new data count for believers as significant "signs of the times"?

Thus the recent coalescence of this new form of prophecy belief into a major force in American religion cries out to be taken as a reading of recent times. Inasmuch as it targets believers looking for meaning, and further makes extensive use of an end-time scenario, this kind of prophecy belief likewise has every sign of being a kind of overtly religious analogue to cyber-noir apocalyptic narratives such as *The X-Files*. In both instances, the turn to cultural pessimism is striking.

Now in the pages immediately below, the former of the two coauthors according to the title page (Stroup) engages in dialogue with the previous work of a specialist on dispensationalist prophecy fiction, that specialist being, of course, the latter of the coauthors (Shuck). The intent here is to take Shuck's detailed investigation as a kind of starting point and to use it as the basis for going further—not by detailed reinvestigation of dispensational prophecy fiction as such (for which Shuck is the specialist, and which this present chapter makes no claim to examine in micrological detail) but rather by placing it and Shuck's treatment of it in a wider and deeper context, the context of contemporary popular cultural pessimism and its rooting in the social and political environment of contemporary America. Shuck will then, of course, have his own part to play in the unfolding of subsequent chapters, chapters which will constitute an unfolding and a modification of the present chapter. That approach—signaled here to the reader in the present chapter with various verbal formulae departing from the simple "we" or "the present authors"—allows the chapter (and us) to engage in internal critique of perspectives and, we hope, in the end to follow out the strong and significant parallels between different strands in popular culture. For what the present authors intend—in this chapter and throughout this book—is indeed to pursue comparisons and contrasts between outwardly divergent products of recent popular culture and to do so in detail and in ways that can move the understanding of these matters beyond the point where Shuck's monograph had left them. But that advancing will take place, not by any further detailed study of contemporary prophecy fiction as such (which the elder of the two present authors does not intend to undertake), but by relying on the work of Shuck and others as the secured basis for a view that now needs to be placed into analytical and comparative context. Shuck's detailed study of prophecy fiction highlights three themes that readily link that fiction with more secular varieties of fantasy cultural pessimism: the possibility that it can function as a "safety valve" under certain circumstances, the possibility that it can under certain circumstances play a role in energizing for political activism, and the possibility that its extreme apocalyptic scripting can connect with a diminished sense of contact with reality (in other words, efficacy of the individual self) at a time when such concerns are not unknown in the wider culture. These three themes in Shuck's book strongly suggest that his study is a major point of interconnection between apocalyptic studies and the study of contemporary culture at large.[11]

At the beginning, then, allow the former author first to say something more about the method to be followed here. Next, in order to avoid misunderstanding at the very outset, the author will remind the reader of some very significant differences between secular or New Age cybernoir cultural pessimism on the one hand and on the other hand evangelical Christian pessimism oriented toward the Rapture and the coming Tribulation.[12]

Now by *method* here the main point to be made concerns sources and evidence. Just as with the cybernoir devotees, so also here the chief interest is not in poll data concerning attitudes or intentions in correlation with socioeconomic data. Here again the primary focus is on products of the imagination as indicators of deep concerns, especially concerns that point toward an image of the near future. Once readings have been taken on these deep concerns, the study will of course look to see whether real life movements and events currently suggest human movement toward the future encoded in the images and language of those deep concerns. As for the method of examining this material, more will be said on it a bit later.

What then needs to be borne in mind initially as one considers the pessimistic attitudes of two analogous audiences, those who follow *The X-Files* and *The Matrix* on the one hand, and those who follow the volumes of Left Behind on the other? Both attitudes view current conditions in America and the world as corrupt, perhaps even corrupt beyond repair (though stay tuned here, as finality on this topic is not yet to be had). Both attitudes indulge in elaborate escape fantasies that, we shall argue, finally serve to help the distressed and literally or figuratively homeless individual to find comfort and a certain community and compensatory distraction so as to continue to operate in this comfortless environment for the foreseeable future. Both attitudes and their related cultural products create a mental and social world in which reminiscence of home and even of compensatory resistance to current corruption can be sensed. [13]

In the long run, however, in empirical experience and even in fantasy narrative the actual end of this present age does not arrive very effectively for either group. Even if narrative may depict the disappearance of millions of believers, those left behind must still struggle with mundane matters such as house payments and flu vaccinations. And, as coauthor Glenn W. Shuck's recent monograph argues in detail, the long-term emphasis is on those who must cope here below. Indeed, reading Shuck's detailed analysis of the LaHaye-Jenkins narratives, the sense repeatedly emerges that the obsessive treatment of problems faced by those not taken in the Rapture is so detailed that it begins to function as a comfort for contemporary believers troubled by two thousand years of the nonappearance of the Second Coming. [14]

On the more secular side of this comparison and contrast, Mulder and Scully still must cope with their emotions and the wrecks of their careers for the indefinite future—all the more so as after nine years of *The X-Files* there is still no certainty that alien takeover will indeed infallibly occur at the next turn of the Mayan calendar. Thus throughout this study the growing tendency has turned out to be a foregrounding of the aspect of latent function[15]—that is, a decision to emphasize the compensatory and distracting quality of these dark products of popular culture, and to do so in a way that challenges any crass version of the older belief that (with regard to the most extreme versions) their first result is to encourage genuine revolt by saucer cultists or conspiracy nuts—or real *War Games*—style self-triggering of literal nuclear apocalypse by religious maniacs eager to lift a helping trigger finger for Christ. In this crass sense, at least, the predominant tendency toward compensatory fantasy and comforting hope for escape ordinarily does not encourage overt action of this blatant kind. (Other kinds of activism are not so excluded—and, as a later chapter will argue, the growing influence of Armageddon-enthusiasts on American geopolitics may call for greater concern than the present authors initially thought with regard to mushroom clouds invested with a sacred aura.)[16]

Yet that having been said, still one must concede real differences in the potential for political and social impact on the part of the two groups. Evangelicals, especially those oriented toward Rapture and Tribulation or other activation of prophecy belief, are close to constituting a multifaceted movement, religious, cultural, and certainly political. The partial overlap with the right-wing evangelical moral majority and later organizations is obvious. Furthermore, this tendency is not random or casual. Judeo-Christian monotheism in many of its versions has historically tended very strongly toward taking the form of a movement, and a highly exclusivistic and active movement at that. Later on it will be necessary to say more on this paradoxical tendency toward action while the world hurries to a dramatic end.

Secular cybernoir addicts following William Gibson and *The X-Files* and similar darkly technoid visions are far more shapeless as a group or "community." Probably even an investigation limited to the audience specifically targeted by investors and advertisers supporting this genre would find appreciable overlap with at least the more passive consumers of LaHaye-Jenkins works. Yet the feel of the cybernoir group is obviously not at all evangelical. Its ambience is rather amorphous New Age/Christian-liberal/conspiracy-theorist—but only in a nonbinding way. For *most* of that audience the cultivation of conspiracy and related narrative is not zealous, not inner-circle-nut-group-activist. The fondness for conspiracy and for weird hypotheses serves rather to keep the world at bay, to help avoid dangerous commitment. Mulder wants to believe at the outset—a stance that at some points during his nine years probably does not preclude atheism in religion or skepticism with regard to UFOs.

This group, like the presumably far smaller group of Right-extremist conspiracy adherents who may also watch *The X-Files* despite the show's left-liberal framework, could conceivably provide material for a movement under just the right circumstances. But for the larger of these two groups, those who do not hold to conspiracy hypotheses with enough zeal to embolden them to action, the impulse to cohere and agitate simply seems absent, at least at the present moment. Further, the key narratives are not locked in to a human structure so as to allow easy activation. Even the depiction of intense resistance in *The Matrix* is not so "plugged in."

What does characterize the cybernoir perspective is ambiguity with regard to political engagement, along with a sense of defect in the efficacy of all human agents and great uncertainty about the connection between any human action and the situation thereafter. The liberal commitment to civil rights, the residual nostalgia for an untroubled bond with the American government and its actions worldwide, the sense of loss and betrayal are presumably present in a good part of the target audience for cybernoir. Some occasional political involvement is certainly to be presumed here—but to suppose that a movement of anxious libertarians and New Age Democrats is coalescing around worldview issues or a nonexistent revolutionary subtext in the cult of Keanu Reeves or David Duchovny stretches the imagination. Cybernoir devotees are ill-suited to turn into a serious and lasting political movement or agitation group of a readily identifiable stripe. Ambiguity, with the use of improbable conspiracy theories to keep single-minded commitment at bay, is the foundational attitude in cybernoir. To be sure, it is not the entire story—when personal situations demand, a Mulder or a Neo or any other cybernoir antihero can defend the heroic role quite effectively. The possibility of resistance is formally upheld—but the organization for it is not at all in place on the cybernoir side of things.

The situation is extremely complicated. As the former Yale University president and commissioner of major league baseball A. Bartlett Giamatti—whose brief term of service in the latter capacity was darkened by the Pete Rose affair and tragically interrupted by heart disease which sent him into the cosmic postseason—indeed really may have said: "If you can't handle ambiguity, you shouldn't be at Yale."[17] The package of similarities and differences can be approached with the observation that cybernoir university types and dispensational Protestants view American institutions and American culture with equal degrees of bitter nostalgia, recalling days of old when one could cherish a kind of unmixed bonding love directed toward the country and its government and institutions, organized religious groups included. However, the two audiences ordinarily show somewhat different attitudes toward the contemplated destruction of the world as they have known it, corruptions and conspiracies included.

The contrast can be seen most clearly by following up on the previous chapter and remaining with *The X-Files* series as the preeminent example of cybernoir conspiracist cultural pessimism. Suppose that the projected alien takeover does occur on schedule, with little effective obstacle from either humanity or the antitakeover aliens with their penchant for pyromania. In a best-case scenario on those terms, the human enemies of Mulder and Scully will continue a barely tolerated existence as administrators of the alien devastation of human life and culture. Less likely would be a continuing violent and active resistance by some human minority effectively vaccinated against the alien virus, doubtless with numerous twists, turns, betrayals, and plots.

Now all of these outcomes are highly unsatisfactory. To be sure, Mulder, Scully, and the Lone Gunmen would have the satisfaction of knowing that their suspicions were finally vindicated, in that much of the dying or enslaved human race could see that Mulder's crackpot theories were on target and that their governments had probably been betraying everyone on a scale hitherto unimaginable since the final days of the Nixon administration. Pyrrhic, this satisfaction. In other words, the basic analysis here simply confirms the findings of sociologist of religion Steve Bruce. As he wrote concerning the general prospects for the larger mentality of individualistic and quasipantheistic spirituality represented by New Age followers, "In summary, New Age religion cannot aspire to promote radical and specific change because it does not have the cohesion and discipline of the sect."[18]

The situation of the evangelical devotees of the Rapture is significantly different—different with a positive advantage for the evangelicals compared with the cybernoir devotees. Now in general terms, supposing the initial Rapture occurred, what would be the situation of those left behind? While the lukewarm and unbelieving would continue a very difficult physical and spiritual struggle during the post-Rapture Tribulation, with billions being annihilated (including most of the Jewish population),[19] still the final outcome is, on overt dispensationalist terms, highly satisfactory. The first set of living believers will have been removed from earthly suffering to the eternal enjoyment of divine bliss (heightened by the contemplation of the infinite sufferings of unbelievers, presumably). Moreover, those left behind who manage to avoid serving the Beast and Antichrist and who persevere in faith in the Christian God through Jesus Christ and the Holy Spirit will, in a few short and nasty years, also find themselves transported to not quite so elevated a condition of bliss unending, but nevertheless equally soothed by the same sense of triumph over devils and damned colleagues seen to be tossing in fiery billows of molten pitch for all eternity. While some dispensational believers still struggling here below with the flesh may secretly cherish reservations about how enjoyable all this may be in actuality, nonetheless it does technically count as unalloyed triumph from their point of view. Presumably once the transition to eternity is made, the infinite extent of this bliss will become evident even to those who thought they would find the eternal spectacle of the damnation of friends and relatives unattractive. At least these are the attitudes and feelings that they ought to experience now and forever, same as it ever was.

Yet with all these observations made, the curious investigator is still far from any deep understanding of the cultural pessimism that undergirds current radical prophecy belief, above all its political potential and its alliances with related groups. That potential and its contrast with other currents of cultural pessimism must be on our minds as we explore the features of contemporary prophecy belief. In the course of this exploration we may even find some explanation for why progressive, New Age, and cybernoir affiliates seem more enervated in situations where prophecy believers instead seem on the whole rather emboldened toward action.

Activism, Pessimism, Politics, and Preparation: An Overview

Certainly the readers of prophecy fiction tend toward the same negative diagnosis of American life and institutions, as do hardcore fans of cybernoir. To be sure, many different nuances exist in assessing just how irretrievable the entire situation has become—and whether extreme human efforts may not be called for after all. We have already shown that the more secular or cybernoir group is not equipped to move into an activist or reform mode in any noteworthy manner. What about the hardcore Christians? Here judgments vary, though the degree of political activism among Rapture enthusiasts usually does not come off as high, at least in theory. The point of contrast that establishes this is usually taken to be the contrast of prophecy believers awaiting the Rapture and Tribulation here with a smaller, far more activist Christian group that is not obsessed with the Millennium.[20]

It is well established that one important but small alternative to dispensational prophecy believers is a hardcore and literalistic group of Protestant Christians known as Christian reconstructionists. They reject preoccupation with dispensations or the imminent arrival of the Tribulation and Millennium. They instead expect divine power to assist them in a complete takeover of the culture and government, such that the standards of primitive Christianity and even the Old Testament can be applied generally, a belief system often euphemistically referred to by insiders as "dominion" or "crown rights" theology.[21] This group—a small, fringe group, regarded by many as overtly problematic—has fuzzy boundaries with those strongly influenced by a Christian take on survivalist and militia-style commitment to some imminent, Millennium-based activism.[22] Somewhat similar to nineteenth-century Christian social liberals (although more activist), reconstructionists aiming

for repristination believe that human activism must first prepare the way for
the Second Coming of Christ—but for them the activism is not liberal reform
but an extreme return to the rule of God's Law from the Old Testament.
Imagine for a moment a typical kindergarten celebration of Thanksgiving
complete with cornucopia, dried corn, funny black hats, and large buckles,
featuring cardboard blunderbusses (definitely not imitation in survivalist circles!). With that act of the imagination you are in the general neighborhood,
though of course reconstructionist fashion police may have other suggestions
at this late date. Anyhow then combine this with rigid interpretations of Old
Testament law, such as stoning as a preferred form of capital punishment.
Then one gathers a sense of the sort of reconstruction the reconstructionists
have in mind. As for casual Fridays, they will not be on the calendar, whether
you like the reconstructionist fashion police or not.

The reconstructionist movement with regard to doctrine is a radical
intensification of the theology of Princeton conservative Cornelius van Til
carried out by Rousas John Rushdoony in the early 1970s.[23] These unyield-
ing antimillennialist believers have not been gentle in their condemnation
of prophecy believers interested in the Rapture and related doctrines. That
they are not simply another splinter group to be discounted is shown by
the reports that prominent ministers with reconstructionist tendencies have
ties to the White House of George W. Bush—though where these ministers, friendly members of Congress, and White House staff actually position
themselves theologically is difficult to discern. The groups in question adopt
stances ranging all the way from mild pressure in elections to hyperbolic position statements verging on calls for extreme measures to reassert the "crown
rights" of Jesus Christ as God and the taking of earthly power by the godly
along with enforcement of inequality for nontrinitarian Americans.

Likewise the groups in question show a variety of positions with regard
to a pragmatic alliance with their nominal rivals, the group of dispensationalists most concerned with apocalypse and Armageddon.[24] Now ordinarily it
is thought that, since dispensationalist prophecy believers expect a dramatic
end, probably soon, such multilevel political activism of the reconstructionist
variety will strike most of them as quite out of place. Is this the whole story?

Certainly all contemporary varieties of American cultural pessimists feel
indignant that the culture and institutions of America are in their view now
so corrupt that redeeming them seems difficult. Unalloyed trust in government and institutions is gone for many, at least in any simple way, though
9/11 and the election of the second Bush mitigate this to a degree. Still,
with the continuing currents of globalization and multiculturalism, great

reserve must offset any strong renewal of such trust in institutions. Yet, while this mistrust overtly unites cybernoir libertarian or swing Democrats along with Christian cultural pessimists, the very real strands of nuance need to be recalled constantly. Also—with regard to prophecy believers—one must look beyond the standard notion that prophetic expectation simply works against cultural and political activism.

In point of fact, by and large no group of Christian evangelicals has completely given up the hope of a reconquest or a rechristianizing of America. The rise of the Sunbelt and the procession of more or less evangelical presidents and their hosting of prominent preachers reinforces the possibility of hope against hope here, also on the part of those expecting the Rapture and Tribulation, that political action may yet yield tangible fruits this side of paradise.

Noteworthy here are several points. First, the more adroit of the end-time theorists, duly cognizant of more or less twenty-five hundred years of spectacular miscalls by Judeo-Christian gloom merchants looking for the big one, have spun out the hypothesis of a trial run or dry run in the form of a mini-, early, or pseudo-Tribulation, a category of immense utility for those wise enough to hedge on such an ultimate point. In other words, prophecy-believing exegetes have already built in devices by which the nonarrival (postponement) of the Rapture and Tribulation can be handled, explaining that all now find themselves for the moment in a "pre-Tribulation tribulation."[25] Second, this is, ultimately, an American movement, despite its British origins. Americans may believe in the end of the world, but they are reluctant to elect political leaders who overtly give up hope of doing something with positive results. (And politicians, however much they may share Sunbelt apocalyptic tendencies, are really quite constrained here by the long-established rules of American political discourse, which demands reform, hope, expansion, even a hundred years after the closing of the frontier.)[26] What does all this imply for the coming years in the millions-strong prophecy movement?

The most recent close study of these anxious souls, based in considerable measure on their narrative imaginings in exegetical and social context, comes from intellectual historian Glenn W. Shuck. His 2005 monograph views prophecy believers as poised between two options given the repeated postponements of the Rapture and full Tribulation—the options of intensified accommodation to contemporary culture and of intensified activism to transform that culture with themselves as instruments of God in a premillennial context. Shuck argues that prophecy-oriented evangelicals are acutely conscious of the way time and the environment gradually push them toward a relaxed stance that threatens to make their movement domesticated and indistinguishable from the tepid religion of the wider culture. They are at the moment not only prosperous financially but also quite aware that they "stand on the precipice of overaccommodation, incorporating many of the values of the secular . . . culture they ostensibly resist."[27]

Desiring to preserve their movement and wanting to "re-claim a sense of marginalization" diminished by, for example, having a sympathetic president in the White House, prophecy believers have begun to experiment with a variety of stratagems. According to Shuck's reading of the context of Christian prophecy fiction, the target audience and its leaders not only expect their futurological novels to abound in troublesome miracles that mark out their mental universe as highly distinctive; beyond this, argues Shuck, their leaders for some time have been considering, even engaging in, the possibility of a once unthinkable turn to a sustained variety of intensely political action in today's real world. In this way, given the unknowable length of the pre-Tribulation tribulational period of waiting and testing, they can stake out a claim to be God's preTribulation agents on earth:

> Basically, the injunctions against political activity exist because prophecy believers think they can only do so much before God returns and does everything himself. But LaHaye and Jenkins subtly transform their dynamic protagonists throughout the *Left Behind* novels into actors for God's eternal plan, role-players who take on wider political involvements precisely because they believe they *are* actualizing God's End-Times plan, rather than simply bending its rules but otherwise respecting its limitations. Thus, although prophecy belief may still act as a restraint on large-scale political activity among prophecy believers, the tethering rope may become weaker the longer the End tarries. The *Left Behind* novels suggest that dispensational prophecy believers may be embarking on a slippery slope toward the more unrestrained, reactionary positions of their Christian reconstructionist cousins, albeit for very different reasons.[28]

Now let us hold off here in trying to determine what this all means in detail within the broader context of our present investigation. Enough has been sketched to complete our general orientation of comparing and contrasting cybernoir types with prophecy believers. In both cases, the appearance of full-scale escape is (on close examination) something of an illusion. For the followers of *X*- or *Matrix*-episodes, the struggles of Scully, Mulder, or Neo served to comfort, to assist in fantasy, but hardly to embolden toward political or revolutionary action—distraction, opiates for the technoid proletariat, perhaps—but no pain-killing drink of mead prior to some berserk literal attack on the worldwide System. Nor do the dark versions of science fiction so depress their consumers as to render them incapable of returning to their *Office Spaces,* their lives of Dilbertage oscillating between endless meetings about software upgrades and the ritual congregating around water coolers that provide both the occasion for corporate gossip and also potential vessels for gathering samples in the untimely and constitutionally questionable practice of drug testing.

Likewise the nonfiction empirical Rapture remains elusive for prophecy-obsessed Christians, while (as we shall see below) the fictional Rapture of novelistic narrative more and more is overshadowed by intense and complicated narratives concerning the coping strategies of those who have not been taken up with Christ in the air. More basically, the professional leadership of the dispensational movement is in fact well aware that the end has been failing to arrive now for two thousand years or more, and that the delay evokes much overt skepticism among unbelievers.[29] They are so aware that they have self-consciously built in both narrative and exegetical ways of deflecting such naïve objections on the part of hardened skeptics failing to see the inner wisdom of God's plan.

As Shuck points out, while one wing of prophecy believers shows signs of tending toward hitherto unheard-of activism in politics at various levels and in culture wars, the mentality propelling this new spirit of takeover (if it comes to full fruition) is not one of upbeat optimism. The sense is of a grim falling into line, of conforming to a divine script written before human history, a script that in prophetic revelation now threatens to crowd out all surprises, all divine spontaneity or human innovation. If the prophecy believers must become activists, it is as fully scripted divine marionettes, not as independent agents. In this way, it appears, they hope to hasten the arrival of the Rapture in a move that unexpectedly lacks the logical consistency of their more conservative Reconstructionist cousins.

Thus even the prospect of unprecedented premillennialist activism strikes the observer as an option tending toward grim hopelessness to be rescued only by some divine grace that would make the eternal outcome palatable. In the short term, of course, there is no expectation of spontaneous improvement, of a religious springtime for the Christian message. Certainly neither reconstructionists nor prophecy enthusiasts expect Harvard, Yale, and most definitely not the most recent apostate, Princeton, to return to evangelical Christianity on their own initiative, any more than they really expect Los Angeles and Manhattan to become citadels of piety. Not one of the popular narratives of end-time Rapture and Tribulation has any place for a mass reconversion of

America's cultural elite to Bible-believing fundamentalism (with the possible exception of Larry Burkett's novel *The Illuminati*—although he describes an end that turns out to be a false alarm).[30] In any case the spread of upscale unbelief can be explained away by reference to the scriptures. If God hardens the hearts of those whom former Vice President Dan Quayle (during his days of criticizing the motherhood of Murphy Brown) once famously dubbed the cultural elite, it merely follows the textual archetype of Pharaoh, whose heart was hardened by God unto plagues and damnation. If the Rapture actually does arrive in this generation, however surprising that may be to the more theologically sophisticated—at least among progressive seminarians—the classic "hardening" tactic will explain why so few at Harvard and CBS heeded the words of Christ's end-time message.

On the other hand, if the struggle does continue, if the encouragement of the unending series of *Left Behind* sequels is needed for the truly long haul—that, too, can be digested, though with the passage of time the need will grow for prophecy believers to create a culture amenable to their beliefs and unlikely to disconfirm them.[31] If the prophecy-believing activists have their premillennial way in preparation for the real showtime of the divine endgame—then there may indeed be a fuller legal takeover of institutions by Sunbelt and Midwestern evangelicals; there may be juridical incarceration of the godless in larger numbers on the way to Armageddon—but some things will not change. The divine script will not be seriously rewritten. There will be no spontaneous springtime of conversions among the skeptical godless at the top of the High Modern/Postmodern-posthistorical social pyramid. There will be no place for the spontaneous development of the evangelical message in any sense potentially contrary to the musings of LaHaye, Jenkins, and their cohorts. And there will be spiritual warfare in expectation of the coming full Tribulation and the eventual bitter struggle with the Antichrist, however near or far that episode may be.

Thus in the end, the prophecy believers may turn to sustained, even intense, activism while enduring the preTribulation tribulation. This will, however, not rejuvenate America, if the dark scenarios of the Left Behind series are to be trusted. An inner conversion of America, a true and effective rollback of institutional and societal corruption, is as little expected among evangelicals as an analogous springtime on different terms could be among pessimistic readers of William Gibson.

Moreover, here the program-obsessed evangelicals do have something in common with cybernoir devotees. While the cybernoir types increasingly tend to view the human as an illusion (and with it moral responsibility and nonmechanistic or nondata-processing concepts of intelligence), the prophecy believers have their own devaluation of the human. For them the highest calling of the species is that of marionettes grimly executing the scenario and moral imperatives of a mysterious God, allegedly merciful and loving, but little given to encouragement of freethinking.

Thus the chapters below argue that in the end, important strands in both groups part company with the heritage of both secular and religious modernity based as it has been on varying strands of the eighteenth-century Enlightenment. This can be seen with regard to the central issue of human freedom, or free will—or spontaneity in deciding and acting. A quick survey of options at the first high-water mark of Western modernity, the eighteenth-century Enlightenment, shows that it knew many possibilities here, both secular and religious and ranging from the concept of human beings as near angels fallen into sickness and ignorance (early Enlightenment nonDeist Christianity) to humanity as a collection of machines (Julien Offray de La Mettrie).

Yet as any American familiar with political and inspirational rhetoric knows, the American consensus has, by and large, been built on a rhetoric of freedom, free choice—as James Russell Lowell put it:

> Once to ev'ry man and nation
> Comes the moment to decide
> In the strife of truth with falsehood,
> For the good or evil side.[32]

Notably, American Roman Catholics, who retain infant baptism rather than requiring corporeal and mental maturity for church membership, are much more open to free will than the hyperAugustinian first generations of Protestant reformers, especially Luther and Calvin—an openness that for a long time has allowed Catholics to fit in rather well as the American enterprise has unfolded.

Options religious and secular that did not provide scope for this outlook have—up to now, at least—not done well in the American marketplace of ideas. Thus it is quite typical that, at the end of the trajectory, in the fantasy world of *The X-Files,* it counts as a sign of total resignation and defeat when the hallucinating Mulder hears the image of a dead character tell him to abandon his guilt and go on to personal enjoyment because, as Mulder hears it affirmed, he (Mulder) is emphatically "not the hub of the universe, the cause of life and death" because both he and the sepulchral speaker are "merely puppets in a master plan"—"[n]o more, no less."[33]

What Mulder hears denied (human importance, human nonpuppethood) must be denied because otherwise it is taken for granted—since being puppets runs so thoroughly against received American wisdom, whether rationalist secular or freewill Christian sacred. That is, American noneccle-siastical modernity has thus far been committed to some version of human spontaneity apart from the purely mechanistic working out of the laws of physics and data processing—precisely what (after two hundred years) is most threatened in *The Matrix,* and also challenged in much of *The X-Files.* Likewise with regard to religious worldviews, the distinctive Protestant heri-tage of the nascent American republic moved early on toward a stress on free will. More and more it had abandoned the quasiManichaean radical dualism of Luther and Calvin, specifically repudiating Calvinism's hyperAugustinian rejection of human free will, and (with seventeenth-century Dutch freewill Arminianism) defending free choice in religious matters. Only with a few nineteenth-century exceptions, the double predestination of Calvin and early Calvinists was unpopular; it found few takers willing to accept the status of damned to the glory of God forever on the basis of divine decrees laid down before the creation of the world. Free choice and hard work were axiom-atic, were more than slogans, were perhaps a Protestant ethic, after all—but in industrial America an ethic adopted quite eagerly by immigrant Roman Catholics engaged in practical ecumenism in the workplace.

Now contemporary high-intensity American Christianity still tends to issue no overt challenge to the bedrock Arminianism (freewill tendency) that is at the base of most American religiosity. Formal repudiation of freedom of the will in matters of individual ("personal" as American evangelicals like to say) salvation is not usually carried out even at this late date. Nonetheless the would-be defenders of American Christianity find in their prophecy-centered version of divine revelation an overwhelming emphasis on deterministic and fatalistic themes—not simply an overall divine script that is not to be varied, but also (as Shuck's important study of the new thematizing of the "Mark of the Beast" shows) a slide toward determinism in end-time salvation options. This shift in effect returns us (during the Tribulation at least, which is in any case a narrative model of the "here and now," and not so much of the life to come) to a kind of grimly fatalistic world just as demeaning as that in Calvin's eternal decrees of damnation issued before the foundation of the cosmos. How this plays out in the imagined future of Left Behind we will see below.

There can be little surprise, then, that these scenarios of escape, help, and comfort are unlikely to deliver any definitive solution. Neither the promised escape nor a fully human self-conception seems likely to result from either the cybernoir universe or the damnation-headed Tribulational earth depicted in prophecy fiction. But here we get ahead of the story—only after a fuller look at the frustrations inherent in current popular Christianity and its parallels with the frustrations of technoid escape will we be in a position to look at such pictures of true revolt, of real rebellion, as prove possible on the terms of contemporary American society. The immediate task is to retrace the outline of points just traversed, furnishing greater detail and wider perspective.

How to Read Christian Science Fiction

The last paragraphs immediately above have been spinning out a loosely conceived approach to reading Christian prophecy narratives and their cognate works. Now the assignment is to tighten the theoretical aspect even as we apply it to both products of Christian imagination and the real-world setting for those narratives. First, and to repeat with variation what was said above: the chief documents for the internal status of premillennialist prophecy believers are products of the imagination, above all the Left Behind series and its relatives. While the content of this material has been studied (most recently and in detail by Glenn W. Shuck), the issue of temporal perspective and its relation to real-life events must now be dealt with explicitly.

The next cue here comes from another novelist and expert in lateness and decadence, albeit one who would be abhorred by contemporary American evangelicals—that is, the Nobel prizewinning novelist Thomas Mann. His famous novel *The Magic Mountain* is celebrated for its mixing of time perspectives. It is not precisely accurate to say, as one sometimes hears loosely proclaimed, that Mann's narrated years 1907–1914 are "really about" the dissolution of democracy and decency in the crises of the Weimar Republic leading to Hitler (so, the years after 1918). It would be closer to the truth to say what Mann himself essentially said: that he portrays the unfolding of ideological obsessions in ways that imply simultaneous awareness of the origins, the spread, and the end result of the various points of view adopted by the leading characters. In this way the real-life involvement of characters and readers is targeted in many different ways. As Mann says with regard to his characters who are "heightened" or "enhanced" versions of the ideas they represent, the narrative in which they appear provides:

> [t]he mystery of the time element, dealt with in various ways in the book. It is in the double sense a time-romance. First in a historical sense, in that it seeks to present the inner significance of an epoch, the pre-war period of European history. And secondly, because time is one of its themes: time, dealt with not only as a part of the hero's experience, but also in and through itself. The book itself is the substance of that which it relates: it

depicts the hermetic enchantment of its young hero within the timeless, and thus seeks to abrogate time itself by means of the technical device that attempts to give complete presentness at any given moment to the entire world of ideas that it comprises. It tries, in other words, to establish a magical *nunc stans,* to use a formula of the scholastics [the present outside time, eternity—JS]. It pretends to give perfect consistency to content and form, to the apparent and the essential; its aim is always and consistently to *be* that of which it speaks.[34]

Now after nearly a century of time experiments, flashbacks, not to mention Proust criticism and New-Wave film, this kind of authorial playing with time perspectives can come as second nature even to those who do not offer credentials in comparative literature. In any case, it is evident that the LaHaye-Jenkins series, like Mann's quasifictional recounting of the tumultuous precursors of the Weimar disaster, overtly concerns not only time but also the trajectory toward the end of an age, indeed of time itself—and that quite self-consciously and with hints of reflection on two thousand years of failed prognostications about the end. Moreover, most of the pages in the series are dedicated to the difficulties of characters coping with harsh circumstances following the Rapture along with explicit consideration of the problems and possibilities of evangelical involvement in politics based on thirty years of mixed results from the Moral Majority phase of evangelical reentry into late modern political culture.

The multitude of perspectives on time and events in the series is further enhanced by the fact that the characters, if killed off, are replaced by what are in effect renewed instantiations of the divinely managed archetype that each represents for a limited number of printed pages.[35] Thus here the proposal is to read the novels transtemporally in such a fashion that they address first of all the immediate and current concerns of their consumers here and now, not the needs of a fictitious group stranded after the disappearance of millions. Such assumptions have long been standard with exegetes dealing with the living consumers of ancient apocalyptic belief or with Christian apologetics ostensibly directed toward nonbelievers (who do not buy apologetic works) but more practically targeting believers (who do purchase such items).

Second, the perspective adopted here is clearly one outside of the novels themselves, however absorbing these fantasy products may be. That perspective is necessary above all because here the aim is an eventual direct application of findings about the novels to clues, events, hints, and stirrings in the real world of contemporary politics and culture. Such a reading with an eventual search for a contemporary objective correlative has its own self-evident logic as a means of getting at the mood and inclinations of a sizable reader-ship. That one here deals with fantasy products enhances certain difficulties but by no means disqualifies the novels as evidence.[36]

The Reading: A Contextual and Analytical Approach

Contemporary prophecy fiction is not first generation. As Shuck's *Marks of the Beast* shows, the twelve volumes of Left Behind (before the pre-quels) represent a reflective advance on earlier, cruder novels and take into account the current economic well-being of many evangelicals. Also on the agenda are the mixed results of thirty years of moral majority-style reengagement in politics that reversed the disengagement following on the original fundamentalist controversies of the early twentieth century. Beyond that, one may readily suppose that generations of audience expo-sure to science fiction, cybernoir, and political conspiracy theory is taken for granted by contemporary authors and opens up possibilities in religious narrative fiction not readily available previously.[37] In the section that fol-lows immediately below, the voice of the elder of the two coauthors seeks to weave a lifetime of personal observation of the historical anxieties of post-Reformation evangelicals and his view of the Left Behind novels into a fabric further adorned with several points that specialist Shuck dangles in front of his readers.

Shuck's monograph depicts the mental (or at least fantasy) universe of contemporary prophecy believers, some now immensely wealthy and with many connections to federal and state government. For Shuck the still-appearing Left Behind volumes provide a window into the concerns of a movement that worries about its distinctiveness vis-à-vis the larger secular culture. This movement also wonders whether thirty years of renewed politi-cal engagement have brought much in the way of satisfying results, a worry Shuck finds faithfully mirrored in the post-Rapture debates concerning what kinds of resistance legal and illegal can be attempted versus the one-world system instituted by the forces of the Antichrist.[38]

Above all, argues Shuck, the novels show us an activist mentality among those left behind but hopeful of salvation. Innovating in the direction of American hope, LaHaye and Jenkins break with earlier dispensationalist prophecy writers to contend that mortals left behind after the Rapture are not almost always damned. Instead, they have a single hope, one chance and only one remaining to escape eternal hellfire—a chance discarded if they accept the number or the mark of the Beast offered, commanded by the postRapture one-world government. That mark, of course, is required to buy and sell in the world of the Tribulation.[39]

Clearly here is a narrative impulse for strenuous resistance despite torments and executions on a fading planet. Yet all in all the impression of tremendous determinism prevails, not least because it turns out that, post-Rapture, those who take the mark of the Beast cannot remove it (although this does occur once in the novels).[40] This fact (with the issue of reconversion to God's Elect being uncertain, unlikely, and wholly hidden in the mysterious counsels of God) points toward growing acceptance of fatalism and determinism at the tactical or individual level in contemporary dispensationalists. The same indications are given at the sweepingly strategic level. There one encounters the analogous tendency to regard the divine apocalyptic script as essentially unvarying so that late-blooming Christians must carry it out slavishly—a theme growing ever stronger in recent prophecy fiction, according to Shuck.[41] Though the narrative by LaHaye and Jenkins concerns post-Rapture existence during the Tribulation, it is hard to see how such attitudes, dealt with in excruciating detail, can fail to spill over to the way evangelicals are encouraged to regard life here and now.

The combination of these factors means that, from the outset, it is highly problematic to suppose that Christians could ever effectively "escape" on these terms—except for those in the unknowable future who might get caught up in a heavenly updraft lifting their bodies (conspicuously absent of jewelry, clothing, prosthetics, and other assorted terrestrial accoutrements) straight toward heaven in a mighty wind. As for everybody else—well, in the Left Behind novels the situation is as follows:

Before the Rapture, the American conservative Protestants generically portrayed by the novels are so overtly successful in material and political terms that they must work hard to achieve a uniquely self-marginalized position of victimhood, as they are all obviously in danger of succumbing to worldliness. One notes here their megachurches equipped with bowling alleys, their suburban cable networks giving advice about online trading and the latest in designer antioxidants, along with the latest hints on maintaining a Martha Stewart, Stepford-style, perfect palace of domestic placidity.[42]

After the Rapture, those left behind amid the turmoil of the Tribulation are in a far worse condition (although, unlike their raptured colleagues, they at least get to retain possession of their clothing and metal objects). They are further bedeviled (or one could say be-angeled) by a double problem. On the one hand—if they are aspiring believers organized against the Antichrist in the so-called Tribulation Force—they risk further conforming to worldliness by taking on the militancy, guile, religious blood-lust, and power-hunger of the forces of the Antichrist—even at times beating themselves at their own hellish game. On the other hand, they are more and more sentenced to appear simply as puppets working out an unvarying divine script, with no convincing sense of personal responsibility, all spontaneity long since destroyed—becoming essentially the opposite of anything recognizably human on the terms of freewill evangelicalism of the American Enlightenment. Thus the possibility of a truly satisfying "escape" for Christians is largely vitiated by overlapping circumstances that conspire to weaken the Christian's personal sense of responsible selfhood—that is, the believers, like the doomed unbelieving masses enslaved to the Antichrist, are relieved more and more of active choice or what the skeptic might recognize as significant moral responsibility. A novelistic flood of miracles and omens removes the uncertainty aspect of faith in God for those now "sealed in the Spirit" postRapture and thus incapable of contravening God's commands. The earthly damned are likewise under Satan's sway to such a degree that disobedience seems unlikely even as psychological feelings of responsibility remain rudimentary.

In the course of the novels the authors do indeed break with dispensationalist tradition in that they portray a desperately Christian resistance movement fighting the Antichrist with some limited but real and unexpected success, utilizing all the technological apparatus of the world they had grown to condemn as satanic in its techno-centralization. The consistent successes of this movement (despite a high casualty rate) lead Shuck to conclude that in the end what threatens the sense of self and of efficacy in the portrayed survivors is not the daunting powers of the Antichrist at all. What threatens their sense of selfhood and of effectiveness is rather an overpowering sense of being absorbed by the immutable purposes of a God whom believers are constrained to regard as somehow beneficent.[43] (That he is more feared than loved is perhaps an erroneous conclusion on the part of non-dispensationalist interlopers—but then again, being feared is on the whole more advantageous than being loved, at least for those masterminding spectacles of disaster, plague, holy war, and infinite torment in a style outdoing what any Renaissance condottiere could possibly match.)

Shuck further contends that the series as a whole is tremendously preoccupied with the interior self of prophecy-oriented Protestants. This preoccupation goes so far that from one perspective the tectonic cataclysms here narrated are but epiphenomena serving the narrative needs of an obsessional religious clientele, unsure of its salvation, its identity, and its relation to the nonreligious in America's elites. From another perspective, of course (as just observed), the selves and actions of the resisting post-Rapture believers become mere epiphenomena of the omnipotent God, whose script shapes not merely final outcomes, but the daily parts assigned to mortals. As LaHaye and Jenkins are committed to an American-style hands-on activism on the part of technosavvy members of the antiAntichristian Tribulation Force, and as they are equally devoted to the inerrant mandate encoded in the book of Revelation, the later volumes of the series show Christians totally caught up in armed and computerized struggle. In it their inner spontaneity and imagination are quite reduced to unquestioning efforts at carrying out the long-term scenario of struggle provided in (their reading of) the Apocalypse of John (Book of Revelation). This reduction is further enhanced by the way characters become interchangeable cogs, or perhaps interchangeable instantiations of the archetypes favored by both the authors and the divine Author himself, with the executed martyrs readily replaced: "Certain roles, in other words, replicate, albeit with different personalities. The Tribulation Force never lacks pilots, spiritual authorities, medical staff, technological consultants, or even economists."[44] This dispensability of characters, along with the growing sense that action is legitimate only as the unfolding of God's detailed script, means that the new theme of partial human success in resisting the Antichrist counts for little. Rather than enhancing the consolidated identity of a character or strengthening the sense of human efficacy, these factors paradoxically reduce it.

The bipolarity of perspectives here—the interior self entirely trumping all epiphenomena however earthshaking, the omnipotent Godscript absorbing all mortal efforts however strenuous—reminds us of how great is the debt owed by Western Christianity to that nonmillennialist founding father Augustine of Hippo, theological progenitor of Jean Calvin and original Puritanism, who is remembered for saying that he desired to know "God and the soul" and "[n]othing more."[45] The converted Christian's strong debt to Augustine's earlier flirtation with Manichaean dualism and determinism is equally celebrated.[46] Now in the Left Behind narratives it is striking that, despite the enormous countervailing debt of American Protestantism to Enlightenment Arminian doctrines of mitigated free will, nonetheless general fatalism and even irreversible determinism in salvation now begin to return to visibility, though of course in constant struggle with Enlightenment free-will currents. So great then must be the end-time pressures reflected in *Left Behind*—and they are not pressures resulting in a strengthened sense of self, identity, and confidence in human efficacy.

The full force of Shuck's portrayal can be conveyed only if we look at one or two key aspects of the narratives more closely. For attention to detail here confirms how strongly the fantasy life of dispensationalists now tends toward subsuming all human striving under the overpowering rubric of a divine plan or even a divine code—and to such a degree that the doctrine of free will in individual conversion, the bedrock of American Protestantism, moves into a shaky position.[47] Attention to detail also supports the further impression that real-world evangelicals in the early years of the new millennium moved toward favoring unprecedentedly intense political and cultural engagement. They are indeed emboldened in this respect, however much the reliance on God's purposes tends to reduce their personal sense of identity and efficacy.

Consider, for example, the issue of individual salvation. The novels reveal a considerable tension or confusion on this issue. On the one hand, LaHaye and Jenkins certainly register the imperative of free choice in American Protestantism, and that so strongly that they actually revise the grimmer early currents of prophecy fiction to allow a single chance of conversion and salvation to mortals after the Rapture has left them behind. And with the case of one appealing protagonist (Chang), they even allow the mysterious counsels of God to be so moved by prayer that the damning mark of the beast is removed from him. Ordinarily, however, this is not expected and apparently not possible—though in this one case, at least, the authors have paid the necessary postRapture homage to the heritage of free will in American Protestantism.

However, other indicators point in a fatalistic direction. Thus for LaHaye and Jenkins in the postRapture mode, those who under duress take the mark are regarded as damned even though they wish to assent to the promise of salvation extended to the human race—for apparently they now cannot move into effective assent.[48] Clearly the authors have in mind the classic scriptural passages (such as Exodus 7:3f. and John 12:39f.) on God's "hardening" of the heart of those habituated to evil such that they can no longer desire what is good—though in fact the authors seem to portray numerous of their menagerie of damned as psychologically desiring what they cannot attain through adequate fiduciary trust.

The repellent absurdities here cannot escape the reader—least of all the believer in dispensationalist versions of the afterlife. Thus this situation, combined with the unfolding horrors of earthly torture and tribulation, leads one key character explicitly to reflect on the distasteful aspects of it all:

> Rayford knew the prophecy—that people would reject God enough times that God would harden their hearts and they wouldn't be able to choose

him even if they wanted to. But knowing it didn't mean Rayford understood it. And it certainly didn't mean he had to like it. He couldn't make it
compute with the God he knew, the loving and merciful one who seemed
to look for ways to welcome everyone into heaven, not keep them out.[49]

However much Left Behind may fluctuate on the issue of Calvinistic determinism versus modern Protestant voluntarism with regard to conversion
and salvation, the picture is far less muddled when we turn to the level of
overall script and the nature of activist engagement postRapture. Here the
books' authors unhesitatingly opt for the position that Christian action in the
endgame can be significant only as the unquestioning and slavish execution
of roles written before all time and handed out for flawless execution by a
demanding God who (to be sure) is willing by miraculous means to empower
His servants to carry out the most difficult of tasks.[50]

At an earlier point, mention was made of the likelihood that some particular circumstance or constellation of conditions was driving the sudden
wave of interest in dispensational prophecy. From references in Left Behind
and from analogous references in fiction and out of it, one may readily
list some of the main factors causing alarm among potential consumers of
prophecy fiction. Much more than the approach of Y2K has been at work
here. The growing size and complexity of populations, the globalization and
multiculturalism of official culture, the rise of electronic databases and centralization of world currencies, the escalating distance of high government
officials from the general population, the technology-driven intensification
of means for surveillance of the population, the spread of unfamiliar religions in North America, the secularization promoted by the Supreme Court
and the American Civil Liberties Union (ACLU)—these all now mix to produce a heady and alarming brew for those conservative evangelicals who perceive themselves as Left Behind. Combine this with the heartland heritage
of populist distrust of government, along with cable television coverage of
the upscale trend toward marginalizing Christianity in public life, and one
has an unprecedented group of converging or overlapping triggers (if triggers
can overlap). The penchant for reading all these developments as satanic is
spurred not only by the more general spread of conspiratorial thinking after
Watergate, but as well by recurrent signs that high-level academics and public
leaders espouse nontheistical approaches—the so-called secular humanism of
its religious critics. The original or Renaissance form of this would be alarming enough. But that is not the end: add to it feminist and gender-studying
academic approaches together with deconstruction interpreted as the triumph

of nihilism in the universities where future leaders are trained, and then one sees why prophecy believers have such extreme anxiety, especially where the potential identity of children in school and college is concerned—even if one abhors such archconservative perspectives.[51]

Thus it is to be expected that precisely these kinds of worries figure prominently in Left Behind. There, for example, secular humanism is represented by the religion of the Antichrist, which amounts to a smokescreen covering human self-deification, moral relativism, generic nihilism, and a satanic centralization of communications and government serving the purposes of the Antichrist.[52] In particular, it appears that LaHaye and Jenkins themselves are chiefly motivated by "culture wars" types of issues.[53]

Looking outside the text from LaHaye and Jenkins to more mundane and timely expressions of evangelical opinion in the preRapture present, one finds that the same basic concerns are prominent in calls for political activism from the Religious Right.[54] The strength of this current of activism is noteworthy, as it now embraces large numbers of prophecy believers who—as a type—traditionally had tended to avoid politics in view of the presumed shortness of time before the Rapture and its dramatic aftermath, an avoidance traditionally supported as well by the conventional assumption that God would handle all matters of significant importance, especially during the end-times.

In other words, it appears that LaHaye and Jenkins speak for prophecy believers rather accurately when they call for political struggle of a kind once thought superfluous by those anticipating a quick and convulsive Rapture.[55] In today's Long March to the Rapture, the purpose given for new political engagement of course is ensuring that American culture does not become totally antiChristian well in advance of the Antichrist's appearing—the uncertainty about remaining time apparently encouraging prophecy believers to act so that the milieu for soul-winning and morality-enforcement does not deteriorate catastrophically well in advance of the truly serious trials that the era of Tribulation must ultimately bring. In the end, argues Shuck (in a sense following Susan Harding on this point), the necessity of protecting evangelical identity over a haul perhaps increasingly seen as long overrides the historic reluctance of dispensationalists to undertake much in the way of political action. It is in this general territory that one may also look for reasons for the partial convergence in matters political between dispensationalists and postmillennialist reconstructionists despite the differences in eschatology.[56]

Moreover, judging from what appears to be the tone of consensus discussion, apparently it is already well-documented, first, that in real American life this religiously-driven activism is born of what we have described as cultural

despair at evangelical loss of influence among top elites; second, that it flour-
ishes best when fear of change and bewilderment at the delay of the Second
Coming are operative; third, that this activism now has begun to constitute a
premillennial parallel to hardcore Christian Reconstruction; and fourth, that
it is often moved by impulses to act as an uncritical instrument of God's eternal purposes as encoded in scriptural prophecy filtered through an ardently
antihumanist dispensational clergy.[57]

At this point, it is possible to break off this close look at contemporary prophecy belief in order to expand the framework for its interpretation
beyond that supplied in the specialized research of scholars like Shuck and
his predecessors.[58] Certainly one finds ample support for the comparison and
contrast with the cultural pessimism of cybernoir fans. The sinking sense that
cultural and political decline are far along, the difficulty of imagining much
improvement under ordinary circumstances, the hope for escape by extraordinary means—these are all paralleled, shared between the two groups, as
is (out of different impulses) a strong consciousness of diminished human
identity and agency linked either to human-cyborg interplay or to supernatu-
ral-human interplay.

Yet the parallels cease when one looks closely at the readiness for aggressive political and cultural engagement among both groups. Indeed, the immediate original working hypothesis here appears to have considerable support
behind it, in that prophecy believers are able to combine a weakened sense of
personal efficacy with a militant sense of political engagement. This capacity
is in no way matched among the cybernoir-inclined, science fiction-driven
ranks of bookish (geekish? virtual?) souls otherwise presumably libertarian, a
conclusion that is not to be shaken by periodic waves of Left-liberal involvement in the occasional strongly motivated or single-issue election—shaking
this conclusion would require far more than some ephemeral "tsunami" of
temporary negative reaction to some perceived Right-wing excess. At the
superficial level, this difference in Right and Left is readily accounted for
by the obvious fact that prophecy believers stand in a two-thousand-year-
old tradition of religious movement organization, of political engagement by
organized churches. Moreover, this same religion-mediated tradition of political empowerment has often been historically linked with a sense of human
impotence and consequent reliance on supernatural omnipotence. One does
not find—at least not often and not yet—a similar nonironic faith in the
salvific power of new technologies and neocapitalism among contemporary
atheists (if indeed anyone in post-9/11 America besides Michael Newdow is
willing to admit to atheism).

Conclusion: Religion as the Continuation
of Politics by Other Means?

The practical spin-off from these changes is highly significant. For by this point, we recall, both the audience of *The X-Files* and the audience of any of the more spectacular end-of-the-world televangelists now have something in common. In both camps there now shows up a similar drift toward calling human free will into question. The radical French (mechanistic and rationalist) Enlightenment on the eve of the Revolution had on occasion proclaimed human beings to be machines—at the time, an extreme and exotic view, since both medieval Catholicism and later Reformed theology had recoiled from extreme determinism, even as most believers in the Age of Enlightenment tended toward a combination of mitigated free will and divine grace. Contrast the situation at the millennium: now, with the unstoppable forward gallop of technology and cyberengineering, any claim of human spontaneity, responsibility, and uniqueness seems constantly under attack in advanced circles, an attack only marginally repulsed by "defenses" of it such as one sees portrayed by Mulder's interior monologues or by *The Matrix.* How these issues of agency and identity can fare given the growing interest in uniting DNA and microchips to produce technohybrids (cyborgs) is pure guesswork, as the outcome would seem to be beyond good and evil, beyond ethical and psychological evaluation in any conventional sense.

Likewise the pragmatic downplaying of human free choice in Dispensationalism, and with it a growing taste for uncompromising confrontation in cultural and ethical wars over sex, education, gender roles, and a host of other issues all must be registered as pointing toward confrontation. For the Left Behind phenomenon looks to be merely a part of something larger at work, a self-identified and far-ranging conservatism that is intent on managing the tactics and strategy of an American confrontation with modernity and globalization.[59] This is an attitude both political and religious—and one that, well aware of the risks of too large a bet on the imminence of the Second Coming, by now has found theological justifications for attempting a kind of Christian reconquest of large segments of American culture and society, in practical coalition with nonapocalyptic evangelicals and with extreme reconstructionists. Here is not Calvin's Geneva—but it is not Kennedy's Camelot either.

The precondition for this set of developments is a demographic fact. Recent years have seen the emergence of a wealthy and politically powerful conservative movement in the New South or Sunbelt—a movement prepared to make political alliances on key social issues with Roman Catholic Republicans, Jewish voting blocs, hard-line evangelicals of whatever stripe, and even previously shunned Mormons in many instances. The newly confrontational coalition has been condemnatory of the direction that liberal religion, social thought, and politics have been taking for decades.

As for the broader problems raised by this variety of self-definition, those only start with the utility of this activism as a way of reasserting group distinctiveness despite financial success—though it is evident that uncertainty and even guilt about the degree of financial prosperity and media exposure gained by evangelical superstars has led to a compensatory counterimpulse toward what Shuck terms "frequent attempts at self-marginalization"—what the elder of the present authors has here tended to describe as a desperate search for a credible posture as victim and martyr—bringing the catacombs, as it were, to Orange County.[60] The celebrated instance of long-term patient Terri Schiavo and similar cases, puzzling to many observers, can to some degree be understood as part of the search by newly empowered evangelicals for marks of their victim status at a time when they exert a near unprecedented influence over American politics: not only does the contemporary mind-set call for victim status as a means of attracting further legitimacy and preferred legal standing, beyond this, there stands a long tradition in Protestantism of according theological and ecclesial legitimacy to persecuted segments within Christianity.

Yet to the eye of the careful observer—or so it seems to the former of the authors, perhaps more cynical than careful at times—these two overlapping criteria for victim status turn out to be distinct in a noteworthy way, at least in contemporary use. The historic Christian criterion of suffering under persecution ascribes value to loss suffered on account of lived, personal faithfulness and, under ancient Roman conditions, counted in the eyes of survivors as entitlement to a (contested) claim on positions of church leadership. This claim functioned in the primary instance as a credential for people who actually lived through persecution leading to exile or execution (or as a credential for the posthumous cult of those who died under it without lapsing from the faith). Contemporary evangelical victim status in the United States, however, is far more many-splendored. Originating in personal experiences of faithfulness under unfavorable conditions such as loss of control of historically Christian colleges or loss of status due to association with affairs like the Scopes trial, it appears to be infinitely transferable to other members of the same group or even capable of rubbing off on those outside the group who can find ways of associating themselves with its superior status. Thus the victim status invoked by contemporary evangelicals associated with cable networks and megachurches has a strong aura of having been prepared in advance and packaged for widespread application over an indefinite period of time, a time separated by generations from the initial loss of status in the America of H. L. Mencken and Clarence Darrow. This evangelical victimhood, while certainly a claim to entitlement, shows every sign of representing what social scientist Stjepan G. Meštrović in another context has spoken of as "curdled indignation," a kind of stored-up victimhood based on events long in the past.[61] To be sure, hardcore evangelicals are not very welcome on the board of the Yale Divinity School: but how significant is this in a time when the President of the United States invokes lightly camouflaged evangelical criteria in order to discourage sex education and stem cell research?

Thus it appears that the real function of the evangelical obsession with their historic loss of Harvard and Yale and even the historic loss of control over what science can be taught and public affairs may well lie in legitimating a complex and long-lasting strategy for regaining control over as many of those lost areas as feasible—not all of it, certainly, but as much as possible. But meanwhile, since in fact they are anything but persecuted, since a fair amount of their most visible segment enjoys great financial advantage, their gravest problem is one of internal legitimacy, that is, of convincing themselves that they are true representatives of a faith historically credentialed by subjection to fire, sword, stake, rack, mockery, imprisonment, and the literal fangs of literal lions. Of that list, only mockery by columnists in *Salon* and the occasional bribery investigation with threat of imprisonment appear to be real dangers at the moment—hence the need for as much infinitely fungible, prepackaged victim status as possible. But more will be said about this complex theology of reshaping America in an allegedly conservative image in later chapters.

The true problem here emerges from the way the media and clerical representatives of intense evangelicalism and Dispensationalism instinctively go well beyond mere pro forma efforts at looking countercultural, in that they often appear determined to reverse all trends toward the secular version of modernity. Bent on asserting an identity against a secularizing society, and further realizing that their apostolic-age credentials for credibility as martyrs and victims may be difficult to obtain when surrounded by bowling alleys, swimming pools, and chrome-plated weights in the fitness center of the nearest suburban megachurch, they at times position themselves and their movements into an extreme activist stance using all the techniques of closed-door influence, a stance fully congruent with conspiracy theory at its most intense—yet with cultural and political ramifications more tangible than (and perhaps more far-reaching than) the sorts of comparable conspiracy she-nanigans one typically finds in the melodramatically hyperbolic scripts of *The Prisoner, The X-Files, The Matrix,* or even the cyberpunk novels of William Gibson. This is not, of course, to deny that waves of evangelical disgust at what the attainment of power requires have not convulsed evangelical subcultures, or that a close chronicle of these matters over decades would not show much ebbing and flowing, debating, hand-wringing, and hemming and hawing over how far to go in reversing the early twentieth-century evangelical decision to turn aside from overt political striving after the loss of influence to theological liberalism in the wake of the original Fundamentalist controversies enshrined forever in films like *Inherit the Wind.* But in our own day the die was cast, and evangelicals decided, with great success, to go heartland and Sunbelt activist. But what in fact has this entailed?

It is precisely at this point that the analysis becomes difficult, uncertain, and tantalizingly suggestive in spite of (or because of) its elusive aspect. The activism, the secrecy of leadership conventicles in prophecy-driven evangeli-cal movements, the quasiwartime uncertainties and doubts, the occasional quests for traitors within the ranks of the presumed elect, the hints of ties to the very highest levels of the federal government—these themes in dis-pensational fiction and in the public career of real-world Christian move-ments suggest that the analogies with conspiracy publications may not be far-fetched. Indeed, Mark Fenster's path-breaking 1999 study[62] cataloged the beginnings of this assimilation or cross-fertilization, though without know-ing how much further it was to proceed in recent years. It is not simply that dispensationalist tracts and novels share much of the Right-wing politi-cal outlook of conspiracy theory. In some ways, as Fenster shows, proph-ecy fiction functions as a variant on conspiracy theory, that is, as a variant on the view that a small group has illegitimately taken control of a much larger entity so as to misappropriate and misdirect it for narrow and wrong-headed purposes. The interplay between conspiracy tracts and dispensation-alist thinking can be explicitly illustrated and in fact Fenster does so, citing chapter and verse of various works—of which the most spectacular is perhaps a 1991 Thomas Nelson novel by Larry Burkett. Entitled *The Illuminati,* this work of Christian fiction chronicles the march toward world government by the Antichrist with the drumbeat issuing from a mysterious organization linked to "the Druids, the Freemasons, and the Illuminati" along with "Mao, Lenin, and Hitler."[63]

Now the most important aspect of Fenster's parallelism lies in the way that conspiracy theory—whether as either totally fictional narrative in right-wing novels or otherwise as popular "philosophy of history" for mass consumption reportage in the exposé or nonfiction genre—in either case usually turns out to have a problem. It experiences great difficulty in achieving a satisfactory end, any satisfying result, or some effective closure. Neither the protagonist's moment of horrible realization about the deep dimensions of what has gone wrong nor the fantastical heroics of anticonspirators in overt fiction is really capable of registering the aforementioned outcomes effectively with the reader so as to score a direct hit. As Fenster notes, conspiracy accounts (fictional or not) generally close with a broad hint that there are plenty of conspiratorial slugs awaiting discovery under a myriad of stones yet unturned, thereby perpetuating a publishing industry much more than fomenting revolution.[64]

In other words, inherent within the limitations of the highly personal genre of conspiracy narrative is a concentration on private illumination and unmasking and a limited, highly personal view of the nature of change or struggle. As a result, at least within purely human limits, the positive political outcome of all this is disappointingly limited—at least for the (secular) true believers. In human terms, nothing on a scale akin to Marxist revolution can be conceived. (Of course, purely human terms are what evangelicals discount here.) Now it is highly significant that specifically Christian authors have adopted many elements of generic conspiracy theory and narrative as they begin to deal with political and cultural themes: they have thereby gravitated, instinctively or not, to a form that gives them little effective help in presenting a full triumph of the forces of good in any definitive way. In other words, to the degree that nonreligious conspiracy narrative models operate in an evangelical (overtly religious) context, we may speak of an inherent predisposition to construct narratives with an inconclusive outcome and with the heavy burden of residual frustration—unless, of course, the literal out-of-text Rapture should occur while the narration is in progress.

If the inner model of narrative operating in these circles inclines toward built-in lack of completeness, what does this imply for the new political activism in these groups and how it may affect others? It implies that the repeated Christian narratological choice of a conspiracy mode deficient in opportunity for total closure is highly significant. That instinctive move toward narratives favoring incomplete closure reflects built-up evangelical frustration with intractable obstacles presented by social change, pluralism, relativism, and the resultant insurmountable barriers to full membership in America's highest elites (outside the White House and Senate). But still the broader results here are very much open to discussion. Certainly one could indeed conclude that, over time, the implications will be extreme after all—that is, that a new drive for theocracy aimed at quick, decisive (and perhaps bloody) overcoming even the objections of cultural anthropologists and theologians at Harvard or Chicago is the best characterization of these developments. This is not far from the conclusion reached by Kevin Phillips in his book *American Theocracy;* and in the last chapters below, the present authors experiment with scenarios equally total in their goal, though probably whether the theocrats could ever obtain the prize of controlling Harvard as well as the Senate and the Pentagon appears dubious.

What is important to note here is how the present authors have moved back and forth between various positions as different constellations of evangelical and political phenomena have come to the fore demanding greater and greater imaginative ingenuity in trying to discern what may be the plausible limits to mainstreaming extremism in the American future. We have consistently found it quite plausible to reason in the opposite direction—that is, instead to take the evangelical gravitation toward the unclosed world of conspiracy narrative as highly suggestive of a diagnosis of the difficult nature and long duration of the struggle—and as an implicit endorsement of unspoken evangelical consensus on the opportunity and need for continued overt and energetic activism in cultural and political contestation.

That is to say, the evangelical affinity for the closure-unfriendly universe of the "conspiracy community"[65] seemingly reinforces and parallels what we have seen already: hardcore prophecy believers are by now quite realistic—within their frame of reference, anyhow. The careful use of narrative and theological devices such as the preTrib Tribulation suggests that in their sober heart of hearts the leaders of this movement expect neither triumph nor quick closure, at least not in any verifiable future within any normal horizon. Just as the turn to postRapture coping themes in fiction illustrates the empirical need here and now to find a way of living in a corrupt and aging world, so likewise the move toward conspiracy narrative paradigms implies a half-conscious expectation of long and complex struggle in the immediate future. No let-up in pressure for reshaping culture and politics in a strongly moralistic and Rightist direction is to be expected given these indicators—despite the constant talk of eschatological signs of the end. In all likelihood, the impossibility of obtaining total Theocracy or of experiencing actual Armageddon will in no way diminish organized evangelical pressure for movement toward Theocracy in some sense. As for pressure to help God along on the path toward Armageddon, perhaps that is a discussion best postponed.

In broad perspective, the twenty or thirty years of increasingly evangelical crusading for a politics of cultural conservatism in millennial America does not appear all that unusual given the past history of this almost-Christian nation, of this national quasichurch with the soul of a stock exchange. Numerous authorities[66] have commented on how inventive and resourceful evangelicalism has proven in devising updated modes of coping and surviving. The kinds of political and cultural activism here dealt with fit fairly well within this last rubric, that of modes of survival by updating and adapting. Nonetheless, as noted above, there are also features in this picture that could point in other directions, toward cultural control unprecedented in the recent past. It is not inappropriate to recall that hardcore Calvinism was so effective a worldview for struggle during the English Civil War that Michael Walzer has portrayed it as the first instantiation of a modern ideological movement, a direct ancestor of revolution-inducing elites from Robespierre to Lenin.[67] Whether such potential could again become actualized in the context of evangelical disaffection is simply, at this moment, unknowable. As a counterformation to offset secularism and militant forms of political Islam, such actualization does not appear implausible.

What is known, however, is that the kinds of political views advocated by the Left Behind novels have at least some correlate in actual, everyday evangelical behavior, such that the possibility that prophecy believers may become even more politically active in the coming years seems quite probable. Indeed, from a public policy standpoint, those who oppose such viewpoints (Norman Lear's *The People for the American Way* comes to mind) have ample reason to shake their lengthy mailing lists for still more funding to fend off this very real and very determined adversary.

Yet as we have seen in this chapter, prophecy belief maintains inherent limitations. In the end, do the novels really make much more difference than their noir predecessors? Although the question is so new as to preclude a definitive answer, it certainly seems likely that Left Behind, with its numerous internal contradictions, is the perfect vehicle for diagnosing the rage of white middle-class SUV-driving evangelicals, bringing their vehicles in increasing numbers to nearby polling stations. But it perhaps, even probably, leaves us no closer to an immediate outbreak of evangelically-driven social tumult and armed confrontation of the domestic godly with the domestic ungodly than our previous examples—all the more so, some may argue, as creeping authoritarianism with a heavily Old Testament flavor may have captured Congress and the presidency already. However this may be, prophecy fiction features a vast amount of billowing smoke and more than a few metaphorical mirrors for individuals desiring to reflect on the states of their souls. But as for the motivation of individual souls to meditate on political philosophy in connection with the evolution of the nation-state—well, that much seems as alien to the genre as Mulder's adversaries in *The X-Files,* even though the top strata of evangelical leadership certainly would seem to include a certain number of players with an interest in the pragmatic side of such meditating. In any case, with the clientele that purchases Left Behind, we have not yet arrived at a condition of total rage and complete despair. Up to this point that total pessimism, that point of absolute rage at the condition of things, has yet to manifest itself in the consumers of either the religious or the secular works of popular culture as we have met them. We will, however, reach that point shortly in the next chapter as we discuss the most controversial of all such works of popular cultural pessimism, *Fight Club.*[68]

Chapter 4

God's Unwanted:
Fight Club and the Myth of
"Total Revolution"

"Maybe self-improvement isn't the answer. . . . Maybe self-destruction is the answer."
— *Chuck Palahniuk,* Fight Club

"We are God's unwanted children. So be it!"
— *Tyler Durden,* Fight Club

Introduction—Illegimate Children

Many Americans do not fit into any of the ironic categories thus far described. Instead, an ironic rage fills them that has neither official rhyme nor corporate reason. It seeks the destruction of the given order, perhaps with the ghost of primeval hunter-gatherer life hovering in the air. But this too is illusory, both in empirical politics and in compensatory fantasies that may mislead the unaware into taking their narrative universes literally. Thus the protagonist in the sensational film *Fight Club* at least *seems* irrevocably to abandon even the nostalgic ideal of reintegration into bourgeois normality and instead cultivates rage, frustration, and fantasies of the utter destruction of the entire economic and security apparatus. And for good reason: he initially suffers from insomnia, enslavement to corporate consumerism, and extreme deprivation of affect and vitality—in other words, from an extreme case of defective human agency— same song, different verse. The protagonist, however, passes into full-scale dissociative disorder and so makes contact with what remains of his will and his libido—and with it a growing group of similarly deprived followers who, once awakened from their zombie-like existence, dream of replacing drone society with clan-like groups based on primal instincts of male bonding.

Those bonds are cemented by savage initiation rites centered on ritual-ized physical violence and brutality. So do the followers regain contact with human passion and human boundaries, all shown as retrievable on the indi-vidual and immediately interpersonal level. But in so doing, intoxicated by the rush of feeling and sense of empowerment, they abruptly blossom into a nihilistic movement that wanders off course, misunderstands the nonpub-lic point of experiential violence in a society where all sexes are castrated, and ultimately passes into fascist overdrive as its stored-up rage finally erupts to the untoward and unanticipated end of senseless violence provoking ever greater violence, all the while losing sight of the underlying, original socio-cultural concerns.

Far from being a threat, however, this film and the novel behind it sug-gest that real revolt can result only in sustained episodes of individual and collective delusion. The power of the film is only enhanced when the further realization dawns that the despair of *Fight Club* leads only to an exhilarating re-creation of the carnivalesque feasts of misrule that once served as safety valves and fantasy leveling tools in premodern society—a kind of re-creation of the feast of fools for contemporary purposes. In short: the compensatory fantasy of anarchy and the empirical retreat from real reform and real revolu-tion are the message here. Yet the whole business simultaneously suggests the limitless capacity of Americans for combining despair with reasons for hope.

Fight Club: The Protagonist[s] and the Plot[s]

The protagonist of the work is—at least in his "normal" life—essentially nameless: "Jack," as he comes to be known, works for a major automobile manufacturer. He must estimate product liability totals for particular models in order to decide (on purely financial grounds) whether a recall is advis-able. Oppressed by job and boss, increasingly washed out due to chronic insomnia, isolated from companions of all ages and sexes,[1] he takes refuge in high-end, upper-middlebrow yuppie consumerism (such as Ikea) in order to pin down an otherwise fleeting sense of identity. The plot of the work centers around Jack's search for a good night's sleep and some reality of existence, some satisfaction in life, some capacity to register feelings.

Increasingly troubled by insomnia, although basically healthy, he becomes a nightly "tourist" at emotionally charged support groups for the severely ill or disabled. There he poses as a victim (sometimes under the name Cornelius) to gain recognition and sympathy from others and to bring repressed emotions to the surface. They emerge only in the cry-and-hug-on-command sessions that conclude each group meeting. Only with this release (otherwise denied) can he sleep and ward off his growing tendency toward waking hallucinations, a release all the more important as conventional healthcare professionals fail to take him seriously.

Even this solace, however, is threatened. The recurrent appearance of a fellow "tourist," equally healthy and equally disturbed—but female—again unsettles Jack. Since he is then in the presence of someone who knows him to be a fraud like her, she puts him on the spot. Suddenly his therapeutic version of method acting in group process no longer functions—he cannot cry and hence cannot sleep. In desperation, he eventually persuades Marla to divide sessions with him to avoid fatal overlap and procures her phone number for troubleshooting purposes.

Nonetheless his psychic state remains tenuous in the extreme. On a routine flight he meets one Tyler Durden, his repressed shadow side now tangibly visible to Jack. His shadow emits a seething and inexhaustible supply of long-denied drives for physical and sexual aggression, not to mention the love of domination. Tyler is good-looking, athletic, flippant, irresponsible, and the constant center of attention, pushing not the envelope but the manila folder, indeed the filing cabinet, at every opportunity. (By the way: his identity as shadow alter ego to Jack is not overtly revealed to viewers and readers, or the narrator, until quite late.) Tyler informs Jack that he lives from the sale of boutique soap and hands him a business card—then disappears from view with a quip. Much later, once Jack has realized that Tyler is the visible instantiation of his own denied impulses, and that he has allowed Tyler to carry out an astonishing series of outrageous acts, Tyler will retrospectively sum up the action with the much-quoted words: "You were looking for a way to change your life. You could not do this on your own. All the ways you wished you could be . . . that's me! I look like you wanna look, I fuck like you wanna fuck, I'm smart, capable and most importantly, I'm free in all the ways that you are not."[2]

All that is, however, still in filmic future at this point. On returning to his nameless city after the first encounter with Tyler, Jack discovers his high-rise condo and his Ikea furniture have been blown to bits by a mysterious explosion, perhaps from a slow leak of natural gas. He ends up telephoning new acquaintance Tyler and telling him his troubles over beer in some smelly dive. After commiserating and letting out a few anticonsumerist rants, Tyler invites homeless Jack to spend the night with him in his ramshackle quarters. Having accepted the offer after Tyler's repeated reassurances, Jack is in Tyler's debt. At once, on the deserted parking lot behind the bar, Tyler collects. He asks for a favor that cannot be denied and then specifies: "I want you to hit me as hard as you can." As Jack begins to comprehend the request, the movie soundtrack here suddenly features a pulse-like drumbeat to signify that here, now, and in this particular way (and not at support groups for testicular cancer), he is suddenly awakened from the dead—suddenly alive.

The exchange of blows that ensues in the film largely occurs between two distinct actors, but here and there one discovers visual cues that, by the latter part of the film, might allow the viewer to guess that Jack is beating himself— an unusual sight that attracts remarkable attention from passers-by. After the fight, the two actors are shown in postcoital mode, with beer bottle and cigarette in action. Jack moves in with Tyler, who is squatting in a condemned former mansion now in the most polluted and industrial part of the city.

In the action that follows, the main character[s] unfold[s] in various ways. The good spirits of Jack are now directly linked to his close association, even molding, by Tyler—and are linked above all to his growing involvement in bare-knuckle "fight clubs"—the informal founding of more and more geographically diffused groups of men who fight each other, men who share with Jack this means of reviving some part of themselves. Then an ongoing sexual connection develops between Tyler and Marla, one that shows Tyler's intensity and taste for extreme encounters, while at the same time suggesting that Jack is not totally comfortable with what he feels as competition for Tyler's attention (for Jack fails for some time to realize that he and Tyler are one).

Ambiguity surrounds and permeates Jack's character. Above all, one cannot determine with certainty whether he begins to show some capacity for bonding with people outside his alter ego Tyler, although in any case his fascination with Tyler is so great as to occupy most of the plotline. As the circles of bare-knuckle fighters multiply, Jack and Tyler as founder(s) remain active participants. One cannot, however, readily discern whether Jack derives much support from these connections or instead is simply buoyed up by identification with Tyler and Tyler's role as Alpha Male Leader. In any case Marla is a source of tension, with Tyler critical of her and women in general and insisting that Jack not discuss Tyler with Marla (who, as is not said explicitly, could hasten Jack's discovery of who Tyler actually is, since to her eyes Tyler and Jack are the same physical person, a perspective never offered to film viewers who instead see actors Ed Norton and Brad Pitt.

The multicoded plotline proceeds along multiple tracks. The official investigation into the destruction of Jack's old apartment suggests an inside job—arson using homemade explosives. Then in an elaboration of a track already established (pointing ahead to the rapidly approaching theme of neoFascist tendencies in the now numerous fight clubs set up by Jack and Tyler), the theme of male bonding and initiation is developed, but first developed as occurring between Jack and Tyler as the necessary precursor to the founding of fight clubs as secret societies. The initial bonding ritual is tied to Tyler's means of livelihood, the manufacture of homemade soap for sale at exorbitant prices to boutiques. Along the way we learn that the soap is made from stolen liposuction fat (so the play on Nazi imagery can foreshadow the nihilistically authoritarian turn that the fight club movement eventually takes), with the setup providing an opportunity for Jack to serve as Tyler's sidekick by assisting in the theft. Yet the more important initiatory scene takes place after the theft and immediately before the actual manufacture of soap in Tyler's decrepit kitchen.

A key scene features Tyler as he gives lye to the lie by using the soap-making chemical to plant a caustic wet kiss on unsuspecting Jack's hand, a drawn-out moment of scarring pain. This white-hot moment of conscious intensity lets Tyler drive home to Jack the need to "hit bottom," to give up, to face the reality of onrushing death and destruction and the fact of one's essential unimportance—and thus the need to give up on earlier stages of meditation as a means of avoiding the pain and roughness of living (anesthetic meditation as "premature enlightenment"). The pain and vulnerability Jack experiences in boxing is set in fuller context by this initiatory scene, a context clearly implying sympathetic Western appropriation of Asian traditions in spirituality.

At this point it becomes clear that the redemptive character of violence somehow derives from pain and from an associated dismantling of inappropriate claims to special or elevated status in the universe—a Western appropriation of what presumably counts as Eastern views. This motif does not, however, prevent the work from associating redemptive violence with other emphases—for example, cutting through postmodern and postindustrial distractions and counterfeits to the immediacy of living—an immediacy given in experience of the purely physical and intensely human. Moreover that simplification, that drive to the primal, is shown as linked (female-linked, indeed, decadent and effeminate) with rejection of consumerism. (For all the denunciation of this film by would-be cultural conservatives who did not view it—such as former Reagan education czar William Bennett—in fact the work is permeated with the stereotypes of nineteenth-century antidecadence cultural criticism, with Friedrich Nietzsche and self-overcoming even explicitly named by Ed Norton at the Yale Film Society in a retrospective of the film.) Were the film not so negative toward technology, it could be mistaken as a meditation on Spengler (and his critiques of the decadent West), or even a withdrawal from tainted public life, as Ernst Jünger would have it.[3]

The motif of primal roughness as antidote to artificiality and decadence runs throughout the work (although the work does not go so far as to quote Nietzsche's *Gelobt sei, was hart macht* (praised be what makes hard) [*Beyond Good and Evil*]). It even widens into a more fundamental calling into question of the practice of allowing boys to be raised and socialized by contemporary American women—apparently because such child rearing cannot produce men capable of standing for any principle or outlook based on internal direction-finding.[4] Paluhniak's apparently misogynistic misgivings aside, it is evident his anger (even if ill-directed) is shared by many Americans.

The unfolding of Jack's character also traces his growing involvement with Tyler the Trickster. For example, the latter has a penchant for urinating into lobster bisque in hotel dining rooms and splices single frames of pornography into Disneyesque animation epics. With Tyler and his sidekick Jack, these games widen into a broader project of playing major pranks amid the icons of capitalism. In a spectacular scene, Jack beats himself to a bloody wreck in his boss's office, doing so in such fashion that security holds the boss responsible. Thus Jack can blackmail his company into bankrolling his life as a paid and nonworking consultant, well-supplied with funds and airline tickets. So—with money and temporary housing as squatters in a ramshackle mansion—Tyler and Jack devote their childish energies to expanding the antibourgeois activities of a growing chain of fight clubs.

The reader or viewer of *Fight Club* must determine when the character of this initial improvement or rejuvenation in Jack's life turns negative—but it appears that the audience is meant to feel that it indeed does so despite Jack's initial perking up. This downturn is so amply encoded and embedded that one must despair of critics who find a simpleminded approbation here of Tyler's megalomaniacal bent for aggression and domination of others in his anticonsumerist Mayhem movement. That is, at some juncture the movement in Jack's life radically alters its tone and becomes definitively unpleasant—with deciding when becoming a judgment call made more complicated by the exaggerated and ironic aspects of the later stages on life's way here. Essentially the condemned mansion becomes a parody of a Zen monastery for Tyler's disciples—each of whom has been involved in a fight club, each of whom passes discouraging admission rituals, and each of whom becomes part of the new, nihilistic, quasifascist "Operation Mayhem," the details of which Tyler keeps from Jack. Whether at any point Jack experiences supplementary bonding with the live-in disciples is unlikely but not safe to exclude;

in any case his main tie (and his main potential for jealousy) is with his shadow side, Tyler.

The escalation of Mayhem involves increasingly serious tricks, even arson against the icons of corporate America. It culminates in a grandiose plan to blow up the skyscrapers housing America's computerized credit reports en masse—but by night, with fight club members on duty for maintenance and security, such that no one is to be killed.

Movement toward this climax brings with it a definitive marker in the violent death of disciple Robert Paulson, who had earlier bonded with Jack in a support group. His death from a gunshot wound panics the clone-like disciples ("space monkeys," Tyler dubs them), who no longer retain their given names. At first, they are intent on burying Paulson in the garden to obscure any evidence of crime. Jack intervenes, insisting that Paulson's name (and identity) return to him at least in death. This scene underscores how, once the personal rejuvenation mediated by Tyler has given way to something more public or collective, old issues of identity loss and pallor of individual character reappear, now cloned and institutionalized. Initially, physical contact, some kind of bonding, and the hypnotic *Penis Monologues* (what else to call them?) of the Alpha Male Leader had seemed to solve the problem—but no longer.

The central place of the intensely personal is further emphasized with the repeated appearance of a jealousy motif. It always revolves around Tyler. Tyler, wanting to avoid too overt a confrontation between himself and the other aspect of the protagonist, has warned Jack not to talk about him to Marla (who is by now Tyler's steady lover, without grasping how complete is the dissociation of personalities in her companion). Nonetheless, Jack comes closer and closer to letting too much slip to Marla about Tyler's split-off career. Meanwhile, Tyler's plans and movement become grotesquely grandiose, involving flights across the country and increasingly militant "pranks." At a key moment, Jack sees that Tyler and some of the disciples are carrying out extreme "pranks" of which he is unaware. Moved by envy and the sense that all this is, after all, a joint enterprise, Jack gives his jealousy free reign.

The final segment is introduced as an elaboration of the jealousy theme. During a boxing sequence, Jack takes on one of the younger disciples heavily involved in the pranks, one who (perhaps because of his youthful good looks) receives a good deal of Tyler's affection. Jack beats him so severely that his face is permanently scarred despite a trip to the emergency room. In reaction, Tyler confronts Jack, asking whether the underlying issue is not finally whether Jack has surrendered enough of his remaining sense of self-worth or self-importance. To underline the point, trickster Tyler wrecks the limousine in which they are speeding.

When Jack awakens, he is in his ramshackle bedroom—alone. The disciples have disappeared and so has Tyler, though extant records allow Jack to reconstruct Tyler's airplane flights. As he frantically follows Tyler, a suspicion dawns on him: people are treating him like Tyler—perhaps he is Tyler? From records he learns of the plan to free America from credit card debt as a first step toward taking us back to a hunter-gatherer society—and is horrified at the excesses of what the movement has become.

So begins the conclusion, with Jack trying to short-circuit Tyler's plan to blow up the skyscrapers housing America's credit records. He fails: but in a remarkable final scene he does rid himself of hallucinated Tyler (who has finally gone too far) by committing a near-suicide with a handgun. Nonetheless, his earlier plan to sequester Marla (fearing the movement will have to kill her) in a sense pays off: with Tyler gone, with skyscrapers exploding, Jack and Marla stand hand in hand, ready for a try at fulfillment in a personal future of heterosexual private life together—at least in the film version. While the suicide can be read to mean that happiness in the current situation or freedom in it comes only once one is dead and rid of current society,[5] the novel—in contrast—makes future bliss a bit more uncertain by ending with the salvaged Jack still in custody in a mental ward looking to get out. Nevertheless, one still finds a happy ending of sorts—and a return to normal society after a fashion. The bitter taste of Thorazine takes the place of sweetly scented rose and geranium soap as the socially prescribed way to cleanse one's soul.

The Central Argument

Fight Club appears as a mass of contradictions. Is it a merely a protest against consumerism and wealth voiced by Brad Pitt, or perhaps something much, much more? Regardless of the answer, it is a work reeking of cynicism and despair that has achieved cult status for a certain segment of American popular culture that permeates several generations. Many respectable film critics have nevertheless panned it as a total failure. Spokespersons for the political Left and Right join the critics, ironically holding hands in their condemnation of the film, much the same way the work itself appears to end happily with lovers hand in hand united against the world. Clearly much is going on both within the cinematic universe of *Fight Club* and in its reception among elite viewers.[6]

Progressive charges of failure to imagine a realizable political and social alternative are justified. *Fight Club* depicts fantasy, and a fantasy of public catastrophe at that. It does make frequent use of revolutionary, ideological, and public concepts and images from the past three hundred years, in particular the mythical rebellion and reversal of decadence imagery characteristic of European Romanticism and especially the writings of Nietzsche. According to one perspective, *Fight Club* features an imaginary future of regression with the unstoppable detonations of Mayhem designed to feed shriveled male egos in the audience; however, this reading is more often trumped by critics' outrage at the portrayal of violence and politics as an impasse exited only through the fascist door.

Such is the sentiment from betrayed progressives: led on by the familiar, by the use of revolutionary themes, left-leaning critics of the standing order feel betrayed by *Fight Club*.[7] Thus the critics, like *Fight Club*'s character(s), reject what they know and instead want something more satisfying—but *Fight Club* delivers instead a virtually uncharacterizable parody or deconstruction of public satisfactions and revolutionary politics. And to make matters worse, it does so in ways that (worse still) cannot even be read as a more reactionary endorsement of the status quo. Thus if one reads *Fight Club* as advocating political action, the action depicted appears to be what some term "microfascism," with the movement portrayed in colors that make it appealing only to a very suspect subaudience.[8] For most viewers of a reflective tendency, of course, the activism depicted qua mayhem politics is depicted as a cautionary tale and not an endorsement for skinheads.

Thus one begins to see why *Fight Club* evokes such intense reactions, such loyalty, such rage, and such claims that it is an incompetent, puerile, and morally degenerate failure, albeit one with a cult following. For its fans and the adepts of Palahniuk's "cult,"[9] the work conveys a mysteriously electrifying message beyond brutality, adrenaline, and buff bodies—a non-formulaic take on what faces younger Americans here and now. The work remains enigmatic, for it operates on many levels in dealing with a current situation that can be only grasped in elusive, oblique imagery. And this leads to a central paradox: *Fight Club* appears to trash all hopes for the continuation of bourgeois, suburban life, but somehow it energizes fans. Critics find it too violent, too bloody, too nihilistic, too negative, and perhaps in an ironic twist, too realistic.

But why does it evoke such strong condemnations? To be sure, the film is periodically linked with the fad of unlicensed fighting clubs, some involving the illegal sale of fight videos with resultant hospital trips: but to impugn the film without mentioning the growth of a massive culture of ritualized violence in America over the last quarter century seems absurd and logically skewed. Beginning at least in 1989 with the transatlantic hit serial *American Gladiators,* and perhaps dating back to the 1982 film *Conan the Barbarian* featuring the later Republican governor of California Arnold Schwarzenegger in the title role, a complex and spectacularly popular culture or cult of brutalization has swept the country. This is further linked with an increase in undereducated and unemployable youth searching for some lost and probably mythical sense of masculinity.[10]

The especial condemnation of *Fight Club* after decades of success for martial arts training and the now ubiquitous teen-slasher film genre makes such criticism especially suspect. *Fight Club* hits too close to home, or so it seems. It at least has the distinction of treating violence on both an individual and a group level, and with it the possibility that it may serve as a cautionary tale before conditions in the American underclass become far too volatile. *Fight Club* in this sense retains a redemptive quality, at least for those willing to endure it without the all too typical critical cut-and-run routine. *Fight Club* does indeed have an attitude problem, and it is central to how the work functions: the film's uncovering of thorny issues and the possibility of difficult albeit doable redemption (perhaps not total, depending on how one views the end of the work, but near-total nonetheless) very likely has something to do with the work's bad reputation. Again, it blurs the line between fantasy and near-term cultural prophecy.

Thus the film's defenders are certainly on to something when they point out how films with more violence, even with more verisimilitude in rendering violence, encounter less in the way of total rejection. Defenders do speak up in the discussion of the work, who report they thought prior to viewing it that it was simply about bludgeoning, a kind of *Texas Chainsaw Massacre* without the chainsaw or Texas. The tribal clan or male bonding side, the quest for authenticity aspect, the attempt to come to grips with contemporary life using classic concepts of nineteenth-century high-culture Romanticism and the worn but potent and generically appealing clichés of philosophy of history—none of this seems to have been known at first, according to the narratives of the converted—but after viewing or reading *Fight Club,* enough of these weighty issues made it into their fields of vision to change a negative to a positive for many critics.

While *Fight Club* is so multicoded as to evade formulaic summing-up, precisely this quality can take us to its significance. For it does have a certain intended payoff, one that its fans ordinarily home in on, however disconcerting this may be to critics. This phenomenon has not escaped critical notice. One of the more lucid writers on the work, Kate Greenwood, sees this payoff as she uncovers highly contradictory, tension-laden aspects of what the novel and film seem to commend (that is, individualism together with priority of an authoritarian group). Looking at these paradoxes overall, Greenwood—citing the French theorist Gilles Deleuze—justifiably points to "the fact that according to *Fight Club* the struggle for authentic subjectivity under late capitalism is a dubious objective to begin with, that 'maybe it's a mistake to believe in the existence of things, persons, or subjects.'"[11]

With elegant clarity, Greenwood follows contradictory threads in the work, in particular that of self-discovery or Nietzschean self-overcoming on the one hand, and a kind of Western everything-is-illusion disdain for issues of meaning and uniqueness—both themes that are well-represented in the lapidary pronouncements of Jack/Tyler.[12] Thus she judges that:

> *Fight Club* is fundamentally ambivalent towards all of the issues it would explore. It promotes a discourse of 'finding yourself' while simultaneously insisting "you are not a beautiful and unique snowflake." Does it all simply dissolve into postmodern irony, or does a kernel of significance remain? Beneath the contradictions the message regarding subjectivity seems to be this: the only 'authentic' thing about contemporary subjectivity is that at its heart lies a void. Embracing this void, while a bleak prospect, rather than frantically trying to compensate for its absence, is the only authentic gesture that remains.[13]

Greenwood follows important lines of tension and/or paradoxical self-contradiction. First she observes: "The notion of pain as a portal to 'your true self' is recalled when Tyler gives Jack a chemical burn. Tyler expounds: Without pain . . . we'd have nothing. . . . This is the greatest moment of your life. . . . It's only after you've lost everything that we're free to do anything." However, as Greenwood notes, this view is fully counterbalanced. Thus she can observe:

> This ideology of abandon, of 'losing it all,' is contradicted throughout *Fight Club* by Tyler's equal appeal to rules and structure. Furthermore, Jack's description of the feelings he experienced after fighting—"when the fight was over, nothing was solved, but nothing mattered"—seems to be embracing the converse: if nothing was solved and nothing mattered, surely 'finding yourself' is not important.

Greenwood is onto something. The work is complex in dizzying ways that send the reader/viewer swinging and spinning in divergent directions. With good reason, then, Greenwood makes an interpretative virtue of this para-doxical necessity, steps back from the oscillating canvas, and invokes a con-temporary authority on these matters.

> Slavoj Žižek's consideration of the postmodern individual can stand as a summary of the depiction of subjectivity in *Fight Club*. Žižek posits a sub-jectivity that knows no limits, when
>
> > [t]he inherent obverse of 'Be your true Self!' is . . . the injunction to cultivate permanent refashioning, in accordance with the post-modern postulate of the subject's indefinite plasticity . . . in short, extreme individualism reverts to its opposite, leading to the ulti-mate identity crisis: subjects experience themselves as radically unsure, with no 'proper face,' changing from one imposed mask to another, since what is behind that mask is ultimately nothing, a horrifying void they are frantically trying to fill in with their com-pulsive activity. . . . [14]

Greenwood closes in upon the mark when she applies these principles to *Fight Club*:

> In this sense, the narrative on subjectivity in *Fight Club* becomes extremely complicated, conflating extreme individualism ("follow your dream"), extreme collectivism ("you are not special"), and an endless shifting from mask to mask to mask (Cornelius—Jack—Tyler . . .) where no mask is privileged as more authentic than another. [15]

And it is on this substantial basis, textually, that Greenwood concludes, as we noted above, that the real position of the work with regard to identity or individual "subjectivity" amounts to the "bleak prospect" of "[e]mbracing [the] void"—the demand of "authenticity" here and now—the "only authen-tic gesture" under the circumstances, surely being preferable at least to a mistaken and potentially harmful activism ("rather than frantically trying to compensate for its absence"—which activist impulses have led, as we see, to the Mayhem movement and its regressive detonations).

Yet Greenwood's points, while spot-on, are not fully adequate—she gives us much of the story, but not all. On the one hand, as we have previously contended, *Fight Club* and its sleep-deprived schizophrenic protagonist (pre-Tyler) stand at the end of a wider trajectory. Insomniac Jack very plausibly stands for the end station on the line toward diminution of effectiveness, of utter impotence in postmodern life. Yet somehow what this work shows manages to draw in readers and viewers seeking an alternative, an escape—though how it does this (aside from those who fetishize violence) is difficult to determine at first. Greenwood is correct that much of *Fight Club* can be subsumed under the postmodern theme of resignation to the void, the end of the individual subject self, however little this registers with many in the audience. Further, to the degree that it is not read as overtly discrediting all public action, one can envision *Fight Club* as winking at those who enjoy a rerun of fascism and other authoritarian movements, this time with a brutal irony garnishing the whole item.

What then does *Fight Club* offer reflective readers and viewers, those whose needs are not satisfied by surreal fantasies of masculinist triumph? Clearly the work appeals to those who dream of a return to a hunter-gatherer stage of life in which males suffering from attention deficit disorder will require no amphetamines but will instead now blossom as alpha males, perhaps even replacing presidential security advisers and risk avoidance consultants under contract to public school hockey teams. But what can *Fight Club* possibly offer more reflective fans? The short answer is, paradoxically, that to these and to others of very different outlook and hormonal balance, it offers both utter despair and an emblem of hope—if the audience wants to find it and take it home.

What *Fight Club* attempts is difficult. The work is crafted with great skill, however many brain halves went into the versions of this project. It targets a very real but elusive, undefined audience—not simply white males of a certain age, as perceptive feminist critics have noted[16]—but an audience under forty, perhaps even under thirty. Those who work with younger people will readily sense the screens and masks put up and the kinds of cues and tokens required for members of this subgroup to recognize each other—with the work under discussion being one such token. It is a group that prides itself on equanimity in all situations but which harbors deep doubts about all aspects of the System and the system's prospects for delivering happiness, satisfaction, or even security. That is, *Fight Club* undertakes to evoke attitudes that cannot be openly avowed these days (lest one be summarily fired from most jobs)—attitudes so negative, so critical, so distanced, that even to hint at them is to disqualify the speaker from being heard.

But author Palahniuk intended *Fight Club* to be read and discussed, and so it has and will continue to be, in part thanks to acid-free printing and DVDs. But it is part of a larger phenomenon. After all, while unique, it does not stand alone. It is one of several films that have made an impact by chronicling personal dissatisfaction on the part of young Americans apparently (and paradoxically) doing fairly well (*Office Space, American Beauty,* and—in a greatly extended sense—the *Matrix* series come to mind). Like those films, *Fight Club*, too, means to be heard. *Fight Club* means to reach its audience not simply by oblique references and knowing glances that are code for unpleasant topics otherwise best avoided. It aims to legitimate itself[17] by suggesting that the kind of outlook it conveys can make the situation in one's personal space a bit better, a bit more tolerable, and even from a certain angle almost exhilarating—but only up to a point, for in essence nothing significant can be done, nothing can really be improved. (Or as the text puts it, "Self-improvement is masturbation.")[18]

It is always risky for a film with such a grave undertone to depict a playful and upbeat exterior. Presumably such films tap into a vast, undefined, and largely repressed and denied reservoir of discontent, primarily among young people who by and large are unlikely to admit to any such hypothetical discontent. After all, today's youth have been socialized from birth onward (in unprecedented ways) not to betray to any traceable or attributable degree any serious doubts about institutions. They are brought up to keep a close check on their emotions to ensure that institutional functioning never gets derailed by counterproductive outbursts.

This novel mode of socializing the young has been studied in detail by the social thinker Stjepan Meštrović. Meštrović argues that the social manipulation of emotion, often with internally debilitating results, is the hallmark of our current situation, one that constitutes an intensification of the "other-directed" culture discerned fifty years ago by sociologist David Riesman. Anglo-American culture, it follows, is based upon the constant adjustment of personal and collective goals on the basis of a peer acceptance driven by the norms of corporate domination. Now, decades after Riesman elaborated his vision of other-directed conformism, argues Meštrović, the cultivation of commercially useful attitudes is paramount in the socialization of oneself and one's peers. Moreover, it also involves the sequestration of emotions into a reservoir that can be tapped by corporate elites for the desired aims. Think here of the frequent wartime recitations of patriotism buoyed by performances of country singer Lee Greenwood's unforgettably forgettable unofficial national anthem, "God Bless the U.S.A."[19]

Films such as *Fight Club* and *The Matrix* are made by people intensely aware of precisely this ongoing intensification of peer-oriented social control in a corporate cultural context and with it the foreclosing of alternative approaches to personal and public life. Such films constitute intricately encoded attempts to ameliorate or even escape the loss of meaning in contemporary life. The films may even restore hope—at least for a time. Films such as *Fight Club* must operate in many domains, transmitting messages about religion, private life, economics, society, and politics. They are not "about" any one of these domains; they address the far-reaching, cumulative losses that touch everyone but which are most acutely felt by those between twenty-five and forty years old, in the sprawling suburban demographic. This generation simply lacks a language suitable to express their amorphous outrage at a lifestyle that is slipping, sometimes quite violently, away—hence *Fight Club* and its imitators.

This consciousness of loss and the partial repression of it could be traced at great length in a separate study. Here we find ourselves constrained by the larger topics. It is clear that circa 1973 the income and career prospects for young white males began to worsen, such that, as one young economist has noted with regard to the retrospective picture today, "for those age 25 to 34, there has been a decline of median income of fourteen percent since 1973."[20] Likewise it has become axiomatic that younger voters tend to abstain from voting at a rate higher than that of the general population, although this trend does fluctuate.[21] Further, the fact that voter participation in any or all segments may increase dramatically at times of perceived crisis certainly does not—in and of itself—indicate any increase in felt legitimacy of the politico-social system. It may merely indicate an increase in anxiety and in the immediate, superficial (not necessarily long-term) stability of the politico-social system. Superficial stability and perceived legitimacy, while not necessarily much explored in their interconnections, are not identical—indeed, their potential disjunction is foundational to this investigation. We postulate an increase in short-term, superficial political stability linked with a decrease in perceived legitimacy, within which increasingly extreme scenarios of escape increase in importance.

At all events, while individuals are trained not to express papable discontent, one finds abundant signs of disaffection. For example, in a poll from 2003:

> Remarkably, 53% agreed that "America's youth find more 'truth' in Eminem's lyrics than in President Bush's speeches," according to the survey conducted by the New York advertising agency Euro RSCG.

> Even though the lyrics of Eminem, a white rapper, have been branded homophobic and misogynistic, only 19% disagreed with the statement [above]. Among 18- to 24-year-olds, almost two-thirds of respondents believed that Eminem was more truthful.[22]

Even these minimal clues indicate that filmmakers and writers have a wealth of discontent into which they can tap. Thus it is not surprising that we recently have encountered an emerging genre of film that targets the repression of felt discontent, repression as an externally imposed burden. The cultural place of all this emerges if we compare the films mentioned above with Mark Fenster's anatomy of emplotment in classic conspiracy narratives out of the realm of recent politics and metapolitics. Here Fenster works with the key concept of "narrative pivot"—the moment when scales drop forever from the innocent eyes of the protagonist, who from that moment forward must devote everything to reversing or at least mitigating a terrible set of wrongs and injustices for the public benefit:

> This is a complete transition for the character: he becomes alienated from an increasingly defamiliarized political and social order, and his everyday life is suddenly vulnerable to extreme danger and violence. The uncovering of this evidence is nothing less than a totalizing conversion, affecting the character's engagement in the social world and his private life. Information has forced on the character a cognitive crisis, and every current and past event becomes subject to reinterpretation in light of a changed world.[23]

Note that Fenster's pivotal moment occurs in both small-circle, "nut-case" conspiracy narratives serving small, highly committed but marginal groups, and in definition to broad-based, domesticated, keep-the-world-at-a-distance versions that do not insist upon blind allegiance as the only option (so-called "commodified" conspiracy, such as *The X-Files*). Further, even in these more accessible, more generally-distributed pop culture narratives, Fenster finds a portentous sense of meaning just as with the life-involving narratives used by real (nut) groups: the protagonist(s) and society need each other for a vast historical drama. This sense of epic struggle, even if not carried on with the insistence that consumers of the narrative immediately obtain their membership card in the applicable nut group, runs through the more intense varieties of both paranoid cult and later more general (but in essence hypothetical or optional) versions of conspiratorial self-understanding.

Here in the latter mass genre (nonparanoid, *X-Files*-related), the same portentous sense of world-historical mission rubs off on protagonist and viewers/readers alike. And whether the main debt is to Christian eschatology or to modern ideology is not decisive. The point is that grandiosity and a play for epic salvation remain very much alive in the struggles of the various protagonists against inhuman powers that threaten human survival and human uniqueness (machines in *The Matrix*, aliens in *The X-Files*, and so on). But precisely this point does not hold with regard to *Fight Club*. *Fight Club* is unique in that it plays with this sense of mission and trashes it decisively (at least for those capable of irony), puts it into the dustbin of history (perhaps along with history itself). For *Fight Club* reveals the utter emptiness of Tyler/ Jack's obsession with a way out, what some critics term "micro-fascism."[24] That is, *Fight Club* exposes the escape genre as mere flailing on a grandiose scale, all the while failing to formulate a more "moderate" political alternative. Escape, as we have seen before, is not possible, at least in the universalized, metaphysical sense characteristic of escape narratives.

Second, and closely related, is the way such mythic or fictionalized narratives view society and life before the fateful moment of pivotal disclosure, before the "cognitive crisis." And here *Fight Club* is not unique, but rather a prime example. While it is true that popular narratives of conspiracy and disaster from the 1950s forward did note the danger of extreme and irretrievable loss as themes, they were by no means necessarily negative about the situation before the fateful moment of pivoting. The novelty and inner-circle cachet of early science fiction noir products like *The Prisoner* did indeed derive from the negative take on existing society, unlike other, coexisting narratives that contrasted a satisfying daily normal American life with its destruction by atomic warfare, mutant insects, aliens, human puppets, and their ilk.

But by the millennial time of narratives like *American Beauty* or *The Matrix* (or perhaps even with comedic treatments like *Office Space*), the center of gravity had begun to shift. In the *Matrix,* protagonist Neo has long secretly engaged in illegal and dubious infotech activities.[25] These activities allow Neo to move toward a pivotal moment even as they alert conspirators from the underworld of human reality to Neo's ripeness for initiation, for pivoting. Once that occurs, once he ingests the red pill given him by the human underground, the truth emerges and happy daily life in the days before appears in a new aspect, as an untrue hallucination concealing the horrible fact of human impotence in a world run mercilessly by cybermachines. It was tainted, irrecoverably contaminated, all along. However, while Neo may be a maverick, and while the world he thought he knew is revealed to be illusory, things could be much worse: there is no suggestion that the world prior to machine takeover was itself corrupt beyond redemption. That last step in cultural pessimism is taken by other films, notably *Fight Club.*

While the contemporary film *American Beauty* operates far differently in its American appropriations of Buddhist attitudes, the take on daily life is ultimately darker than in *The Matrix:* here we find a strong condemnation of normal Anglo-American idealized middle-class existence—and here, as with

The Matrix, now what was once segregated at the exotic periphery (Allen Ginsberg's *Howl, The Prisoner*) is mainstreamed in upscale suburban movie theaters. This condemnation echoes unrelentingly in *Fight Club,* where all the techniques of extremism and irony must be used in the effort at recapturing freshness for a condemnation owing much to Nietzsche and perhaps a certain amount as well to Allen Ginsberg's opening lines in *Howl.* Thus spake Tyler Durden, at least in the film script, wherein Tyler gets to say things that sometimes emerge in the novel from the mouths of his helpless disciples:

> Man, I see in fight club the strongest and smartest men who have ever lived. I see all this potential—God damn it, an entire generation pumping gas and waiting tables; they're slaves with white collars. Advertisements have them chasing cars and clothes, working jobs we hate so we can buy shit they don't need. We are the middle children of history, man. No purpose or place. We have no great war, or great depression. Our great war is a spiritual war. Our great depression is our lives. We've all been raised by television to believe that one day we'll all be millionaires and movie gods and rock stars—but we won't. And we're learning slowly that fact. And we're very, very pissed off.[26]

At other moments the Nietzschean mode predominates over the Ginsbergesque in *Fight Club,* for instance, as Tyler gives Jack the chemical kiss at the at the moment of initiation:

TYLER
Shut up! Our fathers were our models for God. And if our fathers bailed, what does that tell you about God? . . .

Listen to me. You have to consider the possibility that God doesn't like you. He never wanted you. In all probability, he hates you. This is not the worst thing that can happen . . .

JACK
It isn't?

TYLER
We don't need Him.

JACK
We don't, we don't, I agree.

TYLER
Fuck damnation, man. Fuck redemption. We are God's unwanted children. So be it![27]

This, coupled immediately with

TYLER
It's only after we lost everything that we are free to do anything.

JACK
Okay . . .[28]

At this point Tyler finally extinguishes Jack's searing wound with a dose of vinegar. Here the shooting script of *Fight Club* self-consciously echoes semi-familiar, rebellious, bohemian, promethean slogans from nineteenth-century Romanticism and ideological radicalism. They have been associated with revolution, dandyesque protest, even stylized nihilism and are known from Turgenev, Laurent Tailhade, Nietzsche, Dostoyevsky, and so on. However, in the context of *Fight Club,* the ultimate outcome of these incantations is a unique and complicated condemnation of our current situation, one that finally discredits political and public ideological activity en bloc while at the same time remaining relatively consistent in its condemnation of the triumphant neocapitalist order. The lovers do indeed remain standing, hand in hand at the close as they witness the smoking triumph of—something non-descript—perhaps a return to the Bronze Age. But to begin with, they hold that satisfaction may only be found in the private sphere. This is plausible, that is, unless they get too curious about what lurks under masks, unless they develop a nihilistic taste for staring into the void.

But our analysis has barely scratched the surface thus far. Misogyny, a powerful hatred of consumer capitalism, and fear of aggressive multinational corporations cannot bring us to a full understanding of the anger in *Fight Club.* To go deeper we need to understand Jack's hallucinated shadow side, the brawling, risk-taking, libidinously irresistible Tyler. Why is this figure necessary as a complement to Jack's needs, and what exactly does needy Jack stand for in sociocultural terms?

Put succinctly, the interplay between zombie Jack and aggro Tyler targets the repression of outrage and disgust triggered in contemporaries by precisely the changes in social control and risk avoidance uncovered by Riesman and his later interlocutor Meštrović. This is not to say that the creators of the work have necessarily studied either social scientist; it suffices to say that perceptive observers of different backgrounds see the same things and express them in their favorite ways. Note how the distinctive features of postmodern or extreme "other-directed" social control are both enumerated by the research of Meštrović and rendered in *Fight Club.*

In Meštrović's expansion of David Riesman, the full quality of contemporary social functioning cannot be seen if we confine attention to the overtly cognitive domain.[29] Transnational corporations and globalizing governments operate within a situation in which a highly effective form of emotional control or training functions to put strict limits on troublemaking and dissent so far as most of the population is concerned. This analysis represents an outgrowth of Riesman's classic fifties contrast between modernizing "inner-directed" personality types and later (contemporary) "other-directed" personality types. Reformation theologians, Enlightenment rationalists, Romantic rebels, and metapolitical ideologues (such as Marx) instantiated a type of leadership dependent on rules and ideals instilled at an early age, applied to concrete situations with varying degrees of creativity and flexibility, but useful for effecting social change by attracting followers who replicated the program according to their own basic rules.

After World War II, "other-directed" types, by contrast, were free-floating, opportunistic, capable of rapid political and ideological shifts, and constantly attuned to the emerging new consensus of the moment as their antennae picked it up from peers and colleagues. The hallmark of this emergent style and its intensification is social adjustment by emotional preemption, so to speak. Persons socialized in this manner suppress spontaneous outbreaks of emotion and are trained constantly to rehearse emotional display with an eye to how it will be received and its effects on career and the perceived smooth functioning of the greater system.[30]

Beyond this immediate picture stands, for Meštrović and *Fight Club*, the broader issue of a society tending toward complete control, with security cameras, digital tracing, polygraphing as credo, and the occasional application of force supplementing the preemptive emotional control already learned in kindergarten. The sociological works of Riesman and Meštrović depict a society in rapid transition to a condition of greater and more insidious social control. If we turn to *Fight Club* with this picture in mind, we find that the work precisely renders these features and findings. Just as Meštrović homed in on precognitive emotional training as the fundamental hallmark of this transition, so likewise does *Fight Club* depict in detail the same feature. Protagonist Jack (preTyler) is essentially a zombie in search of a sufficiently normal equilibrium of the psyche to allow him to overcome insomnia, register the world in shades other than pale gray, and recognize that within him unacknowledged emotions are backing up at a fantastic rate. His sleep-deprived condition somehow snaps into the hallucination of his embodied shadow side, reckless, uncontrollable, risk-seeking, libidinous, charming, and altogether dangerous Tyler. Once that encounter occurs, the results are explosive, from the dynamiting of his

Ikea-stocked condo to Tyler's unstoppable detonating of the credit card towers of America.

Note further that, if Jack (before Tyler) is a miserable representative of Meštrović's postemotional society in extremis, so likewise is sex- and aggression-god Tyler a throwback to something much like Riesman's inner-directed type. What principles his dubious father implanted we cannot know—but they were certainly not those of Calvinist or Jesuit inner-directed ideologues of early modernity. In any case, fast-talking, persuasive, hormone- and pheromone-driven Tyler behaves very like Calvin, Loyola, Robespierre, and any Romantic agitator one cares to name—he founds a movement based on obedience, audacity, and (a remarkable amount of) violence as an instrument of social change and recruitment.[31] Furthermore Tyler's perspective on the changes and conflicts going on is pointed and (for him) reflective: as we can readily piece together and translate into sociological terms, he views the ongoing shift to other-directed, consumerist, group-conforming attitudes as signs of decadence and effeminacy, of decline and fall.[32]

Such then, at the most basic level, is the set of problems targeted in *Fight Club*. The details, the fact that the entry into this seething mass of unclaimed spontaneity and resentment is here gained by using material from resentment-laden contemporary males, is—just as Susan Faludi and Madeleine Bunting argue—secondary for a comprehensive evaluation of the work. Nor is it surprising that the work uses powerful images, an ironic tone, and a convoluted plotline. Its task is to render a deep-seated and probably irreversible process that affects real people in all segments of our society. The work can do this only by targeting and immersing itself in a particular setting. It does this credibly because the author and the primary audience do have ties to males, young, largely white, in a particularly vulnerable set of social strata (office workers, service personnel, professionals on the edge of slipping downward).

Moreover, as *Fight Club* targets issues of social and emotional control and the impossibility of rational political change, note how these issues are brought into high relief. As niceness is the social lubricant most required in the emergent society investigated by Meštrović, cinematic niceness is jettisoned as Jack comes under Tyler's tutelage. As the impossibility of rational political action is a given in view of the power of multinational corporations, normal politics is nearly invisible for *Fight Club*, with corporate structures and attitudes being the overt target. As the work breathes the atmosphere of an America moved by invisible movers and hidden causes, the work is structured in the mode of Fenster's conspiracy narratives (the pivotal moment, after which the protagonist awakens to realize the fraudulent nature of his entire context, corresponds to Jack's first Tyler-session), here further decked out with what Riesman and Meštrović term "inside dopesterism"—a stream of conspiratorial insights into hidden motives and inner workings slightly compensates for utter loss of meaningful input into the political process. Here *Fight Club* drops a number of broad hints. As security and risk avoidance concerns are the point of contemporary social control in its corporate and socializing forms, Tyler moves pupil Jack into ever more aggressive risk taking and stylized acts of spontaneity in the manner of classic European anarchistic "poetry of the deed."

Thus with *Fight Club* we have—among other things—a kind of enacted parable illustrating the intense difficulty of escape from a tightly woven web of social control, a web so constricting as to render life of dubious value save to those who can quietly relish their subservience, their emotional emptiness, and the machinelike prospects for future life. The work's notorious depiction of violence can now be read on numerous levels; aside from shock value and whatever fetishistic excitement it may hold for the author and some fans, it has two other functions: first, that of a plausible instrument and mark of group bonding within the awakened subculture of the disaffected; and second that of signaling in an unmistakable way that the protagonist has (with that first night of fighting) taken a real and direct step toward cutting through and rolling back the curtains of virtuality and the emotion-absorbing gauze with which his human self has been mummified.

Note further that the possibility of personal escape or redemption opens up, with the drumbeat accompanying the first blow struck between Jack and Tyler, a kind of option not closed off as the work unfolds. Certainly the seductive aspects of Tyler and the absurdly tragic course of the movement of disaffected men, culminating in Jack's quasisuicide to rid himself of the excesses of Tyler, show the difficulties attending any move toward authenticity. In a society like our own, any attempt to live by spontaneous impulse faces extreme resistance from a culture based on total control of every response and every initiative, resting on the infinite prerehearsal of reaction as a means of control.[33] To be sure, the work depicts the later phase of Tyler's Mayhem Movement as unstoppably successful and quite entertaining in its targeting of corporate art works, franchised coffee bars, overpriced retro VW beetles, and personal computer window displays. And quite possibly a certain number of audience members continue to cheer on this movement scene by scene.

However, for fans of a more reflective disposition there can be no easy enthusiasm. For them the work has a clear message flowing from the ambiguity and danger of all public activity: domains other than the intimate, other than the private in contemporary life, are here depicted as fatally tainted, irredeemably lost so far as life and human authenticity go. The desperate effort to go back to an earlier stage of sociocultural development fails (on reflective terms) because, flourishing or not, it simply results in yet another incipient totalitarian movement, the apparently unavoidable perversion of Tyler's human warmth and charismatic appeal—the last thing today's world needs! The basic message is clear enough for audience members incapable of unreflective cheerleading: a purely personal awakening or rollback from desensitized zombie life, from existence as a Dilbert-cum-Microserf, may indeed be possible—but the public domain is a quagmire, a loss: in it one can only waste effort, only increase the suffering. Politics and public life can never be accessible on human terms. It is better to stay really low, beneath all radar.

This take on the domain of the public and the political in *Fight Club* is thoroughly pessimistic, extreme even among the artifacts of popular culture we have thus far examined. It persists—but in tension, as the close of the film version gives no sign that Tyler's demise will weaken the movement. So for those who see flourishing as success, the status of politics is open. But pains have been taken to portray the dark side of this movement; for more reflective readers, politics become exceedingly problematic. The chances for real-world deliverance or escape are extremely limited indeed (unless one can embrace quasifascism). The choices we are given are few and decidedly unappealing.

Conclusion: St. Vitus's Dance on the Big Screen

Thus we come to the riddle of *Fight Club*'s appeal. It is a novel about the quest for identity on the part of a schizophrenic zombie, awakened but thrown into grave difficulties by association with his utterly reckless alter ego, thereby raising the most serious doubts about the possibility of bringing the quest for identity to a satisfying conclusion, especially as that quest turns into a dizzying set of oscillations around the void. Into the bargain we have the confirmation of our worst suspicions about public activity, putting the seal of certainty on the alternative that the realm of politics is either totally fraudulent smoke and mirrors of no benefit to the public, or otherwise it is at most satisfying only to those who ruthlessly misuse it for the shameless gratification of their most primitive instincts for power and unmitigated bloodlust. A depressing prospect! While there is a certain appeal in tearing the mask from the versions of nihilism and oppression that have been camouflaged up to now, and while budding fascists may take comfort from these escapades, still the wider appeal of this work is not easy to explain.

Most puzzling is how a work that counts as among the most pessimistic of our time nonetheless can elicit positive responses and outcries of exhilaration.[34] *Fight Club* does evoke these, and from a widely assorted group of people, and in ways showing that its depiction of hopelessness and activism gone astray somehow can call forth intensely positive reactions. This feature is strong enough to require explanation; such positive appeal cannot be accounted for simply by invoking our established "apocalyptic reflex" in its secularized form, the reflex expectation that when things get unbearably awful, some great new beginning must be provided by the management simply because it is owed us. No, some stronger factor must be at work here as well.

That factor is related to, but stronger than, the appeal of ripping off hypocritical masks all around. What *Fight Club* does with breathtaking skill is to show us the impossible. The work sketches quite neatly the new norms and new social hierarchy of the culture described in different ways by Riesman and Meštrović, implying first that they are inviolable and untouchable. Then, lightning-like, deftly, it turns this new order upside down, revealing that same new order as entirely susceptible to violation and complete transgression. *Fight Club* shows in fantasy how it is possible to carry out a thorough trashing of the operations and emblems of a worldwide System otherwise moving rapidly toward total and irreversible social control.

That is, *Fight Club* (before Tyler's epiphany) does indeed present an utterly despairing distillation of all the oppressive features of an emergent society of total control; but at the same time (after Tyler), it involves the audience in a centrally targeted series of elaborate defacings and violent spoofings, all exhibiting the ultimate weakness of this new worldwide System. And as a kind of enacted parable with cinematic audience involvement, the whole business suddenly begins to operate with a life of its own beyond the screen images. It brings forth in the theater a hypertransgressive and improvised contemporary carnival, a burlesque, a feast of fools, a parliament of misrule and misrulers, a direct and aggressive parody of our new social hierarchy and its kevlar-clad norms.

This official society and its cultural armor presents a tempting target for the irreverent, combining as it does an infinite spectrum of power-moves and a strong taste for brutality with a fetishizing of risk avoidance and an infinitely tedious propensity for lecturing its subject populace on the moral imperative of eliminating all thoughts of resistance to official requirements. After all, *Fight Club* is ultimately about the society that invented class action lawsuits and recalls of candy bars that fail to warn of ambient peanut fragments. (As *Fight Club* could barely be released as a film in 1999, it is evident that an updated, post-9/11 version not only could not be released, but if filmed would probably lead to the arrest and indefinite detention of the entire cast as injurious to the war in progress and a threat to government itself, a likelihood that eliminates all need to speculate on how it could be updated in a sequel, unless it were shot in Guantanamo instead of Hollywood.)

Yes, there is sufficient clarity about the kind of official norms ridiculed in *Fight Club*—emotional dressage, insurance as a way of life, the suppression of any spontaneity as too risky, the duty to eschew wagering on the adequacy of your body, the duty to prolong your life well into assisted-living senility, the suppression of violence for fear it might prove to be both full of sense and a great shaker-up of everything and everybody. What *Fight Club* provides is not a blueprint for practical revolution (to the disappointment of its critics). It instead improvises an audience-involving and game-like overturning of everything, the classic "world turned upside down." In a society where no pies are thrown and in which mass democracy has rediscovered the ancient crime of injury of sovereign majesty as the worst possible offense (which is the only way we can interpret the Byzantine-like walling off of government officials from the general population, in progress long before 9/11), real feasts of fools are impossible. Society today has zero tolerance for any real version of the classic *Fête des Fous*.

So *Fight Club* as a film provides its fans with a virtual carnival, a cinematic and audience-participatory feast of fools, instinctively sensing the deficit and the resulting absolute need for an update on the ancient custom of burlesque and saturnalia, of a carefully targeted festival of misrule with fools and idiots temporarily ruling the place, in this way providing an experiential illusion of total escape from total prison. What the Romans did with the saturnalia, what the early Middle Ages did with clergy-connected feasts of fools, what urban associations continued in the later Middle Ages (the relentless taunting of every sacred norm and convention dear to the hearts of the masters and power brokers) here reemerges in the only way allowed in the age of the SWAT team—the mode of compensatory fantasy.

Put differently, we have a compensatory fantasy of anarchy that in effect sets the seal of psychic legitimacy upon an empirical retreat from really rebellious politics and really revolutionary revolution, both of which now constitute excluded options in contemporary America. And indeed the way in which *Fight Club* functions overall supports such a reading. The work is presented as a kind of updated feast of fools or carnival of misrule or world turned upside down (explained in the works of theorists such as Georges Bataille, Victor Turner, Mikhail Bakhtin, and Natalie Zemon Davis).[35] Further, exactly this reading is confirmed quite explicitly in the important analyses of the film by Slavoj Žižek, Bülent Diken, and Carsten Bagge Laustsen. Yet, as these last-named three analysts concur, here the enacted fantasy of misrule and extremity—unlike some rituals and fantasies—does not prepare the way for real change, merely for an indispensable psychic adjustment, the prolegomenon to more of the same so far as real politics and economics are concerned, a finding they sense as ratified by the quoted words of Palahniuk himself at the close of the following passage:

> [r]ather than a political act, Fight Club thus seems to be a trancelike subjective experience, a kind of pseudo-Bakhtinian carnivalesque activity in which the rhythm of everyday life is only temporarily suspended. "You know the rage is coming out some way. And if this stuff can be sort of vented in a consensual controlled situation like a fight club, I just see that as an improvement."[36]

Here *Fight Club* provides the capstone in an overarching structure, each stone of which is inscribed *Huis Clos,* No Exit. As we have seen in detail with regard to the emergent genre of popular pessimism, the key examples chosen and analyzed in no way furnish a model of escape from tightening social control that carries with it any real chance for challenging a sociopolitical system already subject to extreme stress, or to seriously increasing the number of active candidates for departure from society under the sign of anomie. Indeed, the special significance of *Fight Club* emerges best from such a perspective. While overtly it offers the most intense challenge of any recent popular work to the standing order, surface appearances can mislead. For *Fight Club,* insofar as it functions as a kind of Turnerian antistructure, a feast of misruling fools of breathtaking intensity, thereby supplies an order-preserving mechanism of a kind not institutionalized in millennial America, a fact reinforced by Jack's bizarre final condition of debilitated reintegration into the heterosexual society of bourgeois consumer capitalism. From this perspective, of course, there is every reason to applaud the brilliant irony here of casting Brad Pitt as the articulator of the most scathing critique imaginable of commodity fetishism, a move that underlines the profoundly ironic aspects inherent in this audacious sendup of all pieties, the revolutionary version included. A genius is at work here, when the media's official sexiest man attired as Nietzschean antihero boldly proclaims for all to hear, and with himself in mind, "We are God's unwanted children. So be it!" (Thus Tyler Durden/Brad Pitt in the script of *Fight Club.*)

Whether this reading, this explanation for the cult success of *Fight Club* (the film) will suffice, only time and readers can assess. To this issue a couple of final observations are worth including. First, no less an authority on the historical aspect of carnivals than Natalie Davis has argued that some of Shakespeare's plays operate as enacted, onstage versions of carnival or charivari, giving us considerable precedent for how such a possibility can be actuated.[37] Second, Davis has likewise held that earlier historical work on the social function of festivities of burlesque or carnival or misrule in various societies has been too limited. To speak simply of a "safety valve," she contends, does not go far enough. Following Victor Turner and Mikhail Bakhtin, she argues that late medieval and early modern carnivals of misrule could at certain times function "both to reinforce order and to suggest alternatives to the existing order."[38] Here, of course, she is at one with Victor Turner.

While this potential may have existed in the past and in eternal theory, still the critics of *Fight Club* are correct about the limited political options it allows—other than fascism and regression to gathering lingonberries, *Fight Club* is not sufficiently creative to get us out of our current varieties of public impasse. It provides an extravagant safety valve; it evokes semisecular echoes of the apocalyptic reflex; it exhilarates by roughly upending the taboos and pieties of social control gone digital, gone emotionally repressive, gone in total. And of course, by reviving some memories of common human traits it points to the distant memory of old dreams of equality and utopia and technology as friend. In so doing, *Fight Club* points to the reality of despair and pessimism here and now, even as it attests to the capacity of people for finding reasons to hope, excuses for imagining resistance, strategies for fantasizing about a major turnaround.

With the case of *Fight Club*, we reach the logical end of a narrative trajectory of recent Anglo-American cultural pessimism crafted for a minority of extremely pessimistic consumers, a minority who feel no need to insist on pasting on happy endings (though Jack's reconciliation with heterosexual domesticity overtly does obeisance to what the millennial equivalent of the classic Hollywood censor currently may require). In the narrative format there can scarcely exist a more despairing work than Jack's story; yet, at the same time the paradoxical effect of exhilaration and release obtained with *Fight Club*, both book and especially film, is noteworthy. The need for such release or escape or distancing is clear enough given the socioeconomic situation of a sizable part of the American population, and emotions of despair and a hatred of neocapitalist structures strongly emanate from this work. Its sense of loss and betrayal fits, by the way, perfectly into the model of the self-undermining of Thatcherism proposed in 1995 by British academic John Gray. Gray argued that transnational corporate economic pressures tend inevitably to evoke a strong counterreaction from displaced identities and displaced social structures, a negative reaction tied up with rational fears concerning diminished chances for survival of individuals and social systems, fears going far beyond worries about economic difficulties.[39] Especially deserving of mention is the total inability of corporate culture in *Fight Club* to evoke loyalty from the protagonist(s), and the ostentatious way primary group bonding is contrasted with the indifference or open hatred exhibited toward one's employer. The long-term practical significance of this circumstance for the economic and political outlook in America deserves much reflection, reflection it is unlikely to receive in corporate boardrooms or in the two permitted political parties.

Yet our story would be incomplete if it ended with *Fight Club* (even though *Fight Club* is for our purposes the ultimate narrative and the ultimate set of rejections). Beyond narratives of pessimism, conspiracy, and apocalyptic magic, or rather beside them, is a genre related but distinct. It is the genre of alternative theory and of alternative pragmatics—not in politics, but pragmatics in the management of the needs of empirical body, soul, self, consciousness, or spirit, *whatever*. Here we shall uncover an equally critical, equally despairing, but more paradoxically optimistic variant on diagnosis and prescription, a variant housed in works of theory and practice, in works of alternative physics and alternative prehistory, in guides to alternative medicine and alternative cosmology. In these assorted works, dealing with everything from alien plots to Atlantis to zoology—[Crypto], we shall find abundant documentation confirming our finding with the case of *Fight Club*—that Americans today possess infinite capacities for combining unprecedented despair and hardnosed pessimism with the most astonishing modes of inducing hope, modes ranging from the herbal medicine to wildly contradictory views on extraterrestrial influence. This is a serious business as befits a nation for whom a sizable part of the sinking middle class faces interlocking reasons for despair, a situation that calls for the most varied kind of analysis, and a situation backing up the words of one of the current generation's most-clued-in therapists, who recently quipped, "You know you're in real trouble when your primary caregiver is an aromatherapist."

Chapter 5

Relocating the American Dream: The Challenges and Ambiguities of Contemporary Cultural Pessimism

This chapter and the remaining ones reexamine the themes of the previous chapters, placing the negative images in popular culture in the setting of wider views of the underlying issues by contemporary thinkers dealing with millennial society and politics. The broader significance turns out to lie in the nature of what it currently takes to keep hope in the American dream alive—and where that dream winds up. Meanwhile, we look at the way survival of American hope more and more comes down to stabilizing the political system and the mass media support on which the two-party system depends.

MILDRED

Hi, Kathie. Aren't they wonderful?
Did you hear what I said? I said
what does that mean—B.R.M.C.—
and he said 'the Black Rebels'
Motorcycle Club.' And I said what
are you rebelling against, Johnny?
Johnny said, 'what have you got?'
What have you got! Isn't that cute?
    —*The Wild One*

Ingredients in Millennial Pessimism:
The Mixed Themes of Protest, Betrayal, Accommodation,
Resistance, Pseudoescape and System Stabilization

Exactly why Marlon Brando's open-ended rebellion strikes Mildred as cute is—if we think about it—the key question. Johnny signals he and his sidekicks intend to raise hell. Mildred thinks it's cute. Real-world, physical revolt breaks out, minichaos ensues, and the System physically restores order. While there is a good deal more to the plot than this, the package does not break out of that formula.

From this case we see that our familiar bundle of themes emerged long before Tyler Durden. Already with leather-jacketed Brando's postwar version of the protest role in *The Wild One,* we can sense the breadth and depth of the rage that will seethe and boil in the America of Eisenhower, LBJ, and Nixon. Already with Mildred, we can sense as well that this protest will have great difficulty in getting itself taken seriously by serious people, that is, in the upbeat world of mainline media dealing with the "real world" of the official culture of American democracy.

Already with Mildred the impossibility of giving any single-serving explanation of what is at stake in this attitude evokes the accepting but uncomprehending first response denying all seriousness by remarking "Isn't that cute?" Pointed, smart-ass, but not cute—that was the intention. Precisely why certain motorcycle-riding misfits and war veterans cannot settle down into the corporate world of other-directedness and economic definitions of well-being may be mysterious . . . but we do not dismiss that possibility that the power and direction of this rebel drift can become obvious. Certainly Brando's Johnny, like Fox Mulder, Rayford Steele, and Tyler Durden, shares with his peers a sense that things are going to hell, and not merely the economy.

Suppose then we try to determine what this package of protest contains and what it amounts to. By this point the reader has looked in detail at *The X-Files,* Left Behind, and *Fight Club*—and has looked at them only after first examining Patrick McGoohan's transatlantic series *The Prisoner.* That series for our purposes anticipates all the big themes of nonconsensus, downbeat pessimism. Not long after Johnny and Mildred, McGoohan and colleague Markstein envisioned something like a full blueprint of the world of contemporary extreme pessimism—the perfectly interlocking system of systems in which no real escape is ever possible from the system of social control now in place, the step-by-step training for suppression of even the imagined possibility of any real revolt in which we now live, information-oriented and globalized.

In the chapter-length treatments of *The X-Files, Left Behind,* and *Fight Club,* we saw emerging the themes of betrayal of promises made with regard to Enlightenment progress, betrayal of participatory democracy in the tradition of civic humanism, and betrayal of (or loss of) a strongly anchored individual self fit for nonservile (free) existence. To a growing degree, the chapters took on the aspect of comic book versions of sociological theory, in particular, variations on the work of fifties classic sociologist David Riesman and his other-directed cast of office-spaced lonely crowders. Whether employed in the high end of automobile liability and risk assessment or in the corridors of irresponsible power inside the Beltway, or more excitingly employed piloting jets as part of God's marionette force rolling back the Antichrist, all these versions appear in retrospect as other-directed, programmable, Dilbert-like, script-obedient—that is, selves that are hollowed out, deprived of substantial context, and, as will be argued below, optimized for mall shopping, online trading, and corporate service anywhere in the world.

In the broader sense, our main documents also turned out to show how contemporary cultural pessimism possesses a latent social function of siphoning off outrage and thereby stabilizing the globalizing social system, with, however, the riddle emerging that *one* of these versions, the dispensationalist Christian vision of near-Tribulation activism, energizes for real-world political activity, whereas the other versions seem to consolidate progressive apathy. *Fight Club* in particular struck us as more than mere pseudoescape, as in fact an example of engagingly, actively enacted, carnivalesque buffoonery of the most serious kind—a kind of contemporary "feast of fools" or "ritual of misrule" let loose upon a totally controlled society—a place which no longer allows actual medieval-style feasts of misrule (applying Victor Turner to *Fight Club*).

Fight Club, we argued in some detail, produces a sense of exhilaration even though overall the work is negative regarding hope for improvement in society as a whole or for politics in particular. A cleansing or siphoning-off function with regard to rage thereby occurs as part of the enacted carnival or burlesque of role reversal that *Fight Club* forces upon its rather willing audience. Along these same lines but more generally, as we have already suggested, the forms of pseudo-escape in these documents of cultural pessimism appear to have the latent function of keeping hope alive and neutralizing rage and frustration, stabilizing the larger system as it comes under strain during some of its more difficult moments. Significantly, the most extreme of all these documents, *Fight Club,* is emphatically not a practical manual for revolution, but the opposite, one of a series of means of graphically evoking and experiencing the illusion of escape or revolt from a sociopolitical and economic system that these works in fact help to stabilize.

Thus from McGoohan's early *Prisoner* to *Fight Club,* the genre of cultural pessimism presents us with a recurrent message: Specifically, first, that advanced modern societies, led by America, have already evolved a self-stabilizing political and social system capable of suppressing dissent and of reshaping identities in increasingly dehumanized ways to obtain a perfectly functioning machine in the service of power and rigidly hierarchical social models camouflaged as progressive democracy in the Enlightenment tradition. Second, it says that by so perfectly keeping disconfirming data, dissent, and imperfect personalities and worldviews from access to power and media coverage, this perfectly closed system risks blinding itself to the possibility of impending catastrophe from unperceived inner revolt or from unperceived external enemies or even from unperceived (misinterpreted) economic or structural or biological or natural data (global warming, for example).

The first part of this message, the loss of freedom and sense of participatory power, we have already documented in our treatments of *The X-Files,* Left Behind, and *Fight Club.* Or to vary the image, the first part of the message presents us with something like the perfectly maintained bridge and first-class dining saloon on the *Titanic,* perfectly heated and lighted, impervious to troublemakers in steerage and rather poorly informed about real-world icebergs. The second part of the message tells us that icebergs and persons both interesting and perhaps dangerous do lurk outside or in steerage, along with a whole host of undreamed-of phenomena, none of them much noticed by the bridge or the diners lingering over peach melba. Notice also that this second message, that of a social system largely unaware of imminent or impending dangers of unspecified varieties, occurs in the last three of our works, *The X-Files,* Left Behind, and *Fight Club.* Mulder and Scully, along with the inner circle of knowledgeable collaborators with the alien invaders, know what is coming in 2012—but the public at large and most mid-level, even high-level, authorities are kept clueless by the System. As for the Left Behind books, they rest on the premise that high-level society is totally incapable of seeing or imagining the hell of Tribulation about to be let loose upon it. Finally, with *Fight Club* we have the paradox that even those who bring about the revolt and the detonation of credit records fail to find the escape they seek, instead regressing into nameless protohumans en route to microfascist careers as hunter-gatherers led by an Alpha Male hypnotizing them with *Penis Monologues.* Thus in the dark vision of this genre, the perfectly self-stabilizing nature of the advanced System in no way excludes the possibility of utter catastrophe. Yet, just to make matters worse, the possibility of utter catastrophe does not open up much in the way of liberation—the Right-wing Christian vision, again, tellingly enough, offering a bit of an exception with regard to the Raptured and the marionettes of the Tribulation Force, if indeed they can be thought of as truly escaping.

Horrific, and horrifically complete, are these successive visions, which again and again offer us the paradox of a social system both perfectly stabilized and insulated on the one hand, yet in fact immensely vulnerable on the other—but vulnerable in ways that offer only quite problematic possibilities of real escape. But these visions do offer the chance that group or subgroup energies may indeed be activated and discharged in search of real and effective escape or improvement, a possibility portrayed as probably useless (Scully and Mulder), possible only for a few fanatical marionettes (Rayford Steele and company), or a road so awful it is not worth traveling (the Mayhem boys in search of an Alpha Male). These documents taken together constitute a *Minority Report;* and it is a minority report on America and its disciple nations, here and now.

Horrifying, yes. Nonconsensus, yes. But significant? Accurate? Meaningful for wider discussion and analysis? Those are the points demanding discussion in our remaining sections. To deal with those points from several angles fruitful for subsequent debate, we propose to stay with our image of the bridge of the *Titanic* as an overarching image, one capable of bringing together this series of horrifying visions. The visions show us a social system proceeding relentlessly forward, taking little note of the workings of the engines below, the crew laboring within, the wretches in steerage, or the icebergs outside, but taking careful note of the sequence of courses in first-class dining and the career advancement requirements of the White Star Line. (This is not to suggest that the James Cameron film of 1997 is a work of cultural pessimism! The culturally pessimistic reading of the *Titanic* image goes, in fact, back to the era of Spengler himself, and owes much not only to the Promethean overtones of the ship's unfortunate name, but as well to the fateful closeness of its sinking in 1912 with the outbreak of world war in 1914. As such, the image of the ill-fated liner belongs to the classic and established emblems and icons of European cultural pessimism, having been brilliantly utilized in a work of unpopular cultural pessimism by filmmaker Federico Fellini.)[1]

To shed light on the importance and accuracy of these horrifying visions seen from the liner's bridge, we intend repeatedly and in different ways to look for answers to two different questions. First, other than our narrative documents of pessimism, what indicators are available for contemporary real-world correlates corresponding to the pessimistic visions now familiar to us? Second, supposing those gloomy real-world correlates do exist, what signs are there that the sociopolitical system works all that well, and works to keep disturbing data out of its field of vision by way of stabilizing itself—or by way of protecting itself . . . (and against what, we may further ask)?

These two broad lines of inquiry by themselves will allow us to consider an entire array of pertinent matters. Work on the reemergence of the actual category of "cultural pessimism," and also work on failing and revised ideologies of social integration from a religious point of view, and even nonnarrative material analogous to our documents of popular cultural pessimism can, for example, throw light on the first issue of accuracy of perception in the pessimistic genre. Do real-world serious correlates exist to the gloomy threats discerned in our documents? Are serious issues repressed so that their political and economic implications do not surface in an accountable fashion?

Likewise, work by scholars, analysts, and journalists on the inner motor or inner dynamic of the contemporary socioeconomic and sociopolitical system can cast light on different aspects of our *second* problem: the functioning, self-stabilizing, and vision-limiting nature of the System. Further, such work may also reveal the perception of dangerously intensifying threats to its stability and the resulting efforts at stabilizing the System at any price.

Accuracy of Pessimistic Perception: Aspects of the Pessimistic Vision and the Search for Real-World Correlates

According to Ivy League oral tradition, shortly after the end of World War II, Yale's outgoing professor of homiletics, Halford E. Luccock, greeted his successor with a handshake and the words, "Welcome to the Yale Divinity School, an institution that has destroyed more churches than the *Luftwaffe*." This observation can stand here for a view by now familiar in many contexts—the perception that mainline, quasiofficial institutions have proven as much an obstacle as a help so far as advancing human and civilizing and emancipatory aims. At the same time it is a profoundly pessimistic, nonconsensus view of the System and its key religious institutions at the top, at the highest level, and from the inside. The System works by consistently betraying its ideals and its lower-level components—in this case, congregations, presumably undone by the excessive liberalism from clergy trained in elite divinity schools—a bit of inside dope, in sociologist David Riesman's terms.

In previous chapters we have already encountered variations on this pessimistic theme, for example, the FBI in *The X-Files,* voices of theology and church life in Left Behind, and the corporate employer in *Fight Club.* It is already evident that a perception of System-wide institutional and ideological failure—or rather betrayal—is a, perhaps *the,* chief component in pessimistic popular culture's encoded way of rendering a deep popular skepticism. This skepticism can be broad and deep. It is skepticism about basic official direction in America, a popular skepticism about the honesty and clear-sightedness of the System that has fluctuated but never abated, from the death of John Kennedy to the most recent round of American wars, governmental security measures, and debates over job loss, middle-class income loss,[2] immigration, citizenship, and presidential powers.

The breadth and depth of that protest—and its difficulties in getting itself taken seriously in the upbeat world of mainline media dealing with the "real world" of the official culture of American democracy—is, as we know, an integral part of this entire complex. Signaled already in the exchange between Johnny and Mildred in the Brando film, this difficulty or trivialization of protest has its varied causes, not least of which is the real impossibility of giving any single explanation regarding what is at stake in the basic attitude of protest. That difficulty, along with the need ultimately to avoid too much disruption, helps evoke Mildred's off-target response of "Isn't that cute?" And even when we come to share the suspicion of the protesters that things are going to hell, still we may not know all that much merely by being suspicious. This is murky and multilayered territory.

In all the documents of cultural pessimism we have considered, from *The Prisoner* to *Fight Club,* the same sense of complexity lurks. All agree that a host of issues merge to motivate the sense of loss and readiness for rebellion. Moreover, we recall, our treatment of *Fight Club* amounted to a counterargument to offset the implication in some writers that the work is insignificant because it "really" deals with the economic worries of a slender segment of white males from the rust belt. No, we argued. No; here we have to do with a sense of loss and betrayal rooted in the empirical world of society and politics, yet finally one attuned to the broad and wide ways in which our modern world has gotten out of joint. These dark works strain to discern what it all may portend, even as they avoid calling for Left-wing revolt, instead somehow marking a subtle accommodation or adjustment to resignation, to living under the System. (Evangelicals headed for Rapture and the political action committee of choice, as we saw, constitute a subgroup here, however.)

As we have seen, popular culture in its darker narrative mode constitutes a way to evoke an unmentionable cultural pessimism. This is a pessimism mainstream American reportage rhetoric can never foreground in explicit terms, not on an evening news funded by transnational corporations, any more than such a perception of decline can be dealt with in any penetrating way using the language of the two-party political system or the public school civics textbook. This is a good moment to recall McGrath's insistence that *The X-Files* really had to be about mood and nostalgia because nobody could find serious fault with real-world conditions in America. Tyler Durden disagrees, and yet he and other cultural pessimists link outrage at concrete economic and social factors with outrage at other kinds of loss, a loss that shows deep cultural, even religious roots—they have a manifold perception of loss and decline, one that could be undone only by a multifaceted total reversal, one that would allow a definitive relocating of the American dream. Relocating . . . but how? And to where?

Now to commentators deeply embedded in the prosperity thinking of the upper eight percent of today's America, these notions uttered in any decade sound like the ravings of a delusional drug user. Perhaps McGrath was correct after all? Perhaps narratives of cultural pessimism reflect simply some regressive nostalgia for the "simpler" days of the cold war?

McGrath's objection deserves answers. The basic answer is the fact that a variety of pessimistic voices have for years been speaking in unmistakable terms about interlinked domains of intense decline and the need for total reversal of direction in every aspect of the empirical world—and that in material for an audience distinct from that of the backward-looking evangelical Right, and that in a genre not restricted to the ambiguities of novels and screen scripts. As we shall shortly see, its pessimistic readings based on contemporary data are by no means lacking among academics and journalists. Moreover, the same pessimism can be found in a distinct genre not yet considered, one different from standard journalism or social science studies.

New Age Pessimism and Fantasy Escapism: New Age as the Postsixties Attenuation of Hardcore Protest

We realize that a good deal of all this is enigmatic—what precisely do these pessimists rebel against—are they mere latter-day Marlon Brandos, ready to object on emotional grounds alone to whatever the situation has become?

Why are they so "paranoid"—is it not perhaps merely a matter of whining about bad digestion, a.k.a. nostalgia? Our view inclines in quite the opposite direction, ultimately. Thus, for readers who doubt that fantasies of extreme calamity in popular cultural pessimistic narrative actually encode a deep concern about empirical life in real-world American modernity and a call for extreme reversal of direction, we provide material for further reflection. In New Age circles that call for reversal turns out to involve both practice in the worlds of medicine and lifestyle and politics as well as worldview at the level of doctrine or ideology.

That is, we contend, the same dark pessimism we met in narratives above also figures explicitly in the notoriously nonChristian, future-oriented materials of the New Age worldview and spirituality movement. The same pessimism and call for reversal known to us already now turns up in New Age materials that are both pragmatic and related to worldview. That is, it's not just about some vague mood. And New Age materials point to the interplay between theoretical diagnosis and concern with real-life conditions—concerns that can be taken as objective correlates to the worries already familiar in our narrative and script documents.

If this possibility is worthy of serious consideration, our investigation can begin to look more broadly at the possibility of correlative empirical phenomena in today's America, at concrete conditions. Let us therefore turn to the grassroots cultural pessimism of the New Agers, a cultural pessimism that implies a remedy or rescue. For according to our criterion even an overtly upbeat worldview along these lines still deserves the label *pessimistic* if the hope for improvement or upturn comes only from a radical change of overall direction for the society or group in question.

It is this criterion that allows us to consider Christian conservative evangelicals (for example) and New Age mystics in the same breath as parallel varieties of cultural pessimists: for each point of view rejects one or more key elements in the classic modern American consensus outlook. (By "consensus outlook" we mean what might be termed the antemillennial status quo outlook in midtwentieth-century America, the official ideology—one that affirmed conventionally progressive, or Enlightenment-based, views with space for some belief in human free choice and civic participation with or without adherence to a particular religious creed.) By the 1960s, that understanding went along with greater comfort with a secularized take on American identity that affirmed diversity and the increasing separation of religion from public life. In this late stage, the ideology of legitimation, the undergirding outlook for the nation as a whole, had in consequence come to rely on an exceedingly ambiguous relic of civil religion, ambiguous with regard to its basic Christian demands for the entire nation, and ambiguous with regard to how inherently militant, expansionist, and mission-filled it had to be. In the consensus outlook, in any case, there certainly was as well some kind of hope for an economic chance for general upward mobility. Thus with this ideal type of classic consensus outlook, we highlight a worldview finally resting on belief in the easy coherence of Enlightenment doctrines of progress through scientific rationalism and an implicit acceptance of a special role in ordering the world order for the Anglo-American commonwealth. By "status quo" in this context then we mean as a baseline the median level of moderate, progressive culture as one slides from the Eisenhower era to the Kennedy years. And, we stress again, the specifically Christian component in that outlook was multilayered, ambiguous, and increasingly out-of-date for the complex America of the later twentieth century.[3]

In contemporary America, leading up to and moving beyond the millennial years 1999–2001 however reckoned, hard-line evangelicals increasingly challenged this inherited or mainline consensus. They have challenged it with regard to the growing separation of religion from public life as a desirable goal, even as they chomp more and more at the edges of reliance on science—without, however, switching off the air conditioner or insisting on immediate renunciation of depleted uranium as a weapons technology. New Age types, on the other hand, have challenged any number of the other items in the ideal-typical American consensus (its equation of Western with scientific, for example), while on the whole and with certain limits tending to retain a progressive separation of religion from public life—so long as that religion being separated is traditional Christianity. Yet an interest in finding ways to resacralize secularized culture along New Age or Eastern lines was clearly evident in the early days of the New Age movement and still can be sensed in some situations: the scientific positivist outlook of official modernity strikes New Agers as inadequate. (Prince Charles announcing, between ribbon-cuttings at homeopathic hospitals, that he is interested in becoming Defender of the Faiths [plural] can epitomize this vague interest in alternative sacralizing.)

Both groups, evangelical and New Age, then, can entertain an interest in finding some fitting way for reinstalling a religious aura in today's America. Both groups can at times favor some version of what could be called neosacralizing of aspects of contemporary life and culture, surely a complex and murky issue for all parties in millennial America, but one that in the abstract holds out some promise of unifying a core or base. Pumping more of some kind of religion into millennial America seems to them a desirable goal. But from what reservoir? And into what conduits?

In any case, we have here to do with attitudes that by no means simply wish to continue and uphold the classic progressive and consensus view of 1960. Rather, by recommending a strong change in direction with regard to orientation toward the classic premillennial consensus, evangelicals and New Agers qualify as rather different (yet in a sense related) peas in a culturally pessimistic pod. In either case the regnant consensus, from around 1960 or so seen as needing very considerable, even extreme, rearrangement if improvement, perhaps even salvation from doom, is to follow for the nation. However, and here is the key point, despite its use of perennial mystic and older Romantic elements in its worldview, the most distinctive characteristic of New Age material in our times is its status as a greatly weakened and transformed relative of the militantly political antibourgeois protest movements of the sixties. This theme has been developed in considerable detail by specialist historian Christoph Bochinger and need not detain us here for long.[4] To state the matter a bit differently, for Bochinger the apparently incoherent and derivative bundles of new religions, spiritualities, groups, and practices known as New Age in essence represents a cultural or spiritual and lifestyle (rather than explicitly political) continuation of the activist counterculture of the 1960s and 1970s. Once the revolution failed to occur, antibourgeois energies found their way into the remaining areas and channels, giving rise to a vast array of increasingly marketable practices and products, some more group-centered than others, and many initially connected with the European view held prior to the sixties, that far-reaching changes in consciousness were connected with the precession of the equinox. As such New Age, whether still obsessed with epoch change in sidereal perspective or not, represents an attenuation of politics and hardcore cultural criticism, but nonetheless a variant thereon, one rendered relatively harmless, perhaps a kind of analogue to the attenuated live virus used in some vaccines as a mode of immunizing the patient against the real disease.

In this framework we turn our attention to New Age currents. The New Age movement has become a byword for elusive, not surprisingly so since its currents of pessimism intermingle with fantastic optimism in a manner rendering easy diagnosis difficult—even as that mix makes it hard for the novice to assess the degree to which a particular New Age strand represents major fragmentation of society and its culture.

This elusiveness marks the key feature of expectation of a turn in the ages, a turn from old to new. Specialist Olav Hammer points out that the movement's earlier unifying belief in a dawning new epoch keyed to the precession of the equinox has abated, so the movement has somewhat changed from its original instantiation as a cultural prolongation of the political counterculture of the sixties—yet the foundation on the worldview of sixties critique remains.[5] Hammer's turn would mark a second attenuation—having turned from hardcore political protest, New Age currents then began to stray from the obsession with ages of the signs of the zodiac into ever more diffuse versions of worldview, yet always retaining the aura of "alternative" and "countercultural" that allows it an eternal character of being antibourgeois and anti-establishment, capable of giving off a vague sense of being against the System, whether in religion or medicine or in ecological issues at the ballot box. Elusive, yet not incapable of being read.

The same elusive impression characterizes the way varied positions intermingle with New Age phenomena. We find here antiinstitutional outlooks, strong interest in pantheism or Eastern mysticism, often with a reliance as well on both neoplatonic and quantum vibrational models. Yet finally it is a Western movement, stressing the assimilation of such outlooks to a modern mentality that recasts the entire business in the language of scientific paradigms. Running throughout this potpourri is the Western desire to retrieve personal identity in the face of death (reincarnation in a specifically Western or personality-conserving sense). This special blend constitutes a distinctive package of New Age movement markers that point to real changes in the movement's character.[6]

With regard to contemporary or recent versions of New Age outlook, moreover, researcher David Tacey affirms their kinship not only to the cultural pessimism discussed here in detail (pessimisms, but in particular its kinship to pessimism that finally fails to deliver real escape or rescue):

> . . . the New Age movement, which offers glimpses of lost unity and harmony, will prosper and grow. . . . In discussing the various phenomena of the New Age we are not necessarily talking about a consciously adopted ideology or an intellectual philosophy, but about very basic forms of spiritual longing that are denied expression in the dominant secular culture and in the mainstream institutions of faith. . . .
>
> The New Age is a living reminder that the intellectual Enlightenment no longer delivers its promises of liberation and freedom, that the secular humanist experiment has been found wanting, and that people are demanding a newer, more profound kind of existence.[7]

Tacey shares the standard view that the New Age movement has become largely ineffectual politically, often ending in a kind of entrepreneurial

capitalism unlikely to challenge real contemporary enemies in any significant way. Nonetheless for Tacey, New Age necessarily and by definition
retains a key significance as it constitutes the New Age version of Left-wing
cultural pessimism's typical strategy, the strategy of pseudoescape in the face
of diminished political effectiveness. He writes:

> The New Age compensates our consciousness in different ways. It com-
> pensates our secular, materialist society by nakedly displaying the powerful
> longings of the human spirit, even if this compensation is unsuccessful,
> i.e. unacceptable to mainstream secular attitudes. It also compensates our
> established religious traditions by forcing us to attend to what has been
> repressed or ignored by Western religion: the sacred feminine, the body,
> nature, instincts, ecstasy and mysticism. . . .
>
> The New Age, however, does not compensate our consumerist society
> but simply reproduces several of its features in its industry and enterprise,
> creating a spiritual consumerism. It turns the spiritual realm into a com-
> modity, packaging ancient wisdoms, indigenous cosmologies and spiritual
> psychologies in order to satisfy our spiritual longing. But because the New
> Age operates in this consumerist mode, it rarely meets our spiritual needs,
> often providing a 'fast food' service, a kind of McSpirit that fails to satisfy.
> The human spirit calls for an authentic response, not simply for a symp-
> tomatic or artificial quick fix. Therefore the New Age itself is a kind of
> parody of the authentic spiritual life that longs to be realized in our time.[8]

Contemporary New Age thinkers interest us here on account of the way their
effort at some kind of "compensation" under current circumstances necessarily involves two elements. First comes the built-in respect for science-related
paradigms in all New Age thought. Then comes, at the same time, the distinct requirement of retrieving premodern versions of holistic ascription of
overarching meaning or ultimate significance—precisely the kind of (un)holy
union between the two cultures that has proven so problematically unattainable since the triumph of positivistic science in the nineteenth century.

The last truly great challenger of the clean separation of meaning from
science was the German thinker Johann Wolfgang von Goethe, who died
in 1832. Recent high-end representatives of this genre are scarce—and no
wonder, for we speak here of a genre in New Age that, at its most demanding,
seems to place impossible demands on anybody. For if properly carried out,
a work in this genre would involve the self-conscious combining of science
in an academic framework with New Age models and narratives both primal
and personal that can supply higher meaning.

Now certainly there are any number of physicists and cosmologists who
regularly make the cover of *TIME* by discovering vague traces of divine order

in remote galaxies and in the unpredictably synchronized meandering of sub-atomic particles. But this kind of recombining meaning and science is so vague and so weak-toothed that it offers little payoff to anybody save the physicists and the science journalists intent on yet another rediscovery of God.

Here, however, we are interested in recombiners whose work has teeth that bite into the contemporary world and its worldviews. In this sense the list of current candidates is short. On the list would be the gracious and learned William A. Tiller, a lattice crystallographer at Stanford whose spiritual journey in its earlier phase involved meditation in the style of Edgar Cayce. But the title of most sweeping New Age theorist goes not to a gentleman at Stanford, but to one formerly in the philosophy department at Georgia State, Professor Mark Woodhouse. Dr. Woodhouse's work brings together not only the effort at reintegrating science and superscientific taste for ultimate meaning, but as well ambiguous themes of cultural collapse and sources for renewal—the mix of pessimism and optimism that finally makes New Age materials important. At the same time, though, it makes them elusive and potentially the markers of a kind of cultural fragmentation that insists on donning the vestments of sociocultural reintegration. Woodhouse, in a word, takes up the same themes of decay and hope for dramatic escape as do pessimistic novels and scripts, but he does so in the nonfiction section of your local bookstore. His work constantly attempts to connect with real-world correlates yet in the end proposes kinds of escape that edge into the fantastic. In this way, it points as well to the increasingly ambiguous character of all countercultural protest these days, an ambiguity and lack of definition increasingly shared by Left-wing political groups deprived of clear identity given the ebbing of sixties protest and the collapse of Marxism.

The New Age Importance of Being Earnest:
Real Darkness and Fantasy Dawn in Contemporary
Nonnarrative Pessimism from New Age Sources

New Age materials depend for their overall impact as a worldview on a sense of pessimism that its various outlooks and nostrums can help overcome, or at least compensate for. In other words, New Age materials are important because they are meant to be taken seriously—the importance of being, well, e[a]rnest! They want to be read as pointing to big solutions to big, and very real, problems.

Take as a prime example Dr. Woodhouse's book, published in 1996. It is a very serious book. It offers more thematic statements elaborated from more New Age points of view than nearly any other book—a grand theoretical vision that at the same time explicitly invokes this-worldly concern for practical issues of "empowerment" and reform.[9] For that reason it serves here as our main document of high-end popular culture in a vein combining science and philosophy of science with grand narratives of cosmic significance and hints of intensely personal spiritual exploration. It is serious indeed in diagnosing major problems in the real world and the disjointed outlooks that require overcoming.

Woodhouse is a trained scholar, and one convinced not only that modern science and philosophy in their respectable forms have failed by their limitations and inability to deliver compelling and humanly convincing ultimate answers, but also that they are doomed in the long run. They will lose their war to keep respectability (and perhaps also grant money?) out of the hands of New Age and mystical thinkers who wish to broaden the boundaries of science to include controversial approaches dear to New Agers.

For as it turns out, what these controversial would-be reshapers of "science" usually want to retrieve, and the secret perhaps of their broad appeal outside scientific guild circles, is themes and approaches fraught with the kind of human meaning long banished from respectable science. In particular, they want to retrieve vibratory and quantum-analogy-ridden paradigms, the kinds of models that help New Agers relocate the scientific results formerly supported by the hypothesis of an aether and other, earlier, tools for perceiving cosmic harmony, neoplatonism included.[10] That the New Agers are engaged in a bizarre parallel retrieval to what evangelical creationists are doing seems obvious, all the more when Atlantis research overlaps as it sometimes does with the search for Noah's ark.

In order to appreciate what Woodhouse is up to, some further preliminary remarks are in order. One may ask how neoplatonic notions can reappear in an age of quantum physics given the disappearance of Mesmer's ether or "invisible fluid" that could support types of matter of varying fluidity and allow for human consciousness to connect with events and entities far away, even as it, in the words of historian Catherine Albanese, "eroded the distance between matter and spirit."[11] Similar notions of harmony, she notes, and also notions of correspondence and divine influence on matter were common in many influential thinkers, for example, Emanuel Swedenborg (d. 1772).

Albanese argues in this connection that that paradigm of twentieth-century respectability Werner Heisenberg himself showed the way by undermining the solidity of matter and by replacing certainty with probability in matter/energy transformations. Indeed, claims Albanese, Heisenberg himself readily moved into metaphysics, indicating that, in her words

> the Platonic world of forms reflected reality: the smallest units of matter were ideas that could be articulated in mathematical terms. [Heisenberg] thought, too, that a "sharp separation between the world and the I" could no longer be possible. . . . The new physics, [Heisenberg] explained, was "a part of a general historical process that tends toward a unifying of our present world."

Comments Albanese:

> Amid the speculation, the irony was that the new physics had generously supplied a metaphoric base that could lead some to the reconstitution of the mesmeric and Swedenborgian worlds. If matter and energy were moments in a continuous natural process, phases or appearances of an essential and dynamic substrate of the world, then—for some—body and mind, substance and spirit, could be construed as part of a single continuum. The invisible fluid [of Mesmer—JS] could emerge as highly visible, and its pulsing, wavelike motion in the old etheric world could be reborn in the vibrating quanta of the twentieth century.[12]

On this basis, concludes Albanese,

> [the] stage was set for a latter-day synthesis that would make the past its prologue to a dawning millennium. In this synthesis, the blurring of matter and energy at the subatomic level would be linked in principle to the occult romanticism of the mesmeric-Swedenborgian habit of mind. The manipulative potential of minds that could control self and others would be joined to a matter that followed laws of harmony. Thus, acts of harmony would become, simultaneously, acts of power and control. And the world in which these things would happen by the late twentieth century would belong to the New Age.[13]

From current scholarship it seems evident that the multitudinous currents of twentieth-century New Age share certain features, each supporting the other. First is the willingness to move from quantum physics as science to a metaphorically linked domain of strongly held worldviews—worldviews that tend toward a comprehensive overcoming of the troubles of conventional modernity.

In this domain, one is allowed to get away with all manner of remarkable suggestions, in particular the claim that physics after Einstein and Copenhagen gives scientific support to outlooks associated with Asian religions in their Western reception, particularly a reaction against a Western worldview denoted simply as "Cartesian mind-body dualism." There are over-statements and logical leaps in all this, for example, imputing to Descartes an attainment of certainty far greater than that of which he would have approved.[14] Then there is willingness to rely on an appeal to an undifferentiated and prob-lematic category of experience that is held up to transcend the religion-science gap so long as the religion is nonChristian, a view stemming it from an anticolonial ideology pioneered in so-called Neohinduism.[15]

Second, it is evident that this outlook mixing spiritual and worldly atti-tudes readily gives rise to to what historian Christoph Bochinger terms a new professional group, "the group of secular mediators of religious contents."[16] Thus one encounters figures like physicist turned spiritual teacher Fritjof Capra, author of the *Tao of Physics*. Similar secular credentials and a similar role can describe the stance of Professor Woodhouse.

Third, New Age writing on science even at a high theoretical level is just as likely as its crasser relatives to contain myths of history, the millennium, the apocalypse, or some kind of big, overall, perceptible transformation or so-called "Turning Point"—both the stick and the carrot, hell and heaven, catastrophe and utopia, just as with any typical religious big narrative.

Whether accentuating the bad news or the good, New Agers can claim to offer a multifaceted account of what is really going on, an adequate truth. In a time of pluralism, relativism, postmodernism, distrust of institutions, voter disaffection, New Agers using variations on their theme of vibrational advance to universal harmony claim to offer scientifically grounded yet reli-giously satisfying (and comfortably antiinstitutional) explanations—a truth progressive and yet ancient, predicting eventual convergence and multidi-mensional transformation.

Obviously, the variability of the New Age message extends to its view of the difficulties believed to lie in the foreseeable future. While some schol-arship suggests that most New Age scripts do not expect so grim a set of tribulations as do the grimmer of the American dispensationalists, there is no shortage of New Age scripts calling for shifts in plate tectonics, invasion by aliens with or without the assistance of human traitors high up in govern-ments, and assorted calamities.[17]

In order to round out our introductory view of the New Age phenom-enon, several additional points are worthy of note. By this juncture, one point is evident: *New Age* is a term that denotes a variable category of world-view. It encompasses metaphysical, cosmological, historical, anthropological, medical, and metapolitical works, along with fiction and prophecy. New Age materials, though rooted in currents from antiquity, the Renaissance, the

Enlightenment, and the nineteenth century, in their mature form represent a cultural or spiritual and lifestyle (rather than explicitly political) continuation of the activist counterculture of the 1960s and 1970s, a theme explored at length by historian Christoph Bochinger.

Thus, although New Age material is exceedingly varied and although it pays attention to astrological theories of time from the nineteenth and early twentieth century and to distinctive themes from Swedenborg and William Blake, in recent practice it constitutes a kind of attenuated prolongation of the imaginative and critical impulses of the Vietnam generation among the educated young.[18] As such it provides an optimal field of potential examples of critical and alternative-seeking thought and diagnosis in and about real-world millennial America. In material from this genre, we can find as good a field as possible for sounding the depth and nature of American counterimaginings and dream relocatings today as anywhere else. The darker and lighter sides of contemporary cultural pessimism are as likely to emerge in this domain of investigation as anywhere.

Looking at New Age materials provides, then, a dizzying perspective. They reflect their times, so that examining them and their calls for big change can allow us to take account of the way recent cultural pessimism connects with the mood and circumstances, even the deep sense of purpose or lack thereof or sense of crisis, in a particular segment of the postmodern educated public. That audience—like the very creators of these pessimistic documents—finds its concrete and its ideological situation unfolding in ways it sees as unfavorable, even if highly placed figures among the pessimists may be wealthy celebrities (all protest movements, like all political movements, and likewise all pseudoescape movements must have an elite leadership).

For a recurrent strand in all recent cultural pessimism assumes worsening prospects for the current generation—worsening compared with the prior basis for believable optimism in the economic, social, and creedal assets of their recent ancestors. These assets had comprised the raw material for the historic America once described by historian David Potter as *People of Plenty.* For Americans approaching the millennium, looking at diminished prospects, however, the given outlook was not and currently still is not, one of automatic high expectations. In this regard one can identify popular documents that mark off the change: the 1990 (post-stock-market downturn) film *Metropolitan* marks one high point, or low point, in this aspect of the genre.

The fact that an audience with limited education can also be the consuming target for some of these popular documents aimed in large measure at those with some education beyond high school reflects not only the theory and practice of postmodern media experts, but as well the life experience of broad segments of the public. Postmodern works are targeted by definition at multiple audiences.

New Age materials can respond as well to a sense that official institutions and their ideologics fail in furnishing even a modicum of a sense of human meaning, here indicting not only official churches, but as well schools and universities—along with a political system perceived to be far beyond accountability and hence capable of being mapped only using the coordinates of conspiracy theory.[19] Indeed, the work by Woodhouse—the most important theoretical statement of American New Age doctrine and history in recent years, itself written by a former head of a university department of philosophy—dovetails in many particulars with contemporary American conspiracy theory at its most intense, and we do not mean a sociocultural model for conspiracy thinking. No, it dovetails with an unmediated and fully developed exploration of the evil intentions of Illuminati, UFO-landing aliens and the like.

That Woodhouse's treatise differs so radically from unalloyed conspiracy tracts above all with regard to the tendency toward a favorable outcome for humanity may assist Woodhouse's political reputation. But this difference will do nothing to weaken the sense that New Age materials build on a foundational sense that official institutions and worldviews have failed in realizing the promise of modernity and the Enlightenment, so that therefore help needs to come from exotic quarters, such as Tibet, meditation, crystals, alternative science, and (with Immanuel Velikovsky or Zecharia Sitchin) the revival of officially rejected catastrophist hypotheses about prehistory.

The sense of deep crisis and catastrophe affecting the physical as well as the cultural and political world, and then the attendant need for extreme forms of hope deeply stamps New Age materials and of course connects it with cultural pessimism in general—though cultural pessimism certainly need not involve alien implants, mysterious rays, and impending sudden shifts in plate tectonics. Still, the sense of crisis that links domains characterizes our earlier documents even as it characterizes New Age treatises.

That point deserves attention. Previous chapters have dealt with popular culture's pessimism in the face of recurrent loss, loss tangible (economic and social mobility challenges to the survival of the so-called middle class) and intangible (challenges to all manner of conventional aspects of personal and group identity). In earlier chapters, likewise, we have met the corresponding (or underlying) theme of the human self under multifaceted attack as it attempts a defense of its historic idealized status as a freely choosing entity, a self with an identity internal to itself yet external in its necessary social and civic presentation.

This theme—a weakening self—is one we have seen frequently appearing in the most varied of popular documents. Typically these documents have portrayed the millennial American self as coming under strong and varied, foundationally significant attack or essential and persistent threat, a threat connected with an intensifying sense of impotence and disorientation on the part of individuals that never fully leaves even once the protagonist undergoes a kind of negative illumination. The nature of the danger here usually registers as a fatalistic, deterministic, mechanistic, or cyborg-information-technological, even the divinely scripted sense of utter powerlessness, a sense of impotence bordering on a sense of loss of meaning (or leading directly to it, as with *Fight Club*). And while some characters acclimate themselves and turn toward activism, the overall outlook for a reconstitution of society and identity along precrisis lines appears grim in the pessimistic genre as a whole.

We have hitherto uncovered a variety of perceived underlying sources for this impotence, this complex of popular cultural threats to any continuing American sense of morally responsible choice with regard to what passes for the human self as an agent increasingly deprived of traction. Portrayed is a self in crisis and plunged into crises. Typical threats from the works considered above include the conspiratorial manipulation of the population's DNA by government scientists collaborating with powerful and exceedingly malignant aliens aiming at the enslavement or even extermination of the human race; the apocalyptic scripting carried out by an omnipotent God obsessed with torturing his conscripted human actors in an eternally unvarying drama enacted for his good pleasure by his helpless but allegedly responsible mortal pawns; and the info-techno redefinition of human beings as replicants and cyborgs infinitely fungible and mutable, existing ultimately to serve the financial well-being of a transnational elite of exceedingly wealthy and select leading shareholders acting in concert with the purportedly democratic government of the United States.

Similar perceptions of deep crisis shape many New Age documents. As we learn immediately below, like popular narratives of cultural pessimism, New Age documents share the pessimistic sense of deep misdirection. Further, like the activist groups in today's Washington think tanks, New Age documents often point to scenarios of extreme redirecting for society in holding out some sign of hope. Here, however, the redirecting and the activism largely take place in a realm of fantasy, albeit often in ways that do begin to blur the line between empirical reality and the necessarily imaginary and fantastic (in theory this is different from what goes on in Washington, D.C.).

Of course a very sizable public consumes these New Age documents (and buys the products pushed in conjunction with a good many of them), even as a more limited number actively join groups, even cults, that live out the alternative views of their adherents. In this respect the New Age groups and their documents formally resemble much from neoconservatives and representatives of the Christian Right.

But thus far, New Age devotees have not succeeded in moving close to making any real impact on public policy, let alone capturing the levers of state power in order to try to reintegrate the commonwealth along their lines. If we leave alternative medicine and nutrition out of consideration, much of the public arena at first glance seems remarkably unaffected by New Age currents. This contrast is more obvious with the more outrageous of the New Age proposals precisely because they are so impossible to realize as a sociopolitical blueprint in empirical America, most likely winding up in the index of some handbook of bizarre-gonzo cults. Nonetheless, Americans are not deterred from engaging in thought experiments with New Age methods of relocating the American dream in a time of stress or from arriving at less hard-edged ways in which New Age currents can begin to move toward a tentative relocation of dreams in the empirical world of religion and values.

So far as methodology is concerned, here looking at the New Age we keep an eye constantly on mechanisms by which documents of popular culture may have positive functions for their consuming audience, functions that the audience in question and its authors learn by means of complex interactions and communications explicit and implicit. In other words, to make quite clear what we have been doing all along, we are reading films, popular books, and television programs in much the same way as does the German school of *Begriffsgeschichte* (conceptual history) founded by Reinhart Koselleck, assuming that concepts and other units of complex discourse are neither dead nor passive, but capable of serving as "indicators" and "factors" alike, as signs of the changing sociopolitical situation and ways of affecting that situation in complex ways.[20] Just as this approach has helped free contemporary European historiography from a static and elite-centered notion of how ideas operate in high culture, so also a similar set of instruments can open up new perspectives on the latent sociopolitical function of popular documents.

Thus we turn to New Age proposals for a revision of positivist science, such as the one embedded in Woodhouse's book. Such proposals understand

themselves as scientific, so they do not exclude verifiability and intersubjec-
tive checking on principle—in fact, since they are part of a movement that
has embraced scientific language and models, they in fact call for it.[21] (To be
sure, some New Age theoreticians do call upon subtle extra senses for additional monitoring of data.)[22] The most interesting difference lies elsewhere.
It is rather that the use or misuse of quantum metaphors, scalar and vibratory paradigms, resonance language, and the like is with New Age writers
set within a script or narrative of human labor, suffering, and elite victory, a
script far more overtly religious or meaning-laden than the carefully pruned
script of human evolution and progress fostered in positivistic official science. The conventional and austere drama of human advance in mainstream
science, on the other hand, is often hardly a drama at all—more a kind of
neutral wisdom that sometimes seems maddeningly devoid of human satisfaction or point.

On the other hand, the New Age script chronicling scientific progress
is far vaster and extends much further forward and backward in time. Its
heroes and villains can include cosmic entities, interdimensional beings,
helpers and hinderers from distant universes, times, dimensions—the flavor
of the whole thing is redolent of Hellenistic Alexandria, or perhaps a bit
reminiscent of Renaissance Florence. It is pretty well the opposite of the
atmosphere of the Scottish Enlightenment! New Age revisions of science are
full of a sense of mission to limited and suffering intelligences (ours, to be
exact) and must be read as such—as Steve Bruce puts it, "New Age science
has more in common with religion than with science."[23] Like the ancient
spirituality of Hellenistic Gnosticism, which specialist Eduard Schweizer
argued was a response to the failures of earlier politics and religion in the
Hellenistic world, with the gods of the polis inaccessible and imperialism
making government less and less accountable, so also now, it might be held,
as then, does a religioscientific worldview attempt to overcome the material world. New Age does this, not so much by a gnostic escape of the soul
from the body as from a thoroughgoing transcending of matter itself. This
it achieves not only by techniques of meditation and channeling but by
invocation of quantum formulae of indeterminacy in which the dualisms of
Plato and Descartes dissolve along with the modern reliability of the world
altogether. In this sense, at least, political and economic failures are overcome in the rhetorical world of the New Age.[24]

Nevertheless, actual narratives of expected escape, remedy, and help also
assist the New Age community in coping with the difficulties of this present
life. All this we can see in the proposal for revision of positivist science and

much more furnished us by Professor Mark Woodhouse. It is enframed within a remarkable New Age metanarrative and thus readable as cultural criticism. It works, as we might expect, with rhetorics of resonance and vibration within a cosmic context—and is by no means devoid of overt pessimism.

Woodhouse's *Paradigm Wars* is a complex survey of challenges to academic and scientific orthodoxy, a summary of New Age hot topics from quantum physics to transpersonal psychology, and a prophecy of the coming eclipse of materialist skepticism. Here Woodhouse has in mind views of the kind we associate with doubters like Carl Sagan or Stephen Jay Gould. Woodhouse's acknowledgments thank well-known academics like Huston Smith and Michael Zimmerman along with "various interdimensional beings," all of whom have helped him. By the end of the book, Professor Woodhouse and one cameo contributor are defending the reality of an alleged giant constructed facial image on Mars.[25] For those who balk at his extraterrestrial scenarios, Woodhouse consistently leaves open an option of doubt he himself seems not to utilize.[26]

Woodhouse on science will sound familiar—the stress on quantum thinking and energy, the distrust of mere matter. The villain is "mechanistic science." The solution is "vibrational modeling," "frequency modeling," and attention to "deep patterns" of "resonance, harmony, or interference" rather than "changes in the spatial configuration of discrete underlying things."[27]

Along with this goes a kind of obsession with "the quantum connectedness of distant particles," that is, Bell's theorem (the thesis "that the predictions of quantum mechanics [QM] differ from those of intuition") taken to delegitimate local causation (in the sense that "deep reality" is asserted to be of necessity "non-local").[28] For Woodhouse Bell's theorem is important because he thinks it "may force us to acknowledge domains outside of conventional space time to account for presumed action-at-a-distance exceeding the speed of light." For Woodhouse all this advances "a convergence of science and spirituality" based on the work of the physicist David Bohm. That Woodhouse unfolds as "Energy Monism," which "views energy and consciousness as dual aspects of a neutral ground." Here he finds himself allied with Buddhism, Taoism, and Spinozism, not to mention Carl Jung, Carlos Casteñeda, Paracelsus, Wilhelm Reich, and Swedish radiologist Björn Nordenström, all of whom he invokes leading up to affirmation of a "bipolar" oscillating life "energy or ch'i visible" to "psychically sensitive individuals."[29]

Now such a revision of science makes sense only within a metanarrative once more invoking distant intelligences and a mighty process of human transformation into "a new human species . . . *Homo noeticus*," "on the planet after the millennium manifesting greater wisdom, love, empowerment, and psychic awareness." A new science and a new consciousness are required if we are to "enter into constructive relations . . . with positively oriented extraterrestrials" while being able to "live at peace" and "find our place in the larger galactic community." As more people grow in consciousness, Woodhouse finds cause for hope in objective data: sensitive individuals report what is confirmed by "telepathic transmission" from friendly aliens "indicating their willingness to assist in human progress at this 'evolutionary turning point.'"[30]

While all this sounds upbeat, a kind of interdimensional or interspecies relocation of the cause for hope in some version of the American dream, the underlying tone of Woodhouse's metanarrative is darker. Citing *Humanity's Extraterrestrial Origins* by former Yale Professor Arthur Horn, Woodhouse suggests earth was colonized as a genetic experiment involving improvement of body and soul. Various competing extraterrestrials still keep in touch not only by abduction, telepathy benign and malign genetic work, and malign enslavement, but also through "'secure' radio channels of NASA."[31]

Now the evil element among these aliens, it seems, has helped keep the human race ignorant of its origin and the extent of its psychic powers. As for the good aliens, they often are "more energetic than solidly physical" and are in part "interdimensional," fearing "adverse intergalactic consequences" from nuclear war or even because of earthly "interdimensional portals that facilitate space-time jumps" and hence intervene to prevent nuclear war and to further "spiritual upliftment." Their adversaries are the Rigelians, an evil subgroup of aliens known to aficionados as Reptilian Grays. They aim to control and enslave earth through human allies without ever overtly showing their hand, using implants and secretly controlling governments and religions. According to Professor Woodhouse, the Grays made contact with the U.S. government through "Nazi intelligence circles" and use our species for genetic experimentation.[32]

The good aliens are gradually becoming more visible and encouraging knowledgeable humans in government to turn against the Rigelian plot. As Woodhouse writes, "extraterrestrial and real UFOs and extraterrestrials are *attracted* to our evolutionary turning point in order to play their respective roles . . . within a larger galactic unfolding." While Woodhouse is ultimately optimistic, expecting light rather than darkness, even God is said not to know the details of the outcome.[33] Christ, if he returns, will appear as a quasignostic republisher of higher knowledge as part of the vast process of restoring what was once known to advanced but vanished ancient civilizations such as Atlantis.[34]

This is, then, an optimism upheld only with difficulty, in the face of a skepticism ending in conspiratorial hypotheses extending even to the thesis of JFK's Dallas driver as an active player in the assassination drama—not to mention plenty of mention of secret governments.[35] While overtly within the domain of New Age mixing of science with spirituality, Woodhouse's work also functions as a diagnosis of the profound and interlinked causes of disorder and galloping disarray in the eroding world system—and as such, however etheric and cosmic its conceptual instruments—intends to be read on one level as dealing with structural causes of interlocked impasses in today's society. Its elaborate talk of plots and secret groups reinforces the impression that it means to deal with real events in the real world—even though it sounds for all the world like a compendium of situations from *The X-Files* episode guide.

Indeed, the work is little removed from the atmosphere of rampant conspiracy books like journalist Jim Marrs's *Rule by Secrecy: The Hidden History That Connects the Trilateral Commission, the Freemasons, and The Great Pyramids* (HarperCollins Perennial, 2000).[36] Marrs, in his flamboyant late period, has moved into a kind of conspiracy hyperbolism, managing to combine Skull and Bones, The Bilderbergers, Nazi occultists, the Templars, the Illuminati, alien genetic experimentation in ancient Sumer, and ancient advanced civilizations possessing atomic energy, all in support of his grand alternatives by way of conclusion:

> It is the immense and ancient power of the [alien-derived—JS/GS] knowing elite . . . that has sought to usurp and control virtually every major movement toward the development of full human potential, from long before early Christianity to the New Age. Since it has been demonstrated that this knowledge—or view of the world—is still tightly held within the inner sanctums of the secret societies, there appear to be but three possibilities: the small inner elite continues to accumulate wealth and power in the hope of contacting our ancient creators (nonhuman intelligences); or they have already achieved such contact and are being guided or controlled; or they *are* the ancient creators. . . .[37]

The New Age narratives in Woodhouse and the conspiracist narratives in Marrs could be merged without extreme exertion by a third writer, though Woodhouse with his upbeat tone and need for happy outcomes is not interested in the Bilderbergers in the way Marrs is. Marrs's ultrahigh level of concern with conspiracy hypotheses at first might seem, to some observers, to point to an extreme alarmism akin to that in primitive conspiracist outlooks,[38] but in fact our overall take tends in another direction. Here we are instead inclined (specifically with regard to Woodhouse, not necessarily with Marrs, who is not a New Age theorist as such despite the overlap, and who is not so studiedly quietistic in his persona as Woodhouse) to see something closer to the diffuse "commodified conspiracy theory" known to Birchall.

By that we mean something not unlike Fredric Jameson's celebrated popular analogue to postmodern theories of deconstruction—a mechanism that accounts in some way for the fading of Enlightenment-style rational explanation, clear responsibility, and attendant political or moral accountability.[39] Here, however, in the specific case of Woodhouse, the narratives function to place blame for things gone wrong in the real world within so murky and complex a pattern of responsibility that political and juridical accountability becomes impossible. The adherent can practically speaking look only to some kind of generalized uprising of attitudes and obscure forces, though against what and with what hope of success remains exceedingly obscure. (One thinks, not only of Jameson, but also of Fenster, Birchall, and Peter Dale Scott on this issue of explanation and accountability.)[40]

To be sure, Marrs the hard-edger does advocate pressing for revelation of the truth by failing to trust government experts and not participating in government-sponsored lotteries, but it is evident he holds out little hope of any dramatic breakout. Woodhouse, overtly more optimistic, puts his faith in a process of long-term cooperative evolution, though one with many twists and turns, in many respects so unknowable as to elude comprehension, at least at this stage. *The result, at least for Woodhouse, is a transfer of both hope and accountability out of any domain that current politics can do very much to affect.* Thus, as it were by default, existing institutions, though undermined in important ways with regard to credibility, still need fear no storming of the Info-Bastille or real revolution or putsch from below. Yet at the same time, Woodhouse's book—which doubtless numbers many inveterate *X-Files* viewers among its readers—certainly has to do with far deeper and more concrete kinds of concerns than the mere cold war nostalgia for simplistic explanations invoked by McGrath as a means of dismissing any connection between televisual cultural pessimism and real-world difficulties.

Moreover, a work like that by Woodhouse offers a surprisingly large payoff to the New Age true believer. It is highly useful if the reader can accept its claims—this one book, functionally speaking, supplies in one way or another some version of all the genre-specific desiderata earlier enumerated. That is, it provides a variety of strategies to allow cultural pessimists to deal with betrayal or loss—extreme strategies that may deliver what is wanting (by alternative science and transformation of consciousness), that in other cases may celebrate a loss as a gain if but correctly perceived (it is all part of a grand process for the ultimate good), and that in still other cases may assign the fault for failure to causes and sources so far beyond ordinary reckoning as to relieve existing institutions of real revolutionary threat, even though they do come in for a good deal of linguistic blame.

In other words, with Woodhouse (the work by Marrs is capable of a more outlandishly pragmatic interpretation) we find a shifting of hope and blame to areas of explanation capable at best of pseudoclarification; the result here, is no significant challenge to the standing order.[41] However "extreme" his strategies may be, however much empirical or real-world conditions may be envisioned, in the New Age variant the strategies of rescue ordinarily do far more, it would appear, to siphon off discontent and keep hope alive within the system of transnational capitalism, than they do to foster overt revolt—which, indeed, they more often than not tend to retard.

To be sure, a certain potential does exist for other kinds of more activist and even extreme developments on the periphery. The possibilities along this line do exist, as may be seen if one meditates on the permutations and combinations inherent in the spectrum of oppositional alternatives treated explicitly and implicitly in relevant scholarship, some of which could be applied (one supposes) to variants ranging from offshoots of Marrs all the way to some strands related to the militia movement.[42] But for the moment, any serious coalescing of such oppositional forces as a political or parapolitical force appears remote. In the meantime, for our purposes, Woodhouse as the quintessential New Age text illustrates how perfectly New Age materials fit our more general model of extreme pessimisms that keep hope or at least the functioning system alive even as their very existence signals the demise of serious political protest. Woodhouse fits into this mold by providing channels for the diversion of energy away from overt rebellion in the empirical world.

Chapter 6

The Quest for Real-World Correlates: Sightings of Cultural Pessimism in the Domains of Scholarship and Journalism

Understanding the Escapist Point of Departure

While New Age theoreticians, Right-wing dispensationalist resistance heroes in fiction, and Tyler Durden may differ on exactly where to put the accent marks, they all want to accentuate the negative. Economics gone bad for the average citizen, outsourcing, loss of traditional community, Nietzschean death of God, the Antichrist unleashed in the United Nations, worldwide terrorism, uncontrolled immigration, suspension of habeas corpus, the ever-encroaching tentacles of big government, war on the middle class (allegedly the yeoman mainstay of both democracy and republicanism, yet subverted by the Beltway), the untrustworthiness of secret government and its technological research programs—these manifold empirical phenomena, though susceptible of differing analysis, strike pessimistic observers as reason for extreme diagnoses and extreme therapies.

In the remaining sections, we seek to understand the implications of that pessimistic take. We have already met the objection that this material merely targets some vague mood. On the contrary, as our look at the attenuated version of countercultural protest politics embalmed in New Age materials demonstrates, their contemporaries (are they writing nonfiction or fiction with their versions of extreme pessimism?) can enjoy a substantial sales volume while propagating their versions of decline and renewal of the empirical world, and that in terms mostly identical to those of the "fictions"

143

enshrined on-screen or in novels—though the real world envisioned in the New Age subgenre has an alarmingly high population of reptilian grays rubbing appendages with real-world generals and senators.

Having shown that the empirical world in some optic can be and often is envisioned in the modes of extreme pessimism, we feel free to turn to standard works of observation and analysis in the search for real-world correlates. Now we can look in the works of journalists, academic historians, and social scientists so as to move back and forth between the cultural pessimist's typical view of real-world problems in narrative or script and the apparent real-world objective correlatives to those pessimistic views.[1] Those correlates can be distilled from rather prosaic material in scholarship and journalism.

The ways in which the perceived causes for depression and pessimism find their remedies for Americans both fictional and real-world are varied indeed. This place is as good as any other to point out that throughout this study, we ascribe a therapeutic, safety-valve, distracting, or relieving property to a seemingly astonishing collection of notions, stratagems, and movements—items that often lack any overt title to the therapeutic. As we move forward through our list of objective correlates and models of driving impulses in the System, the reader may well find this ascription of therapeutic power puzzling at times. What do we say to this bewilderment?

Certainly, as the previous chapters underscore, in the decades since the killing of John F. Kennedy, American popular culture has found striking ways to show the depth, extent, and variety of cultural loss and of political and institutional failure and betrayal. Remarkable however is how those same ways also provide ingenious tries at keeping alive the dreams and hopes for fulfillment at issue here, and along with them the ideal claim that the political and social system can still hope to provide some tangible movement toward fulfillment—loopholes of escape and portals of hope remain built in to the pessimistic take on the situation.

That overall impression has served us as the foundation for elaborating hypotheses and trying on comparisons from an early point in this investigation. We are impressed not simply by the ubiquity of themes of loss and betrayal, but as well by the ways that these works readily fit into models of *latent function,*[2] that is, they function in channeling and easing personal and social transition at a time when cultural hiatus mixes with socioeconomic downturn and repeated complaints of loss of political accountability. And it is in this standard sociological concept of latent function that we advise the reader to take refuge when a particular alleged therapy or purported loophole or siphon for rage at first appears unlikely.

Another methodological difficulty deserves brief mention. The religious dimension has faded in and out of our chapters on pessimism like a kind of Cheshire cat. *Where's the religion?* The reader may well ask, having finished with the Rapture enthusiasts and feeling a growing appetite for more examples of true faith in action. Here our advice is to remember how, ultimately, everything is connected with everything else. For example, perceived institutional betrayal in American society does not stand in clinical isolation for pessimistic observers. If it did, this entire line of investigation would have failed to develop. Rather, the individual instance of loss or betrayal leads the pessimist to reflect, not only on similar cases, but on the broader significance of the instance at hand. For the pessimist, the single case brings up wider and deeper issues of moral, ethical, and metaphysical consequence . . . even as that aspect turns out, by definition, to involve not merely a spiritual (that is, chiefly private or individual) but as well a religious (that is, public or social, and therefore potentially binding) aspect affecting the status and future of the commonwealth.

This point holds in particular for phenomena leading to meditation on spectacularly catastrophic or pessimistically apocalyptic scenarios envisioning mass destruction and large-scale change. Here in particular the note of betrayal has predominated, a take intensified by the implicit contrast with the optimistic, utopian, progress-oriented character of the official worldview or "civil religion" that from an early stage has helped bind Americans together in an ultimately ambiguous enterprise founded on rather different versions of the eighteenth-century Enlightenment.[3]

These considerations lead to yet a third methodological observation, or rather a general remark on the character of the phenomena we examine here. That character remains in the end enigmatic, even though we seek to force it into explanatory models of a misleadingly mechanistic type. Thus in the end, we do not really want to suggest that (to pick one aspect of this material) mere outrage at perceived loss, betrayal, and failure is the simpleminded and single-voiced take on the matter in the pessimistic segment of recent popular culture. To be sure, these attitudes, appropriately hidden by encoding, are detectable in documents from recent American decades, decades characterized by perceived remoteness of government and growing disparities in wealth distribution and falling prospects for upward mobility. Yet as hinted already, other attitudes do vie for attention as well (even in the most pessimistic American material targeting a popular audience)—the sense of bewilderment at the inadequacy of any explanation including even simplistic conspiracy theories (Scully and Mulder, who favor both complex conspiracy theories and simple narratives of outright betrayal), the perverse inability of simple group reaction to correct the problem (Jack struggling with Tyler over when enough is enough by way of self-assertive protest), the way that escapes and exits prove inadequate (ubiquitous, cunningly lurking in all the examples considered), futher the sense that paradoxical narratives may be the best statement since rational expositions in the mundane prose of the official Enlightenment-derived public world are bound to prove utterly misleading (the shared assumption of both Christian apocalyptic enthusiasts and unclassifiable fans of works of cybernoir, not to mention readers of the novels of Palahniuk—along with allied assumptions in all versions of conspiracy theory, strangely akin to academic deconstruction).

These repetitive themes of bewilderment, taken together with the popularity of works like *Left Behind* indicating perceived movement into an unfamiliar and threatening new era, suggest the difficult, indeed, enigmatic nature of the phenomena we examine here. After all, the topic is escape into the future, and the future cannot be known with certainty. Still, ultimately each style of cultural pessimism must offer some kind of comfort to its consumer, whether that comfort be merely a sense that all explanation and accountability have become illusions to be cast off, or the more traditional comfort of suggestions that God or the government or the people can somehow be in control however outrageous the fortune confronting the targeted consumer who pays taxes and tithes.

The mood of millennial pessimism has its puzzles, above all its boundless capacity for conveying some sense of pattern and meaning while confronting the portal to an era with unknown features, features perhaps to be tolerated only if they can be invested with a questionable sense of familiarity. If they can somehow look familiar, they may not shoot down our hope that institutional and group continuity will somehow make it over the threshold, will arrive still functioning despite being however redefined—and permit our further hope that, once over some threshold or other, in some space or hypercyberspace somewhere or sometime, the dream of enlightened progress, abundance, and freedom can become tangibly accessible, located in its relocated location, so to speak. Moreover, if these comforts fail, hardcore cultural pessimism always can offer the final consolation that such an outlook is by definition a minority outlook, a worldview so extreme and intense that only a limited clientele (a true elite of the discerning) can ever possibly share it. However, no guarantee exists that any one of these spun-off scenarios will offer comfort to other observers. They may offer quite terrifying consequences, especially when they go all the way and actually promise to reintegrate a fragmenting society at the cost of a message of high intensity and exclusivistic extremism.

Whether the outlook be terrifying or beguiling, it does indeed appear that the American portion of Atlantic modernity remains capable of contemplating extreme developments with a positive outlook. We cannot overemphasize, looking back at the pessimistic material surveyed, how impressed we are by the inventiveness of Americans determined to keep alive some version of hope—most literally doing what a generation-ago *Esquire* magazine summed up with its famous slogan, "Smiling through the Apocalypse."[4]

The Question of Objective Correlative: An Age of "Cultural Pessimism" as Diagnostic Label

If we rely on common-sense media and academic accounts about perceived loss of effectual agency and its broader framework, we move toward the interpretive big picture by looking at a number of obvious topics. First there is the explicit use (outside fiction and fringe tractates) of the revived category of *cultural pessimism* to refer to our own time and place. If this is not some kind of evidence of real-world correlation to the disaster/renewal scenarios of our fictional narratives, perhaps none exists.

Of interest to us here are observers—academics, high-level journalists—who utilize some version of the category of "cultural pessimism" in ways that suggest it has attained contemporary viability on account of descriptive usefulness. It sums up perceptions of diminished hope and lowered expectations based on empirical, pragmatic, real-world concatenations of phenomena. The issues here overlap to a degree with those tied up with other specifically American questions of political legitimation and social integration. Also in play are questions of diminished economic and social mobility expectations on the part of the young and often educated target audience for nonconsensus works in the genre of pessimism.

But it gets much hotter. "Cultural pessimism" as a category takes us into the murky territory of comparisons and contrasts with perceptions of failing community and need for revival or restoration in societies and cultures other than that of millennial America.[5] The fascination of this category stems from the ominous earlier associations and diagnostic significance of that phenomenon in Europe, especially nineteenth- and twentieth-century Germany. Noteworthy here is the rarely mentioned fact that low socioeconomic expectations for the young and the educated long ago attained axiomatic status as causal elements in the complex of factors taken to have led to the popularity of fascism and National Socialism.[6] This fact makes dismissing current pessimists as whiners and losers with no appreciation of the glories of the invisible hand a tad on the facile side—unless the possibility of an American fascism is taken as inherently impossible.

So the new interest in "cultural pessimism" is no simple item, and new interest is evident. Among responsible observers of millennial America, indeed the millennial West, somber tones now resound, tones reminiscent of earlier ages of worry about European decadence and pessimism. For example, Paul Craig Roberts, Assistant Secretary of the Treasury under Ronald Reagan, has recently published a series of gloomy projections about the omens for the immediate American future, underscoring how reliance on undifferenti-ated policies of free trade in relation to labor threatens American political and social stability. He fears such policies can create a highly educated but futureless "academic proletariat" driven to frenzy by the outsourcing of even high-level jobs in technology and engineering, a situation made more alarm-ing if seen within a wider context of alarm indicators with regard to matters tangible and intangible. Roberts writes:

> Twenty million evangelical Christians, who once focused on saving their souls, now [April 2005–JS/GS] seek an avenue to heaven through war in the Middle East, which they believe will bring on Armageddon and the Rapture. . . . America's financial preeminence is based on the dollar's role as reserve currency, a role threatened by the dollar's long downward slide in value as the result of trade and budget deficits. . . . Patriotism's place is being taken by a dangerous nationalism . . . . US executives, with an eye to quarterly earnings and their bonuses, . . . force their American employ-ees to train their foreign replacements and then fire their American work-ers. . . . American capitalism is destroying itself by dismantling the ladders of upward mobility that have made large income inequalities acceptable. By rewarding themselves for destroying American jobs and manufactur-ing, engineering and scientific capabilities, US executives are sowing a whirlwind. American political stability will not survive the turning of an American university degree into a worthless sheet of paper. . . . Whither America is a question that deserves a lot more attention than it gets.[7]

Commentators have not failed to press home how they detect an undercur-rent of multivalent pessimism more generally, both in the United States and in the Western world at large. This detection of pessimism has shown up in various places and times in ways highly pertinent to our study here. Worth mentioning to begin with is a study from 2006 by long time Republican strat-egist Kevin Phillips, who in his recent book (hyperbolically entitled *American Theocracy*) draws a predictive parallel between the attitudes and policies of the contemporary United States and other past dominant powers. Their military, religious, and financial policies allegedly doomed them to painful declines in ways that, to Phillips, resemble the contemporary situation of a millennial America. According to Phillips, America faces military overstretch, religious zealotry, and financial calamity camouflaged as unprecedented debt.[8]

Moreover, Phillips's analysis not only extends its pessimism to scenarios of overextension and decline. It also takes its pessimism even further to make the charge of an underlying and in some sense unprecedented U.S. turn to lack of clear thinking that (Phillips implies) corrupts the democratic process beyond likelihood of recovery. The downturn for Phillips derives from the nature of geopolitics and from a domestic politics centered on the intersection of oil and religious zeal. Phillips argues:

> . . . U.S. preoccupation with the Middle East has two dimensions. In addition to its concerns with oil and terrorism, the White House is courting end-times theologians and electorates for whom the holy lands are already a battleground of Christian destiny. Both pursuits, oil and biblical expectations, require a dissimulation in Washington that undercuts the U.S. tradition of commitment to the role of an informed electorate.[9]

Worth mentioning as well is a study much older than that by Phillips, one indeed going back some years, a work that points to a gradual and long-term shift in popular mood. Here we mean the study already discussed, the one from Tom Engelhardt, his *The End of Victory Culture: Cold War America and the Disillusioning of a Generation.* This work, like the later study of UFO imagery by political scientist Jodi Dean,[10] rank as pioneering, exploratory, probing efforts at connecting the themes of popular culture with underlying shifts in mood and (by implication) with the possibility of locating sources for such mood shifts.[11]

Now if Engelhardt's book concentrates on the immediate popular culture aftermath from Vietnam and Watergate, another study approaches these themes more broadly (that is, not concentrating exclusively on the United States, and not unduly limiting itself in temporal scope either). In this way it foregrounds a covering concept that can threaten to evoke distasteful and dubious comparisons and contrasts with interwar Europe: cultural pessimism, a phrase that instantly takes the alert reader into the world of comparative studies of fascism and the like signaled with the names of Fritz Stern and George Mosse.[12] The work in question is a study by the English critic and cultural theorist Oliver Bennett.

While Oliver Bennett's book[13] has a certain immediately interesting focus on late twentieth-century cultural pessimism, in some places it deals with earlier forms of the mood in ways designed to aid in achieving perspective. And while at first glance it seems to trivialize the concept and the underlying attitudes as ultimately dependent on ephemeral and malleable matters of mood, such is not its overall message. For concern with shifting mood gives way gradually to careful interest in socioeconomic circumstance and viewpoint. Bennett elevates the concept's importance by showing it possesses both wide resonance in time and broad distribution over space. Furthermore, Bennett's study strengthens the reader's suspicion that socioeconomic circumstances are on the whole likely to favor the diffusion of cultural pessimism in the near future. While much of Bennett's study looks at the role of neoliberal capitalism or Thatcherite economics in precipitating contemporary cultural pessimism, it in fact goes far deeper in its analysis.

On closer inspection, Bennett's work has multilayered ultimate implications, ramifications transcending economics. Indeed, Bennett makes the case that, changeable or not in its urgency and appeal, cultural pessimism of late has shown a surprising propensity for reemergence in the most diverse domains of advanced and progressive contemporary Western life, notably high-end reflection on meaning in religion, in science, in art, and in political economy. Reading between the lines, it is not difficult to see that Bennett's study amounts to *a generalized revalorization of the category of cultural pessimism.*[14]

General and intangible factors not immediately dependent on income mingle with economic and social categories in this kind of analysis. For Bennett, the upshot is a plea for taking the category of cultural pessimism seriously. He in effect leads the way by beginning to look at the concept outside the inherited narrow domain of studies of cultural and economic factors leading to Hitler. Furthermore, what at first appears as Bennett's tendency to reduce pessimism to factors of treatable brain chemistry turns out to be an ironic suggestion that the Spenglers and Cassandras of our time may be on to something, or on something, depending upon one's perspective. Reading between the lines, what emerges for immediate purposes from Bennett is the wisdom of keeping one eye focused on socioeconomic factors in the strict and narrow sense, and another eye focused on more intangible indicators and factors of mood when trying to grasp the significance of a particular bout of cultural pessimism. That doubletracking strikes the present authors as sensible, as does Bennett's repeated attention to neoliberal or globalizing economics as a causal element in the resurgence of popular pessimism at levels below that of the transnational boardroom.

Can this reemergence of pessimism as a slogan be justified? Certainly here we have to do with something that labelmakers recognize as conceptually related (however distantly!) to the cultural pessimism or despair or ideology of crisis we know from older looks at interwar Europe or Weimar Germany (by Fritz Stern and George Mosse).[15] For Americans its appearance as an *American* category for potentially serious discussion may at first seem not quite justified, a mischaracterization of a blip in mood, an exaggeration rather akin to those paranoid discussions of "American fascism" one used to encounter in the hyperventilating sixties. One could argue that the grimly sardonic portrayal of frustrated escapes from bureaucratic surveillance in *The Prisoner*, for example, represents merely a temporary phenomenon of the sixties, an early and essentially naïve overreaction to phenomena of social control now taken largely for granted in far more extreme forms in Britain and America after 9/11.

One could argue that—if one were capable of blotting out the fact that the *Prisoner* series moved into perennial classic status in the later years of the twentieth century, and that among an audience obviously as outraged at the growth of more than Benthamite techniques of universal surveillance as it was puzzled about how to beat back those intrusions. More broadly, however, reading the appearance of the category of cultural pessimism outside Weimar Germany as far more than a a temporary blip makes sense if its appearance and persistence over the last forty years is taken together with, for example, current American debates learned and popular concerning the limits and difficulties of secularization or deChristianization in connection with legitimation of the American political system at large.[16] For the obvious issues of political legitimacy and identity underlying the unending debates about the Christian Right in politics connect with critical use of the concept of cultural pessimism: where the country is headed, how viable its social contracts currently are, how many unpaid mortgages burden its economic and ideological account, and above all the nature of national identity and community in a time when borders are perceived as porous and culturally diverse immigration patterns as unfounded, all turn out to be interconnected topics constantly threatening to reenter any and all American debates at the moment.

Or, to rephrase the point: the resurfacing of the old category of cultural pessimism (in the wake of Vietnam, Watergate, growing bureaucratization, and lack of a strong sense of popular participation in government, along with the multicultural anxieties symbolized by 9/11, a context a continent away from cultural pessimism's usual intellectual home in Weimar Germany) serves as yet one more pointer to a deep crisis in American, even North Atlantic or Western, public and private identity—and to the fact that the ongoing sociocultural coping with this crisis justifies not merely the preceding chapters, but further study and debate along these lines, as well.[17]

Overtly, the emergence of a school of thought searching for generic typologies of fascism based on ideology as well as on criteria of political structure[18] might seem to be simply a development belonging to the history of history writing. After all, the work of George Mosse and his followers ordinarily concerns early twentieth-century Europe and largely ceases with 1945 so far as the main topic of study is concerned. The most recent historian in the general tradition of Mosse, Roger Griffin, also drawing on the work of Emilio Gentile, has however extended the study of "international fascism" to include the mores and facets of locally differentiated movements of national community, going on then to broaden his field of vision to encompass topics of "redemptive violence," "political religion," and sacral experiencing of entry into a new kind of time. The outcome of the development of this school of study remains intriguing and uncertain, yet potentially of interest for the evaluation of contemporary renewal movements. To be sure, even Griffin's own school includes critics who caution against excessive attention to the component of ideology in studying interwar Rightist movements. Significantly, Griffin himself when dealing with the postwar effort at keeping fascism alive among fringe extremists stresses how marginal pure continuation of prewar movements has become. In this sense, while study of interwar movements of radical renewal of allegedly failing senses of community and national identity based on basic perception of "cultural pessimism" or "cultural despair" remain stimulating, still the young leader of the current school, Griffin himself, stresses how true continuations of European-style fascism always uphold some ethnic component, a point that prohibits any simpleminded carrying-over of analytical modes from the study of authoritarianism in interwar Europe to contemporary America. America in its overt grounding rests on the premise of shared or common humanity and universal human rights that hardcore renewal movements of the interwar European Right were at great pains to deny, a general point that Griffin takes very seriously.

In this sense, one is at first sobered by how little the overtly promising parallel of prewar and contemporary movements to revive flagging senses of community turns out to offer: finally, judged by contemporary criteria of politically progressive students of comparative fascism, America and Tony Blair's Britain cannot count as fascist, whatever the secret hopes of their critics may be.

At another level, more theoretical and more general still, however, this kind of comparison of revival movements may prove suggestive for a study of this kind. Recently one of the first to speak of ideological currents of cultural despair or pessimism, Fritz Stern, surely no ignoramus with regard to the American rejection of European interwar Rightist use of ethnic categories in shaping political community, has nonetheless spoken up concerning what he (Stern) regards as legitimate paralleling of contemporary U.S. communitarian revival movements with surges of national revival in interwar Germany. Given Stern's long and distinguished international academic record, he must be listened to when he speaks out.

Here what Stern focuses on is not the use of biological or ethnic criteria in Germany and their ignoring in American Rightist currents; what Stern foregrounds instead is the use in both instances of a Christian religious aura to invest Rightist and authoritarian moves with a kind of providential and communitarian necessity, albeit one that excludes much of the population from the reforming of an intensified and reconstituted version of national community.

Stern, the original authority on "cultural despair" as a source for protoNazi currents, has made this parallel at least twice publicly, and has done so forcefully.[19] In a brief German-language interview (February 2, 2006) Stern, encouraged by interviewer Theo Sommer, pursues a parallel between Rightist agitation in thirties Germany and Rightist moves in contemporary America, and does so with a strength that would startle many Left-wing publicists in America who themselves would hesitate to use such language in nonacademic discourse. In this interview Stern criticizes an American "Christian plutocracy" that is "supported" and "praised" by evangelical fundamentalists while the government linked to all this puts "real liberties . . . in America" in "danger," "systematically exploiting" 9/11 in order "to strengthen its political power," all the while carrying out a "narrowing" of democracy in America.[20]

Earlier, in a speech delivered in accepting a prize conferred by the Leo Baeck Institute, Stern dwelled in detail on what he regards as the fatal mixing of religion and politics in Nazi Germany, a characterization that the *New York Times* account of the speech makes plain was intended as an implicit (but not subtle) paralleling of thirties Germany with religiopolitical rejuvenation movements of a Rightist and exclusivist kind in contemporary America. In various media statements spinning off from his Leo Baeck address, Stern has made it plain to American reporters that he fully intends such a parallel and that he has grave concerns about the future of the Enlightenment-anchored liberal outlook of the American Republic and the future of the related Bill of Rights—even going beyond this on one occasion to criticize the alliance between neoconservatives in today's America and the Christian Right as being likely to lead to unfortunate consequences.

In all of this, Stern speaks and writes as a Jewish observer whose identity was brought forward by his contact with the Nazis as a boy, an identity at first covered over by his family's prior conversion to nominal Protestant Christianity. Stern, the cofounder of postwar ideological analysis of the seedbed of Nazi popularity, does not shy from seemingly extreme parallels between interwar Germany in the grip of Nazi fervor and millennial America with its religiopolitical rejuvenation movements, even though he is obviously aware that American movements reject ethnic exclusivity of the German type and that America has yet to take any irreversible turns in the direction of extreme authoritarianism and total repression.

It is obvious from Stern's comments in the *Zeit* interview and from his longer remarks in the Leo Baeck speech that his scholarly standpoint here is one interested in analyzing reliance on the irrational power of rejuvenation movements mixing appeal to traditional religious images with contemporary political and communitarian imperatives—the "appeal of unreason," as Stern put it in his Leo Baeck address. On this basis, Stern does not shy from distinctly limited but real paralleling of contemporary American with Nazi rejuvenation currents, stating "There was a longing in Europe for fascism before the name was ever invented. . . ." Or again: "There was a longing for a new authoritarianism with some kind of religious orientation and above all a greater communal belonging. . . ."[21]

What are we to make of this paralleling? The present authors regard it as a suggestive but dangerous oversimplification, one that rightly points to the need for great concern about American authoritarianism and the decline of regard for civil liberties—but at the same time as an oversimplification in that it does not reach for ways of taking account of unique factors in the current American situation rendered by documents of cultural pessimism. Here we do not simply mean that mass executions and concentration camps in the fifty states are not in evidence despite obvious threats given the prevalence of theories of growing executive power. Nor do we simply mean that paralleling Germany and contemporary America can be done only by ignoring the American commitment—at times a rather artificial, government and media-elite driven commitment—to a unitary vision of human identity, though it is in the vision of human identity that we see an area requiring explicit and comparative exploration in order to arrive at an adequate characterization of contemporary revisions of the American dream and perhaps of American ideologies of sociopolitical cohesion.

For if the distinctive feature of Nazi dreams was the racist one of fostering an exclusivist utopia of Aryan overmen and overwomen, perhaps the distinctive feature of millennial American dreams (or nightmares) may lie in an analogous area, a variation on the Judeo-Christian and Stoic-Enlightenment vision of an essentially unitary human nature. Perhaps, as already suggested, differing segments of American "plutocracy" are tending toward deterministic rather than voluntarist (free will or classic civic humanist) redefinitions of a shared and universal human nature—one version being Christian supernaturalist and relying either on extreme Calvinist predestination (among the reconstructionists) or extreme service as puppets in a divine apocalyptic script (dispensationalists), another version being more secular and technocratic (with humanity defined as information processing capacity in a perfect interface, dare we say, with cyborg existence and the infinite manipulability of all energies for the services of global capitalism).[22] The significance of the developments will require expansion in the pages below.

The Question of Objective Correlative in an Age of Failing Political Integration: Civil Religion and Integrative Ideology

What then is the current big-picture connection between pessimism, religious sensibility, and the complex mosaic of daily life in a millennial America held together in part by worldview and outlook? Immediately indicating the situation in real-world America—and the reflection thereof amid academic pulse-takers—is the condition of what has come to be known loosely as "civil religion." Here is an area of undeniable significance for seekers after correlation between fantasy pessimism and real-world concerns, one that the observer can reasonably expect to reflect the kind of worries about society and cohesion evident in our now-familiar narratives.

For academics and journalists in the know, civil religion signifies the religiously connected set of beliefs and axioms that function to undergird and help define politicocultural legitimacy, personal and group identity, and the sense that individuals and groups belong to and participate in the bigger whole known as the United States of America (or whatever your modern nation may be).[23]

More technically, as Rolf Schieder argues in his massive retrospective treatment of debates over civil religion, the civil religion worldview is held to function in the real world to provide identity, integration, and legitimation in situations of growing social differentiation[24] and secularization.[25] It thereby takes over the supportive function formerly exercised by an established and institutionally anchored religion now too narrowly held to perform the overall task of integration, identity formation, and political legitimation for a differentiating and diversifying sociopolitical entity.[26]

As is well known, though the pragmatic use of such beliefs goes far back into the American past, the precise term civil religion gained reflective currency in Robert Bellah's application of the sociological theory of Talcott Parsons during the 1960s. It is now clear that Bellah's work on "civil religion" was largely an attempt to shore up a rickety structure of semi-institutionalized worldview beliefs that, though not directly anchored in specifically Christian institutions, still derived to some degree from Christian belief and had served for some time prior to Vietnam and Watergate to undergird the American package while institutional secularization (separation of public life from Christianity) proceeded apace. With the advancing differentiation, segmentation, and pluralization of American society, however, this compound of beliefs and values—already at the time when Bellah and like-minded associates began to focus on it as a useful object deserving to be refurbished for further use—started to become so worn and outgrown that its continued functioning appeared highly problematic.[27]

Nonetheless, as was obvious from the words of mainstream liberal defenders of "civil religion" from the 1960s on, the notion seemed worth rescuing for practical use outside the academy, since the beliefs in God, American exceptionalism and mission, millennial chosenness, and divinely grounded American liberty as an example for the world (and other associated notions in a loose and ever-varying catalog) were required in order to support an American structure suffering ever greater stresses. The challenges of the later cold war, the economic difficulties of Americans after 1970, and cultural and demographic shifts also pointed to such growing requirements—most obviously to the need for shared assumptions that could help integrate into American life an ever more diverse set of arriving ethnic groups whose particular beliefs and values increasingly appeared only marginally compatible with those of earlier Tidewater Virginia or Puritan New England (or even with those of the Deistical and Free Masonry-tinged elite of the early Republic).[28]

Thus the vicissitudes of the nonecclesiastical worldview as a source of desired sociopolitical integration (civil religion), and that worldview's critical elaboration and foregrounding in the academy, appear to correlate positively with intensifying strains on American society and the American religious system in the later twentieth century. Whether that set of nonecclesiastical beliefs can be said to have been sufficiently overhauled in order to make it adequate for contemporary effectiveness appeared somewhat dubious already in 1992 when Catherine Albanese published her magisterial *America: Religions and Religion.*

In it—well before the overt crisis represented by American total confrontation with radical Islam and the associated transformations of the American political system, and also well before the consolidation of full-fledged political evangelicalism in alliance with Right-wing Roman Catholics—Albanese treated civil religion in detail.

Civil religion was, for Albanese, a compound of both Calvinist and classicism-based High Enlightenment elements; and (for her) civil religion turned out to have aspects of considerable interest to an enterprise such as our own present investigation. Above all Albanese emphasized, both with regard to Bellah's project and with regard to America of the approaching millennium, that civil religion could never be fully successful and that the challenges this historically-grounded worldview faced were likely to prove increasingly daunting, whatever its partial successes in assisting some form of communal integration. As she wrote with regard to the period of Woodstock, "The civil religion in some respects was failing, for the many were not being made into one."[29]

Then, in her retrospective on civil religion after Vietnam, Albanese repeatedly emphasized the inherently incomplete, partial, or inadequate nature of a worldview of this kind, one so rooted in America's Christian and classical heritage that though not anchored in institutional denominations, it could never hope to make, effectively, all Americans into one, however much its use might contribute to expressing the urgency and appeal of that continuing task. It is this *inherently inadequate and partial* aspect of American religiously-related integrating ideology that we wish above all to stress for our purposes below, an approach that should not keep us from attending to other useful and significant points that Albanese made back in 1992.

Also of interest is her portrayal of the components of America's classic integrating ideology or Bellahesque civil religion, composed as it is of a rationalist or Enlightenment overlay that rearranges and filters aspects of the original or Puritan-Calvinist layer. For while this integrating ideology is ordinarily portrayed as low intensity and inherently inclusive, in point of fact both layers (according to Albanese) contain a component of dynamism packaged as drive toward historical improvement. That dynamism, in everyday use, could allow conflating Christian apocalyptic millennialism with Enlightenment-era doctrines of human progress and movement toward individual and social improvement or perfection.[30] Over the decades this conflating meant, argues Albanese, that the American sense of exceptionalism and mission could be used in ways that could point to more than a bland integrating of diverse elements. Its sense of mission and the inherent propensity for guilt about shortcomings meant that civil religion potentially could be used (or misapplied) in an effort at legitimating extreme programs and exclusivizing tendencies—though with what success would remain uncertain from case to case. Semisecularized, desectarianized civil religion, while used in a bland and tolerant way in recent decades leading up to the crisis of Vietnam and Watergate, had on earlier occasions shown signs of having within it the potential for developing in ways just as intense as the supernaturalist Christianity from the post-Reformation age of religious wars—or as Albanese writes in shorthand: "Civil religion contained a good deal of the power of extraordinary religion."[31]

In detail, argues Albanese, this meant nondenominational civil religion was a doctrine that, in ways analogous to supernaturalist apocalyptic in the Judeo-Christian tradition, required "memorable deeds that Americans had performed to initiate an age unknown before in history."[32] This implies (to restate the point) that, however friendly and inclusive a civil religion marketed as stemming from our benign Founding Fathers and from declarations of liberty and rights may have seemed in the presidencies of Eisenhower, Kennedy, and Johnson, still this worldview inherently contained components that could be used to foster acceptance of highly divisive and controversial positions, a point deserving of ongoing discussion.

Without quibbling over details, we have, then, every reason to conclude that the area of civil religion as integrating ideology can feature prominently in a list of indicators of cause for alarm registered by highly respected academic experts. It is, in other words, a first-rate objective correlative matching distress in our fictional narratives of pessimism. Moreover, and more specifically, Albanese's standard account of the unfolding of civil religion contains one further observation of importance. In her explanation of how the American ideology of legitimation and integration blended together Hebraic-Christian elements with Roman-Enlightenment elements, Albanese makes plain that one significant aspect here was the way later Puritans moved from the strict predestinarian and determinist views of Calvin to Arminianism or a position that (for the untutored) gave some scope to human free choice in the outworking of grace.[33] This in turn made practical working together with Enlightenment-era advocates of hard work and progress possible, and in effect cemented an alliance between moderate Enlightenment religionists and potentially secularizable rationalists that (in the view of the present authors) has furnished an indispensable basis for effective collaboration between believers and nonChristians over the decades.

By virtue of this informal alliance in the area of anthropology, believers and even atheists have been able to work together on the basis of an outlook not hostile to a Renaissance-humanist-style unfolding of the inherent capabilities of the human self within the heritage of participatory civic humanism. Moreover, they have been able to do so in an environment not unfriendly to humanist-inspired applications of science and technology, walking as it were a thin and even invisible line of encouragement and limitation that inherently must oscillate between the condemnation of Galileo and the unleashing of Dr. Frankenstein and his monster.

By foregrounding the importance of Arminian, free will-friendly and morally responsible themes in classic American civil religion, Albanese at the same time gives us an informal criterion of sorts for determining whether variants on civil religion are moving significantly out of the classic American outlook deriving from the founding days of the Republic during the age of Enlightenment—and into uncharted, perhaps quasiextremist territory.

Of course, we speak here first of matters of degree and second of recent— that is, incomplete—experiments at producing variants on ideologies of legitimation. These experimental variants may or may not eventually manage to encompass a substantial part of the American population. And certainly we are far from knowing in any way how these variants might relate to the historic view that American projects derive their meaning from helping move toward a new historical era or epoch, whether supernatural or utopian in origin—that is, from decisive patterns built in to the movement of human history, a pattern that alone can give meaning to the entire scope of human existence. Likewise, we do not yet know how these variants may regard the Arminian, free will, independent, and humanistic notion of a strong self. For us, that territory, like many themes here, requires further exploration.

Indicators of Metapolitical Transformation as Correlates to Fictional Dystopian Transformation

Works of narrative cultural pessimism routinely portray society and its structures of order as having undergone a distinctly dystopian, repressive evolution, one accompanied by disaffection and ebbing bonds of loyalty. At the same time, fictionalized reintegration or redemption movements (sometimes negatively, sometimes positively portrayed), do show up—dubious plots to thwart or coopt alien takeover, alliances with the Antichrist or with militant antiAntichrist Tribulation Force movement, Tyler Durden's space monkey fascist band. In this way, radical pessimists experiment with the possibilities in radical attempts at renewal and recovery that would overcome both the low intensity of the political and social bonding which they posit and as well the weak or "hollowed out" nature of the self caught up in the complex transformations of globalization.

It then becomes logical to inquire after real-world correlates in this domain. The multilayered political problem behind the dystopian views of pessimist fiction and script writers, if projected onto a real-world American screen, comes down to a crisis of the American prolongation of the old tradition of civic humanism known from Greece, the Italian Renaissance, and the Enlightenment. Behind that tradition is a whole view not only of participatory politics but of a strong and independent, freely-choosing, engaged self. All that early on in the American tradition, finally rested on practical collaboration between a Christian freewill (Arminian) tradition stemming from the early Enlightenment and a more secular version of the Enlightenment project of human emancipation rooted in ancient Stoicism and Renaissance ideals.

The basis for this historic cooperation, as John Gray argued in 1995, is the basic "humanist" agreement of the Greek philosophical and the Christian traditions that humanity is (in Gray's words) "a privileged site of truth" resulting in both the notion of a universal Church with a uniquely important revelation and a uniquely classical-Western "project of human self-emancipation through the growth of knowledge" in a tradition resting on Greece, the Renaissance reworking of medieval and ancient heritage, and the Enlightenment revolutions.[34]

All that heritage (except that of reliance on technology and a distant, often bitterly disappointed, wish for personal economic advantage) moves in contemporary Anglo-American life into an exceedingly dubious status—at least if we are to trust the direct and indirect testimony of the narrative pessimistic strand in popular culture. Can this entire project now be in real-world trouble as well?

Consider: high hopes, both political and economic, not to mention identity-connected, have attached to the classic versions of this Western project from its inception. Is it not worth considering whether these high expectations of the Western tradition may not now have led to a disappointment, a disappointment accounting for the extraordinary notes of bitterness and betrayal running through recent documents of cultural pessimism? After all, more than personal betrayal may be sensed here. The possibility emerges (if the observer dares connect the dots leading beyond *Fight Club* to a point on the not-too-distant horizon) that the entire Western tradition is in grave difficulties, difficulties beyond the area of economic performance. (Holding to such a view, of course, probably does depend upon a host of precritical inclinations and ingredients in some Matrix, er, matrix not to be rationally defended, and certainly not shared by all, even a majority.)

Note, by the way, in order to be clear in our attempt to locate a real-world correlate, that the key ingredient in our tradition is the concept of the self as effective and independent. Now our description of a perception of changing self-conceptions as increasingly hollowed out, weak, and inclined toward being determined (loosely described in these pages as deterministic or fatalistic) should not be taken as standing in total contradiction with the fact that roots of this self or its perception go back to the original Enlightenment of the eighteenth century, the heritage of Hobbes and Locke. We posit rather a kind of evolutionary continuity based on the unspoken but growing primacy of the economic in the last two hundred years. We recognize here an evolution or development proceeding from early origins in the notion of a self still fully context-situated to the most recent edition of the modern uprooted self in millennial neoliberalism or global freemarket doctrine. That recent version is the consumerist self—eminently suited for flexible choice by virtue of being newly plucked out of significant contextual conditioning and thus globalized; indeed, a certain prior Kantian or free market basis constitutes the paradoxical starting point for this entire development culminating in the contemporary ideal of a universally fungible consumerist self ready for operation in all phases of global neocapitalism. Millennial philosopher and social analyst John Gray has provided us with a brilliant and provocative sketch of the stages in this last development.[35]

But the upshot is that, for all practical purposes, what really survives of the humanist tradition is the economic unit, *homo economicus,* fungible for corporations and optimized for consumerist choice—and hollowed out by removal from contextual attachment, deprived of inherent identity. That reduction lies at the nexus of changes in sociopolitical and personal identity; and, as a perceived reduction, it also lies behind perceptions of loss in pessimistic writers. The fit between fictional complaints (loss of agency) and real-world changes in the economic and political universes is evident. In novel and script, it is up to the writer whether to concentrate on the decay of personhood or the decay of social and political conditions; both regularly show up, and hence both aspects are fair targets for seekers after real-world correlates.

Certainly there is no lack of real-world evidence of correlates here, correlates matching both the perception of decline and the search for methods of recovery. A look at well-known material on the extreme growth of political power on the part of the evangelical Right, and its interconnections with the tremendous growth in political influence by transnational corporations, allows us to put forward a preliminary model of the changes in the real-world American situation now in progress. We do this as an exercise in extrapolation and in order to provoke debate, well aware that such a model cannot appear plausible to all readers. Our exercise proceeds on the assumption that deep cultural pessimism and obvious rejection of the Enlightenment tradition motivate vast segments of the evangelical electorate in America. At the same time, we think, this model drawn from real-world data corresponds reasonably well with recurrent features in pessimistic narrative. Is it true? Is it valid? Agreement on a matter of this kind requires what we do not deliver, a miracle. What we offer is a reading of real-world data with one eye on fantasy accounts of pessimism.

On such a basis, our model abstracted from real-world headlines looks like this. Common to the distinct and limited demographic segments that a real-world pessimistic outlook energizes toward new political involvement (usually on the Right) is a shared capacity for using certain kinds of perceived loss[36] as the emotional impetus toward distinct kinds of reimagining American identity, including personal identity or the self.

Thus we isolate for consideration an entire complex concerning the self—specifically, loss of sense of effective agency or self in a broader sociopolitical and economic context, particularly the notion of an individual self hollowed out by movement away from the inherited context that gave it substance and moral weight and hence inclined toward ready determination by external pressures. That entwined package now must concern us here as a thread of continuity linking perceptions of loss with visions of reintegrating and reempowering targeted segments of the American audience.

In this way, we move toward our most interesting finding as a point for debate, for we sense as already in progress—here and now—*a kind of revisioning of American identity with political implications of enduring significance.* And it is with that re-visioning in sight that *the interim concern here with mechanisms of pseudoescape or siphoning off discontent or relocating of dreams appears now as having a long-term latent social function—that of providing stability and continuity, while identity—personal and group—undergoes transformations as yet uncertain in outcome. This conception of latent function now moves us beyond the earlier, more limited sense of latent function as merely stabilizing the sociopolitical system: now we discern stabilization occurring while major changes go into trial operation, trials at ways of attaining a more effective integration of a fraying social fabric. The strong need for additional sources of stability in this connection is an unmistakable indicator of perceived weakness in the underlying legitimacy of the American political and social and cultural system,* a theme overtly taken up at a variety of levels in the documents of cultural pessimism. In other words, we hypothesize the existence of social mechanisms not yet investigated that help spin out and diffuse fantasy literature of the kind familiar to us in the genre of cultural pessimism, and suppose that in some way the need for the system-stabilizing latent function of such documents helps account for the current popularity of this genre.

As a subsidiary point, we may mention the possibility of group training in "postemotional" storing of sentiment (sentiments of loss) as reserves to be drawn upon on command for production of energizing affects of indignation (after Meštrović's lead as we introduced the theme in discussing *Fight Club*).

If we then attempt a summary of what the evidence thus far implies for transitional changes in American identity on the personal level, the coalescing data we see run along these lines: this reimagined American identity, as we can now discern it in these varied pessimistic circles, emerges as a notion of the self that is perceived as hollowed out, weak, increasingly deprived of real capacity for significant agency, and hence likely to appear as deterministic, fatalistic—though in differing yet compatible ways: one with either a hyperevangelical Christian weakness inclining toward determination by external forces (whether with regard to conversion or with regard to apocalyptic scripting of a detailed and controlling sort) or a secular and technocratic or information-processing weakness inclining toward determination by external forces (representing the inexorable power of technology and capital conjoined).

In either case, that determinism moves to replace the substantial, situated, context-supported, freely choosing and publicly engaged self posited by previous generations of Americans, a substantial self nurtured on the heritage of altruistic, participatory Renaissance civic humanism[37] interpreted against the backdrop of a complex heritage of both Christian and Enlightenment components in the early days of the Republic.

In a general way, this transition has been noted by other observers of the real-world situation, notably the academic Morris Berman, who has commented on the American turn away from public responsibility or communitarian ideals.[38] Of course, this kind of turn toward weakness or diminished agency does not imply that no one is situated in a highly influential sort of decision-making capacity, whether those elite selves be taken as fatalistic in orientation or not.

What then is the emerging bigger picture? Our suggestion is that subsequent discussion must concentrate on an incomplete and ill-understood move to reshape centrally placed American ideals in our time. Further, if that reshaping is taken in context, it appears as part of a change affecting American rhetorics of political legitimation and definition of how government should operate. Given the presence of increasingly authoritarian models of government in America and Britain over the last years, these changes (at times hotly contested) may be part of a move to shove into obscurity the traditional Anglo-American commitment to generalized ideals of altruism and civic humanism as constituents in a larger ideal of truly participatory democracy active among the citizens at large (rather than in some smaller elite group). How this has begun, and how it could play out, loom large as topics for debate.

Millennial philosopher and social analyst John Gray has provided us with a brilliant and provocative sketch of the stages in this last development, tracing in broad outlines the tension between extreme models of optimized consumer choice and traditional models of nonchosen, "given" identity both social and personal.[39] We reemphasize our conviction that such a development can constitute a key shift in ideals of modernity, in that such a shift toward ebbing sense of significant agency (and concomitant "other-directedness") in important opinion-shaping segments can contribute to the advanced decay of notions of generalized public responsibility and participatory democracy (civic humanism), and that under the distracting veneer of continuity—for the function of the "freely choosing" economic consumer and slogan of a universal human self are retained. The possibility of a concomitant rise of crypto-elitist models and practices in real-world contemporary government demands discussion here as well.

Now this model, while founded on many obvious and well-known facts, involves sweeping judgments, judgments subject to objection and to reformulation with nuancing. To be sure, our particular claim about real-world tendencies toward a generalized weakened sense of agency is not absolute. We do not ignore the long-standing Anglo-American importance of possessive individualism after Hobbes and Locke,[40] nor do we suppose naïvely that ideals of community involvement and sacrifice have ever been confused with pragmatic tendencies toward narrow self-interest perceptible at all times and places. Making this claim is a way for us to call attention to the long-standing importance of the interlocked ideals of participatory communitarian involvement (for instance, politics as other than pure securing of economic self-interest) and a self-concept implying the capacity for active, responsible, and morally significant choice—choice in a communitarian and civic context supportive of both substantial personal identity and a real-world context for moral and political decision making.

Furthermore, our contention here is that these presuppositions form a kind of instinctive substrate for a good part of the contemporary population, at least those inclining toward pessimism. Accordingly, we suppose that the composers of works of cultural pessimism today can operate on this basis instinctively. When their reality-grounded instincts take over, and go to work using a skeptical mind-set of a kind obviously not shared by all their fellow citizens, the portrait is largely negative—the creative types in this subset paint in dark colors and come up with the fictional narratives that correspond to their map of daily life. Then they render what they see as recent undermining of the believable status of both the civic context and the independently choosing, morally responsible self as identity-shaping ideals for the general public in our time. Jack asleep at the photocopier is the one result in the fictional version of this, Tyler leading space monkeys the other.

Central to these portrayals is the way they attribute this undermining to transnational corporations, government bureaucracies, social conditioning, and the relentless forward march of technology. In other words, loss of self, loss of agency, and loss of the sociocultural context that supports morally and politically significant decision making appear as parts of the same transformation under the influence of vast forces and are shown as such in the popular culture of pessimism. Moreover, given the deep roots of what is being rejected in this transformation as portrayed, this transformation can be read as a powerful move toward elitist and authoritarian models, models finally implying a profoundly antihumanist and anti-Enlightenment stance, a stance also opposed to the humanist premise of a unique capacity for discerning truth (John Gray).[41]

It is our further contention that the real-world process at issue here—the arrival of the "hollowed out" self, and the systematic undermining of credible ideals of a morally responsible choosing self, reliably embedded within a meaningful context of civic community, with all that implies—moved onto center stage in the fictional narratives of popular pessimism early on. It figured in the script by Paddy Chayefsky for Sidney Lumet's 1976 Oscar-winning film *Network*. There the main character, a somewhat demented television news reporter named Howard Beale, experiences temporary fame as his comments on the money-driven degeneration of American society and politics become more and more outlandish, helped by his promise to commit suicide in front of the cameras at some future point.

In his most famous speech, Beale pronounces a postWatergate eulogy over the entire American body politic and its democracy, opining how "at the bottom of all our terrified souls we know that democracy is a dying giant, a sick, sick dying, decaying political concept writhing in its final pain." After specifying further that he does not mean to prophesy the immediate collapse of American power as such,[42] he explains that rather "[w]hat is finished is the idea that this great country is dedicated to the freedom and flourishing of every individual in it" and again that "[i]t's the individual that's finished." Components of the nation are, he contends, no longer "independent individuals" but instead millions of "deodorized" and "replaceable" units. As a result, worldwide, we are turning into "mass-produced, programmed, numbered, insensate things."

The result, showing up first in the most advanced nation here, is "humanoid—creatures that look human, but aren't" so that, Beale contends on camera, we must come to accept the inescapable conclusion that we are undergoing "dehumanization."[43] Thus Beale encapsulates the thesis for us, a thesis that we find inductively capable of derivation from our sequence of works of popular cultural pessimism—and a thesis abundantly echoed by commentators and journalists observing correlative real-world developments, even as variants on this thesis echo and resound in one document after another in popular cultural pessimism.

This thesis is just that, a thesis for discussion. It is not something that the present authors claim to substantiate by quantitative studies and exhaustive polling. It is highly impressionistic and put forward on a tentative basis, put forward as a reading of emerging trends in popular culture, trends that shift and trends that may well be disconfirmed by developments in the future. We recall that our task here is above all to provide an in-depth reading of the documents of American cultural pessimism, not in the first instance to prognosticate on the possible unfolding of future American possibilities or to demonstrate that a pessimistic rather than a more optimistic basic view is valid (though prophecy based on connected dots can contribute to our reading).

To the reader familiar with philosophical and literary-critical discussions of deconstruction and the allied postmetaphysical or postmodern fate of the subject (acting individual self), this entire discussion may seem intolerably nebulous. But our documents (for example, insomniac Jack and his movement-leading alter ego Tyler in *Fight Club* and especially Scully and Mulder in *The X-Files*) put the hemorrhage of agency and potency into a definite context, that of the economic and political, allowing us to impose limits on our attention to elevated discussions about the metaphysical fate of the Western self from Augustine's *Confessions* to *The Talented Mr. Ripley* and *American Psycho*. It is precisely here that the documents in our previous chapters fit with and take us up to the threshold of recent developments of a highly public, intensely political nature. For making the discussion so political amounts for us to this question: if the sense of agency and potency and effectiveness and power is hemorrhaging, ebbing, flowing out—to where is it moving? Does it simply vanish into some metaphysical black hole, perhaps to be recycled in a parallel universe of Athenian or Florentine civic action or perhaps of rugged frontier individualism in another galaxy?

Probably not, if we are to judge by immediate surface appearances: the simplest way to account for this ebbing is to point to common-sense accounts of changes in the real world of American politics, economics, and social developments. These recent changes imply important and probably lasting shifts of power. We subsume these real-world changes, taken as a whole, under the heading *metapolitical transformation*. What that implies in political categories will occupy our attention in various ways below.

Before sketching some important new features of that metapolitical shift, we remind readers of the System-wide significance of globalizing or neoliberal economics in an age of worldwide competition and eclipse of middle-class earning power. The result in the real world after Thatcher and Reagan has been, after the collapse of the dot-com boom, economic downturn for much (not all) of the Atlantic middle class. Even though (as one can argue following David M. Potter and John Gray) the appeal and even legitimacy of the Anglo-American variety of Enlightenment have depended on the credible prospect of distributed abundance, the system has refused to perform on cue economically. The last thirty years of downsizing of middle-class expectations and the unrelenting outsourcing of even management jobs therefore constitutes a severe strain on such varieties of Western political legitimacy, one that brings to the fore issues and questions previously taken as settled. All this is, in the view of the present authors, linked with the process of eroding conventional notions of self and community and public responsibility—notions encoded as well in the key documents of recent cultural pessimism.[44]

A preliminary assessment of the more than economic significance of these changes can be ventured, with its basis in the work of late twentieth-century economic and political analyst John Gray.[45] For Gray, the starting point is the gradual American and Thatcherite eclipse of noneconomic definitions of both conservatism and Enlightenment-derived emancipation. For the North Atlantic world, by the year 2000 the fate of the Renaissance and Enlightenment projects of human emancipation had for all practical purposes become identical with the destiny of Thatcherite and Reaganite

economics and politics in a globalist setting.[46] That telescoping was a trun-
cation, a reduction of the heritage of humanism into a purely economic
conception of human and social identity.

In other words, the Western promise becomes the promise of corporations *sans* borders or regulation together with trickle-down abundance, the
final edition of the Enlightenment dream of rational progress. The results for
mood, once economic promise and social stability move into the negative,
are equally negative. Gray would agree with the present authors in construi-
ing the negative judgments on mood and economy in millennial America as
a kind of objective correlative to the sullen mood of fantasy documents like
Fight Club.

Likewise, as Oliver Bennett argues in the latest comprehensive study of
cultural pessimism in the developed world, the neoliberal (globalist, out-
sourcing-connected) contemporary reduction in middle-class economic
and social mobility prospects shows every sign of being the major overt
factor contributing to the spread of gloomy outlooks in our time.[47] Thus
highly respectable observers back up our basic sense that a real-world set of
economic and social mobility issues corresponds to a mood of pessimism.
This point deserves emphasis because economic strain and dependence on
corporate demands for surrender of power to corporate management appear
as contributing factors in America's ongoing process of deep metapolitical
transformation. Here again we move into uncharted territory and write to
provoke debate.

But with this we are not finished examining the aspects of metapolitical evolution corresponding to the dystopian images in fantasy pessimism.
Now for fantasy pessimist aficionados, there is no disagreement about the
main target destination for (and main beneficiary of) the vanishing sense of
political and economic clout taken from ordinary mortals in our fictional
dystopias: militarized empires and the upper management of innumerable
high-tech and highly sinister corporations. (Indeed, there are also optimistic
writers of repute who would concur with some of these observations, for
example, Niall Ferguson.) So far as pessimism goes, a vast array of cybernoir
and dystopian science fiction examples await our consideration here (such
as *Johnny Mnemonic*), along with the authoritarian government tendencies
from *The X-Files* and the hatred of corporations in *Fight Club* (nor should
we leave out the unmistakably negative portrait of contemporary American
tendencies in the latest *Star Wars*). There is also no shortage of critical media
coverage of the real-world correlates of growing empire and corporate greed,
which continued to make real-world headlines.

Now in our model of contemporary American evolution (based on a slanted but very substantial selection of data, just as in pessimistic fantasy dystopia, social and governmental and economic reality, under an inherited veneer of egalitarian/democratic rhetoric) rapidly evolves in an exceedingly hierarchical, caste-like direction, with immense political power devolving on small elites. Specifically with regard to our vision of real-world developments gleaned from actual headlines, recent American history sees elites using governmental advantage to downplay economic competition between corporations and to achieve breathtaking extremes in domestic income distribution—the destruction of unions and the calculated driving down of middle-class income by means of an influx of goods and labor from underdeveloped countries we take as a given for our real-world America. In this sense, there is an easy fit between corporate authoritarianism in pessimistic fantasy scripts and the subtext between the lines of backpage financial articles in the real-world newspaper. (Though one could of course assemble a more optimistic reading by excluding vast amounts of data.)

Yet these generalities fail to capture the essence of the metapolitical transformation in progress. There are real-world correlates as well to the heavily military and centralized or imperial governmental flavor of the typical science-fiction intergalactic empire. We posit then a correlative real-world evolution toward special political status for the American military that gives it a kind of religious aura with a latent function, a function of shoring up or supplementing the weakness of conventional civil religion in the face of changes in demographic and income distribution requiring ever-stronger sources of compensatory impulses toward social cohesion: the risk of real fragmentation requires constant attention, requires generating an ideological energy closely related to so-called civil religion. That this evolution reinforces the tendency toward covert hierarchical or caste-like social structure as well fits with our previous model of real-world tendencies.

While we are familiar with the features of globalization and disparity of income distribution in the package of contemporary pessimistic attitudes, the complex political and economic interconnections of the changing role of the military in millennial American society represents new territory. However, for our purposes in getting some grasp on this situation, sufficient work exists to allow us to supply some real-world specifics.

The outlines in the military domain are clear from the publications of well-known commentators like Andrew J. Bacevich and Michael Vlahos.[48] As they and writers like Chalmers Johnson and Kevin Phillips[49] argue, millennial America has developed a public culture, and to a growing degree an overt polity, in which political legitimacy and power are distributed along highly militarized or imperial lines. As Bacevich in particular has shown, the postVietnam military, remade along Christian evangelical and voluntary lines, increasingly has come to bear iconic and morally superior status in the United States, even as at the same time those lacking military-connected credentials increasingly have moved into a position of distinct disadvantage in public life. For some observers, it came to seem that the remodeled U.S. military had become a kind of superior resource or store-house of traditional values and moral standards (which for most of them was a good thing!).

Noteworthy in particular is the way this unprecedented status for the (newly reformed and evangelicalized) American military in the postVietnam era has been, from start to present, explicitly portrayed as the triumphant regaining of a (mythicized) status seen as lost and betrayed during the divisive Vietnam era—one that gave way in the nineties to the military's role as guar-antor of America's status as the "One Remaining Superpower."[50] This theme of loss as empowerment, of troops legendarily spat upon at their return from Vietnam but now become the imperial legions of the free world, should be carefully borne in mind—and along with it the fact that the rebuilding of American military power after Vietnam has been closely linked to the spread of a culture of religion-supported order and meaning based in conservative Christian evangelicalism.[51]

At the same time—well in advance of 2001—the President of the United States began moving into a more and more prominent place. After 2001, that status morphed into the ambiguously militarized role of Commander-in-Chief, seemingly of the entire population whether subject to the Uniform Code of Military Justice or not,[52] and then, finally, in the words of George W. Bush in 2006, into the role of the "Decider."[53]

Thus one may argue that the evangelical quest for restored metapolitical legitimacy and revivified civil religion has gone along with major changes in how American public life and rhetorics of legitimation function at the millennium: whether or not the President and his civilian and military inner circle, and the upper management of Halliburton and KBR or the religious leadership of the evangelical denominations, view themselves as free or rather as deterministic tools of some higher power, there can be no doubt that very special kinds of decision-making power reside in them and their counterparts in Congress and the Judiciary—and with regard to the indi-rect influencing of important opinion, also in conservative religious lead-ers and highly placed policy theorists inside government and in key think tanks. Given this situation, the debates about whether the United States has become an empire are mere word-battles.

It is above all the Presidency that has gained authority and power by the move toward approving the use of imperial and military categories in the daily functioning of the entire political system. Michael Vlahos in particular has argued that the recent move (e.g., Niall Ferguson's) toward "imperial" language in describing America's far-flung military and economic role implies that the powerful presidency of FDR has further transformed the president's role into one eclipsing Congress's, that is, into a role in which moral and political authority to an unprecedented degree shifts to the President as imperial figure supported by his military apparatus and allied power blocs, and that in ways explicitly reducing general stakeholding in the affairs of war and state:

> So the president, through the transformed office of commander in chief, became an emperor. But the war that made this possible was now an imperial war and so his exclusive enterprise. He deliberately denied national participation—"go about your business"—that would have put this war squarely in the tradition of the old republic. Now it was his, and the benefits were great, extending deeply into American society as much as they did across the globe.[54]

Furthermore, as Bacevich notes, the emergence of a clean-cut voluntary military establishment, now largely evangelical in mentality even in an officer corps formerly Episcopalian in orientation (in effect suggesting that alumni of the Fellowship of Christian Athletes now had acquired guns) gave hope to a demoralized, postWatergate nation facing the uncertainties of multiculturalism:

> Since the end of the Cold War, opinion polls surveying public attitudes toward national institutions have regularly ranked the armed services first. While confidence in the executive branch, the Congress, the media, and even organized religion is diminishing, confidence in the military continues to climb. Otherwise acutely wary of having their pockets picked, Americans count on men and women in uniform to do the right thing in the right way for the right reasons. Americans fearful that the rest of society may be teetering on the brink of moral collapse console themselves with the thought that the armed services remain a repository of traditional values and old fashioned virtue.
>
> Confidence in the military has found further expression in a tendency to elevate the soldier to the status of national icon, the apotheosis of all that is great and good about contemporary America. The men and women of the armed services, gushed *Newsweek* in the aftermath of Operation Desert Storm, "looked like a Norman Rockwell painting come to life. They were

young, confident, and hardworking, and they went about their business
with poise and élan."[55]

These observations, taken as a whole, add up, then, to a comprehensive
statement about loss of active participation in the commonwealth accompanied by hugely important shifts in the mode of conferring legitimacy on
the American regime—and at the same time the concomitant registration of
those shifts by sizable numbers of the American population. Such a thesis, if
accepted, would mean that fantasy documents of popular cultural pessimism
over the last thirty years (documents pointing to a loss of traditional sense of
agency) have been indicating, not merely voter apathy or loss of economic and
social expectations on the part of the middle class, but as well a tremendously
significant shift in the political structure of the United States—whether it is
overtly registered in the written text of the Constitution or not.

As for the doubts about the efficacy and viability of conventional
American arrangements indicated in recent works of cultural pessimism,
those same doubts find a posited (but by no means universally accepted)
real-world correlative answer or attempted corrective reponse in the heady *mix
of dispensational evangelicalism and militarized imperial sentiment* recently fer-
menting in millennial, post-9/11 America. Such a situation does not, let us
reiterate, imply that the pessimistic Right-wing consumers of these documents find their outrage and doubt sufficiently and adequately allayed by
the contemplation of Bible-believing military officers communing with their
Commander in Chief! But this picture still does imply a series of important
compensatory changes in the metapolitical dimension of America, changes
bound up with one (Right-wing) variety of coping with cultural pessimism
and its concomitant real-world phenomena.

This then would imply as well that now the notion of a universal human
self rooted ultimately in ancient Stoicism, however revised, does not now and
never has meant that American democracy operates with a fully egalitarian
model. Under the latest arrangement, one suspects, the functioning upper-
most social strata more and more come to include technocrats, the inner-
most circles of government advisers, top evangelical religious leaders, and
perhaps most important, the top management of transnational corporations.
These "selves," whether understood fatalistically or not, suffer no eclipse of a
sense of effective agency but rather appear to blossom under these circumstances. Put these developments into the electoral practice of gerrymandering
to favored incumbents, add the role of the increasingly invisible character of
arriving at key election results, and we have the vision of an elite or caste-like

political structure separated from the general population, essentially invulnerable, locked into place, and in many ways insulated from disconfirming reality. Suddenly we recall our earlier image of the bridge on the liner *Titanic*.

Equally striking are what could be arguably portrayed as highly significant (and related) changes in how internal or domestic political status is defined. Here the theme of mythicized loss as credential for empowerment can be taken as the key to understanding another aspect of the new pattern. Here as good a starting place as any is George Steiner's memorable portrait of American culture as founded on the notion of a place of refuge for Old-Testament-identified exiles (i.e., Puritans) suspicious of high culture and theory, and then refounded in the midtwentieth century as a place of further sanctuary for refugees.[56]

But millennial America is emphatically not the America of Puritan Massachusetts or of FDR. It is multicultural, postmodern—or, as we recall from an earlier point, in the language of David Riesman continuator Stjepan G. Meštrović, *postemotional,* by which he means a sociocultural system (ours) in which spontaneous emotion has been so far as possible replaced by the stored-up and carefully channeled movement of emotional energy in modes designed to optimize the smooth functioning of the socioeconomic and political machine.[57] Operating on a foundation like that described by Steiner, utilizing further the postemotional principles identified by the Riesman School, we can view in retrospect what unfolds in the half century or so after the end of the Second World War as a series of variations on the theme of mythicized loss and historic past injustice as credentialing for subsequent social-segment-specific (not individual) empowerment—an evolving mode of credentialing vital for understanding the millennial domestic role of America's military in the evolving American polity.

But what we think is most significant here is not the customary observation that social justice categories for historically disadvantaged minorities stand in theoretical tension with the Enlightenment ideal of individual performance and individual rights. Far more interesting for America's current metapolitical evolution is the particular application of this group-individual tension in another sector of the population. For in fact, in millennial America the postVietnam volunteer American military takes a new and all-trumping place in the series of superentitled social segments: they move from defeat and contempt to triumph and morally elite status, indeed at times in the popular mind and in mass media lore move into a sacral status not terribly distant from that of the Japanese *Sohei* (warrior monks) or perhaps the Teutonic knights of medieval Europe.

But for contemporary Americans overall, what this translates into is, in the view of Meštrović, a multitude of quarreling segments.[58] These rival factions, he argues, compete by claiming domestic privilege and empowerment on the basis of past status and economic loss now utilizing stylized dead or "curdled" emotions[59] (in place of the earlier Enlightenment ideal of individual rights based on the Stoic notion of universal humanity, with which ideal the group empowerment principle stands in uneasy tension). Noteworthy is the way this development impinges favorably on the status of the military in contemporary society: in this connection, the principle of past suffering and loss as credential for empowerment converts the civilian polity of the republic into a quasi-imperial post-9/11 order in which potentiated legitimacy flows from recovery of the ideal of sacral military glory, with the militarized Executive (Commander in Chief) at the pinnacle of the whole—and mere civilians unconnected with military, high governmental, or high corporate affairs altogether at a disadvantage. Somehow or other, an ancient Roman altar redecorated with the Emperor Constantine's protocrusader Christian vision has got itself installed on the bridge of the *Titanic*. Who is in charge of this script? And who is doing the sets?

But with this, the full picture is not rendered. The Commander in Chief's new key constituency is largely composed of evangelicals and fundamentalists, a group seeking to "reclaim" their place in the political order by associating themselves with the new sacralized status of the superempowered military segment,[60] even as they strengthen their victim status by dwelling on a mythicized destruction of Christian America by activist courts.

Less clear, but certainly deserving of careful study, is the possibility that this metapolitical transformation in America, with its attention to a sacralized military establishment led by an evangelical Emperor Decider in Chief, may also encompass a new (and nonEnlightenment) kind of appropriation of temporal categories borrowed from evangelical obsession with apocalyptic thinking and the approach, not of icebergs, but of literal Armageddon. If those ideational links prove more than temporary and incidental, then to scholars from the school of Mosse, Gentile, and Griffin this entire transformation of American political rhetoric and structures of legitimation could prove unprecedentedly alarming: for the new appropriation of apocalyptic categories in politics could constitute a uniquely American variation on the common-denominator theme of fascisms or postwar authoritarianisms in the Mosse-Griffin school. For in their view, the criterion for an emergent "fascism" now or in the European past is a movement of total national renewal based on indigenous modes of attaining a sacral experiencing of entry into a new kind of time.[61] To be sure, a fair number of Americans have been given to millennial thinking for a good while, except that up to World War I the majority of American Christians did not think in preTribulation, preArmageddon categories because for supernaturalists and liberals alike their eschatology was gradualist, evolutionary, based on working step by step to realize the kingdom of God on earth as an approach to heaven. With the triumph of dispensationalism in popular religion, however, Americans increasingly possess the conceptual tools for totally rethinking their mode of experiencing sacral time, rethinking it in the melodramatic categories of tribulation and literal (and atomic) Armageddon.

Compared with the gradualist eschatology of mainline American Christiaity in the nineteenth century, this tribulationist approach—under a veneer of Christian continuity—can, if applied to the polity as a whole, constitute a major innovation in the public perception of time. It can supply the conceptual material for a forced communal experiencing of entry into a new kind of sacred time and its forced experiencing. (Already, we note, one commentator has argued that the Left Behind novels work by allowing readers to "enact identity," in effect positing a quasiliturgical imaginative function for these innovative fantasies, a function not without parallel in any number of modern rejuvenation movements involving the creation and experiencing of a new kind of meaningful or sacred time—with the festivals and calendar changes of the French Revolution being perhaps the least horrifying in a list of examples.)[62] It can, in other words, furnish the missing ingredient necessary (by the criteria of the world's leading academic specialists in comparative fascisms and authoritarianisms) for the setting up of a peculiarly American authoritarian regime should matters evolve very much further and should a Right-wing variant on evangelical politics institutionalize ways of entering a new kind of sacred time based on the transition from older Protestant evolutionary models (postmillennial) to the increasingly popular, interdenominational, and volatile (Armageddon-oriented) premillennial model—one that, unlike older postmillennialism, makes cooperation between Leftist and Rightist Christians very difficult. Whether such an outcome, should it coalesce at a later point, ought to be termed fascism would be worth arguing about only for those interested in labels. If sufficiently cohesive and demanding, sufficiently authoritarian and New Time-oriented by way of demands for "rejuvenation" of the national community, the label would not matter except to political scientists and historians. If . . .

We stress that this threshold has not been crossed for the polity as a whole. Not only do we still retain a considerable affinity for egalitarian and universal notions of citizenship and humanity; moreover, Armageddon-oriented thinking has not yet become universal—but, on the other hand, some commentators are already speaking with Kevin Phillips of an emerging *American Theocracy.*

While the new version of American polity and legitimacy just sketched may be far from fully accepted by the public and far from complete in its development, while a fully militarized evangelical empire has not yet descended from heaven as a permanent arrangement, it can certainly be regarded as an experiment very much in serious progress in some considerable segments of contemporary America. While as an experiment it may suffer important electoral setbacks, it is not at all dead. That is, it can be read as one of a potential series of current attempts at high-intensity reestablishing of a metapolitical or quasireligious legitimacy felt to have been severely weakened[63] by multicultural and juridical challenge in the later twentieth century—that is, as versions of a postulated revisioning of American identity. As such, it becomes simultaneously a response to late twentieth-century challenges to the conventional Christian component in American civil religion (perceived as weakening and unresponsive to challenge) and at the same time a response to a growing sense of fragmentation of the polity. (Recall globalization and rapid influx of ethnic groups not historically linked to the founding myths of the country.) And that this rise of superempowered segments in a more and more hierarchical model of society has some kind of link with the loss of sense of generalized effective agency chronicled in the works of cultural pessimism seems plausible. (Let us repeat that the present authors do argue that fantasy pessimism responds to certain actually existing real-world phenomena; however, they do not argue that these real-world phenomena are necessarily valid and significant in the sense that they necessarily support the package of pessimistic conclusions embodied in the literature of extreme cultural pessimism, or that these phenomena cannot be outweighed by other phenomena supportive of a conventionally optimistic take.)

Thus we begin to specify a series of changes that represents a considerable metamorphosis. How to characterize them is not an easy matter. That all this may constitute a multifaceted yet tacit abandonment of societal reliance on egalitarian and freewill, civic humanist, Arminian Christian beliefs and slogans from the era of America's founding, the ambiguous Enlightenment of the eighteenth century with its idealization of rationality and its loopholes for freewill Christianity, is the possibility we find we must confront given the overall picture.[64] Vague though it is, it is our current impression of the uncharted territory into which we are heading.

A further word is in order about a particular important aspect of this posited metapolitical evolution. Supposing then that cultural pessimism and dissatisfaction are seething beneath a veneer of American optimism, why does this seething fuel Right-wing activism far more than Left-wing activism? We do not speak of short-term ups and downs or voter rejections of particularly disastrous presidents or wars, but of the obviously enduring fact of an energized and constantly reorganizing evangelical voter bloc allied with various other "conservative" groups. In this connection, so it seems to us, one of the most intriguing and puzzling aspects is the possibility of some inherent connection between the kind of consolation promised by real-world or fantastic sets of ideas and the political tendencies of those most likely to adopt (or consume) that version of proffered consolation.

To examine this issue, we will need to move rapidly back and forth between documents dealing with pessimism, objective correlatives in real-world disappointment, and recent analytical overviews of such material, a set of maneuvers not to be completed in this particular chapter. But a few suggestive remarks are possible at this point. Here again the ultimate stress is on latent social function for the strategies of dealing with disappointment embedded in popular culture—and those strategies offer at the same time fruitful opportunities in our quest for real-world correlates matching the fictional narratives of cultural pessimism.

Those strategies in the fantastic mode have become familiar to us in, for example, the inexplicable universe of *The X-Files* and its New Age relatives. On reflection, we sense how those strategies in some cases promise actually to deliver what is wanting (supplied in alternative worldview and alternative science and transformation of consciousness, in reliance on apocalyptic deliverance or extravagant hope). In other cases, those strategies celebrate the loss as a gain if but correctly perceived, and in still other cases they assign the fault for failure to causes and sources so far beyond ordinary reckoning that the political and social system is in a certain sense spared ultimate condemnation. Again we approach the theme of pseudoescapes, pseudocondemnations, pseudorevolts, anything but the proposal of real rebellion or revolution from below. In this way, it appears, the enormously dissonant cognitive distance between daily experience and the world of corporate-controlled mass media culture gets a bridge of sorts.

Moreover, it is possible to think about the ways in which similar perceptions of a negative situation (in different audiences and different types of American popular culture) lead to widely divergent kinds of political effectiveness or impotence, at least so far as impelling toward overt action within the framework of the two-party system is concerned. Taking this fact into account requires thinking about common perceptions of loss or betrayal simultaneously combined with quite divergent techniques of siphoning off rage, redefining hope, and dealing with vanishing accountability, even as overall the outward shell of the politicocultural system gets preserved and as different political wings receive either effective reinforcement or further confirmation of their ineffectiveness.

In other words, as a thesis for discussion, we can perhaps speak of an interplay or dialectic between various forms of fantastic escape from perceived betrayal (or of fantastic relocating of the quintessence of modernity, that is, the American dream), an interplay that—for the moment at least—seems to support political disengagement for many Americans and at the same moment to support zealous political reengagement and activism for a more limited group or groups who evidently expect to capture and redefine the terms of contemporary culture and politics, some using religious and some using nonreligious (technoid) rhetoric, but uniformly groups on the Right.

Yet common to all of these pessimist groups on both Right and Left or even in between, the present authors contend, is the use of a rhetoric of failure or loss with regard to traditional American dreams and values, for that is the humanist (truth-seeking, in Gray's sense) essence of the modern project derived from notions of the Enlightenment. Here, we assert, it is essential to identify how encoded popular presentation of this sense of loss identifies the issues at stake: for only if we are conscious of exactly what is seen as at stake can we begin to take proper account of how the representation of loss functions for individuals and potential power blocs.

That is, in the unfolding debate about the complex metapolitical evolution now in progress, we need to look for interesting real-world political and ideological alignments within this set of pessimistic perceivers of recent American loss, with the American case as the flagship instance and the most visible marker of the fate of Enlightenment-derived modernity. In addition, we sense that problems with the effectiveness of the rhetoric of legitimation for the American politicocultural system may start to play a part in shaping possibilities for significant future realignment of political power blocs. Put in formulaic language, we can experiment with looking at the issue of differential consequences in political energizing, that is, the connections with both the differential appeal of important variations in traditional rhetorics of political legitimation, and the issue of how different political base groups may be energized or enervated by pessimistic concerns. In the remainder of

the book, we take up precisely these issues of differential energizing and ener-
vating within a multilayered context. But doing so requires a deep sounding
of the powers and motors that drive the entire political, social, and economic
system now in operation, a task assigned to our very next chapter. In other
words, in the company of a couple of experienced engineers, we are about to
descend into the mechanical depths of the *Titanic*.

Chapter 7

The Question of Real-World Correlates to Fantasy Processes of Decline: The Deep Structure of Decay, or, Descent into the Engine Room of the *Titanic*

Not Just Another Tour of the *Titanic*

Previously we pointed to the classic image of the *Titanic* as an established icon of decline and pessimism, known for not quite a century as the emblem of Western civilization colliding with catastrophe, its rational promises and dreams ending ignominiously. By going back to that old image of cultural pessimism, we found a way of evoking key themes that persist and intensify in millennial Anglo-American popular pessimism from the dark side of Patrick McGoohan to the dark side of Brad Pitt, as the series of dystopias and doomed Babylons that have lightened or darkened our screens. The fate of the *Titanic* sums it all up . . . the perfectly secured crew and first-class passengers, immune to ordinary needs and wants, not to be dislodged from power for the duration of the cruise and possibly for the entire coming season; the paradox of a secure and self-stabilizing internal system so perfectly calibrated that it cannot alert itself to life-threatening dangers; the unfortunate passengers and crew deep below, not especially well off during the voyage, utterly doomed once serious trouble begins, but for all that still closer to primal processes of propulsion than the peach melba set up in the first-class dining saloon.

In the previous chapter, we looked at the upper decks of the ship and their correlates in the upper strata of real-world scholarship and journalism that dealt with high-profile, highly visible themes and the social strata pertaining to them—for example, theories about American social cohesion and civil religion, recurrent obsessions with postwar authoritarian and "fascist" bonding and big questions about the role of religion and militarism in America's quest for cohesion and legitimacy.

In this chapter, we return to the ocean liner for a different tour. Now we are going below, deep into the engine room, to look at the processes and structures, in part unseen and little suspected, that drive the entire vessel. Just as the fantasy documents of cultural pessimism portray societies and polities as dystopias in the grip of sinister groups, movements, and creatures often rendered especially terrifying by their interface with advanced technology and their links with half-understood forces, so here, too, we shall seek out their real-world correlates that lie deep underneath. By looking at accounts of deep processes (engines, motors), we do not expect to answer pressing questions of prophecy about coming contingent circumstances. Our previous chapter dealt to the greatest degree possible with facts and contingent concatenations of phenomena. As we lack the gift of prophecy, we shall not press forward into the contingent future—after all, nobody can know details of coming catastrophes, political upheavals, social crises, or coming wars. But a look at overall structural and dynamic factors, at the motors and engines built in to the real-world society and polity of millennial America as the most advanced postmodern society, can nonetheless prove instructive. It can alert us to the drift, the inclination, the built-in tendency of the whole, at least to the limits set for our horizon.

Specifically, then, we hope to gain two kinds of knowledge from this examination of deep processes. First, we hope to gain some clarity about the persistent question of system stabilization and its connection to political tendency in relation to modes of pseudoescape as stabilization on the one hand, and the issue of filtering the field of vision on the other. That is, why does cultural pessimism seem to energize only or chiefly those on the Right for activism and engagement while promoting apathy on the Left? And further, are we correct in supposing that a dangerous obscuring of risks and losses goes hand in hand with the quite novel process of metapolitical stabilization we believe to be now in progress, the process of furnishing an illusion of continuity while means for reintegrating a fragmenting polity are located? Are social, political, and economic risks getting overlooked for reasons connected with the self-calibrating character of a system becoming ever more secure in an imperial kind of way? Thus with the first group of questions, the emphasis is on the relation of ideas to deep processes driving the whole business. Along the way, we hope to look one more time as the issue of the so-called return of fascism and its possible connection with far-reaching changes in American evangelical theologies of time and eschatology.

A second group of questions important to us now goes in a different direction. Our end goes back to our beginning, the beginning with McGoohan and the secret agent/human agency problem. That is, is it possible to throw light on the question of what or who really is in control here? If anything can shed light on this, surely it is study of deep social processes as they touch governments, military establishments, and civilian populations. As no secret agent can dispense with technology, so also here it turns out that deep processes of movement, the engines of the engine room, are highly technical, even technoid, in character. Thus the connection between social process now and the character and tendency of technology comes front and center here. As the self is losing its humanist effectiveness for the eyes of pessimistic observers, its eclipse by our Corporate Agency (to which Borg resistance is futile) emerges as an inevitable topic. Beyond this, we shall finally ask whether putting together issues of deep process about the role of ideas and issues of deep process about diminished individual agency and technology can help us—what happens if we combine the two lines of inquiry?

And so we make our nonepic descent into the engine room and its real-world correlates . . .

Deep Motive Processes and their Reflection in Ideology

Our most important analysis of the deep processes held to drive our System comes from three thinkers. One concentrates chiefly on the themes of technological forward evolution and its connection with the concentration and acceleration of means of control in the framework of militarization and governmental intensification of differing modes of pressure in every sense. That thinker—whose work we take up in the third part of this chapter—is Paul Virilio. Virilio, operating from a phenomenological perspective with regard to philosophical anthropology, has devoted his analytical career to tracing the modern and postmodern undermining of the support systems of self and traditional community by the technology of enhanced speed. The work of Virilio turns out to coincide rather effectively with—and to supplement—the work of our other two analysts of millennial deep driving processes. Our first main analyst, to whose comprehensive work we turn now in detail and at once, is John Gray.[1] His work we consider in direct connection with the related policy analysis by another multitalented contemporary, Edward Luttwak.[2]

To John Gray our analysis owes several items—to begin with, sustained reflection on the way the Enlightenment ideal of a freely choosing self plucked out of sociocultural context morphs in the postReagan, postThatcher era into an abstraction (in fact, *homo economicus*) increasingly difficult to export and increasingly problematic for its globalizing supporters.[3] Gray's finest example of this outside the UK could be Jack, or "Ikeaboy," in the opening of *Fight Club,* with his identity defined entirely by his consumer capability with regard to the lifestyle options of the Ikea catalog on the one hand, and his job of minimizing the consequences of corporate negligence on the other, with chronic insomnia and a tendency toward schizophrenia as the portrayed result.

It is also Gray who already in 1995 brilliantly argued that the neoliberal or Thatcherite-globalist triumph of extreme free-market economics everywhere tends so thoroughly to undermine the support systems of community and identity that its adherents will find themselves paradoxically forced to support free-market worldviews by injecting cultural and religious varieties of fundamentalism in order to shore up sufficient illusions of continuity to allow an increasingly dysfunctional society to function.[4] (Along the way, Gray also cited with approval of accuracy Edward Luttwak's celebrated slogan of fascism as the "Wave of the Future" based largely on neoliberal economics's contempt for the security and well-being of members of the middle class, lower middle class, and working class.)[5]

In so doing, Gray at the same time provided a compelling answer to our question about the apparent inherent affinity of cultural pessimists for extreme Right-wing worldviews and sociopolitical agitation: the perception of approaching collapse, of the impending implosion of social support structures and indeed the substance of personal identity, is likely to bring with it readiness for any measures to keep the cultural framework of society in existence—especially if globalizing economic measures support sustained cultural and social chaos, with only a tiny minority at the top experiencing income growth.

Thus we may preliminarily venture the further observation that, for contemporary cultural pessimists viewed through Gray's lens at least, political and cultural agitations of a Rightist and fundamentalist variety constitute a curious kind of functional parallel to the untidy mechanisms of steam venting and tension release that (up to this point) have appeared as the polar opposite of apocalyptic impetus to political agitation, for each in its different way responds to the increasingly problematic situation of the latest version of the Enlightenment project. As Gray has argued, the extreme intensification of the Enlightenment project of an individual self moved out of sociocultural context into a position optimizing absolute universality of choice (*homo economicus* writ global, i.e., hollowed out to the max) ends (in the perception of much popular culture) in social crisis and a series of dilemmas—tending toward a situation of ideological chaos rooted in refusal to admit that the largely given, unchosen nature of structures of identity and personal constitution amount to a self-limiting mortgage on the expansion of free-market economics and its doctrine of an infinitely exportable rational economic self deprived of serious attachment to its historic society and culture.[6]

In other words, for John Gray, the key to understanding contemporary societies is the perception that the triumph of this unsupported, noninvolved, "hollowed out" or politically lightweight individual self (ideally suited as it is for consumer choosing and fitting into transnational corporate structures) today palpably encounters grave difficulties on many fronts. For Gray, these difficulties result from the tendency of such a self-conception so to undermine the cultural support system of society that both its survival in its Atlantic home and its exportability worldwide become highly problematic.[7]

In this sense, Right-wing myth-activating agitation for "family values" and the like can be read as a desperate effort at to stabilize the sense of identity and the functioning of community norms and myths of system legitimation as they are increasingly done in by the mutability of all things demanded by globalizing free-market liberalism. For those who are equally distressed but socially and culturally committed to Enlightenment emancipation (or cut off from reliable income growth), remaining real-world alternatives grow increasingly limited, with the resort to steam venting and myth generation in popular culture as perhaps the single remaining option short of emotional breakdown for those not in the upper five or ten percent of the economic spread (hence the growing popularity of the genre of popular cultural pessimism in its nonevangelical variety, with evangelical prophecy fiction and military fantasy products remaining for cultural pessimists of the Right). Meanwhile, suggests Gray, the Enlightenment "project" has self-destructed to the point that little else beyond globalism and consumerist ideology remains of it.[8] In consequence, those on the free-market conservative Enlightenment-heritage side also find that they must resort to their own myth-making, exaggerating the rational and robust and exportable quality of globalist economics and making desperate alliances to support the social system, with dubious groups pushing conservative-sounding programs. These programs, which American readers in particular will know how to identify, usually constitute a mythicization of idealized past views in order both to try for hegemony for their faction and to stabilize a socioeconomic system—a system spinning further and further out of predictable control.

This seeming absence of positive alternatives to globalizing free-market neoliberalism for those favoring some kind of continuation of Enlightenment emancipation helps—so it might seem, at least—to contribute substantially to the limitless feelings of rage and frustration at perceived betrayal of modernity's foundational promises (Enlightenment promises with regard to freedom and prosperity, not to mention rational accountability) so often encountered in our primary documents, frustration enhanced by the sinking prospects of the contemporary middle class (heir of Enlightenment hopes) in the outsourced and globalized Atlantic world.

One should recall, as John Gray and with him David M. Potter have argued in different ways and times, that the political legitimation of Enlightenment-derived regimes in their later phases has derived largely from their success in generating apparently limitless economic growth; yet once these regimes encounter sustained economic stagnation or contraction affecting significant segments of society, by definition a severe crisis of political legitimacy (regime viability) sets in, perhaps brought on by the further extension of Enlightenment outlooks of optimized choice in market situations going global, so that outsourcing and cheap labor bring with them falling living standards for much of the Western middle class.[9]

Thus such so-called economic growth when applied to the Western middle classes slides precipitously into an abyss of personal frustration for middle classes and into political and social crisis for governments. This is the situation described over a decade ago by both Edward Luttwak[10] with his talk of fascism and "turbo-capitalism" and John Gray with an eye especially on Britain, and one now apparently replicating itself most notably on the Reaganite side of the neoliberal Atlantic.

Given the deepening dimensions of this set of crises currently, we are inclined to keep asking several hard questions despite the deficit in final answers. What is the deepest structure of America's subcultural undercurrent of pessimism and the difficulties behind it? Does the persistent charge of betrayal in major documents like *The X-Files* have the full significance we might ascribe to such a document taken at face value—does it imply the necessity of giving up on the tradition of civic humanism and its roots in both Christianity and the classical republican tradition? Are these hopes truly frustrated for so much of the population? Is then a radical lowering of expectations the only road to contentment? How then is the system to cope with cascades of outrage at the extinction of an ideal (civic humanism, whether Christian or secular) and the associated way of life?

Or, on the other hand, is any reaffirmation of a strongly situated and supportable individual self and its context of participatory democracy in any sense conceivable in an era of technocracy, multiculturalist relativism, and philosophical skepticism? John Gray has contended that the postmodern, multicultural, and generally skeptical situation today means that one must abandon any serious defense of the primary "humanist" position of the Greek philosophical and the Christian heritage that humanity constitutes (as Gray puts it) "a privileged site of truth" supporting both the idea of a universal Church bearing a quintessentially valid revelation and an essential and distinctive classical-Western "project of human self-emancipation through the growth of knowledge" stretching from Greece to the eighteenth-century Enlightenment.[11]

Here Gray's position on agency and the self could merge with the evanescent "I" of McGoohan's morphing Number Six in the turbulent 1960s, preparing the way for grave crises for so-called exportable Western democracy. For without faith in the human as a unique "site" for apprehending truth (*pace* John Gray)[12] what becomes of the projects of freedom, self-given laws, and participatory governance? Must they be dismissed as delusions to be supplanted in the governing process by reliance on media-driven myths and the hope for wealth and toys? Further, with regard to the possibility of a merely economic foundation of Western political legitimacy,[13] what follows from the fact that—as the rise of the religious Right helps demonstrate—it is evident that such a foundation neither is, nor appears to today's Americans to constitute, sufficient legitimizing basis for regimes born out of the venerable participatory (stake-holding) tradition of civic humanism?[14]

The tension between the answers to these questions cannot be resolved in this paragraph or ultimately in any book, but we need at least to think about the implications of this thesis, in case it should turn out to be sustainable. What if Gray is correct? What if the Atlantic West is tending toward an insupportably ethnocentric tendency toward what Gray alarmingly sees as unalloyed *cultural fundamentalism* in politics—meaning (for Gray) that in reality, forming and upholding the functional identity of people and communities requires a host of given (not chosen) traits, traits that contentless, hollowed out, globalized, "purely economic" identity undermines even as it optimizes the possibilities for mall shopping and online trading among those still solvent. Without an irrational upholding of the local complex of these given traits, society as we have known it breaks down, or so

Gray suggests, with a fair body of evidence in support. Furthermore, people certainly seem to know this, a fact with far-reaching consequences. In the end, argues Gray, they resort to "irrational doctrines" or "fundamentalism" to support the continuation of society—indeed, the very substrate of society required to make possible the functioning of the late Enlightenment economic liberalism or whatever the regnant economic system may be.

In the end, in Gray's model, if globalization sufficiently threatens the continuity of identities and the ongoing functioning of social worlds, even market fundamentalism may be supplanted by extreme cultural fundamentalism or even by Luttwak's so-called fascism. Thus (for Gray) the limits on the expansion of Thatcherism or any other form of extreme free-market/globalist economics are finally given by the alarm signals generated by a social system put under severe stress by allegedly rational economic reform along lines that (in the long run) turn out to favor the extremely wealthy at the expense of society at large—and finally to threaten the overall survival of the society.

What then? What, indeed: Stabilizing this situation, we may speculate, may well push advanced societies toward highly authoritarian models, the "fascism" that Luttwak foresaw as the wave of the near future throughout much of the developed world—and that in Gray's more synoptic take involves as well stabilizing the traditional cultural matrix required for social functioning over generations.

This in turn appears to us as a more sophisticated and far more pessimistic generic model for making structural sense of the special-case turn to intensely Christian/evangelical versions of revised civil religion—the turn commented on in various ways by writers like Thomas Molnar, Kevin Phillips, Richard Neuhaus, and their kin.[15] But (with this dark model) authoritarianism or worse is the likely outcome of a contemporary return to religion, not the benign limitation of powers model envisioned by classic Catholic thinkers yearning after competitive yet supportive dialogue between the Two Swords of Empire and Papacy. Rather, in Gray's extreme situation, we get not the better moments of a balanced medieval situation, but crude use of myth in a heavily authoritarian, rather desperate matrix of raw force. In such a post-globalization situation of extended chaos (envisioned according to Gray's modeling), the fate of the entire heritage of civic humanism and the morally responsible public self must appear dubious indeed, pushed and pulled between massive infusions of religious zeal and technocratic redefinition of humanity as capacity for processing information, perhaps at length succumbing to simple religious excess of the crudest kind, perhaps even hungering for

Armageddon, distracting itself with mass fantasies fed by twenty-four-hour cable television and fundamentalist podcasts that support and filter public perception of what an ideologically driven authoritarian government may be doing to move its clientele along that fateful road. Could such someday be the outcome?

Is such antiEnlightenment "irrationalism" or authoritarian "fascism" or "theocracy" in fact our destination, the place where the tradition of classical civic humanism and Christianity must end among the critically minded of the Western world so as to retain even a tiny bit of human identity and functioning society? Or could it turn out that the notion of a situated self, one not hollowed out by removal of required contents and community support,[16] but properly supported as capable of responsible choice, encouraged by some sign that it can make a political difference, perhaps even given some economic security even if not in the upper four percent of the population—that some such self is capable of being upheld and revived even at this late date, upheld in fact as the *sine qua non* of democratic politics, sustained even after 9/11? Or must we give up on democratic politics as more than an advertising slogan even as we abandon its foundation in the civic humanist self as prime examples of insupportably ethnocentric claptrap?[17]

In this context, the issue of current "metapolitical" attempts to achieve a more effective reintegration of American society and polity, and the specter of authoritarian ("fascist") tendencies now looms as more than a hyperbolic conversational ploy just before the last call for drinks in a closing-time bar. Let us reexamine, and let us rethink, the brief treatment of this theme in the previous chapter.

At that stage, we had already dismissed any facile evocation of the specter of interwar elitist extreme authoritarianism by pointing to America's continuing ideal of a universal human self tied to universal rights. America is not about to embrace Nazi policies! But in retrospect, we do have to admit that the ideal of a universal humanity at the moment appears seriously undermined, not merely by the indefinite curtailing of basic rights (such as habeas corpus), but by the de facto tendency toward an hierarchical structure with regard to serious participation in public life. Here the coalescence of Right-wing Christian or Judeo-Christian credentialing with the exaggerated reverence paid in public to all things and persons connected with the military, and the heavy practical penalties exacted in public life for criticism of the military, suggests that universally valid citizenship as a reality supporting serious participatory democracy is in trouble—especially in the context of grave doubts concerning the reliability of the mundane details of the electoral process. The civilian domain today is regularly trumped by the military, and that in many ways.

We then followed the general thread by arguing elsewhere as follows:

> [T]o scholars from the school of Mosse, Gentile, and Griffin this entire transformation of American political rhetoric and structures of legitimation could prove unprecedentedly alarming: for the new appropriation of apocalyptic categories in politics could constitute a uniquely American variation on the common-denominator theme of fascisms or postwar authoritarianisms in the Mosse-Griffin school. For in their view the criterion for an emergent "fascism" now or in the European past is a movement of total national renewal based on indigenous modes of attaining a sacral experiencing of entry into a new kind of time.

In this context we then argued—and here reiterate the argument—that the late twentieth-century Protestant shift from dominant postmillennial and gradualist movement toward a realization of the kingdom of God (or the ghost of its dominance in the nineteenth century) to ardent expectation of a violent scenario of confrontation and sudden appearing of a hitherto-unrealized kingdom could have extreme significance within the set of criteria provided by Griffin's expansion of Mosse and Gentile against the backdrop of Klaus Vondung. For as Klaus Vondung showed with the Nazis, and other scholars have shown with regard to other extreme authoritarian movements of the enigmatically authoritarian/fascist type, the hallmark of these twentieth-century Rightist movements appears to have been a kind of political cult or liturgy that intoxicates followers by allowing them a psychological and group experience of participating in a new kind of time, a new temporal dimension that transforms, motivates, and colors their activism in days thereafter.[18] As we have written elsewhere with reference to analogous possibilities in contemporary America:

> To be sure, a fair number of Americans have been given to millennial thinking for a good while . . . except that up to World War I the majority of American Christians did not think in preTribulation, preArmageddon categories because for supernaturalists and liberals alike their eschatology was gradualist, evolutionary, based on working step by step to realize the kingdom on earth as an approach to heaven. With the triumph of dispensationalism in popular religion, however, Americans increasingly possess the conceptual tools for totally rethinking their mode of experiencing sacral time, rethinking it in the melodramatic categories of tribulation and literal (and atomic) Armageddon. Compared with the gradualist eschatology of mainline American Christianity in the nineteenth century, this tribulationist approach—under a veneer of Christian continuity—can, if applied

to the polity as a whole, constitute a major innovation in the public perception of time. It can supply the conceptual material for a forced communal experiencing of entry into a new kind of sacred time and its forced experiencing. It can, in other words, furnish the missing ingredient necessary (by the criteria of the world's leading academic specialists in comparative fascisms) for the setting up of a peculiarly American authoritarian regime. Whether it be termed fascism would be a matter of labels.

Here of course we envisioned a possible contemporary American analogue to the experiencing of entry into a new kind of time postulated by certain scholars dealing with twentieth-century European authoritarian movements on the extreme Right (Vondung, Griffin). Supposing then that the recent American fascination with impending dispensational fantasies could potentially supply material for a mass communal sense of joint entry into a new kind of sacralized time for political purposes even today, to what extent overall is one justified in speaking of palpable American approaches to a recognizably authoritarian transmutation of politics and society? Could authoritarian transmutation be the ultimate means of stabilizing a society devastated by extreme globalization? Conceding that the vogue of dispensationalism represents a radical departure that might fill the Griffin-Vondung requirement with regard to changed sense of time, we ask then further where matters stand with regard to American authoritarian trends today, in particular their relation to the results of galloping globalization.

Overall, perhaps the best-rounded checklist of features required for a complete and functioning classic Rightist and authoritarian (quasifascist) regime comes from the work of the eminent Emilio Gentile.[19] While his work chiefly concerns fascist Italy, Gentile himself explicitly observes that neither Italian fascism nor the numerous authoritarian relatives that imitated it in weakened form ever evolved into a completed and perfect condition. In this sense, it is quite legitimate to speak of weak or half-evolved forms[20] of Rightist authoritarianism bearing a strictly limited relation to more fully evolved stages of right-wing authoritarianism both today and in the past. As for the legitimacy of daring to speak of recent American developments in such a context, the present authors do so explicitly with regard to the condition of American civic life in and of itself. That is, they explicitly reject any hint of a suggestion that, by taking up issues of this kind, they could in any conceivable sense be making any observations about the quite distinct domain of external challenges to American security and well-being coming from foreign entities however hostile. The American civic scene here envisioned is one

that has been evolving in particular ways for decades, well in advance of the
emergence of radically politicized Islamic extremism in its unmistakable and
recent forms—a violent phenomenon that the present authors both regard
with great earnestness and insist upon reserving for consideration in a setting
quite divorced from any discussion of the health of American civic life.

Now in the overview of authoritarian movement and regime features put
forward by Emilio Gentile, here also explicitly touching Griffin's concept of
commmunal movement into a new sense of time,[21] Gentile bundles together
a series of characteristics for the comparative study of evolving authoritarianisms which he and his school see as tending to evolve toward fascism in
the sense of an ideal type. As these instances all aim at a "regeneration" or
"palingenesis" of a decadent, fallen, or fragmented national community, it is
immediately clear that no objection can in principle prevent one from comparing them with recent American experiments in high-intensity evangeli-
cal/dispensationalist reworking of civil religion in the hope of an American
rebirth. What about the Gentile checklist?

For Gentile, the evolutionary tendency toward the ideal type of fascism
requires a tightly organized movement aiming at an "experiment" in national
regeneration or "revolution" at an "anthropological" level. The experiment
is all-consuming and in human terms religious or sacral because, having
assigned the "mission" of national rebirth to politics, it makes its political
vision the value-giving determinant of all aspects of life. Quite understandably then, fascist-tending experiments in palingenesis coopt existing reser-
voirs of sacrality (e.g., Christianity, historic traditions) and energy (e.g., the
economic sphere) and begin to subordinate them to the movement's goal of
creating a participatory ecstasy of experienced renewal kept alive by perpetual
public events as "spectacle." In these spectacles the mystical and visionary
source of rebirth (palingenesis) is enacted and evoked by the sacred and military leader in emotional communion simultaneously with the elite guiding
the experiment and with the people.[22]

The entire experiment inherently tends toward elitism because by definition only the leader and the "active minorities" or ideologized elites are at
the outset capable of experiencing and transmitting the transformative vision
to the general public; here sacral, military, and political imagery can readily
intermingle. Noteworthy also is the way the air of creating a unitary and
myth-driven national entity requires homogeneity and spectacle-mediated
agitation into an "organised . . . state of permanent mobilisation . . . to affirm
its grandeur, its might, and its prestige in the world." In the service of this
goal, such collective experiments evolve into one-party states with regard to

political form: "[o]nly a monopoly of power . . . allows the regime to act out an anthopological revolution in order to create a new man and a new civilisation." Of course, because of the all-important sacred vision (which is busy "assigning the mission of regeneration to politics"), these collective experiments tend to play fast and loose with rules and procedures: there is a willingness to mix the legal and the illegal, to utilize a "combination of legal and violent tactics"; likewise, the quest for a myth-based unity in a nation reborn favors the "destruction" or "demobilization" of political structures tending to protect the interests of the working class in order to favor the self-interest of the new ("self-appointed") activist elite now drawn from social strata that had perceived itself as threatened at the outset of the experiment in ideological rebirth of national community.[23]

With Gentile's checklist in mind, we can now venture a more comprehensive inventorying of the features of American Rightist experiments in national rebirth on a Christian evangelical basis during the first years of the twenty-first century. In advance, we already can say that an aura of ominous ambiguity hovers over this entire assessment, an ambiguity hardly calculated to remove apprehensions about the prospects of American democracy as an outgrowth of the civic humanism of the Renaissance and Enlightenment. Can the recent alliance of evangelical power brokers, dispensationalist cable preachers, Republican base energizers, and politically active ex-military lobbyists correctly be seen as a revolutionary cadre? No—but what then is all the talk of carrying forward the "Reagan revolution" or of spreading democracy to Muslims who refuse to let their draped women drive cars? Is the call to turn to Christ before literal Armageddon or the Reconstructionist suggestion that judges and laity should slide toward stoning gays truly a call for entry into a new self-understanding, a call for a high-intensity movement of exclusivists that could forcibly reunite a fragmenting American polity as part of a real movement with popular potential? Is the Christian Right in America politically engaged in trying to propagate a new human society of the converted?

Or again: how can one possibly find any American analogue to Gentile's criterion of a regime installing one political party to the exclusion of others? One must further ask whether this criterion is met or not met with Gore Vidal's celebrated notion of an American "one party" of corporate capital with "two right wings, one called Democratic, one called Republican."[24] Do recent moves toward suppression of press freedom, toleration of torture, international abduction by government surrogates, and restriction of habeas corpus correspond to Gentile's criterion of violent and illegal means of operation? To what degree does the American regime of perpetual war against the concept of terrorism in practice subordinate Christianity to the status of helper in a militarized and ideologized political mission? Likewise, to what extent does this vast undertaking subordinate economic activity to its purposes? In all of these domains, considerable ambiguity reigns with regard to how fully evolved American authoritarianism had become by the time of this writing. Transnational corporations may in the end prove harder to digest than Armageddon-entranced dispensationalists, though even the latter can prove unreliable under some conditions.

On the face of it, two other features in the Gentile list would seem especially hard to match in contemporary America. First is the aspect of mass intoxication by spectacle. Years ago, one heard it said that fascism used to flourish only in places where grand opera was popular, meaning Italy, Germany, and the great cities of South America. Yet, as no less an observer than Fritz Stern[25] pointed out with regard to George W. Bush's televised landing on an aircraft carrier to celebrate the alleged American success in Iraq, a good bit of Leni Riefenstahl could perhaps seem to some observers to lie behind many versions of contemporary political uses of mass media to carry on the Reaganesque tradition of Great Communication in a myth-based rather than reality-based mode. Perhaps some readers will on reflection conclude that American mass media offer an excellent substitute for protofascist open-air rallies, even as others bristle with indignation at the thought.

The second special problem for observers seeking to read American rejuvenation currents as quasifascist or authoritarian lies in the requisite of an elitist or antiegalitarian outlook, the overt antithesis of every slogan necessary for admission to the lottery of American electoral politics. Yet—as we contend elsewhere in more detail—here the contemporary situation may prove surprisingly full of authoritarian promise. The new popularity of an allegedly universal and egalitarian anthropology based on a self-image as dispensational marionette acting according to an eternal script may in fact function to subvert the tradition of humanist free will, in that it opens up space for the elite role of a clerical stratum in society with unique access to the divine script. Again the parallel with the deterministic anthropology of the new technocracy proves suggestive. Here once more we see the elaboration of an anthropology apparently universal and egalitarian, yet in its technodeterminism fitted to undermine the humanist basis of participating civic humanism in the tradition of the Renaissance and Enlightenment. Contributing further to the growth of politically significant hierarchical overlays onto a denatured sense of active self is the recent proliferation of new mechanisms for the production of posthumanist weakened selves suited for frictionless fungibility in the corporate-governmental world of today (for example, "egalitarian" attitude indoctrination through submission to so-called security screening in airports, or politically correct mandatory "sensitivity" training in places of work and education with the latent function of detecting and intimidating potential troublemakers). Another component in the set of overlays transforming egalitarian citizens into denatured entities so deprived of a strong sense of self as to crave direction from a self-appointed ideological elite is, finally, the new cult of all things military with the corresponding sacral elevation of the "Commander in Chief" into a position of undefined but limitless authority over even the civilian population.

For each of the key characteristics on the Gentile checklist, it appears possible to contend that millennial America on the one hand displays significant and worrying movement in the direction of an authoritarian structure of high-intensity political and ideological reintegration or rebirth along Rightist lines. Yet on the other hand, at present this heavily authoritarian alternative still remains an alternative, that is, an incompletely realized possibility of national reintegration still falling very short indeed of its full realization.

These same considerations, this same sense of matters hanging in the balance, all gain reinforcement from other recent developments. To be sure, as we have seen, for some Americans the authoritarianism-enhancing sense of participating in a religiously meaningful new kind of national time can arise from either the innovation of turning from postmillennial to premillennial faith or the novelty of coming to believe in a reconstructionist-led turning back of the national clock to the moral standards imposed upon the community of the faithful in either the era of Calvin or the era of Moses. Yet quite unmistakably this viewpoint turns out to be emphatically rejected by a very large number of contemporary Americans.

This last point, and with it the studied uncertainty and ambiguity of the entirety of American political and cultural affairs these days, emerges for our purposes quite plainly from a look at the immediate consequences of the 2006 midterm elections as those results were being discussed as this book went to press. To begin with, up to a point these results show that the Left has some potential for being energized by community survival concerns linked to a sense of cultural pessimism. Thus we need to begin asking whether any process of reaction could now have been activated that might seek to relieve the pressures on personal and social identity resulting from the turbulent economics of globalization (in effect, an alternative to pressures for greater and greater authoritarianism in politics as a desperate means for stabilizing the social system).

In any case, the fragmentation of Democrats evident soon after their 2006 sweep of House and Senate does not suggest convincing unanimity on the nature of threats to communal and personal survival. While the evangelical bloc among Republicans may have its own uncertainties, they appear to be far outweighed by those of the Democrats. At the moment, we see no good reason to expect a new bloc to emerge that can decisively end the captivity of American politics to John Gray's depressing cycle of oscillation between fundamentalist obsession with community-destroying neoliberal globalization and compensatory obsession with token aspects of the ebbing values of obsolescent community. Thus, for example, there seems, little reason to suppose that Democrats will revise their proglobalization stand on outsourcing and immigration to any serious extent. Yet for any political bloc to alter the cycle described by John Gray, it would need seriously to reassert the primacy of concern for stabilizing and improving the economic and social prospects of a middle class facing disaster due to globalization and corporate control of the economy. Given the strong obligations of Democratic leadership to globalist benefactors, there seems limited reason to suppose Leftist voters will soon be as effectively mobilized into a positive pressure bloc able to compete in the long term with the social conservative bloc represented by alarmed evangelicals on the Right: social values agitation on the Right can seem to offer a compensatory activity potentially satisfying to the threatened middle class without seriously endangering the well-being of transnational corporations that exercise dominant influence over politicians, foundations, media conglomerates, and university administrators.

At all events, alarmed evangelicals, despite electoral difficulties in 2006, certainly are not about to disappear. In fact, growing signs of the spread of worldwide Islamist political extremism appear now to be strengthening the resolve of evangelicals (and concerned Catholics) to find new ways to ensure that Christianity will not be superseded by Islam, by secularism, or by any other aggressive worldview—a resolve that helps explain the depth of the evangelical bond with Israel. The emergence and survival of modern Israel as a political and religious fact (and as an ally of American Christians) serves evangelicals as a very visible piece of evidence refuting the secularist thesis of the modern cultural disappearance of the God of Moses and the Messiah. It serves also as an equally visible bit of evidence refuting the Islamist thesis of the inevitable triumph worldwide of Islam and its antiWestern code of distinctive law. These are hard points, perhaps; certainly they are points that

American liberals, whether Christian or atheist, ignore at their own domestic political peril.

From all these musings and meditations, the present authors leave the reader with two points. America is not yet fully authoritarian, let alone "fascist"—whatever that word could mean in a nation so profoundly antiNazi as ours. And second, having followed recent news stories on the political and military ideas of certain American dispensationalists, the present authors have evolved in the direction of growing alarm—not only about the future of the Bill of Rights, but further about evangelicals' unsettling fondness for getting a religious adrenalin rush while contemplating mushroom clouds enframed with quotations from Ezekiel and the Apocalypse of St. John.

Deep Motive Processes and their Reflection in the Unintended and Unseen Consequences of Technology: Paul Virilio on Acceleration, Militarization, and the Fate of Human Agency

Even deeper in the engine room are the processes that drive society and individuals to augment their power and to seek the connection and collaboration between people and machines. We know already from a thousand scripts and articles that the advance of this process leads in our day to enigmatic questions about who is controlling what and the status of individual versus corporate agency. Here we look, not at replicants and cyborgs in fiction, but at the equally bizarre problem of real-world analysis of technology gone extreme.

From the ranks of political and social commentators looking at these issues one can pick an endless set of observers dealing with issues of economic and social change and political restructuring, all in ways somewhat pertinent to our project. However, if one seeks external confirmation from observers dealing comprehensively with the sense of the self and with processes or imperatives in part beyond the control and full ken of the participants (a definite theme in our popular culture materials), here the selection shrinks radically.

Among those who might fit into this pattern of outside observer one of the best-known, most established, and most provocative is surely the theorist Paul Virilio.[26] His work stands out because of its integrative power, its rootedness in socioeconomic reality, and its long temporal sweep coupled with a sense for recent intensification of critical issues that taken together render the bundle of concerns registered vividly in the documents of cultural pessimism.

To be sure, the writer in question is not an American (though his work applies overtly and with intent above all to processes directed in large measure from American centers) but a Frenchman. Born in 1932,[27] Virilio is a builder, an architectural and urban commentator, and a media theorist—or perhaps more accurately, a media pathologist and diagnostician. His take on matters serves here to amplify and clarify the real-world situation registered in popular cultural pessimism in several ways.

Virilio has summed up his basic view in the thesis that power as social control in our time is moving toward unprecedented effectiveness because with sophisticated technology it has become possible to act on society with unprecedented speed, a speed intensified immensely by the application of electronic and digital techniques. This acceleration has been fostered over time largely because it contributes to military efficacy, but the same acceleration turns out to be a process ultimately of questionable utility because it tends to betray its users.[28]

As Virilio-specialists Jason Adams and John Armitage have shown, for Virilio these techniques of enhancing and accelerating control, brought to bear in a global setting by interlocking corporate, governmental, and military elites upon populations and environments with very limited capacity for resistance, are far along in dissolving personal identities, regional ecologies, and urban environments. Likewise, they are far along in dissolving conventional forms of political or civic community and accountability, even as—with bio- and nanotechnological methods—they now begin to remake or "colonize" individual human bodies themselves. The extent and apparent future intensification of these changes, argues Virilo, is still not fully registered either by ordinary cognitive processes or by officially promulgated ideologies—even though the fact of these changes is well known and though the single-case results are obvious to the recipient of these favors.

While this of the issue at first may seem a trifle dry, not to say bland, resting as it does on Merleau-Ponty and a midtwentieth-century French take on the Christian heritage, its implications are immense. Seen in perspective, Virilio's work synthesizes many recent partial critiques of technical, political, and cultural shifts bearing on the augmentation of centralized power through both centralizing and ostensibly decentralizing (networked rhizomatic, yet still standardizing and synchronizing) modes. His critique shares much with Hubert Dreyfus's more limited phenomenological critique of artificial intelligence and information processing obsessions as being limited and in a sense antihuman or ineffective because they too often rest on unreflective use of a postPlato "mental representation" take on human behavior.

The positions of Dreyfus and Virilio in effect accuse enthusiasts babbling about technoprogress through digital augmentation of power of being naïve in overlooking the devastating attacks on simple platonic dualism inherent in Heidegger and Merleau-Ponty. This overlooking allows enthusiasts for technology readily to ignore the crucial aspects of life embodied and finding meaningful identity in contextual social and civic situations. The cultists of information-processing utopia do not, argue Dreyfus and Virilio, comprehend how a critique of Plato-generated "mental representation" requires a rethinking of what information theory can possibly encompass and must necessarily overlook.

Virilio blends the philosophical take of Merleau-Ponty with his own early experiences of life under bombing and Nazi occupation and his preoccupation with issues of perception and media theory as they affect contemporary spin-offs of military strategy in a global context.[29] Here it is important to see that Virilio's rejection of Plato's soul-body dualism and his use of Merleau-Ponty positions him for seeing why one might regard the outcomes of dualism-based platonic or Cartesian models of human behavior as leading to what we here have tended to describe as "betrayals," that is, to sociopolitical formations that are aimed at liberation ends but result in the opposite. As one leading specialist in Virilio's thought writes:

> Virilio parts ways with the position taken by Plato, that the body is nothing more than a prison of the soul, that confuses its attempts to understand the world, or that it is the body that is the root of social strife and warfare as a result of its uncontrollable 'appetites'—instead he argues that the body is the ecology in which the soul is necessarily embedded, just as the body has a social and territorial ecology in which it is embedded, a conviviality that is the very basis for the new political life he looks forward to. Ironically, his argument is that the true 'prison,' the true basis for the 'confusion,' 'social strife' and 'warfare' is nothing less than that which has been constructed in the naïve attempt to escape these ecologies through the artificial prostheses of speed, those instrumental techniques whose purpose is the mediatization of animal, social and territorial bodies so that they will only come to know themselves within a technical ecology, a non-space controlled by the military, the mass media or both.[30]

Thus in the most basic way, Virilio's view of human history rests on an escalating process of deception, disappointment, and betrayal. Moreover, as Jason Adams notes in his crucial treatment of Virilio, turning from platonism, Virilio adopted from Merleau-Ponty an emphasis on the unity of soul and body and their mutual interconnection with the world as "system," a natural interconnection extending to social organizations. Only by a dualistic outlook that allows the detaching of bodies from their natural ecologies, argues

Virilio, can one turn bodies into neutral objects for manipulation, transforming bodies (as Adams puts it) into items "instrumentalized as objects among
objects, as mechanical bodies-without-souls, as has certainly been the case
in the context of scientistic and totalitarian ideologies in general, and the
empire of speed in particular."[31]

By "empire of speed" Virilio means, as Adams explains, "a worldwide
technological apparatus whose primary function is to undermine the conviviality of animal, social and territorial bodies, such that" democracy gives
way to the rule of technically and digitally augmented intensifications of
power based upon global immediacy of digital counterfeits of presence, with
warfare in the service of this augmentation of power being directed more
against preexisting ecologies at all levels than against individual preexisting
social groups.[32] Further, let it be understood, the premise here is that this
process depends for its plausibility and success on ever-intensifying rates of
acceleration in its worldwide application at all levels, extending down to the
cyborg-like remaking of human bodies in ways that (like digital mass communications) foster an unprecedented uniformity and manipulability in the
perception and behavior of enormous masses of individual units in the political process.[33] The theoretical study of this multilayered process of acceleration Virilio dubs *dromology*. [34]

In a model of this kind, there is ample real-world scope for popular culture's
favorite pessimistic fantasy themes of vanishing accountability of government
and linked agencies such as transnational corporations and military units,
along with the corollary themes of vanishing economic and political power of
subgroups aiming at independent thought or possible resistance to whatever
morphing form the new quintessence of power temporarily assumes.[35] For on
Virilio's terms the worldwide process underway aims not merely at the subjugation and assimilation of preexisting entities and ecologies, but at actualizing
the role attributed by traditional metaphysics to God for the benefit of technology and its allies. Virilio says in a well-known interview:

> [I]t is true that there is something divine in this new technology. The
> research on cyberspace is a quest for God. To be God. To be here and
> there. For example, when I say: "I'm looking at you, I can see you," that
> means: "I can see you because I can't see what is behind you: I see you
> through the frame I am drawing. I can't see inside you." If I could see you
> from beneath or from behind, I would be God. I can see you because my
> back and my sides are blind. One can't even imagine what it would be like
> to see inside people.
>
> The technologies of virtual reality are attempting to make us see from
> beneath, from inside, from behind . . . as if we were God. I am a Christian,

and even though I know we are talking about metaphysics and not about religion, I must say that cyberspace is acting like God and deals with the idea of God who is, sees and hears everything.[36]

Thus we can begin to understand Virilio's tendency to deploy a contemporary application of Augustine of Hippo's ancient concern with "spectacles and shows" according to which one starts as "a secret actor in the tragedy" and is thereby at risk of being transformed. In the setting of contemporary media-dominated and media-centralized political perception, argues Virilio, a certain "loss of personality" fostered by being caught up in alienating modes of collectivized and controlled perception (now technologically mediated as well) is and has been a documented phenomenon for nearly a century.[37]

For Virilio, as Jason Adams has pointed out in his key reading of Virilio's overall work, that sense of loss of personality is only one in a set of interlocking transformations that stretch out before a society in the grip of technological imperatives at the macro- and nano-levels.[38] Moreover, in the context of an ever-accelerating and ever more powerful transformative "empire of speed"[39] we understand how Virilio can move toward theoretical formulations resembling the themes of impotence and conspiracy beloved of popular culture—within the horizon of the Virilian theme of "the contraction of time."[40] In Virilio's view, this tendency, if not in some significant measure checked, will have dubious results. In the same interview he has said:

> What will prevail is this will to reduce the world to the point where one could possess it. All military technologies reduce the world to nothing. And since military technologies are advanced technologies, what they actually sketch today is the future of the civil realm.[41]

Virilio's thought, then, can be seen as a dystopian, against-the-grain reading of the overall significance of technology over time (though he himself certainly sees no simplistic possibility of abandoning technology as such).[42] The overall thrust here finds a clear formulation in the words of Jason Adams in the important and crucial introduction to his own specialized study of Virilio. Put into question is the common assumption that the advance of technology and communications has definitively advanced the effort at spreading worldwide democracy and combating authoritarian or totalitarian trends through spreading the vocabulary of democracy. But, argues Virilio in Adams's summary, that view rests on a great oversimplification:

> What these arguments ignore however, are the ties that bind the Nazi and Soviet forms of totalitarianism to the mass liberal democracies under which we live today through their common embrace of the ideology of

progress, under which all that is external to technology is redefined as raw material for its 'inevitable' expansion. . . . Virilio [taken in context, has argued for the ties joining democracies with totalitarianisms, for he—JS/GS] has demonstrated that technologization has depended upon the uprooting, fragmentation and totalization of the 'animal bodies' of men, women and children, the 'social bodies' of families, cities and nations and the 'territorial bodies' of forests, oceans and mountains. . . . [Fpr Virilio] study demonstrates the bases on which Virilio stakes his claim that the lived bodily experience of the territorial and social ecologies has been subordinated to the artificial prosthetic experience of the technical ecology, thus laying the groundwork for a totalitarian individualism to take over where the conviviality of the 'political body' left off.[43]

Of course, individualism here is very much the opposite of the rugged individualism of frontier myth, signifying the extreme case of the destruction of barriers to control of atomized individual persons or their remnants deprived not only of barriers between themselves and central agencies, but perhaps also of barriers to digital signals from outside the natural body (the conspiracist, cybernoir, science fiction, and New Age obsession with implants immediately springs to mind).

Virilio's dark vision raises the possibility that the human race and its technology are in the grip of a process far larger and more powerful than conscious control can direct, accept, or reject, one that could even overlap with darker visions of definitive destruction or transformation of the species by nano- and bioengineering. These scenarios of betrayal within and without, of "liberation" ushering in hell, flow from the point that Virilio sees militarization and with it accelerating conquest of distance and obstacle, as the driving force in Western history from at least the Greeks onward, with mobile military personnel as the Ur-proletariat and the Ur-monastic order. (What ultimate imperative they serve remains still obscure, as the story is not yet at its end.)

Certain key waystages have, however, long since become clear, at least to the visionary eye of Virilio.

In his view, the power implied by instantaneous technologies means that the human body moves more and more into situations of cocooned inertia, perhaps in preparation for its assimilation to the ultimate imperatives of cyborg and nano-technology as extensions of its natural powers.[44] Along the way, the increasing militarization of society not only eats away at traditional urban spaces, but eats away from within and without modern political structures, modern democracy, and the modern borders of the sovereign national state: the direction of evolution, as Virilio predicted in numerous places before 9/11, is toward a militarized geopolitical unity fighting in sustained fashion against varied hyperguerrilla resistance movements—a situation in which[45] everyone morphs into the situation of worker-soldier in the service of an inexorable process of techno-assimilation with little regard for postures of attempted "resistance."

Recent waystages in this process for Virilio include the Japanese kamikaze phenomenon (speed and explosion overtake the high-tech warrior in a final coalescence); the atomic weapons used in 1945, opening up the possible total coinciding of speed and power with human history; the electronic "synchronizing" of mass emotions through worldwide television, allowing vast movements of simultaneous emotions of hatred and urge for vengeance;[46] a new economy based on a pressing sense of total insecurity in which the main commodity consumed will soon be protection in a way that reorders the entire system of marketing;[47] and penultimately the fact that "the political State dies out,"[48] a development implying the end of the modern world of sovereign states, citizens, significant national borders, and any boundary between civil and military or military and police domains, all undergirded by the emergence of what Virilio does not term a new universal anthropology or concept of the human, but that his verbal assaults on digital gurus and cyborg theorists fully implies—as for example when he writes:

> The suppression of national boundaries and the hyper-communicability of the world do not enlarge the space of freedom. They are, rather, the sign of its disappearance, its collapse, before the expansion of an all-too-tangible totalitarian power, a technological control over civilized societies that is growing ever more rapid and refined. . . .
>
> [T]he reinstitution of torture . . . , the furious multiplication of kidnappings, the scandalous exhibition of Red Brigade prisoners chained in a cage during their trial in Turin, are not by chance: they restore, in mid-twentieth century, the age-old image of the *human commodity*, degraded and reduced to helpless by the military master.[49]

Passages of this kind, taken together with Virilio's frequent indications that he sees the real direction of technological evolution in the digital era to be toward the information-processing cancellation of traditional forms of identity, readily allow the conclusion that Virilio is describing what many cyber-noir and dystopian authors also discern, the emergence of a new definition of the human based on information processing capacity—an outlook meaning that the human species becomes in principle infinitely malleable and regarded as indefinitely capable of interfacing with cyberorganisms of every order of magnitude, a situation in which traditional notions of subjectivity, agency, and free will can be, as it were, indefinitely bracketed out of consideration (along with traditional notions of moral responsibility for those willing to see plainly).

This dark vision raises, by the way, the troubling question of whether the position we have tended to favor here, that of the civic humanism of freely choosing individual selves in the tradition of the Renaissance and moderate Enlightenment, may not itself be as much a way station toward technological obsolescence of the human as a mode of resistance to it: for on the phenomenological terms of Virilio (and his theoretical ally Hubert Dreyfus)[50] a Plato-oriented notion of untrammeled pure (disembodied) intelligence might lie at the base of both information-processing definitions of the postmodern self (i.e., definitions of human obsolescence) and as well behind earlier (inadequate) visions of civic humanist individualism. In such a case, the whole matter could turn on whether a different kind of humanism could be articulated and upheld, one affirming free will while at the same time avoiding the vulnerability of information-processing trumping of all human powers of resistance and the defense of identity-protecting material and social structures.

A word of backtracking and clarification: Virilio's obsession with the growth of centralizing technologies of control does not mean, of course, that he thinks the central government becomes thereby more secure.[51] As he gives ample testimony to in his frequent publications and interviews on terrorism and guerrilla warfare and media manipulation, he in fact sees all borders and command centers as increasingly permeable and vulnerable, so that a situation of accelerating paradox and insecurity in truth exists today. Noteworthy here is how he underlines the growing tendency in various places to erode any distinction between police and military operations (what he has not yet termed the SWATification of police and armed forces). Notable as well is that for Virilio this erosion of administrative and juridical distinctions paradoxically accompanies the actual loss of credibility and authority of the traditional sovereign state in the face of the growing power of transnational corporations[52] and other entities not readily controlled by traditional governments. In this context Virilio speaks of "the breakdown of the unity of political action," and with it the "wildest" kinds of "maneuver" on the part of traditional sovereign states fighting for "survival."[53]

In such a situation, the Virilian state betrays the citizen it is intended to protect, even as leapfrogging technologies lead to a perilous and unending series of new situations in which security constantly morphs into a new insecurity, all undergirded, as we have argued with and aside from Virilio, by the ultimate contemporary betrayal, the sub- and per-verting of the West's universal humanity into a universal fungibility of posthuman identity in which individual selves are infinitely replaceable and redefinable, all at the expense of traditional humanist notions of free will and participatory civic community.[54]

Certain of these contemporary features (such as secret and private intelligence operations) have recently attracted comment by observers, and they could well be denoted by Virilian rubrics like the aeronautical term "wild maneuvers" (or perhaps extreme strategies),[55] signifying the extreme tactics used by prolongations of the sovereign state of high modernity under duress or in its current condition of survival *in extremis,* coping with shocks to the system that signify undermining or basic transformation of the Enlightenment and modern order of sovereign states characterized by real borders and significant distinctions between military and police operations.[56]

Finally here, to the present authors, Virilio's perspective, though intended as a phenomenology-based defense of Western humanism and Christian humanist standpoints, nonetheless shows a certain melancholy convergence with the decidedly posthumanist and postChristian outlook of John Gray.

Convergence of Processes, Convergence of Analytical Perspectives?

John Gray has argued that globalization and neoliberal reduction of Western economic individualism to universally fungible versions of the economic self inexorably ends by destroying the texture of lived community that makes life worth living. Thus in this view (conservative rhetoric and coping mechanisms notwithstanding), the movement touched off by globalist allies of Reagan and Thatcher ends by depriving Western individualism of the heritage of lived community sentiment that its varied instantiations need for truly effective survival over lived generations. In Gray's trenchant formula from 1995:

> The effect of market liberalism has been to run down our common stock of cultural traditions by propagating the absurd view that we do not need a common culture but only common rules, while the patent failings of this . . . view have inspired the vain attempt to recapture a lost cultural unity. Cultural fundamentalism has emerged in a vain attempt to shore up the tottering edifice of market fundamentalism. Neither conservative position answers to our present needs.[57]

Written over a decade ago, these judgments from Gray strike the present authors as highly pertinent in millennial America. His view in context stems from his perception that communities endure only because of a experience gained from life in Virilio-like communities or cultural "ecologies" and that without such a context any worldview, including that of revived economic liberalism, is likely to have little survival power and even less long-term attractiveness as an exportable item outside the English-speaking world. Gray's reflections here involve a denial of what the present authors tend to want to affirm, the long-term defensibility and necessity of the Western notion of an autonomous self enshrined in the parallel traditions of philosophical humanism and Judeo-Christian worldview.[58] For Gray this entire problem, is indissolubly wrapped up with a point that the present authors tend to affirm in conjunction with him (even as they tend to deny his corollary conclusions on the inevitable death of the Western tradition), that is, an affirmation of the identity-shaping priority of cultural heritage.

Gray's formula for this usually runs along the following lines, lines that up to a point support Virilio's insistence on retaining and rebuilding existing human and cultural and even urban ecologies. In the words of Gray (himself far more dubious than Virilio about the prospects for defending humanist identities), the key point is an affirmation of the "primacy of cultural forms," which for Gray is a multiculturalist point inimical to Western humanisms religious or secular as well as to the Enlightenment and its millennial derivative in globalizing economic doctrines resting on an abstract and universal economic self:

> The denial of the primacy of cultural forms is, of course, an implication of any neo-liberal view that makes a fetish of consumer choice, and of any more developed liberal philosophy which accords an intrinsic value to choice-making independently of the goodness of that which is chosen.[59]

Thus for Gray, the primary importance of preexisting contexts and cultural settings does not, as with Virilio, lead to a defense of humanism; it may lead to it in Western humanist domains—but elsewhere it may instead lead to a defense of cultural forms violently opposed to Western humanism and all its postmodern derivatives. Writes Gray turned antiThatcherite:

> The deeper import of the idea of the primacy of cultural forms is that it is not through the activity of choice-making that values are created in our lives. The conception of the autonomous human subject, though it is a central one in contemporary liberal thought, . . . easily degenerates into a dangerous fiction. . . . the idea of autonomy neglects the central role in human life of chance and fate—of the unchosen accidents that confer our identities on us and the further accidents that befall us in life that choice has no part in and, where they are misfortunes, can do little or nothing to

remedy. And it sanctifies that fiction of liberal philosophy, the fiction of the unsituated human subject, which is author of its ends and creator of the values in its life. It is, indeed, this liberal fiction whose emaciated ghost stalks the dim ruins of paleo-liberal ideology, gibbering of global markets and economic efficiency.[60]

Here of course the reader should keep in mind that Gray's own globalizing Thatcherite period and its revival of nineteenth-century laissez-faire economics is his main target. As Gray's important book from 1995 makes clear in many places, he regards Western humanism and its versions (philosophical, Christian, Anglo-liberal individualist, Thatcherite, Reaganite) as a dangerous and indefensible view, dangerous in his opinion with regard to domestic social policy and perhaps more dangerous if used to legitimate the globalizing activities of military-industrial hit-teams on a worldwide scale. For Gray, at most individualist humanism may be a required item for Western populations, illogical though its foundations may prove to be; but as something capable of enduring and general export, it is likely to prove a long-term flop. As such Gray's book from 1995 is a sustained polemic against all postmodern efforts at supporting the continued viability of any version of autonomous choice and its political and economic corollaries, and with it an attack on the economics of Hayek as well as the policies of Woodrow Wilson, and into the bargain a polemic against Huntington, Rawls, and most any defender of the Western tradition.

The views of Gray bulk large at this point because they illustrate in detail and in depth how ambiguous Virilio's traditionalist and phenomenological defense of civic humanist Western individualism can turn out to be. To admit that is to say that not only theoretically, but also pragmatically, the real-world and theoretical basis for defending the continued viability of America as an Enlightenment venture appears highly problematic. Gray, a distinguished philosopher, shows himself quite aware of this implication and in his 1995 work bitterly attacks the blinders of convention required of American intellectuals and academics when they look in this direction.[61] Recall also that Gray does not deal in detail with the issue of advancing technology as a threat to humanist individualism; had he also gone down Virilio's road, his prognosis for Enlightenment's future probably would have been even more unfavorable than it is.

That Gray arrives at so pessimistic a prognosis for the Western humanist outlook (though admitting Western types probably will never give up on some adherence to it as part of their culturally-conditioned mental furniture) indicates then the gravity of the set of problems confronting any serious upholder of American optimism—even one who attempts optimism based on Virilio's strong or phenomenology-based countering of technocratic imperialism. In any case, the perspectives of these two analysts do converge, not perfectly, but in highly suggestive ways. Moreover, this pair of converging perspectives need not strain very much in order to attain further convergence. Let us briefly mention one or two other analytical takes that enhance the sense of aesthetic clicking into place.

To begin with, on the registering of important shifts in the notion of the self, here there is significant convergence with another important analysis. We single out the parallels and differences between our study (with its reliance on Gray and Virilio) and another work on a central subset of themes here. Timothy Melley's impressive 1999 study *Empire of Conspiracy: The Culture of Paranoia in Postwar America*[62] focuses on the notion of recent "agency panic," or the stylized sense that we are losing our sense of self-determined individual autonomy to vague and threatening external structures of immense power and influence. Arguing that the concept serves to keep alive a "fantasy"[63] of the continuing existence and importance of a truly autonomous self no longer sustainable under postindustrial and postmodern conditions, Melley's study examines both an impressive body of postwar social theory thematizing social and psychological conditions contributing to this sense (those of David Riesman, William H. Whyte, Erich Fromm, Vance Packard, Niklas Luhmann, Michel Foucault) and a variety of writers who enshrine the sense of conflictedly paranoiac identity and defiant resistance—a sense closely bound up with feelings of being trapped in a situation of trying to ward off the fact of irresistible passing of the inner-directed or truly autonomous individual self, hence a conflicted identity condemned to irresoluble paradoxes of explanation and accountability manifesting themselves as anxiety and obsession with paranoid and conspiratorial tendencies (manifest in the work of Joseph Heller, Don DeLillo, Thomas Pynchon, and Margaret Atwood).

While cyberpunk (William Gibson, for example) may seem to abandon this nostalgia, its seeming abandonment nonetheless reinforces a central insight of "agency panic" outlooks, that is, the sense that in the era of the postmodern we see a "transference of agency to the corporate body" in connection with a dwelling on "technological and social threats to personhood, while simultaneously resurrecting those threats in corporate form."[64] (Patrick McGoohan seems about the reenter the scene. . . .)

All in all, we take Melley's work as important confirmation that the updated application of Riesman's categories of disappearing autonomy is a highly significant and useful approach—one that seems to the present authors fruitful in leading in several promising and interconnected directions. Beyond this, it seems clear that Melley's study overlaps in significant ways with our own appropriation of Riesman, Gray, and Virilio—yet differs from it in central ways.

Melley aims to illuminate the background, use, and in a certain limited way the function of a concept ("agency panic" connected with sense of loss of autonomy to bigger structures),[65] even as we aim to do similar things for the concept of "cultural pessimism" that we find to be closely linked to related feelings of loss.[66] Moreover, Melley in principle holds a flexible and sophisticated view of how to approach these matters, implicitly distancing himself from the methodology of Fredric Jameson in favor of more nuanced and differentiated approaches, apparently leaving greater scope for evolving modes of interaction between concepts, texts, and society itself.[67]

Nonetheless, in point of fact Melley's study remains chiefly one that oscillates between the twin poles of psychological or individual emphasis and sociological emphasis, without going all the way to explicit and detailed consideration of political and economic factors at each stage of the study.[68] This restraint is quite understandable, as he is after all not a historian or political scientist, but a professor of literature. Here, in this limitation, with the resulting concentration finally on narrative texts and closely associated material, with no strong and consistent push into the overtly political or the civil religious, lies the main methodological differentiation from the present study.

That difference in methodology, together with the fact that the concept under study here (cultural pessimism) consistently leads our investigation far afield from Melley's topic of loss of individual autonomy, underscores the strong contrast between the two works, even while the supporting convergence with the material from Gray, Virilio, and Riesman remains evident. For, as the reader already knows, the present study goes beyond taking account of individual and sociological and literary aspects to press forward and ask questions about the effect of feelings and concepts of cultural pessimism on contemporary politics and ideology, particularly the changing notions of civil religion and the integration and legitimacy of the commonwealth. On the other hand, of enduring significance is the convergence between Melley and Gray: rationally justified or not, people in the Western tradition will and do keep hope alive, even at the cost of potentially insupportable or dangerous-looking illusions or recurrent attacks of panic.

The need for such "illusions" may well be heightened if we consider a further kind of convergence, one between our study's both empirical and analytical registration of a crisis of political and metapolitical legitimacy and a new body of material on empirical signs of the strains and stresses of the contemporary American political, social, economic, and cultural system. This material seems to us to point out the difficulties inherent in the position of conventional state and society in the contemporary situation, for it deals with pragmatic contemporary efforts at "defending" the sovereign state and modern society in its phase of millennial distress. As such this new analytical and descriptive material returns us, after a fashion, to both the "real world" and to the universe of Virilio—with overtones of Bellah and Albanese on civil religion.

Now Paul Virilio[69] attracted our attention on account of his interest in the theme of speed and power, especially the spread of centralizing technologies of control. We noted how, moreover, for Virilio this intensification and growth fails to render the central government more secure.[70] For Virilio, we remember, frontiers and command centers inescapably become more and more susceptible to damage and easier to penetrate. Thus it is correct in his terms to speak of a situation of accelerating paradox and insecurity. Virilio has highlighted the inclination in contemporary society to erode any distinction between police and military operations, surely a sign of both the insecurity of government and its failure to protect the citizens obliged to obey it.

As Virilio sees it, this blurring of administrative and juridical distinctions actually is part of a process of loss of credibility and authority affecting the traditional sovereign state; here he would mention the role of transnational corporations[71] and other entities that readily escape the control of sovereign states. In this regard, Virilio speaks of "the breakdown of the unity of political action," and accordingly of the "wildest" kinds of "maneuver" on the part of traditional sovereign states fighting for "survival."[72]

At this point we want to illustrate—by way of convergence, and in the terms of this study—in what concrete and empirical directions we think Virilio's analysis points. Here we underscore the powerful nature of contemporary challenges to traditional American sociopolitical functioning by making explicit how extreme are the compensatory measures that have sprung up. We do this in part to emphasize our conviction that it is important that the reader not trivialize the novel difficulties facing personal and group mechanisms of coping in today's America. No such trivializing will seem persuasive in view of what we have pointed to elsewhere concerning the domains associated with civil religion and the like (mechanisms of identity, integration, and legitimation).

More broadly, there should be no doubt about the objective existence of extreme conditions that correlate positively with the sustained existence of powerful currents of popular cultural pessimism. Popular pessimism responds to both the fragmentation of American society and politics and the heavy weight of novel compensatory mechanisms that state and society have started to evolve. In other words, the phenomena we foreground at this point (for example, governmental use of private intelligence networks, or again sophisticated instruments of governmental disinformation working in tandem with allegedly private media organs can appear equally well as prescribed remedies and diagnostic indicators of extreme system stress (if not part of the transforming disease of the commonwealth itself).

By the way and furthermore: the fact of this multiple function of the phenomena is, in our view, not a weakness in our mode of argument but a strength. Let us speak then of indicative phenomena (Virilian "wild maneuvers") connected with the state in a situation of extreme stress—and here we could easily expand the list of recent compensatory extreme measures (memoranda justifying thinly veiled torture, indefinite suspension of habeas corpus, executive pressure on bureaucracies and intelligence professionals to produce predetermined results, growing evidence of third-world style manipulation of election procedures in the United States, theories to justify a standing authoritarian regime fostered by the federal government in America, and so forth). These we view as state-connected "wild maneuvers" of response to perceived extraordinary challenges, and we divide them into two broad categories.

The first category encompasses state-connected functional outgrowths or apparatus in the areas of military and intelligence operations that serve the United States government and its surrogates at home and abroad. Here we point—merely as examples—to the massive growth of secret and often private entities for carrying out military and intelligence operations, often utilizing a series of low-profile subcontractors and even highly secret, off-budget entities with obscure channels of accountability. The growth of these entities obviously has brought with it pressing issues and problems—above all, that of effective command and control within a public and responsible framework. The more celebrated of the known instances of problems here include the Bay of Pigs, Watergate, Iran-Contra, and Abu Ghreib affairs, along with various domestic spying and eavesdropping operations after 9/11 that do not yet share one instantly recognizable label.[73]

In a work of this kind, we have no cause to go into detail on these wild outgrowths and markers of fragmentation and privatization of functions vaguely connected with the commonwealth. We simply take the growing interest in and concern with these outgrowths as one highly visible confirmation of the kind of system stress and diffusion of accountability to which, already in the 1960s, Robert Bellah's work on the troubles of civil religion responded. (It is worth pointing out that diffusion or eclipse of political and juridical accountability goes in tandem with loss of capacity for clear, Enlightenment style explanatory models, a point with many implications, some of which are customarily reflected in academic studies of conspiracy theory but which still could profit from additional debate and reflection.) Well beyond issues of economic downturns or upturns we see here in these system-stress outgrowth responses a striking confirmation of the kinds of issues foregrounded in the narratives of cultural pessimism recounted above: the boundaries of the American (or any other postmodern sovereign) state appear just as uncertain as the mode of keeping it healthy and functioning well.

Equally indicative of the presence and proliferation of such concerns is our second category of "wild maneuver" in connection with the state under duress: the emergence and integration into the inner circles of state apparatus of ideologically driven experts or theoreticians professing to have special knowledge. Their alleged expertise takes two forms. It concerns both special doctrines that can guide influential persons in government and key institutions toward a reaffirmation and redefining of American goals and as well the potential elaboration of exoteric views for general consumption that can aid in reintegrating a polity and culture in evident danger of fragmentation.[74]

The initial emergence of this category of specialist is linked from the start with a highly melodramatic and media-covered sense of crisis, an early instance being the "Brain Trust" of Franklin Delano Roosevelt. For present purposes, however, we have in mind two specific groups that recently have cooperated in America and that began as extragovernmental groups in think tanks or advisory councils, only then in short order to emerge in important advisory positions in Washington: the group loosely known as neoconservatives, and the activist or policy group loosely known as evangelicals (not evangelicals in general, but those at the pinnacle of politically active organizations, pressure groups, and the like). That these groups have cooperated and that they each have strong views on how intensely held and exclusivistic beliefs can be used to help reintegrate major segments into powerful but partial blocs capable of capturing the entire machinery of government is a fact of manifold and unmistakable significance. It points out both the importance of trying to reintegrate a fragmenting polity and the difficulty of doing so using high-commitment and exclusivistic ideologies.

Noteworthy here is that each of these groups, moving from the periphery inward to influence and hold offices in the inner circles of federal government, has been driven by ideologies not shared by the population as a whole, though *aspects* of their ideas can be interpreted so as to claim broad appeal. The neoconservatives, as is by now widely known, cannot adequately be described simply by reference to their adherence to free-market economic doctrines; on the other hand, how to describe their ideas positively is problematic, since no real agreement can be reached on labels such as following Leo Strauss, moving to the Right after early Trotskyite indiscretions, and the like. (Be it noted that one of the most impressive studies of Leo Strauss and his significance argues that his legacy is a traditionalist-appearing smokescreen—behind which names and slogans from the Western heritage have allegedly been used as a dazzling cover for a doctrine of Machiavellian power-grabbing by an inner elite with minimal devotion to serious principles but a callous willingness to appear devoted to traditional values—in other words, a doctrine crafted to enable a new elite to seize power from an older, more responsible policy elite in the United States.)[75]

In any case, the so-called Neocons have featured, among the ideologies leading up to their current views, varieties of highly reflective activism of European provenance, dating from the century after Napoleon and strongly marked by Old Europe's interventionist efforts at reassembling a fragmented public life traumatized by the downfall of divine right monarchy and the failure of Napoleon's imperial adventures. This as it were Romantic or perhaps neoromantic debt or tendency has been shared by all strands among the American neoconservatives; perhaps it then can explain what otherwise seems inexplicable, how readily the Neocons have managed to cooperate with zealously sectarian adherents to recent versions of supernaturalist Christianity. Whether or not Beltway neoconservatives described themselves as secular, Christian, Jewish, or whatever, they have shared with the leaders of Christian popular movements a keen interest in high-intensity modes of reintegrating, rejuvenating, and redirecting a society, a polity, and a culture that have otherwise seemed to them (and not without some cause) to be in danger of moving into diffuse decadence.

This interest has a long pedigree going back to the problem of putting Europe back together after Napoleon; it is a reflective interest, one that in postNapoleonic Europe often was heavily shaped by fascination with using religion as an instrument of Right-wing policy—and one with a massive literature, a fair amount of it obviously familiar to contemporary American theorists on the engaged Right.[76] In other words, millennial America has begun to evolve an inner ideological and tactical (if not strategic) leadership of considerable methodological and historical sophistication,[77] with credentials in many areas, but in considerable measure united by a desire to rejuvenate a culture and polity in ways that are by definition elitist or exclusivistic, in that what is sought is a selective recruitment of highly committed and intense followers within the electorate. That this reshaping has at times deliberately recruited followers of several different types (supernaturalist Christian whether dispensationalist or reconstructionist, free-market economics driven, geopolitically theory-driven) indicates its sophistication, its probable staying power despite recurrent setbacks, and its strength (but then also as well its inherent limitations along with the perceived difficulty of the task of reintegrating a fragmenting polity). The veneer of democratic rhetoric need not detain us.

That nonetheless these followers are by definition so intensely committed and so exclusivistic in certain of their views indicates as well that what is envisioned is a relocating of the American dream in directions and places where a large number of other Americans will emphatically not want to follow, a reluctance that will show up in occasional electoral setbacks. In any case, so it seems to us, the growing body of academic and journalistic material on these "wild maneuver" outgrowths constitutes a strong confirmation of this study's general emphasis on the issues of fragmentation and problematical reintegration for the coming decades. As for the further specific convergence with our prior interest in the appeal of authoritarian or high-intensity and extremist modes of political and cultural and social reintegration stemming from self-appointed elites or groups of true believers (that is, evangelical authoritarianism), we register with dismay the fact that all these "wild maneuever" outgrowths do exist and that they do not point in a direction that raises our spirits.

All these "convergences" underscore how on target was our starting sense that the humanist heritage, in all its aspects—religious, political, corporate, individual—finds itself in deep difficulties. We do not suppose this tradition and its grounds for ultimate hope can be adequately reasserted simply by repeating eternal formulae. While it may have sufficed in the Churchillian crisis years around 1940 to take refuge in a return to the roots of the tradition in the outlook of Augustine and the synthesis of Christianity and classicism,[78] it appears that for many now that refuge cannot seem useful. What reasons for hope and what versions of the humanist and Christian take on participatory democracy and individual striving may emerge in the future, we do not know. The future is, after all, not knowable. The present authors, equally intrigued by Enlightenment optimism and by Romantic cultural pessimism, do wonder, however, whether the best is yet to be.[79]

Epilogue: Into the Great Wide Open

"Who Am I; Why Am I Here?"
—Admiral James Stockdale

We are indeed, as the words of singer/songwriter Paul Westerberg indicate, rebels without a clue. As we witness the indictment the President hands down to number forty-eight in *The Prisoner,* we rebel against something we cannot adequately define, even as we seek the cool smugness of the Prisoner who fools himself into believing he is above it all. We also want to believe we will find salvation, whether it is escape via flying saucers, conspiracies that will soon be cleansed by the pure light of day, or flights to heaven aboard express jets that accept only the most elite of believers. And as *Fight Club* puts it, we may have to face the fact that we are God's unwanted, the nonElect. No New Age nostrum promising wholess as salvation and no warmed-over theology can save us from a hell of our own making. No flash of realization, no pivotal and revealing moment, no piece of inside knowledge about the controlling conspirators—however insightful and gossip-worthy—seems really capable of upsetting misaligned power relations and restoring the true balance required for effective democracy.[1]

This need not leave us with a deep pessimism, however. As the old country ballad goes, we may owe our souls to the company store; that is, we may all be mortgaged to the hilt. But it is a battle, a wager against time. The future is about time—borrowed time. Salvation as we view it lies in making our monthly payments, giving our weekly tithes, attending our self-help groups— whatever brings us contentment *for the moment.* The future, as always, is risky. And if we wish to survive it, as tempting as it may be to choose an infantile selection such as blowing up the credit card archival towers and creating total chaos, we must continue to to play the variety of dubious games actually

215

available. For as long as we play, we at least remain in the game. We know in the backs of our minds that the house almost always wins, but we play for the rare chance when it will not.[2]

Since we are forced to play, having little choice, some of us may try to use what slight advantage we can muster against the house—most readily, counting cards, that is, using our memory and our brains. So what have we seen go past us in these recent games, and what does our keeping count suggest for the games still remaining?

Here even the sharpest-eyed will likely attain only partial agreement. Certainly a bewildering variety of cards has been sighted. On the other hand, it will not be easy to agree on either which cards still remain in play or what real value should be ascribed to these cards.

For example, what are we to make of the fact that Americans often prefer good feelings and optimistic predictions in the face of reality-connected hard facts? As we know, in the era of Nixon and Carter the dangers of runaway consumption of fossil fuels received wide attention. Yet from the Reagan era forward these manifold vistas were ignored.

Equally cryptic is the long-term outlook for the conventional American reliance on the ambiguous clichés of Enlightenment, which in one trajectory of tradition allow democracy and divine revelation to coexist, even as in another, divine revelation ends up radically excluded from the public square. As we have seen, at the millennial moment it had begun to appear that only an essentially antiEnlightenment ideology of religious high intensity could any longer reassert the compatibility of revelation and politics, and that only for a distinct minority of the population.

With this divergence has come what now appears as the crisis of legitimacy of one of the hallmarks of Enlightenment modernity, the sovereign state. In particular, as we have remarked, popular culture attaches marks of betrayal to all things having to do with the state even as it paradoxically clings with extreme devotion to its positive attachment to military valor as a last resort. Issues of alien identity, national boundaries, and the like currently get top billing in the media in ways fully illustrative of the manifold crisis of the sovereign nation-state. Where this all may be heading (other than toward an intensified crisis for the overworked notion of civil religion) we do not claim to intuit, but that we should expect a long-lasting tug-of-war between Right and Left and between evangelicals and secularizers we have no doubt. We further expect a resurgence of political influence over the decades to come on the part of a conservative Christianity more and more carefully reshaped as a challenge worldwide to politically resurgent Islam in its militant varieties.

Another group of cards recently in play has thus far received insufficient attention even though it is a group directly deriving from the Enlightenment out of which America had its origins. Immanuel Kant is famous for having summed up the Enlightenment in the command to have the courage to judge for oneself rather than turning each department of life over to the professional specialist in an uncritical manner. The manifold sense of betrayal chronicled in this book consists of various kinds of betrayal by institutions. As such, these multiple betrayals directly reflect systematic and sustained violations of Kant's command: there has been unbounded reliance on government bureaucracy, on scientific experts, on corporate executives, on the clergy, and on nongovernmental philanthropists. As a result, hopes turn out to have been misplaced, lives have been ruined, as institutional professionals have misused the trust placed in them.

Ordinarily when considering this process, our attention goes to the upper level, as it were—to how experts and high-level professionals constitute elites that subvert and trump the sound common sense on which eighteenth-century Enlightenment would have us rely. There is, however, another dimension to this process. In our own millennial era, we also see the elaboration of lower-grade specialists with the social function of humiliating and degrading the members of that middle class whose flourishing is the precondition for the effective functioning of representative democracy. The poorly educated and ill-trained functionaries of the so-called security bureaucracy imposed on air travelers are one noteworthy example of this structure of downward mobility by mass intimidation. A similar latent social function of downward pressure through humiliation is exercised by the instructors in sensitivity and political correctness in corporations, bureaucracies, and universities. These functionaries constitute a highly visible adjunct to the other agencies producing a widespread sense of weakened self or agency throughout contemporary society, subverting equality by constituting themselves an undeclared elite helping corral the middle class for the undeclared aim of galloping globalization in the service of the true elite of high-level management. As such, these functionaries and the resulting social consequences represent a run of cards with values and effects hitherto unencountered and thus incalculable. In any case, these consequences can hardly be expected to make the stabilization of conventional American participatory democracy (to the degree that this exotic species still is extant) a simple matter.

None of these known cards makes us especially optimistic; yet play we must if we are to stay in the game whatever the odds. Finally, real escape is not an option; but neither is surrender.

Bibliographical Essay

GOAL OF THE INVESTIGATION. This book looks at the persistent appearance of pessimistic themes in Anglo-American popular culture in recent decades. In the course of the investigation we pose a series of questions about underlying mood in millennial America and the relation of that subterranean current to both contemporary politics and empirical conditions and expectations over the last thirty to forty years. Here we have in mind the famous post-Vietnam, post-Watergate era, stretching forward through Carteresque malaise, Reaganite optimism, Bush 41 uncharacterizability, Clintonite dot-com boom, through Y2K into 9/11 and beyond into the mental universe of Bush 43. We assume that any enquiry of this kind will touch on a variety of fairly obvious religious issues, including the tension between myth and competing versions of reality and the clash between perception of well-being and progress and the perception of suffering and decline. We do not, however, suppose that all versions of American reality and all perceptions of millennial America can be shown with equal straightforwardness, therefore allowing ourselves some freedom in looking for the more distasteful realities and perceptions. Our favorite angle, moreover, is popular pessimism's suspicion that much in technology and progress has a way of secretly making all it touches into its creatures and servants, controlled by what those creatures fail to perceive as the "alien powers" behind the scenes, omnipotent forces that really run things—including the increasingly elusive selves of the human population.

In a general sense, the book has as its most remote ancestor the old study of misgivings at the heyday of the French Enlightenment by **Henry Vyverberg**, though far greater overt influence has been wielded by the writers mentioned in the section on pessimism immediately below. As for the mood of profound mistrust of modern institutions in its religious mode, the remote or deep ancestor of this book is **Bo Giertz**'s Swedish novel *Stengrunden* from long ago and far away (Småland in 1941).

Our study's particular theme is the outlook and mood of people who have created, marketed, and consumed a particular kind of product: items in mass culture that are (however) not targeted at the entire audience of more or less adult consumers, but at a minority audience defined by a pessimistic outlook not extremely common in an American setting. Working backward from the characteristics of key

219

documents here, we can say: the target group thus consists of those who share a perception that different domains in culture and society are linked, that their common contemporary trajectory is downward in the sense of away from their accepted goal (this feature marking off extreme cultural pessimistic works from mere disaster and dystopian works), and who then understandably are plausible targets for creators and purveyors of books and scripts operating with such culturally pessimistic assumptions. The main evidence for reconstructing the outlook and mood of this subculture here is the mass-marketed documents most characteristic of this subculture (e.g., *Fight Club*). These documents are examined and read against the broad socioeconomic background of the Atlantic world, especially America, in the years from the killing of John F. Kennedy to the assumption of executive power by George W. Bush. The authors have proceeded on the assumption that America today as in the past is notoriously given to a deeply ingrained rhetoric of upbeat optimism; therefore pessimism of this kind is likely under all circumstances to constitute a minority view, and one allowed expression only within strict limits of encoding tending to preserve the superficial integrity of the sociocultural system (see the work of **Arlie Hochschild**). At the same time, since our questions all touch on or veer toward issues of ultimate meaning, the authors take it as likely that particularly religious issues will surface repeatedly and link the documents examined and the issues emerging: and in that expectation, they have not been disappointed. The method of the investigation is deeply affected by the resultant requirement of treating questions of genre and representative technique within documents as a means and not an end in themselves (see below). As for the organization of this bibliographic essay at finding and weaving together the main threads of source material, it follows not from superficial ticking off of a list of chapters but rather from a sounding into the deep structure which the chapters of this book obliquely reflect.

Literature

Giertz, Bo. *The Hammer of God.* Edited and translated by Clifford Ansgar Nelson and Hans Andrae. Minneapolis, Minn.: Augsburg, 2005, revised edition; first edition as *Stengrunden: En själavårdsbok.* Stockholm: Svenska Kyrkans Diakonistyrelses Bokförlag, 1941.

Hochschild, Arlie Russell. *The Managed Heart: Commercialization of Human Feeling.* Berkeley: University of California Press, 1983.

Minogue, Kenneth R. *Alien Powers: The Pure Theory of Ideology.* London: Weidenfeld & Nicolson, 1985.

Vyverberg, Henry. *Historical Pessimism in the French Enlightenment.* Cambridge, Mass.: Harvard University Press, 1958.

PESSIMISM AND CULTURAL PESSIMISM. The classic connection between philosophical pessimism and cultural-political pessimism goes back to the theorizing of Marxist **György Lukács**, who argued that the political failure of the German middle class in 1848 led many to find refuge in a kingdom of resigned aesthetic and philosophical inwardness, for which move the Hindu- and Buddhist-influenced philosophy of Arthur Schopenhauer was the theoretical justification. After World War II, the connection was argued in a less specific way (with much less attention to Schopenhauer and more to his upbeat disciples Richard Wagner and Friedrich Nietzsche and their Weimar-era followers) by **Fritz Stern** and **George Mosse**. Their approach marked off a distinct approach to studying European and Europe-related authoritarian political regimes, one that paid great attention to notions of decline and rebirth and hence to attitudes and ideas and their self-conscious manipulation by ideologues and politicians. Later applications of this approach have sought generalizable versions derived from the German and Italian cases; here we may mention among others **Michael Ledeen, Emilio Gentile**, and **Roger Griffin**—and, from a different perspective, **Klaus Vondung**, all the while stressing that these researchers have very distinct approaches despite limited similarities. Vondung's work follows its own line of argument in stressing the extraordinary lengths to which devotees of apocalyptic (whether supernatural or secularized matters little) are willing to go to force the historical process to yield a meaning imputed to it: destruction of a civilization to make way for a new birth of postulated meaning comes squarely within their sense of mission.

The application of related but clearly distinct categories in a much looser and less theoretical way, whatever the labels and self-conscious drawing of academic lineages, to the specifically postwar Anglo-American scene (aside from the German-American Bund or Lord Haw-Haw and Oswald Moseley) has come above all from the incisive and nuanced work of **Tom Engelhardt** and then in a different mode from his methodological follower **Jodi Dean**. As an example of how a key document on which we were working could be read in a methodologically stimulating way with regard to issues of the ambiguous status of globalization, we mention the important study by **Paul A. Cantor**, surely a model of unearthing connections between clues within the work and empirical situations. It is a work to which we owe much at many points, not only with regard to its own topic (globalization and *The X-Files*), but also generally with regard to methodology. As we noted in chapter 2 above, however, we think Cantor has not grasped the remarkable degree to which the evolving genre of intense pessimism (a minority-report genre, so to speak) has somehow along its way evolved means of self-reflectively registering the possibility of radically tragic outcomes in the American situation, and that in ways that still uphold the imposed code of upbeatness (for instance, the ideal of democracy can never be challenged, and the tension between liberty and equality must formally be treated as manageable.) Beyond this, the quite specific and explicit category of cultural pessimism has been programmatically reinvoked by **Oliver Bennett** with regard to the postwar scene in his indictment of neoliberal (Thatcherite, Reaganite, globalizing) economics. Beyond this, the latest American version of high culture or elitist condemnation of American culture and society, distinguished however by its attention to recent American politics and geopolitics in a highly intelligent way, comes from the hand of **Morris Berman**. (Here we do not chronicle Berman's American and European predecessors, as a mere bibliography of such elite-versus-the-masses literature could well require as many pages as this entire book.)

In a more general sense, of course, the book draws on study of the philosophy of history, in particular the studies on ancient thematizing of decline edited in **Reinhart Koselleck** and **Paul Widmer**. Beyond that, the book bears a certain relation both to **John Stroup**'s work on notions of time and decline in Emanuel Hirsch and his 1995 Montreal paper on late twentieth-century German notions of decline on the one hand, and to **Glenn Shuck**'s book on contemporary American dispensationalist prophecy fiction on the other. .

Literature

Berman, Morris. *The Twilight of American Culture.* New York: W.W. Norton, 2000.

————. *Dark Ages America: The Final Phase of Empire.* New York: W.W. Norton, 2006.

Cantor, Paul A. "Mainstreaming Paranoia: *The X-Files* and the Delegitimation of the Nation-State." Pages 111–98 in his *Gilligan Unbound: Pop Culture in the Age of Globalization.* Lanham, Md.: Rowman & Littlefield, 2001.

Dean, Jodi. *Aliens in America: Conspiracy Cultures from Outerspace to Cyberspace.* Ithaca: Cornell University Press, 1998.

Engelhardt, Tom. *The End of Victory Culture: Cold War America and the Disillusioning of a Generation.* New York: Basic Books, 1995.

Gentile, Emile. *Le religioni della politica. Fra democrazie e totalitarismi, collana «Storia e Società ».* Rome: Laterza, 2001.

————. *The Sacralization of Politics in Fascist Italy.* Translated by Keith Botsford. Cambridge, Mass.: Harvard University Press, 1996.

Griffin, Roger. "Cloister or Cluster? The Implications of Emilio Gentile's Ecumenical Theory of Political Religion for the Study of Extremism." *Totalitarian Movements and Political Religions* 6:1 (2005): 33–52.

————, ed. *Fascism, Totalitarianism, and Political Religion.* London & New York: Routledge, 2005.

————. "The Palingenetic Core of Fascist Nationalism." Pages 97–122 in *Che cos'è il fascismo? Interpretazioni e prospettive di ricerche.* Edited by Alessandro Campi. Rome: 2003.

————. "The Palingenetic Political Community: Rethinking the Legitimation of Totalitarian Regimes in Inter-war Europe." *Totalitarian Movements and Political Religions* 3:3 (2002): 24–43.

Koselleck, Reinhart, and Paul Widmer, eds. *Niedergang: Studien zu einem geschichtlichen Thema.* Sprache und Geschichte 2. Stuttgart: Klett-Cotta, 1980.

Ledeen, Michael. *Universal Fascism: The Theory and Practice of the Fascist International, 1928–1936.* New York: Howard Fertig, 1972.

Lukács, György. *Die Zerstörung der Vernunft: Der Weg des Irrationalismus von Schelling zu Hitler.* Budapest/Berlin: Aufbau Verlag, 1954–1955.

Mosse, George. *The Crisis of German Ideology: Intellectual Origins of the Third Reich.* 1st ed. New York: Grosset & Dunlap, 1964.

Shuck, Glenn. *Marks of the Beast: The* Left Behind *Novels and the Struggle for Evangelical Identity.* New York: New York University Press, 2005.

Stern, Fritz. *The Politics of Cultural Despair: A Study in the Rise of the Germanic Ideology.* Berkeley: University of California Press, 1963.

Stroup, John. "Historical Thinking about Decline in the Twentieth-Century German Quest for Identity: The Troubled Heritage of Rightwing Intellectuals in Today's Germany." Unpublished paper for the 18th International Congress of Historical Sciences. Summarized in Antoni Maczak, "Decline as an Historical Concept," *18th International Congress of Historical Sciences 1995 Proceedings: Reports, Abstracts, and Introductions to Round Tables.* (Montreal: International Committee of Historical Sciences, 1995), 183–95.

Stroup, John. "Political Theology and Secularization Theory in Germany, 1918–1939: Emanuel Hirsch as a Phenomenon of His Time." *Harvard Theological Review* 80 (1987): 321–68.

Vondung, Klaus. *The Apocalypse in Germany.* Translated by Stephen Ricks. Columbia: University of Missouri, 2000.

———. *Magie und Manipulation: Ideologischer Kult und politische Religion des Nationalsozialismus.* Göttingen: Vandenhoeck & Ruprecht, 1971.

POPULAR CULTURE AND THE ACADEMY. Appropriately enough the state of this question is epitomized online, specifically in a (**Wikipedia**) article-concentrating above all on academic discussions of the possibilities and limits of popular genres, particularly neo-Marxist, Frankfurt School, and cultural studies school discussions of the extent to which popular genres can carry out radical change—often a lamentably small extent, it appears. All this theoretical discussion is potentially quite interesting and even useful, yet as a point of departure it misses the point. For us such possibility of genre talk can only be a *means,* not an *end in itself.* We are interested first in analyzing conditions and mentalities within the sociopolitical system, especially their religious aspect. In this sense the potential of particular genres is interesting, but not as such the primary object of study, only an ingredient in a larger mosaic. Likewise approaches akin to the New Criticism or "text-immanent" study of documents have their place—but more as a starting point for subsequent close observation of how documents are produced and how they are received by and installed in reception-traditions by their audiences. Here we take important cues from the work of **John Lyden**, which attains pioneering significance in drawing attention to the active power of audience response to films.

Another way of summing up such an approach is to borrow the formula that a document or a concept may serve simultaneously as an indicator of mentalities and their relation to social conditions and at the same time as a factor in affecting how mentalities and their context are altered in a context changing over time. This formula was introduced by the history of concepts school of **Reinhart Koselleck,** and we see every reason to apply it to the scripts and books in contemporary popular culture. Dynamic interaction of producers attuned to markets and of reception traditions reflecting the changing self-perception of Anglo-American audiences represents an adaptation here of approaches utilized by Koselleck's school in tracing how high-end concepts could be used as instruments of struggle in sociopolitical contests in modern Europe. Such an approach can readily be integrated with the central perception of the sociological perspective employed in the study of early Christian apocalyptic and missionary activity by **John Gager**, according to which subcultures create and maintain "social worlds" through the propagation and alteration of worldviews built on eschatology and apocalyptic, the quintessential building block in Western philosophy of history. And if the eschatological perception that the world is hastening toward its end (**Hans Preuß, Werner Elert**) does not represent cultural pessimism, then nothing does.

Literature

Elert, Werner. "36. Weltende. *Mundus advesperascens.*" Pages 447, 408, xii in his *Morphologie des Lutherthums: Erster Band. Theologie und Weltanschauung des Lutherthums hauptsächlich im 16. und 1. Jahrhundert.* 3rd ed. München: Beck, 1931; rpt. 1965.

Gager, John G. *Kingdom and Community: The Social World of Early Christianity.* Prentice Hall Studies in Religion Series. Englewood Cliffs, N.J.: Prentice-Hall, 1975.

Koselleck, Reinhart. *The Practice of Conceptual History: Timing History, Spacing Concepts.* Translated by Todd Presner. Stanford: Stanford University Press, 2002.

Lehmann, Hartmut, and Melvin Richter, eds. *The Meaning of Historical Terms and Concepts: New Studies on "Begriffsgeschichte."* Occasional Paper, German Historical Institute, 15. Washington, D.C.: German Historical Institute, 1996.

Lyden, John C. *Film as Religion: Myths, Morals, and Rituals.* New York: New York University Press, 2003.

"Popular culture studies," *Wikipedia.* http://en.wikipedia.org/wiki/Popular_culture_ studies (last accessed July 1, 2006).

Preuß, Hans. *Martin Luther, der Prophet.* Gütersloh: Bertelsmann, 1933.

APPROACHES TO THE RELIGIOUS ASPECT AND THE APOCALYPTIC DIMENSION. The scientific study of world-relativizing pessimism inherent in Judeo-Christian eschatology (end of the world doctrines) and apocalyptic (divine hidden plans and messages about the same melancholy topic) dates from the Enlightenment of the eighteenth century and in our own day has attracted interest from the viewpoint of sociology (**Leon Festinger, John Gager**). While this relativizing pessimism is in a sense inherent as a postulate in all studies of prophetism and the message of Jesus (H. S. Reimarus, Franz Overbeck, Albert Schweitzer, Martin Werner), the systematic study of divine end of the world doctrines and a coming "thousand year kingdom of the saints" has formed the theme for several noteworthy monographs, notably those of **Heinrich Corrodi, Leonhard Atzberger, Jacob Taubes, Bernard McGinn,** and **Eugen Weber.** As **Karl Löwith** suggested through the arrangement and unfolding of his classic study of the philosophy of history, at the close of antiquity St. Augustine defused the politically unsettling tendencies of apocalyptic thinking by relegating the onset of the coming kingdom of the righteous saints to the past (i.e., the arrival of the institutional church, for all practical purposes, so recently and uneasily yoked together with the decrepit Roman Empire). The later western Middle Ages and subsequent modernity then saw the reigniting of this volatile material by the unsettling expectations of Joachim of Fiore, the Spiritual Franciscans, the apocalyptic sects of the late Middle Ages and Reformation, the extremists of the English Civil War, the pietists of Germany, the progressive kingdom groups of mainline Protestantism in the nineteenth century, and an uncountable number of apocalyptic and dispensationalist groups thereafter—not to mention the more secularized offshoots of the same, notably Karl Marx.

This entire development of expectations of a coming kingdom of the saints has been chronicled by a host of specialized scholars, notably **Herbert Grundmann, Will-Erich Peuckert, Marjorie Reeves, Sylvia Thrupp, Bernhard Bernhard Töpfer, Wilhelm E. Mühlmann,** and **Norman Cohn.** Particularly noteworthy is **Michael Walzer**'s presentation of the extreme Protestant hardliners of the turbulent English Civil War as the first modern revolutionary cadre, so to speak, fueled by predestinarian and eschatological energies that made them the first, but not the last, group of organized activists to push forward to regicide as regime change. In other words, the observers of the American scene today would be ill-advised to underestimate the explosive potential of Judeo-Christian apocalyptic in any situation.

Literature

Atzberger, Leonhard. *Geschichte der christlichen Eschatologie innerhalb der vornicänischen Zeit.* Graz: Akademische Druck- und Verlagsanstalt, 1970; 1st ed., Freiburg i.B., 1896.

Cohn, Norman. *Cosmos, Chaos, and the World to Come: The Ancient Roots of Apocalyptic Faith.* 2nd ed. New Haven: Yale University Press, 2001.

———. *The Pursuit of the Millennium: Revolutionary Millenarians and Mystical Anarchists of the Middle Ages.* Rev. ed. New York: Oxford University Press, 1970.

Corrodi, Heinrich. *Kritische Geschichte des Chiliasmus Oder der Meynungen über das tausendjährige Reich Christi,* 4 vols. Zürich: Orell, Geßner, Füßli, ca. 1780–1783.

Festinger, Leon, Henry W. Riecken, and Stanley Schachter. *When Prophecy Fails: A Social and Psychological Study of a Modern Group that Predicted the Destruction of the World.* Minneapolis: University of Minnesota Press, 1956. 1st ed. Rpt. New York: Harper & Row, 1964.

Gager, John G. *Kingdom and Community: The Social World of Early Christianity.* Prentice-Hall Studies in Religion Series. Englewood Cliffs, N.J.: Prentice-Hall, 1975.

Grundmann, Herbert. *Studien über Joachim von Floris.* Leipzig: G.B. Teubner, 1927.

Löwith, Karl. *Meaning in History.* Chicago: University of Chicago Press, 1957; 1st ed., 1949.

McGinn, Bernard, John J. Collins, and Stephen J. Stein, eds. *Continuum History of Apocalypticism.* New York: Continuum, 2003.

Mühlmann, Wilhelm E. *Chiliasmus und Nativismus: Studien zur Psychologie, Soziologie und historischer Kasuistik der Umsturzbewegung.* 2nd ed. Berlin: Reimer, 1964.

Peuckert, Will-Erich. "Germanische Eschatologien." *Archiv für Religionswissenschaft* 32 (1935): 1–37.

———. *Die große Wende.* Hamburg: Claassen & Goverts, 1948.

Reeves, Marjorie. *The Influence of Prophecy in the Later Middle Ages: A Study in Joachimism.* Oxford: Clarendon, 1969.

Taubes, Jacob. *Abendländische Eschatologie.* Bern: Francke, 1947.

Thrupp, Sylvia, ed. *Millennial Dreams in Action.* Comparative Studies in Society and History, Suppl. 2. The Hague, Mouton, 1962.

Töpfer, Bernhard. *Das kommende Reich des Friedens.* Berlin: Akademie-Verlag, 1964.

Walzer, Michael. *The Revolution of the Saints: A Study in the Origins of Radical Politics.* Cambridge, Mass.: Harvard University Press, 1965.

Weber, Eugen. *Apocalypses: Prophecies, Cults, and Millennial Beliefs through the Ages.* Cambridge, Mass.: Harvard University Press, 1999.

THE TECHNOLOGICAL AND DIGITAL FEATURES. The historical background to concerns about the effects of technology within the framework of modernity are thematized by many writers, including **Jackson Lears** and **Lewis Mumford.** The connection between technological concerns, specifically digital issues, and issues of anthropology can be found in **Scott Bukatman, Donna Haraway, Kathryn Hayles, Ray Kurzweil, Michael Zimmerman, Hubert Dreyfus,** and the works by and about **Paul Virilio,** esp. **Jason Adams, John Armitage,** and **Steve Redhead.** Given our stress on Virilio and his phenomenological sources, we have given them prominence here (**Dreyfus**).

Literature

Jason Adams. "POPULAR DEFENSE IN THE EMPIRE OF SPEED: Paul Virilio and the Phenomenology of the Political Body," M.A. thesis, Simon Fraser University, 2003. http://www.geocities.com/ringfingers/thesis.html (last accessed June 2, 2006).

Armitage, John, ed. *Paul Virilio: From Modernism to Hypermodernism and Beyond.* London: SAGE Publications, 2000.

Bukatman, Scott. *Terminal Identity: The Virtual Subject in Postmodern Science Fiction.* Durham, N.C.: Duke University Press, 1993.

Der Derian, James, ed. *The Virilio Reader.* Oxford: Blackwell, 1998.

Dreyfus, Hubert L., and Harry Kreisler. "Conversation with History: Hubert Dreyfus: Artificial Intelligence." http://globetrotter.berkeley.edu/people5/Dreyfus/dreyfus-con6.html (last accessed, July 2, 2006).

Dreyfus, Hubert L. "Heidegger on the Connection between Nihilism, Art, Technology, and Politics." Pages 289–316 in *The Cambridge Companion to Heidegger.* Edited by Charles B. Guignon. Cambridge: Cambridge University Press, 1998.

Haraway, Donna. *Cyborgs, Simians, and Women: The Reinvention of Nature.* New York: Routledge, 1991.

Hayles, Kathryn. *How We Became Posthuman: Virtual Bodies in Cyberspace, Literature, and Informatics.* Chicago: University of Chicago Press, 1999.

Kurzweil, Ray. *The Age of Spiritual Machines.* New York: Viking Penguin, 1999.

Lears, T. J. Jackson. *No Place of Grace: Antimodernism and the Transformation of American Culture 1880–1920.* New York: Pantheon, 1981.

Mumford, Lewis. *Pentagon of Power: The Myth of the Machine.* Vol. 2. New York: Harvest, 1974.

Redhead, Steve, ed. *The Paul Virilio Reader.* European Perspectives: A Series in Social Thought and Cultural Criticism. New York: Columbia University Press, 2004.

Virilio, Paul. *Ground Zero.* Translated by Chris Turne. London: Verso, 2002.

———. *Speed and Politics: An Essay on Dromology.* New York: Semiotext(e), 1986.

Virilio, Paul, and Sylvère Lotringer. *The Accident of Art.* Semiotext(e)/Foreign Agents. London: Verso, 2005.

———. *Pure War.* Semiotext(e)/Foreign Agents. New York: Semiotext(e), 1998.

Zimmerman, Michael E. *Heidegger's Confrontation with Modernity Technology, Politics, and Art.* Indiana Series in Philosophy of Technology. Bloomington: Indiana University Press, 1990.

GENRE ISSUES: PESSIMISM, CYBERNOIR, EXTREME CINEMA, POPULAR LITERATURE. The 1960s see the emergence of a genre or set of subgenres in popular culture marked by deep pessimism about the overall direction of society, culture, and eventually politics, pessimism so thoroughgoing that only a total change in direction could possibly yield true improvement. While the television series *The Prisoner* marks the full development of this genre as a phenomenon of the Atlantic world, it of course has roots and ancestry, notably in science fiction horror, certainly in forties noir cinema, and notably in Rod Serling's *Twilight Zone.* The argument here is not that knowledge of or casual consumption of a few items in this category is significant, or that deeply pessimistic works may not attain a notoriety that may make them familiar in some degree to a majority audience; the argument is rather that works fully within this pessimistic category also target and help solidify a subculture that—within the rules of encoding allowed by official upbeatness—repeatedly signals its profound skepticism about the positive direction of Anglo-American modernity. In so doing ,the market is delineated for further ventures along these lines in television, film, books, magazines, and in other areas as well (worldview manuals accompanying alternative medicine, for example).

Literature

Cavallaro, Dani. *Cyberpunk and Cyberculture: Science Fiction and the Work of William Gibson.* London: Athlone, 2000.

Fairclough, Robert. *The Prisoner: The Official Companion.* London: I Books, 2002.

Heuser, Sabine. *Virtual Geographies: Cyberpunk at the Intersection of the Postmodern and Science Fiction.* Amsterdam: Rodopi, 2003.

Lucy, Niall. *Postmodern Literary Theory: An Anthology.* Oxford: Blackwell, 2000.

McCaffery, Larry. *Storming the Reality Studio: A Casebook of Cyberpunk and Postmodern Science Fiction.* Durham, N.C.: Duke University Press, 1991.

Spicer, Andrew. *Film Noir.* London: Longman, 2002.

Sterling, Bruce, ed. *Mirrorshades: the Cyberpunk Anthology.* New York: Arbor House, 1986.

PIONEERING SCHOLARSHIP ON PESSIMISM IN POSTWAR POPULAR CULTURE. While raw-sources reportage on the chaotic era of Vietnam was gallantly collected by **Harold Hayes**, and while the litany of familiar names and phenomena finds its standard edition in **Allen J. Matusow,** one must look elsewhere for a secondary thematizing of cultural pessimistic themes in a reflective and methodologically adventurous sociocultural context. It is above all **Tom Engelhardt** who has tried to evoke the emergence of a public, symbolic, and mythic culture of victory after World War II; how that same culture was transformed into its polar opposite in a postVietnam, postWatergate symbol system of weakness and of defeat and withdrawal constitutes, then, the obvious next stage in the unfolding of this cultural complex. **Jodi Dean** has studied Engelhardt carefully and has applied this general perception to the particular instance of the emergence of UFO culture and mythology as a sinister and horror-permeated phenomenon saturated with signals of passivity and impotence. Giving a deeper and fuller explanation for the growth of a mood of alarm and pessimism at the end of the twentieth century and beyond—outside the immediate milieu of political, academic, and media-connected advocates of unlimited use of state resources to outsource everything—falls to the able word-processors of **John Gray** and **Edward Luttwak** (on whom see **Corey Robin**).

Literature

Dean, Jodi. *Aliens in America: Conspiracy Cultures from Outerspace to Cyberspace.* Ithaca: Cornell University Press, 1998.

Engelhardt, Tom. *The End of Victory Culture: Cold War America and the Disillusioning of a Generation.* New York: Basic Books, 1995.

Gray, John. *Enlightenment's Wake: Politics and Culture at the Close of the Modern Age.* London: Routledge, 1995.

Hayes, Harold, ed. *Smiling through the Apocalypse: Esquire's History of the Sixties.* New York: McCall, 1970.

Luttwak, Edward. *Turbo-Capitalism: Winners and Losers in the Global Economy.* London: Weidenfeld & Nicholson, 1998.

———. "Why Fascism is the Wave of the Future." *London Review of Books,* April 7, 1994, 3, 6.

Matusow, Allen J. *The Unraveling of America: A History of Liberalism in the 1960s.* The New American Nation Series. New York: Harper & Row, 1986.

Robin, Corey. "The Ex-Cons: Right-Wing Thinkers Go Left!" *Lingua Franca* 11:1 (2001): cover story. http://linguafranca.mirror.theinfo.org/print/0101/cover_cons.html (last accessed, July 2, 2006.)

EXPLANATION AND ACCOUNTABILITY: CONSPIRACY THEORY AND ITS RELATION TO LITER-ARY AND CULTURAL STUDIES APPROACHES. The overall scenario is the breakdown of straightforward Enlightenment-style accountability and explanatory power in favor of nonaccountable, remote, vague, oblique, invisible, endlessly deferred models implying the extreme difficulty, perhaps impossibility of assessing accountability and hence of attaining justice or positive change—though of course quasimiraculous "apocalyptic" rescues and escapes can be hoped for. The upmarket version includes deconstruction, linguistic theory, Marxism, and psychoanalytic depth sounding, not to mention aromatherapy and vast worldviews allegedly based on quantum physics together with the I Ching; the downmarket version is so-called "commodified conspiracy theory," which reworks old-fashioned simpleminded nut conspiracy theory (group Y is responsible and should be tarred and feathered) into a much more broadly held and respectable excuse for worrying endlessly, blaming all and sundry but nobody so much as to call for the tar and feathers, and thus doing almost nothing, especially in mainstream American politics. The remarks above are based on a synoptic reading of the works below. It is also worth pointing out that the school of **David Riesman** seems to have a certain connection with all this, in that for them and their master, the exhausting world of other-directedness attempts to compensate for loss of sense of effective power and agency by making a great deal about access to supersecret and allegedly significant secret information about how the world is really run ("inside dopesterism" and similar phrases resound in this school), with Clinton's impeachment and celebrity gossip talk shows as one of the way stations on civic humanism's evolution into whatever it is becoming; see also **Stjepan Meštrović** and his treatment of David Riesman and the concept of the "inside-dopester" or "inside-dopesterism." As for the pure version of conspiracy theory, it is richly elaborated in the works by **Birchall, Fenster, Knight, and Melley.** For conspiracy in the context of a defense of intelligible unraveling of causal factors, see **Scott.**

Literature

Birchall, Clare. "The Commodification of Conspiracy Theory." Pages 205–32 in *Conspiracy Notion: The Politics of Paranoia in Postwar America.* Edited by Peter Knight. New York: New York University Press, 2002.

Fenster, Mark. *Conspiracy Theories: Secrecy and Power in American Culture.* Minneapolis: University of Minnesota Press, 2001.

Himmelfarb, Gertrude. *The New History and the Old: Critical Essays and Reappraisals.* Rev. ed. Cambridge, Mass.: Belknap, 2004.

Jameson, Fredric. "Cognitive Mapping." Pages 347–58 in *Marxism and the Interpretation of Culture.* Edited by Cary Nelson and Lawrence Grossberg. Basingstoke: Macmillan, 1988.

Knight, Peter. *Conspiracy Culture: From the Kennedy Assassination to* The X-Files. London: Routledge, 2000.

———, ed. *Conspiracy Nation: The Politics of Paranoia in Postwar America.* New York: New York University Press, 2002.

Melley, Timothy. *Empire of Conspiracy: The Culture of Paranoia in Postwar America.* Ithaca: Cornell University Press, 1999.

Meštrović, Stjepan. *Postemotional Society.* With a foreword by David Riesman. London: SAGE Publications, 1997. See in particular his discussion of the "insider dopester" in relation to "inside dopesterism" and the heritage of David Riesman on pages 58 and 162.

Minogue, Kenneth R. *Alien Powers: The Pure Theory of Ideology.* London: Weidenfeld & Nicolson, 1985.

Marcus, George E., ed. *Paranoia within Reason: A Casebook on Conspiracy as Explanation.* Late Editions: Cultural Studies for the End of the Century 6. Chicago: University of Chicago Press, 1999.

Pratt, Ray. "Essay Review: Theorizing Conspiracy—Before and After 9/11." http://64.233.161.104/search?q=cache:qDKhce5YEpcJ:mtprof.msun.edu/Spr2002/Pratt.html+pratt+theorizing+fenster&hl=en&gl=us&ct=clnk&cd=1 (last accessed July 2, 2006).

Riesman, David. *The Lonely Crowd: A Study of the Changing American Character.* With Nathan Glazer and Reuel Denney. New Haven: Yale University Press, 1950; rpt. 1961.

Scott, Peter Dale. *Politics and the Death of JFK.* Berkeley: University of California Press, 1996.

PARTICULARITIES OF AMERICAN THEMES IN GENERAL AND THEIR TANGLED ROOTS. The roots and ambiguities of the American political heritage begin to emerge in **Stephen Graubard, J. G. A. Pocock, Athanasios Moulakis, George Nash, Howard Zinn,** and **Erik von Kuehnelt-Leddihn.** The essential uselessness of any contemporary concept of conservatism, long before debates began about Neocons, was already made clear by **Panajotis Kondylis.** The peculiarities of an English Protestant founding imbued with messianism and the desire to reinforce its identity with infusions of refugees can be sensed by a synoptic reading of **Ernest Lee Tuveson** and **George Steiner**. For a learned American take on one of the numerous near-invisible elephants in the many mansions of American platitudinous historiography, specifically the pachydermic question of whether most early Americans ever intended to found a secularized polity at all and what subsequently has become of their intentions, one must turn to the alarmed (but not necessarily insightdeprived) fringe, that is, to **Gary North**, whose reconstructionist or Dominionist, and antipluralist, antiFreemasonic, and free-market homage to Charles Beard suggests much about the uneasy place of Christianity in upscale American culture today. Important and suggestive material on the persistence of an antiexpansionist and antiwar stratum in American society shows up in **Barbara Tuchman, Richard M. Gamble,** and **Samuel McCall**. This material does not lack in relevance for contemporary topics precisely because its clear emergence dates from the debate about war with Spain over Cuba and other matters. For the meeting of conspiracy views with the contours of power blocs in American history, see the work by **Oglesby**.

Literature

Gamble, Richard M. *The War for Righteousness: Progressive Christianity, the Great War, and the Rise of the Messianic Nation.* Wilmington, Del.: ISI Books, 2003.

Graubard, Stephen R. "Democracy." Pages 653–67 in *The Dictionary of the History of Ideas: Studies of Selected Pivotal Ideas.* Vol. 1. Edited by Philip P. Wiener. New York: Charles Scribner's Sons, 1973f.

Kondylis, Panajotis. *Konservativismus: Geschichtlicher Gehalt und Untergang.* Stuttgart: Klett-Cotta, 1998.

Kuehnelt-Leddihn, Erik von. *Gleichheit oder Freiheit? Demokratie, ein babylonischer Turmbau?* Tübingen: Hohenrain, 1985.

Macpherson, C. B. *The Political Theory of Possessive Individualism: Hobbes to Locke.* Oxford: Clarendon, 1962.

McCall, Samuel W. *The Life of Thomas Brackett Reed.* Boston: Houghton Mifflin, 1914.

Moulakis, Athanasios. "Civic Humanism." In *The Stanford Encyclopedia of Philosophy.* 2002 edition. Edited by Edward N. Zalta. http://plato.stanford.edu/archives/win2002/entries/humanism-civic/ (last accessed July 5, 2006).

Nash, George H. *The Conservative Intellectual Movement in America.* 2nd ed. Wilmington, Del.: Intercollegiate Studies Institute, 1998.

North, Gary. *Political Polytheism: The Myth of Pluralism.* Tyler, Tex.: Institute for Christian Economics, 1989. North has expanded his argument for not an economic but a deistical-freemasonic takeover in an online version unabashedly titled *Conspiracy in Philadelphia: Origins of the United States Constitution.* Harrisonburg, Va.: Dominion Educational Ministries, 2004. http://www.demischools.org/philadelphia.pdf (last accessed July 7, 2006).

Oglesby, Carl. *The Yankee and Cowboy War: Conspiracies from Dallas to Watergate.* Kansas City, Mo.: Sheed Andrews & McMeel, 1976.

Pocock, J. G. A. *The Machiavellian Moment: Florentine Political Thought and the Atlantic Republican Tradition.* Princeton: Princeton University Press, 1975.

Steiner, George. "The Archives of Eden (1981)." Pages 266–303 in his *No Passion Spent: Essays, 1978–1996.* London: Faber & Faber, 1996.

Tuchman, Barbara W. *The Proud Tower.* New York: Ballantine Books, 1996.

Tuveson, Ernest Lee. *Redeemer Nation: The Idea of America's Millennial Role.* Chicago: University of Chicago Press, 1980.

Zinn, Howard. *A People's History of the United States: 1492–Present.* 20th anniv. ed. New York: HarperCollins, 1999.

"CIVIL RELIGION" AS FACTOR AND INDICATOR IN THE SOCIOPOLITICAL SITUATION. At various points in the main text we have introduced the concept of "civil religion" in **Catherine Albanese**'s sense as a notion used to invoke a national unity that at each stage represents more an ideal than a reality—and certainly a goal that neither the academic concept of civil religion nor the symbols and rituals associated with it can produce on their own. Here we would mention in particular the works of **Robert Bellah** and **Rolf Schieder**.

Literature

Albanese, Catherine L. *America: Religions and Religion.* 2nd ed. Belmont, Calif.: Wadsworth, 1992.

Bellah, Robert Neelly. *The Broken Covenant: American Civil Religion in Time of Trial.* 2nd ed. Chicago: University of Chicago Press, 1992.

———. "Civil Religion in America," *Daedalus* 96 (1967): 1–21.

———. "Religion and the Legitimation of the American Republic." *Society* 15 (1978): 16–23.

Schieder, Rolf. *Civil Religion: Die religiöse Dimension der politischen Kultur.* Gütersloh: Gerd Mohn, 1987.

AMERICAN EVANGELICALISM AND DISPENSATIONALISM. The general material is in **Sydney Ahlstrom** and **Mark Noll**, the highly technical in **Ernest Sandeen**, the culturally significant in **Paul Boyer** and **George Marsden**, and the currently significant against its context in **Glenn Shuck**. The dominionist currents are surveyed by **Michelle Goldberg**.

Literature

Ahlstrom, Sydney E. *A Religious History of the American People.* Foreword and concluding chapter by David D. Hall. 2nd ed. New Haven: Yale University Press, 2004.

Boyer, Paul S. *When Time Shall Be No More: Prophecy Belief in Modern American Culture*. Cambridge, Mass.: Belknap Press, 1992.

Goldberg, Michelle. *Kingdom Coming: The Rise of Christian Nationalism*. New York: W. W. Norton, 2006.

Harding, Susan. "Imagining the Last Days: The Politics of Apocalyptic Language." Pages 57–78 in *Accounting for Fundamentalisms: The Dynamic Character of Movements*. Edited by Martin E. Marty and R. Scott Appleby. Chicago: University of Chicago Press, 1994.

Marsden, George M. *Fundamentalism and American Culture: The Shaping of Twentieth Century Evangelicalism, 1870–1925*. New York: Oxford University Press, 1980.

Noll, Mark A. *American Evangelical Christianity: An Introduction*. Malden, Mass.: Blackwell, 2000.

Sandeen, Ernest Robert. *The Roots of Fundamentalism: British and American Millenarianism, 1800–1930*. Chicago: University of Chicago Press, 1970.

Shuck, Glenn W. *Marks of the Beast: The* Left Behind *Novels and the Struggle for Evangelical Identity*. New York: New York University Press, 2005.

THE NOTION OF "PSEUDO-ESCAPE." As employed here, the notion of "pseudoescape" makes use of the category of latent function developed in sociology by **Robert K. Merton** and readily combined with the social ritual approach of Victor Turner outlined in **Catherine Bell** and put into a different context by **Natalie Davis**.

Literature

Bell, Catherine M. *Ritual: Perspectives and Dimensions*. New York: Oxford University Press, 1997.

Davis, Natalie Zemon. "The Reasons of Misrule: Youth Groups and Charivaris in Sixteenth-Century France." *Past and Present* 50 (1971): 41–75.

———. "The Rites of Violence." Pages 152–87 in her *Society and Culture in Early Modern France*. Stanford: Stanford University Press, 1975.

Merton, Robert K. *Social Theory and Social Structure*. Glencoe, Ill.: Free Press, 1957.

DAVID RIESMAN, CIVIC HUMANIST PARTICIPATORY IDEALS IN GOVERNMENT, AND THE "WEAKENING SENSE OF EFFECTIVE AGENCY" OR THE "HOLLOWED OUT SELF." While the connection—interface?—between sociopolitical forces and a defective sense of agency emerges in the work of John Gray (considered elsewhere), the ideal of civic humanism sketched by **Athanasios Moulakis** is also worthy of attention. The specifically digital is looked at by many authors, some mentioned elsewhere here; to that list we add the work of **Lisa Yaszek**. For the conspiratorial angle, see **Timothy Melley**; for the literary viewpoint, see the similarly focused work by **Gabriele Schwab**. The classic and clear sociological presentation can be consulted in the work of **David Riesman** and his follower **Stjepan G. Meštrović**. The clear metaphysical accounts in psychological context we find in

William Barrett and **Jeffrey Boyd**; the upmarket account for followers of theory of theory is always already deployed by **Slavoj Žižek**, and quite skillfully by the way.

Literature

Barrett, William. *Death of the Soul: From Descartes to the Computer.* 1st ed. Garden City, N.Y.: Anchor Press, 1986.

Boyd, Jeffrey H. *Reclaiming the Soul: The Search for Meaning in a Self-Centered Culture.* Cleveland, Ohio: Pilgrim Press, 1996.

Melley, Timothy. "Agency Panic and the Culture of Conspiracy." Pages 57–81 in *Conspiracy Nation: The Politics of Paranoia in Postwar America.* Edited by Peter Knight. New York: New York University Press, 2002.

———. *Empire of Conspiracy: The Culture of Paranoia in Postwar America.* Ithaca: Cornell University Press, 1999.

Meštrović, Stjepan G. *Postemotional Society.* With a foreword by David Riesman. London: SAGE Publications, 1997.

Moulakis, Athanasios. "Civic Humanism." In *The Stanford Encyclopedia of Philosophy.* 2002 Edition. Edited by Edward N. Zalta. http://plato.stanford.edu/archives/win2002/entries/humanism-civic/ (last accessed July 5, 2006).

Riesman, David. *The Lonely Crowd: A Study of the Changing American Character.* With Nathan Glazer and Reuel Denney. New Haven: Yale University Press, 1950; rpt. 1961.

Schwab, Gabriele. *Subjects without Selves: Transitional Texts in Modern Fiction.* Cambridge, Mass.: Harvard University Press, 1994.

Yaszek, Lisa. *The Self Wired: Technology and Subjectivity in Contemporary Narrative.* London: Routledge, 2002.

Žižek, Slavoj. *The Fragile Absolute: Or, Why is the Christian Legacy Worth Fighting For?* London: Verso, 2001.

———. *The Ticklish Subject: The Absent Centre of Political Ontology.* London: Verso, 1999–2000.

KEY WORKS: *THE PRISONER*. From the multitude of books, magazines, ephemeral publications, and online items, the authority who stands out is **Robert Fairclough**.

Literature

Fairclough, Robert. *The Prisoner: The Official Companion.* London: I Books, 2002.

———, ed. *The Prisoner: The Original Scripts.* Vol. 2. London: Reynolds & Hearn, 2006.

KEY WORKS: *THE X-FILES*. Details on transcripts of the shooting scripts are embedded in the chapter's endnotes. Readers wishing to buy original scripts can seek them on eBay. The importance of **Paul A. Cantor** here in showing the varied levels of reference to issues of globalization in the series needs repeated emphasis, not only for the varied nature of his stimulating suggestions, but as well for the empirical, pragmatic, and common-sense approach he deploys skillfully to arrive at entirely plausible general conclusions of subtlety and power. The other works listed below deal with various aspects of the series according to the canons of the postmodern academy, the most interesting being the politically oriented of **Douglas Kellner** and the effort at placing the series within the horror tradition by **Jan Delasara**. The articles on religious aspects of the UFO phenomenon collected by **James Lewis** deserve attention as background. Endnotes 13–15 for the main chapter on this series discuss significant online treatments of the series' so-called "Mytharc" or overall storyline. Also important is the discussion of the angle of conspiratorial narrative in **Mark Fenster**.

Literature

Burns, Christy L. "Erasure: Alienation, Paranoia, and the Loss of Memory in *The X-Files.*" *Camera Obscura: Feminism, Culture, and Media Studies* 15.3 (2001): 195–224.

Cantor, Paul A. "Mainstreaming Paranoia: *The X-Files* and the Delegitimation of the Nation-State." Pages 111–98 in his *Gilligan Unbound: Pop Culture in the Age of Globalization.* Lanham, Md.: Rowman & Littlefield, 2001.

Delasara, Jan. *Poplit, Popcult and* The X-Files: *A Critical Explanation.* Jefferson, N.C.: McFarland, 2000.

Fenster, Mark. *Conspiracy Theories: Secrecy and Power in American Culture.* Minneapolis: University of Minnesota Press, 1999.

Kellner, Douglas. "The *X-Files* and the Aesthetics and Politics of Postmodern Pop." *The Journal of Aesthetics and Art Criticism* 57.1 (1998): 161–75.

———. "*The X-Files* and Conspiracy: A Diagnostic Critique." Pages 205–32 in *Conspiracy Nation: The Politics of Paranoia in Postwar America.* New York: New York University Press, 2002.

Lewis, James R. *The Gods Have Landed: New Religions from Other Worlds.* Albany: State University of New York Press, 1995.

Lowry, Brian, Chris Carter, and Sarah Stegall. *The Truth Is Out There.* The Official Guide to *The X-Files* 1. New York: HarperPrism, 1995.

McGrath, Charles. "It Just Looks Paranoid." *The New York Times,* June 14, 1998, late ed. sect. 6, p. 56, col. 1. http://web.lexis-nexis.com/universe/document?_m =b5d07bd6e67d889b851b5a9231684286&_docnum=2&wchp=dGLbVtb-zSkVb&_md5=83dcfb89f0ae4be9273558ba79ec0f53 (last accessed August 9, 2003).

KEY WORKS: *LEFT BEHIND.* Details concerning the series itself are embedded in the endnotes to the chapter. Out of the vast sea of commentary on this series we mention

Joan Didion and **Paul Boyer** as examples of the encounter between dispensationalist material and high-end culture, **George Marsden** for the historical roots of a general kind in American fundamentalism, **Glenn Shuck**'s monograph for its work in bridging several worlds while reading the same set of hair-raising texts, and **Amy Frykholm**'s book for its systematic overview of the culture enframing the phenomenon of contemporary Dispensationalism.

Literature

Boyer, Paul S. *When Time Shall Be No More: Prophecy Belief in Modern American Culture.* Cambridge, Mass.: Belknap Press, 1992.

Didion, Joan. "Op-Ed: Mr. Bush and the Divine." Review of *Armageddon: The Cosmic Battle of the Ages* by Tim F. LaHaye and Jerry B. Jenkins. *New York Review of Books,* November 6, 2003. http://www.why-war.com/news/2003/11/06/mrbushth.html (last accessed July 4, 2006).

Frykholm, Amy Johnson. *Left Behind in Evangelical America.* New York: Oxford University Press, 2004.

Marsden, George M. *Fundamentalism and American Culture: The Shaping of Twentieth Century Evangelicalism, 1870–1925.* New York: Oxford University Press, 1980.

Shuck, Glenn W. *Marks of the Beast: The* Left Behind *Novels and the Struggle for Evangelical Identity.* New York: New York University Press, 2005.

KEY WORKS: *FIGHT CLUB*. Details concerning the novel and the shooting script occur in the endnotes to the chapter. Of the voluminous and at times polemical, at times highly theoretical discussion of the film, we single out the few items below as especially worthy of notice and as having affected our discussion. The two poles around which these selections gather are the question of how general the ultimate targeting of the work is, and the possibility of reading the work using high-end theory with political overtones.

Literature

Bunting, Madeleine. "Fighting for Their Lives: It's Been Called a Male Thelma and Louise, but a Brutal New Film Says More about America Than about Men." *The Guardian,* November 15, 1999. http://film.guardian.co.uk/Feature_Story/feature_story/0,4120,103595,00.html (last accessed June 27, 2006).

Diken, Bülent, and Carsten Bagge Laustsen, "Enjoy Your Fight!"—*Fight Club* as a Symptom of the Network Society." *Cultural Values. The Journal for Cultural Research,* 6:4 (2002): 349–67. http://www.xs4all.nl/~mlab/con_gress/7a4fightclub.html (last accessed, June 27, 2006). Also published by the Department of Sociology, Lancaster University, Lancaster. http://www.comp

.lancs.ac.uk/sociology/papers/Diken-Laustsen-Enjoy-Your-Fight.pdf (last accessed June 27, 2006).

Faludi, Susan. "It's 'Thelma and Louise' for Guys." *Newsweek,* October 25, 1999, 89.

Greenwood, Kate. "You Are not a Beautiful and Unique Snowflake: Fighting and Ideology in *Fight Club.*" http://64.233.161.104/search?q=cache: HKZXpctD60UJ:journal.media-culture.org.au/0302/09-snowflake.php+gree nwood+beautiful+unique+snowflake+kate&hl=en&gl=us&ct=clnk&cd=1 (last accessed, June 27, 2006).

Palahniuk, Chuck. *Fight Club.* New York: Henry Holt, 1996.

Redd, Adrienne. "Masculine Identity in the Service Class: An Analysis of *Fight Club.*" http://www.criticism.com/md/fightclub.html (last accessed June 27, 2006).

Žižek, Slavoj. "The Ambiguity of the Masochist Social Link." Pages 112–25 in *Perversion and the Social Relation.* Edited by Molly Anne Rothenberg, et al. Durham, N.C.: Duke University Press, 2003.

KEY WORKS: NEW AGE MATERIALS. Here we concentrate on the most important secondary presentations while including the programmatic primary works by **Mark Woodhouse** and **William Tiller**. The most intelligent and learned comprehensive study is that by **Christoph Bochinger**; the most provocative hypothesis overall is that of **Catherine Albanese**.

Literature

Albanese, Catherine. "The Magical Staff: Quantum Healing in the New Age." Pages 68–84 in *Perspectives on the New Age.* Edited by J. R. Lewis and J. G. Melton. SUNY Series in Religious Studies. Albany: State University of New York Press, 1992.

Bochinger, Christoph. *"New Age" und moderne Religion: Religionswissenschaftliche Analysen.* München: Chr. Kaiser Verlag, 1995.

Ellwood, Robert. "How New is the New Age?" Pages 59–67 in *Perspectives on the New Age.* Edited by J. R. Lewis and J. G. Melton. SUNY Series in Religious Studies. Albany: State University of New York, 1992.

Hammer, Olav. *Claiming Knowledge: Strategies of Epistemology from Theosophy to the New Age.* Numen Book Series 90. Leiden: E. J. Brill, 2001.

Hanegraaf, Wouter J. *New Age Religion and Western Culture: Esotericism in the Mirror of Secular Thought.* SUNY Series in Western Esoteric Traditions. Albany: State University of New York, 1998.

Heelas, Paul. *The New Age Movement: The Celebration of the Self and the Sacralization of Modernity.* Oxford: Blackwell, 1996.

Tacey, David. *Jung and the New Age.* London: Brunner-Routledge, 2001.

Tiller, William A. *Science and Human Transformation: Subtle Energies, Intentionality and Consciousness.* Walnut Creek, Calif.: Pavior, 1997.

Woodhouse, Mark. *Paradigm Wars; Worldviews for a New Age.* Berkeley, Calif.: Frog Press, 1996.

EMPIRICAL ASPECTS OF MILLENNIAL AMERICA: SOCIOECONOMIC. A variety of secondary supporting material on the economic and social hard times of the segments targeted by producers of cultural pessimism documents appears at various points in the text of this book, material of course selected to supplement the heavily filtered (upbeat) material in the mainstream media. For the estimate that the average hourly wage of the Wal-Mart CEO in 2006 was $12,000 aside from benefits, see **Ralph Nader**. Among the other most noteworthy items are those listed below, with the selection favoring those giving an overview.

Literature

Cox, Harvey. "The Market as God: Living in the New Dispensation." *Atlantic Monthly* 283.3 (1999): 18, 20–24.

Faux, Jeff. *The Global Class War: How America's Bipartisan Elite Lost Our Future—and What It Will Take to Win It Back*. New York: John Wiley & Sons, 2006.

Jeffrey Madrick. *The End of Affluence: The Causes and Consequences of America's Economic Dilemma*. New York: Random House, 1997.

Nader, Ralph. "The Politics of the Minimum Wage: A Congress with Marie Antoinette Values." *Counterpunch*, July 6, 2006. http://www.counterpunch.org/nader07062006.html (last accessed July 6, 2006).

Pollin, Robert. *Contours of Descent: U.S. Economic Fractures and the Landscape of Global Austerity*. London: Verso, 2005.

Roberts, Paul Craig. "Hegemony Lost: The American Economy is Destroying Itself." *Counterpunch*, August 25, 2005. http://www.counterpunch.org/roberts08252005.html (last accessed July 2, 2006).

———. "How the Economic News is Spun: When You Can't Obscure the News, Buy It." *Counterpunch*, March 2, 2006. http://www.counterpunch.org/roberts03022006.html (last accessed June 27, 2006).

ASPECTS OF MILLENNIAL AMERICA, ESPECIALLY MOOD AND MENTALITIES AFTER 9/11. Here we highlight the confrontation between American sense of mission, exceptionalism, and refuge and a world seemingly intent on impinging on its Last Best Hope.

Literature

Barkun, Michael. *A Culture of Conspiracy: Apocalyptic Visions in Contemporary America*. Comparative Studies in Religion and Society 15. Berkeley: University of California Press, 2003.

Berman, Morris. "The Meaning of 9/11." Pages 201–34 in his *Dark Ages America: The Final Phase of Empire*. New York: W.W. Norton, 2006.

Edinger, Edward F. *Archetype of the Apocalypse: A Jungian Study of the Book of Revelation*. Edited by George R. Elder. Chicago, Ill.: Open Court, 1999.

Hulsman, John C., and Anatol Lieven. "The Ethics of Realism." *The National Interest* (Summer 2005): 37–43.

Kleinhenz, Christopher, and Fannie J. LeMoine. *Fearful Hope: Approaching the New Millennium*. Madison: University of Wisconsin Press, 1999.

Lieven, Anatol. *America Right or Wrong: An Anatomy of American Nationalism*. New York: Oxford University Press, 2005.

Potter, David Morris. *People of Plenty: Economic Abundance and the American Character*. Chicago: University of Chicago Press, 1954.

Ryn, Claes. *America the Virtuous: the Crisis of Democracy and the Quest for Empire*. New Brunswick, N.J.: Transaction Publishers, 2003.

Steiner, George. "The Archives of Eden (1981)." Pages 266–303 in his *No Passion Spent: Essays, 1978–1996*. London: Faber & Faber, 1996.

Tuveson, Ernest Lee. *Redeemer Nation: The Idea of America's Millennial Role*. Chicago: University of Chicago Press, 1980.

Vidal, Gore. *Perpetual War for Perpetual Peace*. New York: Thunder's Mouth. Press/ Nation Books, 2002.

Zoja, Luigi, and Donald Williams, eds. *Jungian Reflections on September 11: A Global Nightmare*. Einsiedeln: Daimon Verlag, 2002.

EMPIRICAL ASPECTS OF MILLENNIAL AMERICA: "WILD MANEUVERS" OF GOVERNMENTAL AGENCIES AS SIGNS OF SYSTEM STRESS. While the extreme speed and diversity of government-related outgrowths over the last thirty to forty years is extensively documented in the notes to the relevant section of our text, we single out as especially interesting the items by **Gene Healy** and **Timothy Lynch**, **James Risen**, **Chalmers Johnson**, and **Philippe Sands**. The burgeoning literature on intelligence operations defies cataloging in a work of this kind.

Literature

Healy, Gene, and Timothy Lynch. *Power Surge: The Constitutional Record of George W. Bush*. Washington, D.C.: Cato Institute, 2006. http://www.cato.org/pubs/wtpapers/powersurge_healy_lynch.pdf (last accessed July 4, 2006).

Johnson, Chalmers. *The Sorrows of Empire: Militarism, Secrecy, and the End of the Republic*. New York: Metropolitan Books/Henry Holt, 2004.

Risen, James. *State of War: The Secret History of the CIA and the Bush Administration*. New York: Simon & Schuster/Free Press, 2006.

Sands, Philippe. *Lawless World: Making and Breaking Global Rule*. Harmondsworth, Sussex: Penguin, 2006.

EMPIRICAL ASPECTS OF MILLENNIAL AMERICA: "WILD MANEUEVERS" OF A NONGOVERN-MENTAL SORT AS SIGNS OF SYSTEM STRESS. The sections of the main text document these phenomena extensively. For reflection on the "cult" and "conspiratorial" aspects of the problem, see especially the works by **Michael Barkun, Jeffrey Kaplan**, and **Catherine Wessinger**.

Literature

Barkun, Michael. *A Culture of Conspiracy: Apocalyptic Visions in Contemporary America.* Comparative Studies in Religion and Society 15. Berkeley: University of California Press, 2003.

Kaplan, Jeffrey, and Heléne Lööw, eds. *The Cultic Milieu: Oppositional Subcultures in an Age of Globalization.* Walnut Creek, Calif.: AltaMira, 2002.

Wessinger, Catherine Lowman. *How the Millennium Comes Violently: From Jonestown to Heaven's Gate.* New York: Seven Bridges Press, 2000.

LEGALITY ISSUES CONTRASTED WITH LEGITIMACY ISSUES AND THEIR UNDERLYING RELATION TO RELIGION. The strong measures currently in use in the United States and Britain to ward off acts of terror and to glue together the social fabric suggest that the fit between the framework of law and the structure of society is scarcely adequate and that their underlying compatibility is sensed as increasingly unreliable—that is, that a crisis of legitimacy of the regime is lurking as a possibility under certain circumstances. The underlying tension between Enlightenment-derived polities tending toward secularization and the roots of the societies in religiously legitimated modes of thought and action is, so to speak, the big elephant in the room. The items listed below look at various aspects of this intractable problem, some from a more than American perspective.

Literature

Creveld, Martin van. *The Rise and Decline of the State.* Cambridge: Cambridge University Press, 1999.

"Forum: AMERICAN COUP D'ETAT: Military Thinkers Discuss the Unthinkable." Andrew J. Bacevich, Brig. Gen. Charles J. Dunlap, Jr., Richard H. Kohn, and Edward N. Luttwak. *Harper's,* April 2006, 43–52.

Horton, Scott. "The Return of Carl Schmitt." *Balkinization* [sic] (November 7, 2005). http://balkin.blogspot.com/2005/11/return-of-carl-schmitt.html (last accessed July 1, 2006).

Molnar, Thomas. *Twin Powers: Politics and the Sacred.* Grand Rapids: Eerdmans, 1988.

Neuhaus, Richard. *The Naked Public Square: Religion and Democracy in America.* 2nd ed. Grand Rapids: Eerdmans, 1986.

North, Gary. *Political Polytheism: The Myth of Pluralism.* Tyler, Tex.: Institute for Christian Economics, 1989.

Schmitt, Carl. *Legality and Legitimacy.* Edited and translated by Jeffrey Seitzer. Durham, N.C.: Duke University Press, 2004.

Schwab, George. *The Challenge of the Exception: An Introduction to the Political Ideas of Carl Schmitt between 1921 and 1936.* 2nd ed. New York: Greenwood Press, 1989.

CULTURAL PESSIMISM AND ENERGIZING COMPETING BASES: RIGHT VERSUS LEFT. How one assesses various strategies for energizing different political segments, and how one assesses long-term chances for effective political integration of America, depends of course on many points. Some observers (e.g., **Thomas Molnar**) doubt the survivability of post-Enlightenment political pluralism, while others (e.g., **Richard Neuhaus**) uphold it. There are also varying points of view on whether the secularizing decisions of the Supreme Court and allied phenomena of the later twentieth century were or were not all that causative in the religious reaction now in progress (see **Kevin Phillips** and **Daniel McCarthy**). But that the United States represents a particularly complex case of modernity and religious antimodernity seems beyond question.

Literature

McCarthy, Daniel. "The Authoritarian Movement." *LewRockwell.com,* June 30, 2006. http://www.lewrockwell.com/dmccarthy/dmccarthy60.html (last accessed July 4, 2006).

Molnar, Thomas. *Twin Powers: Politics and the Sacred.* Grand Rapids: Eerdmans, 1988.

Neuhaus, Richard. *The Naked Public Square: Religion and Democracy in America.* 2nd ed. Grand Rapids: Eerdmans, 1986.

Phillips, Kevin. *American Theocracy: The Peril and Politics of Radical Religion, Oil, and Borrowed Money in the Twenty-First Century.* New York: Viking, 2006.

SIGNIFICANCE OF TOTEMIZATION OF THE MILITARY IN MILLENNIAL AMERICA WITH REGARD TO IMPERIAL CENTRALIZATION AND THE SUBVERSION OF EGALITARIAN CITIZENSHIP AND INCLUSIVE INTEGRATION OF THE POLITY. No one author has adequately put together the sociological and political significance of the postWatergate reliance in America on a warrior caste mythologized as superheroic and supersacral and for that reason uniquely necessary for community-validating purposes. **Andrew Bacevich** has seen more than other writers in this direction. **Karen Kwiatkowski** senses the ramifications of the new uses for the phrase "Commander in Chief." **Michael Vlahos** meditates intelligently on the way that empires require emperors. **Kevin Phillips**, in his remarks on dynasty, hints at the degree to which egalitarian norms are in the process of being undercut by hierarchical and plutocratic norms, a process which to my knowledge no observer of contemporary America has connected well with the increasingly sacral status of the military establishment and the explicit sanction of the entire process by the newer varieties of evangelical Christianity. The broader context emerges in **Claes Ryn** and **Chris Hedges**.

Literature

Bacevich, Andrew J. *The New American Militarism*. New York: Oxford University Press, 2005.

Hedges, Chris. *War Is a Force That Gives Us Meaning*. New York: Public Affairs, 2005.

Higgs, Robert. *Resurgence of the Warfare State: The Crisis since 9/11*. San Francisco: Independent Institute, 2005.

Kwiatkowski, Karen. "We Are All Forrest Gumps." *LewRockwell.com*, June 30, 2006. http://www.lewrockwell.com/kwiatkowski/kwiatkowski154.html (last accessed July 4, 2006.

Phillips, Kevin. "The Dynastization of America." Pages 51–72 in his *American Dynasty: Aristocracy, Fortune, and the Politics of Deceit in the House of Bush*. New York: Viking, 2004.

Ryn, Claes. *America the Virtuous: The Crisis of Democracy and the Quest for Empire*. New Brunswick, N.J.: Transaction Publishers, 2003.

Vlahos, Michael. "The Weakness of Empire." *The American Conservative*, May 22, 2006. http://www.amconmag.com/2006/2006_05_22/cover.html (last accessed July 4, 2006).

"FASCISM" IN NORTH AMERICA? While our position here is that tendencies toward authoritarianism in America should not be characterized as "fascist" due to their reliance on a unitary anthropology, one should not overlook the long-term potential of factors tending to offset that anthropology (e.g., ascribing sacral superhuman status to the military, plutocratic fostering of hierarchic norms, political fragmentation resulting from group-based politics). Among those with whom we disagree, that is, those tending to label millennial America as incipiently fascist, we would name **Justin Raimundo** and **David Neiwert**. Background on authoritarianism can be found, for example, in **Karen Kwiatkowski, Donald Shriver, and Elizabeth Drew.**

Literature

Drew, Elizabeth. "Power Grab." *New York Review of Books*, June 22, 2006. http://www.nybooks.com/articles/19092 (last accessed July 4, 2006).

Kwiatkowski, Karen. "We Are All Forrest Gumps." *LewRockwell.com*, June 30, 2006. http://www.lewrockwell.com/kwiatkowski/kwiatkowski154.html (last accessed July 4, 2006).

Neiwert, David. "The Rise of Pseudo Fascism." Six-part online series posted beginning September 19, 2004. http://dneiwert.blogspot.com/2004_09_19_dneiwert_archive.html (last accessed July 4, 2006).

Raimundo, Justin. "A Fascist America: How Close Are We?" *Antiwar.com*, March 4, 2005. http://www.antiwar.com/justin/?articleid=5070 (last accessed July 4, 2006).

Shriver, Donald W. "The Insecurity State." *The Nation,* June 5, 2006. http://www.thenation.com/docprint.mhtml?i=20060605&s=shriver (last accessed July 4, 2006).

THE PARADOX OF THE KEY FACT OF SEARCH FOR SURVIVABLE CONTINUITY: THE ENSHRINING OF MYTH AS A SELF-LIMITING BASIS FOR POLITICS AND POLICY. In a sense the book is an extended meditation on corollaries of **John Gray**'s argument—the thesis that a resort to myth ("cultural fundamentalism") in support of endangered sociocultural sense of identity and perceived survivability becomes necessary due to the advance of community-destroying derivatives of the Enlightenment, notably the derivatives of neoliberal globalized capitalism. Certainly the spread of polity-fragmenting challenges to unitary or egalitarian citizenship (e.g., the totemization of the sacralized military caste, group-based political factionalism) heightens the need for myths of inclusion even as the reliance on intense religious mythology and the totemized military fail to overcome the fragmenting potential built in to their use. The degree to which this process of intensifying use of myth and "cultural fundamentalism" may prove to be traumatically self-limiting is not yet known. Military historian **Andrew Bacevich** presents Ronald Reagan's triumph over Jimmy Carter as a case of intensified myth in action, stressing both Reagan's post-oil-embargo retrieval of the myth of validation through endless abundance purchased by faith in the feasibility of dependence on Middle Eastern oil, and Reagan's post-Vietnam lead in totemization of the sacralized military as Superamericans (indeed, reading Bacevich on Reagan's myth-soaked "overcoming" of feelings of impotence, one senses the intuitive explanatory power of what Engelhardt and Jodi Dean have attempted in as it were showing how the way for Reagan was prepared by the prior elaboration of public cultures of victorious potency and post-Vietnam impotence). Like all myths, these too can be used in ways that turn them into dangerous and expensive illusions—even with a political system made domestically invulnerable and with a domestic mass media system made largely impervious to evidence disconfirming of myth. To exactly what this reliance on myth may lead in a "reality-based" world of real wars, religious passions, and domestic economic hardship is not yet known, but the confluence of factors suggests the possibility for highly problematical outcomes, an ironic development apparently within the imagining capacity of **Ron Suskind.**

Literature

Bacevich, Andrew J. "Chapter Four. California Dreaming." Pages 97–121 in *The New American Militarism.* New York: Oxford University Press, 2005.

Engelhardt, Tom. "Tomgram: Running with the Barbarians: Green Zoning It All the Way." *TomDispatch.com,* June 25, 2006. http://www.tomdispatch.com/index.mhtml?pid=95863 (last accessed July 24,2007).

Gray, John. *Enlightenment's Wake: Politics and Culture at the Close of the Modern Age.* London: Routledge, 1995.

Suskind, Ron. "Faith, Certainty and the Presidency of George W. Bush." *The New York Times Magazine,* October 17, 2004. http://www.nytimes.com/2004/10/17/magazine/17BUSH.html?ex=1265346000&%2338;en=67e5e499d9ce0514&%2338;ei=5088 (last accessed July 4, 2006).

Suskind, Ron. *The One Percent Doctrine.* New York: Simon & Schuster, 2006.

Notes

Acknowledgments

1. *The New World in the Treasures of an Old European Library / Die Neue Welt in den Schätzen einer alten europäischen Bibliothek*, trans. Rand Henson and Peter Mortzfeld, ed. Yorck Alexander Haase and Harold Jantz. Ausstellungskataloge der Herzog August Bibliothek, Nr. 17 (Braunschweig: Waisenhausdruckerei, 1976).

Preface

1. Robert Fairclough, *The Prisoner: The Official Companion* (London: I Books, 2002), 38.
2. Jacob Burckhardt, *Force and Freedom: Reflections on History*, ed. James Hastings Nichols (New York: Pantheon Books, 1943). More broadly, here we take up the topic of wide-ranging and perhaps systematic variations on social, political, economic, and religious (or ideological) processes as they may affect the fate of Enlightenment-related explicability and accountability. In other places below, the present authors repeatedly discuss the proximity of these themes to the current vogue of conspiracy thinking. The specific topic of "accountability" in relation to interrelated processes of sociopolitical degeneration has been popularized by the memorable, and highly controversial work of Professor Peter Dale Scott, notable in his *Deep Politics and the Death of JFK* (Berkeley: University of California Press, 1996), 6–7, where Scott, ever controversial and plain-spoken, explains his key concepts of "parapolitics" and "deep politics," beginning with "the investigation of parapolitics, which I defined (with the C.I.A. in mind) as 'a system or practice of politics in which accountability is consciously diminished.' . . . The term referred chiefly . . . to the world of intelligence agencies and similar organizations, where secrecy and covert operations were adopted as a matter of deliberate policy." Because now Scott favors a broader approach, he continues, "I now refer to parapolitics as only one manifestation of *deep politics*, all those political practices and arrangements, deliberate or not, which are usually repressed rather than acknowledged." See also Scott, "Is This Post-America? Some Thoughts on the Outbreak of War," http://www.socrates.berkeley/edu/~scott/post.html (last

245

accessed November 27, 2006). Finally let it be said that at the time of writing there exists no reliable way of assessing the relatively autonomous effects of radical Islamic pressure to curtail freedom in Western countries separate from the interaction of Western institutions with agents of Islamic groups of all varieties, a circumstance that renders rational assessment of long-term political prospects more or less impossible. See however John Mueller, *Overblown: How Politicians and the Terrorism Industry Inflate National Security Threats, and Why We Believe Them* (New York: Free Press, 2006). See also Mueller, "Some Reflections on What, If Anything, 'Are We Safer?' Might Mean," *Cato Unbound*, September 11, 2006, at http://www.cato-unbound.org/2006/09/11/john-mueller/are-we-safer/ (last accessed November 22, 2006). Also of interest is the material in Peter Lance, *Triple Cross* (New York: Regan Books, 2006). For Willie O'Keefe on fascism, see "JFK Script—Dialogue Transcript," at http://www.script-o-rama.com/movie_scripts/j/jfk-script.transcript-oliver-stone.html (last accessed July 24, 2007).

3. For the works in question see the Bibliographic Essay.

4. See for example Gore Vidal, "The Erosion of the American Dream," interview, March 12, 2003, in *Prometheus* 86 (2003), http://wwww.means.com/gore-vidal-03.htm (last accessed November 27, 2006). At that place: "We have one party—we have the party of essentially corporate America. It has two right wings, one called Democratic, one called Republican." Vidal's writings and interviews in the later years of his life abound in variations on the "one party" formulation. See also Lou Dobbs, *War on the Middle Class* (New York: Viking, 2006).

5. See the remarks of Theodore Dalrymple in his interview at Jamie Glazov, "Our Culture, What's Left Of It," *FrontPageMagazine.com*, August 31, 2005, at http://www.frontpagemag.com/articles/ReadArticle.asp?ID=19293 (last accessed November 27, 2006).

Chapter 1

1. The lingering figure of Norman O. Brown hovers here over the present authors. See Norman O. Brown, *Life against Death: The Psychoanalytical Meaning of History* (New York: Vintage Books, 1959), 230: "The dynamic of history is the slow return of the repressed." The significance of this principle with regard to the conflicting needs of corporeality and allegedly discarnate intelligent consciousness is well brought out in Mark Dery, *Escape Velocity*, 273–77 and 248, with regard ultimately to the return of "modern primitivism" or tribalism.

2. For the first two analysts see n. 3 below. On Virilio, see for example by Sylvère Lotringer and Paul Virilio *The Accident of Art,* Semiotext(e)/Foreign Agents (London: Verso, 2005); Paul Virilio, *Ground Zero,* trans. Chris Turner (London: Verso, 2002); Jason Adams. "POPULAR DEFENSE IN THE EMPIRE OF SPEED: Paul Virilio and the Phenomenology of the Political Body," M.A. thesis, Simon Fraser University, 2003, online at http://www.geocities.com/ringfingers/thesis.html (unpaginated) (last accessed June 2, 2006); Ian Angus, *Disfigurations: Discourse/Critique/Ethics* (London: Verso, 2000); Andrew Feenberg, *Transforming*

Technology (New York: Oxford University Press, 2002); John Armitage, ed. *Paul Virilio: From Modernism to Hypermodernism and Beyond* (London: SAGE Publications, 2000); John Armitage and Phil Graham, "Dromoeconomics: Towards a Political Economy of Speed," *Parallax* 7:1 (2001): 111–23; Paul Virilio, *Art and Fear* (London: Continuum, 2003); idem., *The Information Bomb* (London: Verso, 2000); idem., *The Aesthetics of Disappearance* (New York: Semiotext[e], 1991); idem., *Lost Dimension* (New York: Semiotext[e], 1991); idem., *Strategy of Deception* (London: Verso, 2000); idem., *War and Cinema: The Logistics of Perception* (London: Verso, 1989); idem., *City of Panic*, trans. Julie Rose (Oxford/New York: Berg, 2004).

3. The thematization of prepackaged emotions is the particular contribution of Meštrović. Cf. Jean Baudrillard, *The Illusion of the End*, trans. Chris Turner (Stanford: Stanford University Press, 1995); Douglas Kellner, *Baudrillard: A Critical Reader* (London: Blackwell, 1994); Stjepan G. Meštrović, *Postemotional Society,* with a foreword by David Riesman (London: SAGE Publications, 1997; on Virilio, see the works cited in the note immediately above); also Douglas Kellner, "Virilio, War and Technology," in *Paul Virilio: From Modernism to Hypermodernism and Beyond,* ed. John Armitage; or as Kellner, "Virilio, War and Technology: Some Critical Reflections," in his *Illuminations: The Critical Theory Project,* http://www.gseis.ucla.edu/faculty/kellner/Illumina%20Folder/kell29.htm (last accessed July 17, 2006). Compare George Ritzer, *The McDonaldization of Society,* 4th ed. (Thousand Oaks, Calif.: Pine Forge Press, 2004); Meštrović, *Postemotional Society.* Sociologist George Ritzer refers to the problem of Americanization as a cultural homogenization process labeled as "McDonaldization." See also David Riesman and Reuel Denney, *The Lonely Crowd: A Study of the Changing American Character* (New Haven: Yale University Press, 1950; rpt. 1961), for the first stage in what these sociologists try to describe.

4. Classic discussion of these issues in Joseph Wood Krutch, *The Modern Temper: A Study and a Confession* (New York: Harcourt Harvest, 1959; 1st ed., 1929).

5. Hayles maintains that humans retain subjectivity, but only what she calls "flickering subjectivity." This is a situation of human agency that is not sustained, in other words, but can only be experienced in fleeting moments.

6. Note also the publication of Robert A. Heinlein's *The Puppet Masters* (New York: Doubleday, 1951), a novel that played into the fears of many Americans that they no longer controlled their lives.

7. This was one of the themes the writers and producers of *The Prisoner* tried to accentuate. Despite numerous hints that the mythical Village was somewhere behind the Iron Curtain, in the final episode they reveal its actual location in Portmeirion, Wales.

8. The problematic nature of overlapping issues of identity and agency also figured in a spectacular way in the interplay between the megasuccess of techno-energized cold war hero Bond and his antiheroic challengers in the figures populating the glum counterintelligence-oriented novels of John Le Carré. For

the latter, the real problems usually centered around matters of psychology, ethics, and mood. In the typical Le Carré situation, not only does technology consistently fail to play a glamorous role that might conceal its sinister tendencies; more important issues of loyalty, identity, and purpose for action become so tangled (and moral questions so messy) that there constantly hovers over the entire ambiguous package an unspoken suggestion of the virtual moral equivalence of the competing Systems—if not indeed their convergence into some lower third outcome.

9. See George Markstein, *The Cooler: The Secret That Can Only Be Told As Fiction* (London: Souvenir Press, 1974); Robert Fairclough, *The Prisoner: The Official Companion to the Classic TV Series* (London: Ibooks, 2002); Robert Fairclough, ed., *The Prisoner: The Official Scripts* (London: Reynolds & Hearn, 2005); Bernie Ross, "Training SOE Saboteurs in World War Two: War and Conflict: World War Two," http://www.bbc.co.uk/history/war/wwtwo/soe_training_01.shtml (last accessed March 22, 2006); Dave Healey, "THE UNMUTUAL PRISONER LOCATIONS GUIDE: INVERLAIR LODGE," http://www.theunmutual.co.uk/inverlair.htm (last accessed March 22, 2006) is the bundle of themes connected with the notion of the Secret Agent and secret agency. See "Chapter 4: Secret Agents," in Timothy Melley, *Empire of Conspiracy: The Culture of Paranoia in Postwar America* (Ithaca: Cornell, 2000): 133–60 for a thematization of various topics clusered around the slogan of the Secret Agent; also Melley, "Agency Panic and the Culture of Conspiracy," in *Conspiracy Nation: The Politics of Paranoia in Postwar America* (New York: New York Press, 2002): 57–84. Melley's special topic is stylized alarm at the perceived loss of (especially individual) agency.

10. The Wild West episode "Living in Harmony" did not impress government censors (nicely ironic, given the context).

11. As noted, McGoohan's attempt to escape his spy status at the peak of his success formed a theme in *The Prisoner*, as he abruptly turned down several high-profile films including the possibility of starring as James Bond in the popular Bond films. Also note that many fans of *The Prisoner* assume the title character's name—which is never given—to be none other than *Danger Man's* John Drake, giving the two serials a sense of continuity.

12. See Mark C. Taylor, *The Moment of Complexity: Emerging Network Culture* (Chicago: University of Chicago Press, 2002). With a flair for elaborate puns, Taylor informs us that in the Information Era, data does not simply surround us, it defines our lives and indeed who we *are*. It, in effect, in-*forms* us.

13. Quoted from several episode scripts by Arthur Asa Berger in "*The Prisoner*. The Museum of Broadcast Communications," http://www.museum.tv/archives/etv/P/htmlP/prisonerthe/prisonerthe.htm (last accessed March 22, 2006).

14. For a similar analysis, see Piers D. Britton and Simon J. Barker, *Reading Between Designs: Visual Imagery and the Generation of Meaning in* The Avengers, The Prisoner, *and* Doctor Who (Austin: University of Texas Press, 2003). The authors focus chiefly on design, architectural, and design issues, but their

critique is far-ranging and insightful, especially as regards *The Prisoner.* See especially p. 102 for more on McGoohan's satire of democracy.

15. See Piers Britton and Simon Barker, along with Mark Bould, "This is the Modern World: *The Prisoner*, authorship, and allegory," in *Popular Television Dramas*, ed. Jonathan Bignell and Stephen Lacey (Manchester: Manchester University Press, 2005). Their insights make for an interesting comparison to those of Elanor Taylor below.

16. Elanor Taylor, "Free for All?" *Social Issues Research Centre* (December 2, 2003) http://www.sirc.org/articles/free_for_all.shtml (last accessed July 26, 2006).

17. Fairclough, *Prisoner* (2002), 51.

18. ———, *Prisoner* (2002), 53.

19. ———, *Prisoner* (2002), 107.

20. Britton and Barker, "This is the Modern World," 106.

21. Scott Bukatman, *Terminal Identity: The Virtual Subject in Postmodern Science Fiction* (Durham, N.C.: Duke University Press, 1993).

22. Leo Marx, *The Machine in the Garden: Technology and the Pastoral Ideal in America* (New York: Oxford University Press, 1964).

23. Bruce Sterling, "Science Fiction" (2006), in *Encyclopædia Britannica*, retrieved from Encyclopædia Britannica Premium Service: http://www.britannica.com/eb/article-235733 (last accessed July 31, 2006).

24. Marx, 211–14.

25. ———, 220–21.

26. ———, 222–26.

27. See for example the essays in Hal Foster, ed., *The Anti-Aesthetic: Essays on Postmodern Culture* (Seattle, Wash.: Bay Press, 1983) for a notion of the limits of the emerging discussion. A fuller look at the technical aspects here would shatter the framework of this brief treatment.

28. With apologies to the celebrated words of Tom Lehrer on Wernher von Braun.

29. As Jodi Dean herself explains in detail, her work is in considerable measure a specialized application of a broader cultural studies perspective pioneeringly presented by Tom Engelhardt in his *The End of Victory Culture: Cold War America and the Disillusioning of a Generation (Culture, Politics, and the Cold War)* (New York: Basic Books, 1995); for all this, see Jodi Dean, *Aliens in America: Conspiracy Cultures from Outerspace to Cyberspace* (Ithaca: Cornell University Press, 1998).

30. Dean, *Aliens in America,* 174.

31. Nicholas Negroponte, *Being Digital* (New York: Vintage, 1996).

32. Hans Moravec, *Robot: Mere Machine to Transcendent Mind* (New York: Oxford University Press, 2000).

33. On Pannenberg's career, we have relied on the overview in Peter Heltzel, "Wolfhart Pannenberg (1928–)," in *Boston Collaborative Encyclopedia of Western Theology: Wolfhart Pannenberg*, ed. Wesley Wildman, http://www.bu.edu/wwildman/WeirdWildWeb/courses/mwt/dictionary/mwt_themes_856_pannenberg.htm#top (last accessed July 22, 2006). See also Jenny Wolmark, "Staying with the Body: Narratives of the Posthuman in Contemporary Science Fiction," in *Edging into*

the Future: Science Fiction and Contemporary Cultural Transformation, ed. Veronica Hollinger and Joan Gordon (Philadelphia: University of Pennsylvania Press, 2002), 75–89; on technology and escape, see Gwyneth Jones, "*Kairos:* The Enchanted Loom," in Hollinger and Gordon, 174–89; on religious aspects of cyberpunk, see Veronica Hollinger, "Apocalypse Coma," in Hollinger and Gordon, 160–73.

See also *Beginning with the End: God, Science, and Wolfhart Pannenberg,* eds. Carol Rausch Albright and Joel Haugen (Chicago: Open Court, 1997); F. LeRon Shults, *The Postfoundationalist Task of Theology: Wolfhart Pannenberg and the New Theological Rationality* (Grand Rapids: Eerdmans, 1999).

34. Wolfhart Pannenberg, "Modern Cosmology: God and the Resurrection of the Dead," lecture given at Innsbruck Conference on Frank Tipler's book *The Physics of Immortality,* June 1997, translated from the German by Wolfhart Pannenberg, http://home-1.tiscali.nl/~sttdc/cosmology.htm (last accessed July 29, 2006).

35. See Pannenberg, "Modern Cosmology"; also Frank J. Tipler, *The Physics of Immortality: Modern Cosmology, God and the Resurrection of the Dead* (New York: Doubleday, 1994); see also at http://www.google.com/search?hl=en&ie=UTF-8&oe=UTF-8&q=pannenberg+tipler: "Frank J. Tipler's Web Site," http://www.math.tulane.edu/~tipler/summary.html (last accessed July 29, 2006); Wolfhart Pannenberg, "God and Resurrection—a reply to Sjoerd L. Bonting," home.worldonline.nl/~sttdc/pannenberg.htm (last accessed July 24, 2007). Cf. John D. Barrow, *The Anthropic Cosmological Principle* (New York: Oxford University Press, 1988); Sharon Begley with Anne Underwood, "Religion and the Brain," *Newsweek,* May 7, 2001, http://findarticles.com/p/articles/mi_kmnew/is_200105/ai_kepm314664 (last accessed July 26, 2006).

36. Tipler, *The Physics of Immortality.* Cf. Barrow, *The Anthropic Cosmological Principle.*

37. See nn. 33–34 above.

38. After the defeat of Napoleon and the French Revolution, nineteenth-century religious revivalists and Romantics, in cooperation with frightened elites in Europe and Britain, had seen to it that in religious enclaves skeptical questioning was itself repressed. See Robert M. Bigler, *The Politics of German Protestantism: The Rise of the Protestant Church Elite in Prussia, 1815–1848* (Berkeley: University of California Press, 1972). In other words, late in Pannenberg's career what has emerged from the subterranean depths of Christian repression is, once again, the bad conscience of modern faith, its embarrassment when confronted with a secularist scientific worldview that proclaims with Laplace that it has "not needed that hypothesis," i.e., the hypothesis of God. Here cited from Stephen Hawking, "Public Lectures—Does God Play Dice?" http://www.hawking.org.uk/text/public/dice.html (last accessed July 29, 2006).

39. Standard popular account in, for example, Shaun Begley with Anne Underwood, "Religion and the Brain." *Newsweek* (May 21, 2001) at http://findarticles.com/mi_kmnew/js_200105/ai_kepm314664 (last accessed July 24, 2007)

40. Frank Tipler, "The Omega Point and Christianity," http://home.worldonline.nl/~sttdc/tipler.htm (last accessed July 29, 2006). This website is a main host

to Tipler-related materials. Apparently it has replaced much Tipler material that went offline in the wake of Hurricane Katrina, which physically impacted Tipler's home university. Here he defends the "improbable event" view.

41. Pannenberg, "Modern Cosmology," page # needed
42. Krutch, *The Modern Temper*, 18.
43. ———, *The Modern Temper*, 16.
44. ———, *The Modern Temper*, ix.
45. Bukatman, *Terminal Identity*.
46. Mark C. Taylor, *The Reál* (Chicago: University of Chicago Press, 1997). CD-ROM.
47. Here is as good a place as any to observe that our discussion of these matters will pay particular attention to issues of how to read mass media and popular culture—popular culture (film, television, popular novels) that, as John C. Lyden writes with particular regard to "film as religion," "conveys . . . beliefs and values" enhanced by an additional kind of "ritual power to provide catharsis of the emotions associated with . . . life problems and situations" (*Film as Religion: Myths, Morals, and Rituals* [New York: New York University Press, 2003], 246).

Chapter 2

1. Cf. Peter Knight, *Conspiracy Culture: From the Kennedy Assassination to* The X-Files (London: Routledge, 2000): 223: " . . . without the moment of ultimate revelation, the show remains in epistemological free fall, permanently floating between revealing everything and coming up with nothing." Background to conspiracy mentality: see, for example, George E. Marcus, ed., *Paranoia within Reason: A Casebook on Conspiracy as Explanation* (Chicago: University of Chicago, 1999), 6. For modern apocalyptic thinking in these kinds of political connections, see the German examples in Klaus Vondung, *Die Apokalypse in Deutschland* (Munich: dtv, 1988) [ET, Vondung, *The Apocalypse in Germany*, trans. Stephen D. Ricks (Columbia: University of Missouri Press, 2000)]; Stefan Breuer, *Ästhetischer Fundamentalismus: Stefan George und der deutsche Antimodernismus* (Darmstadt: Wiss. Buchges, 1995); John Stroup, "Political Theology and Secularization Theory in Germany, 1918–1939: Emanuel Hirsch as a Phenomenon of His Time," *Harvard Theological Review* 80 (1987): 321–68; broader context: Heinrich Corrodi, *Kritische Geschichte des Chiliasmus Oder der Meynungen über das tausendjährige Reich Christi*, 4 vols. (Zürich: Orell, Geßner, Füßli, ca. 1780–1783); Leonhard Atzberger, *Geschichte der christlichen Eschatologie innerhalb der vornicänischen Zeit* (Graz: Akademische Druck- und Verlagsanstalt, 1970; 1st ed., Freiburg i.B., 1896); Will-Erich Peuckert, "Germanische Eschatologien," *Archiv für Religionswissenschaft* 32 (1935): 1–37; Jacob Taubes, *Abendländische Eschatologie* (Bern: Francke, 1947); Will-Erich Peuckert, *Die große Wende* (Hamburg: Claassen & Goverts, 1948); Karl Löwith, *Meaning in History* (Chicago: University of Chicago Press, 1957; 1st ed., 1949); John Gager, *Kingdom and Community: The Social World of Early Christianity*

(Englewood Cliffs, N.J.: Prentice Hall, 1975); Sylvia Thrupp, ed., *Millennial Dreams in Action,* Comparative Studies in Society and History, Suppl. 2 (The Hague: Mouton, 1962); Bernhard Töpfer, *Das kommende Reich des Friedens* (Berlin: Akademie-Verlag, 1964); Wilhelm E. Mühlmann, *Chiliasmus und Nativismus: Studien zur Psychologie, Soziologie und historischer Kasuistik der Umsturzbewegungen,* 2nd ed. (Berlin: Reimer, 1964); Norman Cohn, *The Pursuit of the Millennium: Revolutionary Millenarians and Mystical Anarchists of the Middle Ages,* rev. ed. (New York: Oxford University Press, 1970); idem., *Cosmos, Chaos, and the World to Come: The Ancient Roots of Apocalyptic Faith,* 2nd ed. (New Haven: Yale University Press, 2001).

2. On *The Prisoner,* see our discussion in our text above. For the quotation, see Ian Kitching, "The Prisoner FAQ," http://iankitching.me.uk/articles/prisoner-faq. html (last accessed June 23, 2006.)

3. Allison Graham, "Are You Now or Have You Ever Been? Conspiracy Theory and the *X-Files,*" on *"Deny All Knowledge": Reading the X Files,* ed. David Lavery et al. (Syracuse: Syracuse University Press, 1996): 54–62. Note how the theme of not simply betrayal but of mutual betrayal is overtly telegraphed with the use of the word itself in the key monologue of Cigarette Smoking Man (see the central first episode of the segment "Two Fathers"): "Smoking Man: 'This is the end. . . . I could never have scripted the events that led us to this. . . . All the brilliant men . . . the secret that we kept so well. . . . We had a perfect conspiracy with an alien race. Aliens who were coming to reclaim this planet and to destroy all human life. Our job was to secretly prepare the way for their invasion. To create for them a slave race of human/ alien hybrids. They were good plans. . . . Kept secret for over 50 years, ever since the crash at Roswell. Kept secret from men like Fox Mulder. Plans that would have worked . . . had not a rebel alien race come to destroy them. Had not my own son chosen betrayal. Or chosen to betray more wisely,'" transcript online at http://www. redwolf.com.au/xfiles/season06/6abx11.html (last accessed June 23, 2006).

4. Andy Meisler, *Resist or Serve: The Official Guide to* The X Files, *created by Chris Carter* (Harper Entertainment, 1999), 284. For such was the statistic for people watching a particularly celebrated midpoint episode on November 2, 1997 (episode title: "Redux"; figures source: Nielsen Media Research).

5. "Redux," episode #5X02 online at http://www.insidethex.co.uk/transcrp/ scrp502.htm (last accessed July 24, 2007).

    The closeness of this material to the overtly theological can again be sensed when one considers that, had Mulder played the entire tape, he would have watched former Harvard Divinity School Dean Krister Stendahl offering his positive assessment of very close encounters with alien life on the same occasion.

6. See for example http://www.netlingo.com/right.cfm?term=cybernoir (last accessed July 24, 2007) and http://dc-mrg.english.ucsb.edu/WarnerTeach/ E192/bladerunner/cybernoir.stoy.htm (last accessed July 24, 2007).

7. See the online script at http://www.insidethex.co.uk/transcrp/scrp515.htm.

8. Knight, *Conspiracy Culture,* 221, citing episode "Patient X" (#5X13)—originally March 1, 1998. The play is of course on Churchill's characterization of Russia

and its way of dealing with war and policy: "It is a riddle wrapped in a mystery inside an enigma," broadcast of October 1939, http://phrases.shu.ac.uk/meanings/31000.html (last accessed June 17, 2006). The phrase is also played upon in Olive Stone's *JFK*.

9. See the online script at http://www.redwolf.com.au/xfiles/season05/5x14.html.

10. See http://x-files.host.sk/csmetc.php#WMM (last accessed July 24, 2007).

11. "Musings of a Cigarette-Smoking-Man," http://www.insidethex.co.uk//transcrp/scrp407.htm (last accessed July 24, 2007).

12. See http://x-files.host.sk/csmetc.php#CSM (last accessed July 24, 2007).

13. This reading of the overall Mytharc or plotline makes use of the hard work of many fans and experts. The initial popularity of *The X-Files,* and the coalescence of its enduring cult phenomenon, had and has much to do with the once novel power of the internet. Therefore it is fitting, and anything but surprising, that some of the most impressive efforts at making "sense" of the series have their home in cyberspace. For a guide to these see "Mythology of X-Files," http://scifi.about.com/od/themythology/. Perhaps the most useful guide for our purposes, and the one to whom I owe the most, is the one appearing under the names Andy Guess and Anthony Leong, "The Mythology," http://scifi.about.com/gi/dynamic/offsite.htm?zi=1/XJ&sdn=sci fi&zu=http%3A%2F%2Fwww.geocities.com%2FTelevisionCity%2FStudio%2F9 013%2Fmyth.html (most readily accessed through the hyperlink on the previously cited Web site, last accessed July 24, 2007). Also very important for our reconstruction here have been the attempts and suggestions in the following careful and creative places: "Ritterson's Episode Guides: *The X-Files* Guide," http://www.geocities.com/TelevisionCity/Studio/4469/xguide.html (last accessed June 21, 2006; see also http://www.geocities.com/vittersonkeys/xguide.html, last accessed July 24, 2007); "Mike Marek, *"The X-Files* Timeline," http://www.themareks.com/xf/finale.shtml; MBush, "A Comprehensive Guide to the X-Files Mytharc," http://scifi.about.com/gi/dynamic/offsite.htm?zi=1/XJ&sdn=scifi&zu=http%3A%2F%2Fwww.geocities.com%2Fmbush1us%2FTheMytharcIntro.htm (all last accessed ca. June 21, 2006; as of July 24, 2007, see http://scifi.about.com/od?once=trne&; likewise of the same date, http://www.geocities.com/xanderfrohike/archives/jan13.html). For the argument that Scully is presented with aspects of the ambiguously bad and good cyborg, see Lisa Parks, "Special Agent or Monstrosity? Finding the Feminine in *The X-Files,*" in Lavery, *Deny All Knowledge,* 122–34.

14. For example see the Guess/Leong and Ritterson material cited in n. 13 above.

15. A stronger interpretation, favored for example by the *Ritterson Episode Guides* online at http://www.geocities.com/TelevisionCity/Studio/4469/xguide.html, holds with considerable script evidence that "[t]he aliens first landed here on Earth millions of . . . years ago. They Colonized, then went to explore the universe. Those aliens that did not leave remained underground in the form of an evolved pathogen—a virus, unstoppable and unpreventable in almost every way which would later be known as Purity. It waited to be reconstituted when the alien race from which it came returned to Colonize the planet. . . . Mankind and everything we know of our past was created by the aliens. The DNA of Purity (therefore, the DNA of the

aliens) lives in all of us—but it is dormant. However, in some, the DNA is active and this gives these people the ability to read minds using a part of the brain which we are only just beginning to learn about—the God Module. This indicates that the Colonists are psychic. The Colonists, it should be said, are the classic image of the Gray alien. After the Colonists left or went underground, the human species expanded and took over Earth. Humans were created by the Colonists, presumably, as an experiment which snowballed. Thousands of years later, the Colonists returned in secret and, through observing us with UFOs and advanced technology, they were able to examine our society. They then informed the world leaders that they intended to wipe out mankind and Colonize Earth. A timetable for Colonization was set. . . . Though the alien Colonization of Earth was fifteen years away, plans have already begun. The aliens plan to Colonize Earth by unleashing a virus called Purity which is, in essence, their very life force. When humans become infected with the virus, they fall comatose and then the virus creates a new alien entity inside the human. The entity kills the human, and then gradually evolves into the familiar form of the Grays. . . . The Colonists are Colonizing because they were the original inhabitants of the planet, though they left to explore and take over the universe using their virus. Now, they have seen humans as an impurity in their bloodline, and they will wipe us all out. Colonization will happen on a holiday, when people are away from their homes. The President will declare a national state of emergency at which point FEMA—the Federal Emergency Management Agency—will suspend constitutional government, and all government agencies will come under the power of FEMA. The virus will be unleashed, and the aliens will kill everyone except those immune to the virus—people who have been vaccinated and alien / human hybrids and clones. . . . Colonization will begin when a race of successful hybrids has been created, in order for the Colonists to use as slaves."

16. Attention is called to the parallel here with "Mrs. Keech's extra-terrestrial adaptation of Christian apocalyptic in Leon Festinger, Henry W. Riecken, and Stanley Schachter, *When Prophecy Fails: A Social and Psychological Study of a Modern Group that Predicted the Destruction of the World* (New York: Harper, 1964; 1st ed., 1956).

17. Also needing discussion is the very issue of congruency of DNA if, as some interpretations concludes, life on earth was either seeded in toto by the aliens or at least manipulated from a very early point.

18. See the material in n. 13 above.

19. As is noted by essays in Lavery, for example Lisa Parks, "Special Agent or Monstrosity: Finding the Feminine in *The X-Files*," 121–35; also Bridget Brown, "'My Body Is Not My Own': Alien Abduction and the Struggle for Self-Control," in *Conspiracy Nation: The Politics of Paranoia in Postwar America*, ed. Peter Knight (New York: New York University Press, 2002): 107–29.

20. For details, see *Fight the Future* [*X-Files* movie script], http://www.insidethex. co.uk/transcrp/scrpftf.htm (last accessed July 24, 2007). Book version: Chris Carter, adapted by Elizabeth Hand, *The X-Files: Fight the Future* (New York: Harper Prism, 1998).

21. Among whose practitioners we are to be numbered. Preliminary comparison of conspiracy and related thinking in science fiction and *The X-Files* with Christian apocalyptic in Mark Fenster, *Conspiracy Theories: Secrecy and Power in American Culture* (Minneapolis: University of Minnesota Press, 1999), esp. 145–79. It should be noted that Fenster's typology is somewhat at variance with that of Michael Barkun, who sees a resurgence of dangerous, militia-like tendencies in adherents of very elaborate contemporary conspiracy theories. See Michael Barkun, *A Culture of Conspiracy: Apocalyptic Visions in Contemporary America* (Berkeley: University of California Press, 2003).

22. Also note here the relation to Tom Engelhardt, *The End of Victory Culture: Cold War America and the Disillusioning of a Generation* (New York: Basic Books, 1995); also see Dean, *Aliens in America.*

23. For the Mytharc ostentatiously draws upon New Age theory-building and New Age use of prophetic themes from all world cultures, in the end even casting its reading in a narrative framework of television prophecy of sorts, one that in shape mirrors many features of Jewish and Christian apocalyptic literature. Furthermore, the overall trajectory of *The X-Files* series makes some rather clear statements about the problems facing conventional understandings about human identity and human agency and human limits. Thus it invites an opening up of its outlook and its main concerns as they can be read to reflect contemporary America and a comparison of them with analogous material.

24. Fenster, *Conspiracy Theory;* Knight, *Conspiracy Nation;* Cyborg/technical and economic aspects of the emergent situation are surveyed in David Brande, "The Business of Cyberpunk: Symbolic Economy and Ideology in William Gibson," in *Virtual Realities and their Discontents,* ed. Robert Markley (Baltimore: The Johns Hopkins University Press, 1996): 79–106. See also Bruce Sterling, "Cyberpunk in the Nineties," http://www.streettech.com/bcp/BCPtext/Manifestos/CPInThe90s.html (last accessed July 24, 2007).

25. See the remarks on similar yet not identical readings of the limited human prospect among conspiracy advocates and Christian dispensationalists in Fenster, chaps. 3, 4, 5, and 6; and Glenn W. Shuck, *Mark of the Beast: The* Left Behind *Novels and the Struggle for Evangelical Identity* (New York: New York University Press, 2005). On attempts to read the vague anxiety connected with the work of Mulder and Scully, see Charles McGrath, "It Just Looks Paranoid," *The New York Times Book Review,* June 14, 1998, sect. 6, p. 56, col. 1.

26. Cf. Knight, *Conspiracy Culture,* 223: "endless deferral of the ultimate signifier"; "perpetually withholds the keystone . . ." and similar with regard to *The X-Files.*

27. See chapter 3 for a more complete exploration of dispensational thought.

28. And here they have had many predecessors in wondering, beginning with the early Christians noted in 2 Peter: "There shall come in the last days scoffers, walking after their own lusts, And saying, 'Where is the promise of his coming?' For since the fathers fell asleep, all things continue as they were from the beginning of the creation" (3:3–4). Background: Erich Gräßer, *Das Problem der Parusieverzögerung in den synoptischen Evangelien und in der Apostelgeschichte,* 3rd ed. (Berlin: de Gruyter,

1977); Kurt Erlemann, *Naherwartung und Parusieverzögerung im Neuen Testament: ein Beitrag zur Frage religiöser Zeiterfahrung* (Tübingen: Francke, 1995). Also Gager, *Kingdom and Community.*

29. See for example episodes 19 and 20 from season 9 ("The Truth") available in fan transcripts online at http://www.insidethex.co.uk/transcrp/scrp919.htm and http://www.insidethex.co.uk/transcrp/scrp919.htm#truth_part2 (last accessed June 23, 2006). There Cigarette Smoking Man confirms to Mulder that the long-planned alien invasion (with connivance of secret units of the government) will unfold on the date the Mayan calendar cycle ends, December 22, 2012. With regard to the theme pursued a bit later, human action and effectiveness, note the exchange of dialogue between Cigarette Smoking Man and Mulder in episode 9.19 concerning power and powerlessness in the face of the gigantic and probably unavoidable alien invasion.

30. "One Son," http://www.insidethex.co.uk/transcrp/scrp612.htm (last accessed June 23, 2006).

31. "The Truth" (second part), http://www.insidethex.co.uk/transcrp/scrp919.htm. (last accessed June 23, 2006).

32. "The Truth" (second part).

33. "The Truth" (second part).

34. Indeed, this theme of defective human agency indeed may actually have enhanced the appeal of the series, at least for the subgroups at which the program was targeted.

35. On the notion of network culture or network society, see Manuel Castells, *The Rise of Network Society* (Malden, Mass.: Blackwell, 2000); also Taylor, *The Moment of Complexity.* This supposition (the coping/compensatory significance of materials from *The X-Files* and *Left Behind*) becomes all the more plausible when we take account of one additional factor: the weakening sense of effective human agency apparent in these emblematic documents of popular culture, about which a good deal more will be said below. As Mark Fenster has observed, in narratives about locating and redressing imbalances in power and control (of which metanarratives of conspiracy and of religious salvation from alienation are variants with some kinship to the crassest thriller) there are certain basic requirements for a satisfying conclusion. In particular, the story must lead to some "coherence" or "emplotment" making sense of the imbalance and its redress; beyond this, the account must move toward "some form of resolution that reaffirms the protagonist's agency. . . ." See for example Fenster, *Conspiracy Theories,* 129–30. As we shall see, it is precisely here, exactly with the issue of effective agency by human actors with whom the target audience identifies, that difficulties arise throughout the latest forms of the contemporary dark genre. Whether Mulder and Scully can ever assist the human race in outwitting whatever its ultimate enemy may be (or even determine finally whether the real problem is government cover-up or alien implant-lust) were points all roughly as uncertain at the end of the series as at the beginning (and that despite the later revelation that yes, aliens really did exist). Likewise

and in perfect parallel, we shall also find that contemporary popular accounts of millennial tribulation strive mightily but at last in vain to affirm effective human agency within the unfolding apocalyptic plan of a God seen from the outset as in every sense omnipotent and at the same time remarkably interested in very fine details. For details, see the next chapter below and cf. Fenster, 162f.: "If 'history' moves without human influence, if the realm of human history is merely the stage or the visible level of the supernatural powers that determine events and chance, then Lindsey and popular eschatology in general seem to posit a world without human agency. This suggests that observing as events unfold within the 'biblical' patterns outlined by 'professional' eschatologists is the correct collective response to the narrative frame that [Hal] Lindsey constructs. . . . Human agency, removed from the historical narrative through the metaphysical power of the supernatural, returns in a limited way in the individual's decision to . . . ensure that she takes her place in the more desirable part of the narrative, the rapture rather than the tribulation. . . ." See also Shuck, *Marks of the Beast*. Beyond this but similarly, we shall also find that nonnarrative kindred material pertaining to New Age visions of science and cosmic catastrophe put the effective human actor in an equally perilous position, sacrificing that human effectiveness sometimes to truly inexorable impacts and plate tectonics little fazed by human agency, and at other times to technoid evolution of intelligent life with little place for the spontaneity that is customarily regarded as the hallmark of the human. Behind all this turns out to lurk the most unwelcome of outcomes, the inability of imaginative thinkers to spin out a plausible scenario for how satisfying political participation and truly democratic community harmonized with liberty could possibly be instituted in societies as large, complex, and bureaucratized as current conditions demand. Such are the uninviting prospects that feed into the kinds of popular culture at which we have been looking. What kind of compensation contemporary popular culture seeks for the frustrations and aggressive drive stored up once the sober reality of such prospects sinks in—that will be the installment of our story dealing with *Fight Club*.

36. Thus, among other things, we put up for discussion the possibility that various outlooks recently come to prominence may well be looked at as mechanisms for personal coping with the latent function of stabilizing the emerging sociopolitical and economic status quo in millennial America. For example, one could think about Rapture-culture from at least three angles (each, equally applicable to the postmodern or postChristian universe of *The X-Files* and the hyperChristian repristinating universe of contemporary evangelical Rapture-culture): first, the absorption in an endgame scenario that promises escape from a mundane world of total bureaucratic control yet endlessly defers delivery of that escape; second, the custom of explaining situations by reference to a generalized conspiracy theory that has escaped from marginal subcultures at the price of abandoning all realistic hope of either penetrating the veils of disinformation or of restoring health and accountability to a sociopolitical system now taken as altogether

beyond repair; third, the use of endgame or apocalyptic language and images to comment on and distance one's inner identity from a sociopolitical situation perceived as repugnant in the extreme. Yet, as we shall argue below and further, one of these options offers at the same time hope for restoring not so much control in the system as a feeling of stake-holding in it on a basis of reconstitution of the commonwealth, and that along intensely evangelical, Right-wing Christian lines: on such terms, and apparently only on such terms, for the moment at least, one and only one of these variants seems capable of doing much by way of political energizing. The interconnection here with an emerging sense of self radically different from that of America's Enlightenment roots and the results for a politics of exclusions versus a politics of inclusion (despite universal themes in the emergent sense of denatured self) will require exploration below.

37. "Patient X," http://insidethex.co.uk/transcrp/scrp513.htm (last accessed July 27, 2007); "The Red and the Black" (episode 5X14), http://insidethex.co.uk/transcrp/scrp514.htm (last accessed July 27, 2007).

38. See http://www.themareks.com/xf/1999.shtml (details in n. 13 above). Also reference to "One Son" is in episode 6X12 at http://insidethex.co.uk/transcorp/scrp612.htm (last accessed July 24, 2007).

39. See http://www.insanity.com.au/x-files/mythology06-syndicate.htm (last accessed June 20, 2006).

40. The relation of searching for a meaning to deliberately "creating" a meaning and its differential employment in ancient, medieval, and modern Western situations is usefully dealt with by Klaus Vondung, esp. 87–105 of the English edition, where he supplies one of the more exact stage-by-stage documentations of the move from medieval apocalyptic to Pietistic and prototheosophical speculation on reading the divine plan for future catastrophe and future improvement—and thereafter the transition to postNapoleonic quasireligious socialism and the move to dialectical materialist doctrines of revolution, destruction, and transformation. Indeed, here at some points Vondung has surpassed in clarity and breadth even the treatment of these matters by the late Hans Frei, in his *The Eclipse of Biblical Narrative: A Study in Eighteenth and Nineteenth Century Hermeneutics* (New Haven: Yale University Press, 1974). Vondung has succeeded in moving the entire question of religious and nonreligious doctrines of historical goal and meaning well beyond the point it had reached with Hans Blumenberg's stimulating but unsatisfactory attack on the interpretation of such doctrines from the point of view of a critique of blanket doctrines of "secularization" in his *The Legitimacy of the Modern Age,* trans. Robert M. Wallace (Cambridge, Mass.: MIT Press, 1983).

41. See "All Things," http://www.insidethex.co.uk/transcrp/scrp717 (last accessed June 19, 2000) for example.

42. See *"Amor Fati,"* http://www.insidethex.co.uk/transcrp/scrp704.htm (last accessed the June 19, 2006).

43. See for example the opinion of William Gibson as quoted in Antony Johnston, "Waiting For the Man," *Spike Magazine,* http://www.spikemagazine.com/

0899williamgibson.htm (last accessed July 24, 2007): "I really don't think I'm dystopian at all. No more than I'm utopian. The dichotomy is hopelessly old-fashioned, really. What we have today is a combination of the two, with all the knobs turned up to max."

44. See Donna J. Haraway, "A Cyborg Manifesto: Science, Technology, and Socialist-Feminism in the Late Twentieth Century," in *Simians, Cyborgs, and Women: The Reinvention of Nature* (London: Routledge, 1991): 145–82; Kathryn Hayles, *How We Became Posthuman: Virtual Bodies in Cyberspace, Literature, and Informatics* (Chicago: University of Chicago Press, 1999).

45. Douglas Kellner, "*The X-Files* and Conspiracy: A Diagnostic Critique," in *Conspiracy Nation: The Politics of Paranoia in Postwar America* (New York: New York University Press, 2002): 205–32, here 227.

46. *KillSwitch,* http://www.dthomasmaddox.com/killsmith.htm (last accesssed July 24, 2007)

47. Background: see for example Tipler, *The Physics of Immortality;* also the various papers on Tipler online, http://www.math.tulane.edu/~tipler/; Pannenberg, "Modern Cosmology"; Pannenberg, "God and Resurrection"; Graham Oppy, "Critical Notice: Frank J Tipler (1995) 'The Physics of Immortality,'" http://www.infidels. org/library/modern/graham_oppy/tipler.html (last accessed June 24, 2006).

48. Jake Horsley, all "Gnosticism Reborn: The Matrix As Shamanic Journey," http://www.mindmined.com/public_library/nonfiction/jake_horsley_gnosticism_reborn.html (last accessed June 11, 2006). We are greatly indebted to suggestions in Horsley's work on *The Matrix*.

49. Jake Horsley, *The Blood Poets: A Cinema of Savagery 1958–1999:* Vol. 1, *American Chaos;* Vol. 2, *Millennial Blues* (Lanham, Md.: Scarecrow Press 1999).

50. See http://www.divinevirus.com/matrixcontents.html (last accessed july 27, 2007). See also Robert Aziz, *C.G. Jung's Psychology of Religion and Synchronicity* (Albany: State University of New York Press, 1990). The theme of energy behind all phenomena is also central to George Lucas's *Star Wars* trilogies (1977–2005). *The Force* is very Jungian indeed. Lucas's thought seems almost neoLuddite at times: destroying "Death Stars" as a recurrent theme, and the machine versus the organic flesh theme in Vader. Indeed, *The Dark Side of the Force* is associated with the technological, both in the sense of manipulation of circuits as well as persons. Note the in-joke of Darth Vader using "1138" as a landing code for his shuttle in *Return of the Jedi* (1983). Remember also that Lucas named his first escapist fantasy film *THX-1138* (1971). Moreover, he founded his own technological-corporate juggernaut, calling it THX. One then sees the profound irony of Lucas's very technologically oriented statement questioning technology. Lucas, to his credit, is not unaware of this irony.

51. Jake Horsley, "Gnosticism Reborn: *The Matrix* As Shamanic Journey," http://www.mindmined.com/public_library/nonfiction/jake_horsley_gnosticism_reborn.html (last accessed August 22, 2006).

52. Horsley, "Gnosticism Reborn." Increasingly negative about wasted potential in the series then are Horsley, "*Matrix Reloaded,* The Bitter Truth," June 2003, http://www.divinevirus.com/reloaded.html (last accessed July 27, 2007); and

Horsley, "Red for Blue and Blue for Red: *Matrix Revolutions*, or How a Movie Franchise Sabotaged Itself," http://www.divinevirus.com/revolt.html (last accessed August 3, 2006).

53. Harriet Klausner, quoted in online review of Horsley's book *Matrix Warrior: Being the One* (New York: St. Martin's Press, 2003); http://www.amazon. com/exec/obidos/tg/detail/-/031232264X/qid=1075723723/sr=1–1/ref=sr_1_ 1/002–5156156–5245642?v=glance&s=books (last accessed June 23, 2006).

54. Steve Bruce, *Religion in the Modern World* (New York: Oxford University Press, 1996), 225 (after long discussion of New Age): "In summary, New Age religion cannot aspire to promote radical and specific change because it does not have the cohesion and discipline of the sect."

55. See for example William Martin, *With God on Our Side: The Rise of the Religious Right in America* (New York: Broadway, 1996); Kevin Phillips, *American Theocracy: The Peril and Politics of Radical Religions, Oil, and Borrowed Money in the 21ˢᵗ Century* (New York: Viking, 2006).

56. But here the contention is NOT that evangelical dispensationalists are overtly abandoning a free-will position in conversion—only that the determinism in other features of their outlook now begins to overshadow the Arminian or Enlightenment heritage rather spectacularly. The interesting possibility is the emergence of a pragmatic coalition between dispensationalists (techni- cally Arminian, but with a tendency toward fatalism in endtime scripting that overshadows freewill tendencies at many points) and Dominionists or Reconstructionists (predestinarians), whose beliefs now find wider and wider acceptance in formerly nonpredestinarian circles. The two groups agree on most issues of conservative social policy and hence are inclined to seek a theological truce. See chapter 5 and 6 below. The true significance of all of this lies not so much in formal weakening of "free will" as in registering a growing sense of loss of power and substance in the individual self as a necessary constituent of any version of participatory government in the tradition of civic humanist democ- racy or republicanism. In that sense, whether the packaging for impotence be dispensationalist or techno-digital, the result is the same, that is, a great weaken- ing of the credible ideal in American government up to this point.

Chapter 3

1. See Sydney E. Ahlstrom, *A Religious History of the American People* (New Haven: Yale University Press, 1973), 808–11, on "dispensational premillennialism." In this place, Ahlstrom deals with the full elaboration of dispensationalism by John Nelson Darby (1800–1882) in relation to the Plymouth Brethren and then the transformation of this culture-critical evangelical eschatology into an interde- nominational Protestant phenomenon anchored in the Scofield Reference Bible put out by Cyrus Scofield (1843–1921) and in the Dallas Theological Seminary. The prehistory of this movement in the seventeenth and eighteenth centuries cannot detain us here.

2. George A. Mather and Larry A. Nichols, "DISPENSATIONALISM (Christianity)," in idem, *Dictionary of Cults, Sects, Religions and the Occult* (Grand Rapids: Zondervan, 1993), 90: "A dispensation was defined by the Scofield Reference Bible as 'a period of time during which man is tested in respect of obedience to some specific revelation of the will of God.' By this Cyrus Scofield (1843–1921) meant that God has set aside certain ages or 'dispensations' for specific activities that may differ from before or after; there were seven ages or dispensations in all: (1) the age of innocence, prior to the Fall; (2) the period of time up to the Flood when the race, governed by conscience, again failed; (3) the era of civil government, ending with moral collapse and the destruction of Sodom and Gomorrah; (4) the promise to the Patriarchs, ending in the destruction of the Egyptians in the Red Sea; (5) the time of the Mosaic covenant up to and including the crucifixion of Jesus; (6) the age of grace (church age), in which we are currently; (7) the final dispensation or Millennium, which is yet to come."

3. First Thessalonians 4:17. For other verses claimed by dispensationalists see Thomas Ice, "Examining an Ancient Pre-Trib Rapture Statement," http://www.greenspun.com/bboard/q-and-a-fetch-msg.tcl?msg_id=00Bxvs (last accessed July 30, 2006); idem., "Morgan Edwards: A Pre-Darby Rapturist," http://www.conservativeonline.org/journals/01_01_journal/1997v1n1_id01.htm (last accessed July 30, 2006). Here we do not intend to present a history of interpretation of the New Testament and early Christian writers on this point: simply registering the fact that the dispensationalist take on eschatology has been and is a minority position over time and space.

4. In particular, the escape scenario constituted something of an innovation. Already the nineteenth-century founder of this view, J. N. Darby, was accused of innovating with belief in two separate comings of Christ, one for the living believers, another visible to all at the Last Judgment. In any case (so far as most specialists are concerned) this whole view is modern, in that it provides a comfortable apocalypse for believers, rather in contrast to the feel of the ancient readings of the book of Revelation.

5. The doctrine of the Rapture or snatching away of living believers is a strong reading of 1 Thessalonians 4:17: "Then we which are alive and remain shall be caught up together with them in the clouds, to meet the Lord in the air: and so shall we ever be with the Lord" (AV). While this passage can support a strong reading of the so-called Rapture, and while that doctrine had occasional defenders fairly early, still until recently a focus on it was very much a minority position. Early occurrences of a Rapture orientation or doctrine detailed at "Tim LaHaye Ministries—Pre-Trib Perspectives," http://www.timlahaye.com/about_ministry/index.php3?p=newsletter&section=Pre-Trib%20Newsletter (last accessed July 29, 2006).

6. For details see, for example, Shuck, *Marks of the Beast,* 1–52; Amy Johnson Frykholm, *Left Behind in Evangelical America* (New York: Oxford University Press, 2004), 13–66.

7. Here meaning, of course, the Left Behind series by Tim LaHaye and Jerry B. Jenkins. Joan Didion gives the following overview of figures: "In the past eight years the eleven installments that so far make up the series (*Left Behind, Tribulation Force, Nicolae, Soul Harvest, Apollyon, Assassins, The Indwelling, The Mark, Desecration, The Remnant,* and *Armageddon,* which made its first appearance on *The New York Times* fiction best-seller list last April as number one) have together sold some fifty-five million copies, a figure which includes hardcover and trade paperbacks and mass-market paperbacks and compact discs and audio books and e-books and comic (or 'graphic') books, but does not include either the study guides to the series ('using excerpts from the *Left Behind* novels and pointing readers to the prophetic passages of Scripture') or the *Left Behind* military thriller series ('story lines of its own, but parallels the *Left Behind* books'). Neither does the fifty-five million figure include the merchandising of calendars and devotional readings, or the companion series for children between ten and fourteen, '*Left Behind: The Kids,*' thirty-some volumes in which 'four teens are left behind after the Rapture and band together to fight Satan's forces.'" Joan Didion, "Op-Ed: Mr. Bush & the Divine," review of *Armageddon: The Cosmic Battle of the Ages,* by Tim F. LaHaye and Jerry B. Jenkins, *New York Review of Books,* November 6, 2003, http://www.why-war.com/news/2003/11/06/mrbushth.html (last accessed July 29, 2006).

8. Paul S. Boyer, "When U.S. Foreign Policy Meets Biblical Prophecy," *AlterNet,* February 20, 2003, http://www.alternet.org/story.html?StoryID=15221 (last accessed July 29, 2006).

9. See "Is Bush Getting Apocalyptic Advice? MSNBC with Ashley Pearson." Excerpt: "Is the Bush administration turning to a televangelist doomsayer for political predictions? Apocalyptic preacher Jack Van Impe is claiming that he was contacted by Condoleezza Rice's office and the White House Office of Public Liaison for an 'outline' of his take on world events," http://www.msnbc.com/news/943879.asp (posted August 13, 2003) and archived at http://smirkingchimp.com/viewtopic.php?topic=28423&forum=13 (last accessed July 29, 2006).

10. Otto Böcher, "Das beglaubigende Vaticinium ex eventu als Strukturelement der Johannes—Apokalypse," *Revue d'historie et de philosophie religieuses* 79.1 (1999): 19–30; Stephen O'Leary, "Rumors of Grace and Terror," *USC Annenberg Online Journalism Review,* April 2, 2002, http://www.ojv.ojv/ethics/1017782038.php (last accessed November 29, 2006); Gager, *Kingdom and Community;* Otto Plöger, *Theocracy and Eschatology,* trans. S. Rudman (Oxford: Blackwell, 1968); Norman Cohn, *The Pursuit of the Millennium: Revolutionary Millenarians and Mystical Anarchists of the Middle Ages,* rev. ed. (New York: Oxford University Press, 1970); Festinger et al., *When Prophecy Fails;* Otto Böcher, *Die Johannesapokalypse,* Erträge der Forschung 41 (Darmstadt: Wissenschaftliche Buchgesellschaft, 1975); Wilhelm E. Mühlmann, *Chiliasmus und Nativismus: Studien zur Psychologie, Soziologie und historischer Kasuistik der Umsturzbewegung,*

2nd ed. (Berlin: Reimer, 1964); Jacob Taubes, *Abendländische Eschatologie* (Bern: Francke, 1947); Sylvia Thrupp, *Millennial Dreams in Action,* Comparative Studies in Society and History, Suppl. 2 (The Hague: Mouton, 1962); Bernhard Töpfer, *Das kommende Reich des Friedens* (Berlin: Akademie-Verlag, 1964); Michael Walzer, *The Revolution of the Saints: A Study in the Origins of Radical Politics* (Cambridge, Mass.: Harvard University Press, 1965); Eugen Weber, *Apocalypses: Prophecies, Cults, and Millennial Beliefs through the Ages* (Cambridge, Mass.: Harvard University Press, 1999); J. Nelson Kraybill, *Imperial Cult and Commerce in John's Apocalypse* (Sheffield: Sheffield Academic, 1996). The road from prophecy retroactively commented on events contemporaneous with its time of composition to apocalyptic and world-denying fantasies as elaborate and figurative commentary on conditions of the world and processes of decline is a crooked one with many paths and turnings, running through Schopenhauer and beyond . . . we do not map it here.

11. Shuck, *Marks of the Beast,* 200f. ("safety valve"), 56–57, 81, 200 (political activism), 81, 170 (apocalyptic puppetry), 92f. (larger cultural concern with issues of loss of sense of individual efficacy).

12. In making these observations, we are acutely aware that, as a recent detailed study of current prophecy believers by Glenn Shuck demonstrates, the views of prominent interpreters are evolving and are to a surprising degree contained most seminally in imaginative narratives—evidence of the power of the phenomenon (for though no inspiration would be claimed for these recent novels, the tendency is to work directly on the precritical mind of the audience very much in the mode of ancient scriptural texts and the visions that may have underlain them). See Shuck, *Marks of the Beast,* 41–52.

13. Gager, *Kingdom and Community;* Festinger et al., *When Prophecy Fails.*

14. See, e.g., Shuck, *Marks of the Beast,* 197: "LaHaye and Jenkins imagine a continuum of outcomes in their novels, attempting to navigate a fragile balance between an overaccommodation to the world that leaves prophecy-believing evangelicals culturally irrelevant, and a violent, destructive quest to wrest meaning from what they perceive as an increasingly meaningless world. What is most striking in each scenario, however, is the absolute failure to achieve what the narratives ostensibly seek: escape from the mundane world of rapid cultural change. Deliverance, ultimately, does not indicate escape, but becomes instead a tense, ongoing process of negotiations with the forces of modernity."

Years pass, both in the "real-time" of publishing and in the narrative world of the Left Behind novels, and escape always seems promised, but never quite delivered. The novels constantly defer the apocalypse. Yes, we know it has to end sometime; even the authors and their publisher know as much. Yet the escape promised by Left Behind ultimately proves ironic because outside of the first few pages with the Rapture and the last few with presumably the glorious appearing and return of Christ, life on Earth continues, just much more chaotically—hence worse—than before. Thus as tempting as it would be to describe the Left Behind series as a flight of fancy away from the mundane world, the novels prevent this, depicting characters who must remain and struggle against the forces of evil. Not unlike late twentieth-century science fiction productions such as the cyberpunk of William Gibson or the film noir of Patrick McGoohan's short-lived 1960's serial, *The Prisoner,* the novels tantalize with escape but instead prepare their readers for an adjustment phase that will not be easy. Hence I have chosen to treat the novels—despite their unmistakably escapist sentiments—as "adjustment narratives," rather than "escape narratives." Perhaps, in the world outside of LaHaye's and Jenkins' narrative universe, the long-promised airlift to heavenly bliss will finally come, perhaps not. In the meantime, believers must make the best of what they have, and the novels suggest numerous ways to do this." On the "pre-Tribulation Tribulation," see Shuck, *Marks of the Beast,* 70 and 170.

15. See Robert K. Merton, *Social Theory and Social Structure* (Glencoe, Ill.: Free Press, 1957).

16. A word of explanation: This book, like all studies of such contemporary matters, necessarily alters its sense of context, depending on what possibilities may emerge from the way the topic of investigation appears to signify an unfolding package. Concretely, then, taking emerging developments and subculture behavior into account, the authors began their investigation inclined to view liberal waves of anxiety at the domestic and geopolitical real-world payoff of Armageddon and Rapture fantasy as greatly overstated in view of the firm grip of cold war-era Yale- and Harvard-trained hands on the key-sockets of the launch silo, so to speak. At the time of the conclusion of this book (summer 2006) we are a bit more concerned both with regard to domestic and geopolitical spin-offs from the extremist fantasies of apocalyptic enthusiasts, and that also with regard to the real world.

17. A. Bartlett Giamatti's references to ambiguity and the underlying context requiring understanding of ambiguity are so frequent (from his early career forward, as the elder of the present authors knows from personal contact with the late scholar-commissioner) that one may well despair of tracking down this attribution, which the elder of the two present authors thinks was handed down as oral tradition, possibly from some assembly in which Giamatti spoke, perhaps one of his denunciations of the morally unambiguous. If Giamatti did not say it, he said it in a parallel universe not far distant from the current one.

18. Bruce, *Religion in the Modern World,* 225: "In summary, New Age religion cannot aspire to promote radical and specific change because it does not have the cohesion and discipline of the sect."

19. Gary North, "The Unannounced Reason Behind American Fundamentalism's Support for the State of Israel," *LewRockwell.com,* http://www.lewrockwell.com/orig/north7.html (last accessed July 29, 2006). Here, concerning the Tribulation and persecution as dispensationalists currently conceive it "is the opinion of John F. Walvoord, one of dispensationalism's leading theologians, who served for three decades as the president of Dallas Theological Seminary (founded, 1924), the movement's main seminary. The purge of Israel in their time of trouble is described by Zechariah in these words: "And it shall come to pass, that in all the land, saith Jehovah, two parts therein shall be cut off and die; but the third shall be left therein.

And I will bring the third part into the fire, and will refine them as silver is refined, and will try them as gold is tried'" (Zech 13:8, 9). According to Zechariah's prophecy, two thirds of the children of Israel in the land will perish, but the one third that are left will be refined and be awaiting the deliverance of God at the second coming of Christ which is described in the next chapter of Zechariah. (John F. Walvoord, *Israel in Prophecy* [Grand Rapids: Zondervan, (1962) 1988], 108.) North continues: "Nothing can or will be done by Christians to save Israel's Jews from this disaster, for all of the Christians will have been removed from this world three and a half years prior to the beginning of this 42-month period of Tribulation. (The total period of seven years is interpreted as the fulfillment of the seventieth week of Daniel [Dan 9:27].) In order for most of today's Christians to escape physical death [in the Rapture—JS], two-thirds of the Jews in Israel must perish, soon. This is the grim prophetic trade-off that fundamentalists rarely discuss publicly, but which is the central motivation in the movement's support for Israel. It should be clear why they believe that Israel must be defended at all costs by the West. If Israel were militarily removed from history prior to the Rapture, then the strongest case for Christians' imminent escape from death would have to be abandoned. This would mean the indefinite delay of the Rapture. The fundamentalist movement thrives on the doctrine of the imminent Rapture, not the indefinitely postponed Rapture."

20. For the low view of dispensationalism among Reconstructionists and the maxim of incompatibility between the two approaches, see esp. Gary North and Gary DeMar, *Christian Reconstruction: What It Is, What It Isn't* (Tyler, Tex.: Institute for Christian Economics, 1991).

21. See, e.g., North and DeMar, *Christian Reconstruction.* Likewise Mary McCarthy, "Reconstruction Theology in Home Education," http://www.geocities.com/ Athens/Atlantis/8616/reconstruction.html (last accessed March 10, 2006): "Many of the leaders of the so-called hard or Christian Right are followers of the teachings of Rousas John Rushdoony. Rushdoony is the spiritual leader of Chalcedon Foundation, a California organization dedicated to Christian Reconstruction. According to the Foundation, a Christian Reconstructionist is a Calvinist, holding to the principles that God, not man, is the center of the universe and beyond; a Theonomist, believing that God's law is found in the Bible; a Presuppositionalist, believing that he holds to the Faith because the Bible says so and has no need to prove it; a Postmillennialist believing that Christ will return to earth only after the Holy Spirit has empowered the church to advance Christ's kingdom in time and history and a Dominionist taking seriously the Bible's commandment to the godly to take dominion in the earth. The Christian Reconstructionist believes the earth and all its fullness is the Lord's; that every area dominated by sin must be 'reconstructed' in terms of the Bible. This includes, first, the individual; second, the family; third, the church; and fourth, the wider society including the state." The Dominion theology movement places Judeo-Christian biblical law above any and all constitutional law, including the U.S. Constitution. "Postmillennialists believe that righteous human beings, essentially servants of Christ, must achieve positions of influence in societies in order to prepare the world for the Messiah's return." She

further cites here William Martin, *With God on Our Side: The Rise of the Religious Right in America* (New York: Broadway, 1997). Also F. Clarkson, *What is Christian Reconstructionism,* in "Pat Robertson," http://www.theocracywatch.org/pat_robertson.htm (last accessed July 29, 2006).

22. See Michael Barkun, *Radical Religion in America: The Origins of the Christian Identity Movement* (Chapel Hill: University of North Carolina Press, 1997); and Jeffrey Kaplan, *Millenarian Movements from the Far Right to the Children of Noah* (Syracuse, N.Y.: Syracuse University Press, 1997).

23. See Gary North, "Religious Freedom Coalition Presents Christian Reconstructionists: Theocratic Dominionism Gains Influence," http://www.tylwythteg.com/enemies/reconstruct2.html (last accessed July 29, 2006).

24. See, e.g., Chip Berlet, "The Christian Right, Dominionism, and Theocracy," *Talk to Action* (posted December 26, 2005), http://www.talk2action.org/story /2005/12/26/154442/94 (last accessed July 29, 2006); John Sugg, "A Nation under God," *Mother Jones* (December/January 2006), http://www.motherjones.com/news/feature/2005/12/a_nation_under_god.html (last accessed July 29, 2006). Berlet does a careful job of rendering the bewildering penumbra of varieties of this movement. See also Michelle Goldberg, *Kingdom Coming: The Rise of Christian Nationalism* (New York: W. W. Norton, 2006).

25. See Tim LaHaye, *You Are Engaged in the Battle for the Mind: A Subtle Warfare* (Old Tappan, N.J.: Revell, 1980), 217–18.

26. The clear index for this was the persistent reluctance of liberal critics of the second Bush president to go too far in identifying the radical apocalypticism that may be at work here, a reluctance eventually overcome, but only well into the crisis of American geopolicy. Critics from the outset well aware that the Bush lease on the White House is financed by a coalition of neoconservatives, Protestant prophecy believers with a strong interest in Israel, and conservative Roman Catholics. In spite of this the safest critical approach for most appeared to them for months and months simply to be identifying neoconservative theorists as recent converts from Trotskyite radicalism rather than as in danger of being "caught up" (believing or not) in the internal logic of pathological apocalypticism that could dismantle all natural revulsion against doomsday measures. See Andrew Higgins, "Holy War: A Texas Preacher Leads Campaign to Let Israel Fight: Mr. Hagee Draws Evangelicals by Arguing Jewish State Fulfills Biblical Prophecy," the *Wall Street Journal,* July 27, 2006: A1, http://online.wsj.com/article_email/SB115396305776618640-lMyQ-jAxMDE2NTIzNzkyNjczWj.html (last accessed July 30, 2006).

27. Shuck, *Marks of the Beast,* 192.

28. ———, *Marks of the Beast,* 201.

29. So big an issue is this delay as a theme that German scholars even invented a special term for the delay of the full return of Christ: *Parusieverzögerung.*

30. See Shuck, *Marks of the Beast,* 8–9, 56, 16–170, 223 n. 12.

31. Here the classic marks of millennialist movements under long-term pressure according to cognitive dissonance social theory; see Gager, *Kingdom and Community;* and Festinger et al., *When Prophecy Fails.*

32. James Russell Lowell, 1845, cited according to hymn 519 in *The Hymnal of the Protestant Episcopal Church in the United States of America 1940* (New York: The Church Pension Fund, 1961).

33. "The Sixth Extinction II: Amor Fati (7X04)," http://www.insidethex.co.uk/transcrp/scrp704.htm (last accessed July 29, 2006).

34. Thomas Mann, "The Making of 'The Magic Mountain,'" in his *The Magic Mountain,* trans. H. T. Lowe-Porter (New York: The Heritage Press, 1962), xv. The essay first appeared in the *Atlantic Monthly* in January of 1953.

35. See Shuck, *Marks of the Beast,* "Introduction," 15: "Certain roles, in other words, replicate, albeit with different personalities. The Tribulation Force never lacks pilots, spiritual authorities, medical staff, technological consultants, or even economists."

36. Whether in today's world invoking the example of analyst C. G. Jung dealing with the dreams and nightmares of patients on the verge of Nazi Germany can render our undertaking more legitimate may be questioned—but the example is worthy of consideration. See, e.g., Jung, "The Fight with the Shadow," in *Civilization in Transition, Collected Works,* vol. 10 (Princeton: Princeton University Press, [Year]), 220.

37. Shuck, *Marks of the Beast,* e.g., 55–57, 96f., 106–7. Earlier paralleling of science fiction with prophecy fiction is done cursorily in Fenster, *Conspiracy Theories,* 145–79 (stops before *Left Behind*). See also Paul S. Boyer, "The Apocalyptic in the Twentieth Century," in *Fearful Hope: Approaching the New Millennium,* eds. Christopher Kleinhenz and Fannie J. LeMoine (Madison: University of Wisconsin Press, 1999), 149–69; Michael Barkun, "End-Time Paranoia: Conspiracy Thinking at the Millennium's Close," in *Fearful Hope,* 170–81; Boyer, "When U.S. Foreign Policy Meets Biblical Prophecy," *AlterNet,* February 20, 2003, http://www.alternet.org/story.html?StoryID=15221 (last accessed July 29, 2006) .

38. ———, *Marks of the Beast,* 53–195.

39. It should be understood that, once the Beast system of the Antichrist is firmly installed postRapture, much more than mere buying and selling are implied for those who are solidly enrolled. As Cindy Crosby writes in a review of volume eight of the series, "In Tim F LaHaye's *The Mark,* it's the dawn of the Great Tribulation, 'the bloodiest season in the history of the world.' After lying in state for three days, Nicolae Carpathia has risen from the dead. As the world responds in awe, statues of the potentate and 'god' are erected in every major city, and a new religion, 'Carpathianism,' is in full swing. Followers of the Antichrist are branded with a loyalty mark on their right hands or their foreheads, and 'vaccinated' with a biochip embedded with personal information. Those who refuse the mark take a one-way trip to the guillotine. The second coming of Christ is only three and one-half years away. But can the Tribulation Force hang on?

"'The God who calls you to the ultimate sacrifice will also give you the power to endure it. No one can receive the mark of the beast by accident. It is a once-for-all decision that will forever condemn you to eternity without God,' writes Tsion Ben-Judah in his daily newsletter with its cyber-audience of more than a billion. Heavenly power may be the only hope for the Tribulation

Force [Christian underground resistance—JS], as it struggles to survive amid new terrors." See http://www.amazon.co.uk/exec/obidos/ASIN/0842332286/ ref=pd_sxp_elt_l1/202-0028454-1595060 (last accessed July 29, 2006), for an editorial review of Tim LaHaye and Jerry Jenkins, *The Mark: The Beast Rules the World* (Wheaton, Ill.: Tyndale House, 2001).

40. Tim LaHaye and Jerry B. Jenkins, *Are We Living in the End Times?* (Wheaton, Ill.: Tyndale House, 1999), 196.

41. Shuck, *Marks of the Beast,* esp. 170, on the tendency: "Instead, prophecy believers despair of their abilities to bring about any large-scale differences of their own volition, all the while following the dictates of a seemingly inexorable apocalyptic framework. *Left Behind* protagonists no longer encounter the world dynamically and accommodate to it, but become instead mere actors on the apocalyptic stage. They lose their dynamic, individual characters, becoming temporary players of eternal roles, ironically condemning themselves to follow slavishly their own interpretations of ancient texts . . . the third possibility of a politically engaged despair . . . commands evangelicals to remake the world, buttressed by the strength and certainty of a fixed heavenly mandate."

42. Cf. Shuck, *Marks of the Beast,* 13: "*Left Behind* contains constant references to the high status of its protagonists. Ivy-League educated characters work alongside economists, engineers, computer technicians, and airline pilots in the elite Tribulation Force. LaHaye and Jenkins imply that if such high status 'hubs' can accept the evangelical message, ordinary people ought to as well."

43. See, e.g., Shuck, *Marks of the Beast,* 168–70.

44. Shuck, *Marks of the Beast,* 15.

45. "7. A. Behold I have prayed to God. R. What then wouldst thou know? A. All these things which I have prayed for. R. Sum them up in brief. A. God and the soul, that is what I desire to know. R. Nothing more? A. Nothing whatever," Augustine of Hippo, *Soliloquies,* http://www.newadvent.org/fathers/170301. htm (last accessed July 29, 2006).

46. For the intensification of this theme in the Reformation, see especially Harry J. McSorley, *Luther—Right or Wrong?: An Ecumenical Theological Study of Luther's Major Work, The Bondage of the Will* (New York: Newman Press, 1969).

47. Stephen O' Leary, *Arguing the Apocalypse: A Theory of Millennial Rhetoric* (New York: Oxford University Press, 1994), cited in Shuck, *Marks of the Beast,* 55–57, 61, 189–93, 196–98.

48. Shuck, *Marks of the Beast,* 141–66.

49. Tim LaHaye and Jerry B. Jenkins, *Armageddon: The Cosmic Battle of the Ages* (Wheaton, Ill.: Tyndale, 2003), 17–18, cited in Shuck, *Marks of the Beast,* 190.

50. Here the hardened cynic may be tempted to wonder whether Cecil B. DeMille and other masters of Hollywood special effects in the service of biblical epic have not perhaps exercised an unwholesome effect on the God-image of contemporary prophecy believers. Whether the autocratic style of the older studio system has not similarly tainted the operative theology is a prospect too alarming to entertain at length.

51. Shuck *Mark of the Beast,* chaps. 2 and 4 in particular. During his time in theological circles, the elder author has met parents who have changed schools or even moved from one city to another because of "humanism" and sex education in the schools. This future identity concern is (anecdotally at least) so prevalent that it as a theme and motivator among Christian parents deserves rigorous study by sociologists.

52. ———, *Marks of the Beast,* esp. 34–36 55, 67, 136.

53. ———, *Marks of the Beast,* 139: "LaHaye and Jenkins are much more concerned with what they consider problematic cultural changes than they are with one person." See also William C. Martin, *With God on Our Side: The Rise of the Religious Right in America* (New York: Broadway, 1996).

54. See, e.g., Martin, *With God on Our Side.*

55. Shuck, *Marks of the Beast,* 56–57, 200; see 200 on the pragmatic approach to Reconstructionists.

56. ———, *Marks of the Beast,* 56–57, citing Susan Harding, "Imagining the Last Days: The Politics of Apocalyptic Language," in *Accounting for Fundamentalisms: The Dynamic Character of Movements,* ed. Martin E. Marty and R. Scott Appleby (Chicago: University of Chicago Press, 1994), 57–78; also Shuck, 200.

57. Here relying on the general sense of Shuck, *Marks of the Beast.*

58. See especially Paul S. Boyer, *When Time Shall Be No More: Prophecy Belief in Modern American Culture* (Cambridge, Mass.: Harvard University Press, 1992); Robert C. Fuller, *Naming the Antichrist: The History of an American Obsession* (New York: Oxford University Press, 1995); Susan Harding, "Imagining the Last Days: The Politics of Apocalyptic Language," in *Accounting for Fundamentalisms: The Dynamic Character of Movements,* eds. Martin E. Marty and R. Scott Appleby (Chicago: University of Chicago Press, 1994), 57–78; Susan Friend Harding, *The Book of Jerry Falwell: Fundamentalist Language and Politics* (Princeton: Princeton University Press, 2000); and Martin, *With God on Our Side*; Michelle Goldberg, *Kingdom Coming: The Rise of Christian Nationalism* (New York: W. W. Norton, 2006); Frykholm, *Left Behind in Evangelical America.*

59. For the take on globalization in popular culture otherwise, see esp. Paul A. Cantor, *Gilligan Unbound: Pop Culture in the Age of Globalization* (Lanham, Md.: Rowman & Littlefield, 2001).

60. But perhaps not to Stamford and Darien. For "self-marginalization," see Shuck, *Marks of the Beast,* 8 and 171.

61. Here an important parallel in the creative use of overtly dubious victim status can be found in the contemporary portrayal of the sacralized American military as somehow empowered and put beyond criticism due to their having been stabbed in the back and then legendarily spat upon during the Vietnam era. See below, chapters 6 and 7. For "curdled" emotions, see Meštrović, *Postemotional Society,* 1. See also (for the exaggerated reports of Vietnam-era spittings upon returning troops and contemporary reality) Jerry Lembecke, *Spitting Image: Myth, Memory, and the Legacy of Vietnam* (New York: New York University Press, 2000); see also Kevin Baker, "Stabbed in the Back: The Past and Future of a right-wing myth,"

Harper's (June 2006), http://www.harpers.org/StabbedInTheBack.html (last accessed November 23, 2006).

62. Fenster, *Conspiracy Theories.*
63. ———, *Conspiracy Theories,* 166.
64. ———, *Conspiracy Theories,* 106–31, 223f.; 183–88.
65. Thus Fenster, *Conspiracy Theories,* 181–98.
66. For example, Fenster, *Conspiracy Theories,* in this connection cites George Marsden, *Fundamentalism and American Culture: The Shaping of Twentieth-Century Evangelicalism, 1870–1925* (New York: Oxford University Press, 1982); see Fenster, 259 nn. 15 and 150.
67. Michael Walzer, *The Revolution of the Saints: A Study in the Origins of Radical Politics* (Cambridge, Mass.: Harvard University Press, 1965). This reading of genetic and sociopolitical connections here reflects in part the elder of the present writers' original exposure to this work over thirty years ago under the influence of his teacher J. G. A. Pocock and with it Pocock's take on religious struggle in the early modern period.
68. What we lack, and very much need, is a look at evangelical prophecy fiction of the coming generation, fiction written well after the lengthy hold of evangelical-oriented Republicans on national political power has had time to sink in to the minds of potential authors. How well the exercise of power will sit with these authors we cannot know at this stage.

Chapter 4

Epigraph is from Chuck Palahniuk, *Fight Club* (New York: Henry Holt, 1996), 49.
1. On poll data documenting in the detail the dramatic growth of extreme social isolation in the United States, see Shankar Vedantam, "Social Isolation Growing in U.S., Study Says: The Number of People Who Say They Have No One to Confide In Has Risen," *Washington Post,* June 23, 2006, A03, online at http://www.washingtonpost.com/wp-dyn/content/article/2006/06/22/AR2006062201763_pf.html (last accessed June 26, 2006).
2. *Fight Club: The Final Screenplay,* by Jim Uhls, "based on the novel by C. Palahniuk," online at http://www.geocities.com/weekend_game/final_scr4.htm (last accessed July 27, 2007).
3. See "Edward Norton: Interview," where Norton says: "And there were other very provocative ideas that were discomforting in the sense that, well we're at Yale so we can talk this way, but it was more like there's stuff about it that are kind of classically Nietzchean almost. I thought this is a piece about the challenge of individual self overcoming. Of making yourself evolve and of shattering old value systems and received value systems and institutional kind of hierarchies to free yourself individually," "EDWARD NORTON YALE INTERVIEW," http://www.bradcolbourne.com/norton.txt (last accessed June 27, 2006). Cf. Heinz Ludwig Arnold, *Krieger, Waldgänger, Anarch: Versuch über Ernst Jünger* (Göttingen: Wallstein-Verlag, 1990).

4. Thus the celebrated line of Tyler: "We're a generation of men raised by women. I'm wondering if another woman is really the answer we need," http://www. geocities.com/weekend_game/final_scr2.htm.

5. The interpretation of Jack's shooting himself to kill off Tyler has of course elicited many interpretations. Applying theory of ritual behavior here would lead us astray—but certainly a discussion of leaving and entering society in connection with the anthropologist's categories of rites of passage, symbolic death, rebirth, liminality, and the like could well be of interest here (e.g., Arnold van Gennep, Max Gluckman, Victor Turner).

6. For examples of these kinds of views, follow the leads beginning with the discussion of *Fight Club* and related topics between Roger Ebert and David Edelstein in "the movie club: critic vs. critic," *Slate,* December 17, 1999, http://slate.msn. com/id/2000134/entry/1004223/ (last accessed June 27, 2006). For samples of the spectrum of views, see n. 7 below.

7. See, for example, the readings by Giroux and the other entries having to do with the fascism charge; also Kevin Hagopian, "Film Notes: Fight Club," http:// www.albany.edu/writers-inst/fnf04n1.html (last accessed June 27, 2006).

8. For example, see Diken and Laustsen.

9. Thus the Web site title: "The Cult—The Official Site of Chuck Palahniuk," www.chuckpalahniuk.net/ (last accessed June 27, 2006).

10. Paul Farhi, "On the Web, Punch and Click: Amateur Fight Videos Are Proliferating Online," *Washington Post,* June 22, 2006, A01, http://www.washingtonpost.com/wp-dyn/content/article/2006/06/21/AR2006062101780. html (last accessed June 11, 2006); "American Gladiators," http://en.wikipedia. org/wiki/American_Gladiators (last accessed July 27, 2007); Andrew J. Bacevich, *The New American Militarism: How Americans Are Seduced by War* (New York: Oxford University Press, 2005). Bacevich would probably claim to be horrified by the connections asserted in the text at this point, but anyone who thinks that American volunteer troops could tolerate what they put up with in Asian wars, legally or otherwise, without years of prior psychic preparation of a kind not known since frontier days of Indian wars, is living in a dream world. A somewhat too narrowly defined and too class-concentrated but useful analysis of the film along male-identity and employment-possibility lines is presented by Adrienne Redd, "Masculine Identity in the Service Class: An Analysis of *Fight Club,*" http://www.criticism.com/md/fightclub.html (last accessed June 23, 2006).

11. Kate Greenwood, "'You are not a beautiful and unique snowflake'": Fighting and Ideology in Fight Club," archived at http://64.233.161.104/search?q=cache: HKZXpctD60UJ:journal.media-culture.org.au/0302/09-snowflake.php+gr eenwood+beautiful+unique+snowflake+kate&hl=en&gl=us&ct=clnk&cd=1 (last accessed June 27, 2006), citing Gilles Deleuze, *Negotiations: 1972–1990* (New York: Columbia University Press, 1995) and Gilles Deleuze and Felix Guattari, *A Thousand Plateaus: Capitalism and Schizophrenia,* tr. Brian Massumi (Minneapolis: University of Minnesota Press, 2002).

12. ———, "You are not a beautiful and unique snowflake": Fighting and Ideology in Fight Club" (see previous note; original URL http://www. media-culture.org.au/0302/09-snowflake.html). Also online at http://journal. media—culture.org.an/0302/09-snowflake.php (last accessed December 4, 2006).

13. Greenwood, Bit 14.

14. ———, citing Slavoj Žižek, *The Ticklish Subject: the Absent Centre of Political Ontology* (London: Verso, 1999), 373.

15. Greenwood, Bit 13.

16. See n. 7 above.

17. Of course, that is, with its target audience (and that audience by definition regards itself as a minority, but an elite minority, in the know, comprehending of the winks that *Fight Club* so abundantly provides).

18. Thus Tyler: "Ahh, self-improvement is masturbation. And self-destruction . . . ," http://www.geocities.com/weekend_game/final_scr2.htm (last accessed July 27, 2007).

19. Meštrović, *Postemotional Society;* David Riesman, *The Lonely Crowd: A Study of the Changing American Character,* with Nathan Glazer and Reuel Denney (New Haven: Yale University Press, 1950; rpt. 1961).

20. Sean McCrossin in a private communication, citing for example material in the "Historical Income Tables," online at http://www.census.gov/hhes/income/ histinc/p08a.html and http://www.census.gov/hhes/income/histinc/incperdet. html (both last accessed June 27, 2006).

21. See for example "Press Release: The Forgotten Half Revisited: American Youth and Young Families, 1988–2008," *American Youth Policy Forum,* http://www. aypf.org/pressreleases/pr18.htm (last accessed June 27, 2006).

22. Gary Younge, "Youth Find More Truth in Eminem than Bush," *Guardian,* July 18, 2003, http://www.guardian.co.uk/international/story/0,3604,1000344,00.html (last accessed June 27, 2006). Another account: "EMINEM is 'more truthful' than PRESIDENT GEORGE W BUSH, according to a new survey. . . . Questions relating to trust were posed to 1,016 Americans, and 53 percent of those found the rapper's rhymes more credible and believable than Bush's speeches. . . . According to Los Angeles radio station KIIS FM, almost two-thirds of those involved in the survey preferred Eminem to Bush and 55 per cent of 35–44 year-olds thought the same. . . . The survey was conducted by advertising agency Euro RSCG . . . Published: 25–07–2003–12–38." Online as: "EM'S PEOPLE," http://www.nme. com/news/105678.htm (last accessed June 27, 2006; requires internal searching).

23. Fenster, *Conspiracy Theories,* 112. On the concept of "commodified" conspiracy theory, see Clare Birchall, "The Commodification of Conspiracy Theory," in *Conspiracy Nation: The Politics of Paranoia in Postwar America*, ed. Peter Knight (New York: New York University Press, 2002), 233–53, esp. 237f.: "Taking 'belief' out of the equation means that conspiracy theory can be marketed, and [periodically] adopted by those concerned with a generalized, rather than specific, conspiracy or injustice . . . the representational attributions 'true' and 'false' are exposed as unstable once metanarratives are questioned";

Birchall, 238: "A commodified version of conspiracy theory highlights the way conspiracy theory provides us with no line of action, or renders its disruptive potential impotent." See also Fenster, 219; also the important related remarks (on which we have relied here and elsewhere) in Douglass Kellner, "*The X-Files* and Conspiracy: A Diagnotic Critique," in Knight, *Conspiracy Nation*, 205–32.

24. See Diken and Laustsen.

25. Like his Keanu Reeves-like sibling in *Johnny Mnemonic*, where the data piracy is so risky that he must sacrifice his personal memory so brain space can be gained for archiving forbidden official data.

26. Text of the shooting script online and searchable at: "*Fight Club*. The Final Screenplay. By Jim Uhls. Based on the Novel by Chuck Pahlahniuk," http://www. geocities.com/weekend_game/final_scr2.htm (last accessed June 27, 2006). At this point, the script intersects rather violently with the empirical life experience of the target audience in an age of neoliberal globalization, outsourcing, and spin control with regard to economic news so far as it is presented by official culture, the media, and even academic economics. Cf. on this point the words of Paul Craig Roberts, formerly in the Treasury Department under Ronald Reagan and former associate editor of the *Wall Street Journal* editorial page, published as "How the Economic News is Spun: When You Can't Obscure the News, Buy It," *Counterpunch,* March 2, 2006, http://www.counterpunch.org/roberts03022006.html (last accessed June 27, 2006): "[After indicting Wall Street economists, government report writers, think tank economists, and economists and media experts in general as deliberate and unwitting falsifiers of the realities of outsourcing and low pay in middle class jobs, and after discussing in detail the economic facts he contends are spun or ignored in defending neoliberal economics, free trade, outsourcing, and a visa policy detrimental to expensive American labor, Roberts makes plain that for him the conclusion emerges that] In America 'truth' has long been for sale. We see it in expert witness testimony, in the corrupt reports from forensic labs that send innocent people to prison, and even in policy disputes among scientists themselves. In scholarship, ideas that are too challenging to prevailing opinion have a rough row to hoe and often cannot get a hearing." Thus behind Tyler Durden's address to his peers lies a massive generational sense of mendacious betrayal by institutions and experts, universities and foundations prominently included. See also Gabor Steingart, "A SUPERPOWER IN DECLINE: America's Middle Class Has Become Globalization's Loser," *Spiegel Online,* October 24, 2006, http://www. spiegel.de/international/0,158,439766.00.html (last accessed October 24, 2006). See furher Antonia Juhasz, *The Bush Agenda* (New York: Regan Books, 2006).

27. Online at http://www.geocities.com/weekend_game/final_scr2 (last accessed July 27, 2007).

28. Ibid.

29. Meštrović, xi, 2,4, 17, 26, 31–40, 43–46, 55, 78–79, 86, 102, 108, 123, 127, 140.

30. While ideologies do not vanish here, their effective deployment depends upon proper triggering of a chain of emotional reactions according to cues and rules

assimilated by all parties at an early age. Though values and ideological principles are, for these personality types, ultimately quite changeable and in theory infinitely fungible, in practice such fundamental change requires an immense amount of shared energy. As a result, for example, within the contemporary world of political correctness that alarms Meštrović (as well as the contemporary males represented by Tyler Durden, since they are denied such perks) there is little tendency for quick alteration. The limited repertoire of officially sanctioned victims and the conserved outrage and fossilized stocks of appropriate indignation cued to official memory of past injustsice does not change very often or very fast, nor is there any rapid change in access to most-favored-victim status in the sociogovernmental awarding of standing and income that corresponds to these tendencies.

31. As for the emotions of followers in such movements, well, here of course there has always been room for debate about the channeling and reworking of such energy.

32. Note carefully: libidinal, aggressive, compelling, charismatic, relentless Tyler is certainly not other-directed—and he knows it! Tyler is just as inner-directed as Hitler or Calvin. He may hate, despise, and wish to fight his father, but by some method he did acquire his own set of values, values that demand tangible and quick gratification and that finally lead him from entrepreneurial capitalism (which he practices while denouncing the consumers who buy his soap made from their own class's stolen liposuctioned fat) to leadership of a quasifascist men's movement. Whether Palahniuk reads Veblen and Riesman or not, by design or by instinct he has yoked together two extremely divergent personality types in the figure[s] of Jack/Tyler, figures representing an era of builders and individualists and tyrants and charmers, most of them either male or representatives of classically "male" traits—and then as well an era of team players, consumers, attitude adjusters, and representatives of stylized "female" traits. And there can be no doubt that the work tends to link these cooperative, worried, consumer-oriented traits with decadence, lateness, ineffectiveness, indecision, and effeminacy in what Tyler famously terms "a generation of men raised by women." Thus in the by-now celebrated "bathtub scene" Tyler, taking a long soak, discusses with Jack the disappointments of their two life trajectories and the difficulties with the father, at the end of which Jack says, "I can't get married, I'm a thirty-year-old boy!" Tyler responds, "We're a generation of men raised by women. I'm wondering if another woman is really the answer we need." See online text at http://www.geocities.com/weekend_game/final_scr2.htm (last accessed June 27, 2006); and see n. 23 above.

Precisely the same typological and chronological contrast lies behind the closely related series of scenes in which Jack and Tyler discuss who out of a gallery of celebrities living and dead would be an honorable and worthy opponent, tending here always to favor males known because they did something, accomplished something, especially if they also acquired a reputation as good at combat—Lincoln, Hemingway, and the like. This preference is put in close proximity with what to many viewers appears at first as a puzzling put-down of the physical type favored in Calvin Klein underwear ads—curious as the film's own iconography is not too far removed from the same aesthetic. But the point is that Lincoln and Hemingway (and by implication Tyler and Jack as their peers) do not stake their standing in history on an infinitely marketable six-pack and dimples, but on aggressive modes of making a difference, not least of all by founding a volatile and successful metapolitical men's movement.

33. Reading according to Meštrović but supported in context by the compensatory excursions into the outlandishly spontaneous in, for example, employment situations.

34. Victor Turner, *The Ritual Process: Structure and Anti-Structure*, 2nd ed. (New York: Aldine de Gruyter, 1995); Georges Bataille, *Theory of Religion*, trans. Robert Hurley (New York: Zone Books, 1989), 43–63; Max Gluckman, *Politics, Law and Ritual in Tribal Society* (Chicago: Aldine, 1965); extensive conceptual-history background on which this account relies in Catherine M. Bell, *Ritual: Perspectives and Dimensions* (New York: Oxford University Press, 1997); Natalie Zemon Davis, "The Reasons of Misrule: Youth Groups and Charivaris in Sixteenth-Century France," *Past and Present* 50 (1971): 41–75; idem, "The Rites of Violence"; in her *Society and Culture in Early Modern France* (Stanford: Stanford University Press 1975): 152–87; Mikhail Bakhtin, *Rabelais and His World* (Cambridge, Mass.: MIT Press, 1968); Johan Huizinga, *Homo Ludens: A Study of the Play-Element in Culture* (Boston: Beacon Press, 1955).

35. On all this, see the comprehensive account in Bell, *Ritual*, esp. 38–40. There Bell shows how these views evolved, taking clear shape in the work of Max Gluckman on "rituals of rebellion" that affirm social cohesion and work by "releasing social tensions, thereby limiting discontent," even as "temporary suspensions of the usual order . . . dramatically acknowledge that order as normative." Next, as Bell documents, Victor Turner portrayed such rituals as "a mechanism for constantly re-creating, not just affirming" social cohesion, such that ritual contributes to "the ongoing process by which the community was continually redefining and renewing itself." According to Bell, central here was for Turner's ritual capacity to "act out . . . conflicts and the dominant values holding the group together"—a function that did more than simply provide for "a cathartic easing of social tensions" along the lines set forth by Gluckman. On these terms, *Fight Club* presents an improvised analogue to such rituals (in a society quite intolerant of any real-world rituals of inversion), but one in which the contribution to broadening or rearranging or reshuffling the normative social world post-fight-clubbing turns out to be zero, the function in this particular case being simply that of catharsis and reaffirmation in the most non-revolutionary of ways. (Full comprehension of the issues here in Turner's schema requires taking into account his basic distinction between normal social conditions and those in liminal, initiatiory, or re-constitutive situations.) See Turner, 96:

"What is interesting about liminal phenomena for our present purposes is the blend they offer of lowliness and sacredness, of homogeneity and comradeship. We are presented, in such rites, with a 'moment in and out of time,' and in and out of secular social structure, which reveals, however fleetingly, some recognition (in symbol if not always in language) of a generalized social bond that has ceased to be and has simultaneously yet to be fragmented into a multiplicity of structural ties. . . . It is as though there are here two major 'models' for human interrelatedness, juxtaposed and alternating. The first is of society as a structured, differentiated, and often hierarchical system of politico-legal-economic positions, with many types of evaluation, separating men in terms of 'more' or 'less.' The second, which emerges recognizably in the liminal period, is of society as an unstructured or rudimentarily structured and relatively undifferentiated *comitatus,* community, or even communion of equal individuals who submit together to the general authority of the ritual elders." For author Palahniuk's own explicit interest in the work of Victor Turner and liminality, see Michelle Bourdet, "Ranting with Chuck," *The Rebel Yell University of Nevada,* Las Vegas, November 6, 2006, http://www.unlvrebelyell. com/savearticle.php?ID=9984 (last accessed December, 11, 2006).

36. Bülent Diken and Carsten Bagge Laustsen, "Enjoy your fight!—*Fight Club* as a symptom of the Network Society," http://www.xs4all.nl/~mlab/con_gress/ 7a4fightclub.html (last accessed July 12, 2006) or at http://www.lahrs.ac.uk/fss/ sociology/papers/diken_lanston_enjoy-your-fight.pdf (last accessed July 27, 2007), with the final words of Palahniuk cited from S. Tomlinson, "Is It Fistfighting, or Just Multi-Tasking?" (1999), http://www.salon.com/ent/movies/int/1999/10/13/ palahniuk/index.html (last accessed June 27, 2006). See the approving citation of this passage in Slavoj Žižek, "The Ambiguity of the Masochist Social Link," *Perversion and the Social Relation,* ed. by Molly Anne Rothenberg et al. (Durham, N.C.: Duke University Press, 2003), 112–25, here 121.

37. C. L. Barber, *Shakespeare's Festive Comedy: A Study of Dramatic Form and Its Relation to Social Custom* (Princeton: Princeton University Press, 1959); also Robert Hornback, "Emblems of Folly in the First Othello: Renaissance Blackface, Moor's Coat, and 'Muckender,'" *Comparative Drama* 35 (2001), http://www. questia.com/PM.qst?a=o&d=5001048474 (last accessed June 27, 2006).

38. Davis, section 4 of her "Reasons of Misrule."

39. John Gray, *Enlightenment's Wake: Politics and Culture at the Close of the Modern Age* (London: Routledge, 1995).

Chapter 5

Epigraph is from *The Wild One,* screenplay by John Paxton and Ben Maddow after *The Cyclists' Raid* by Frank Rooney is taken from 1953. It can be accessed online at http://www.weeklyscript.com/Wild%20One,%20The.txt (last accessed July 12, 2006).

1. *E la Nave Va* (1983).

2. See for example Robert Pollin, *Contours of Descent: U.S. Economic Fractures and the Landscape of Global Austerity* (London: Verso, 2003); Jeff Faux, *The Global Class War: How America's Bipartisan Elite Lost Our Future—and What It Will Take to Win It Back* (New York: John Wiley & Sons, 2006).

3. Here of course it is important to realize that this outlook on the one hand assumed the rightness of progress and a certain secularization while at the same time leaving as yet undefined the definitive stance on the limits of social change.

4. Christoph Bochinger, *"New Age" und moderne Religion: Religionswissenschaftliche Analysen* (München: Chr. Kaiser, 1995).

5. Olav Hammer, *Claiming Knowledge: Strategies of Epistemology from Theosophy to the New Age,* Numen Book Series 90 (Leiden: E. J. Brill, 2001), esp. 73–74.

6. It is noteworthy that expert David Tacey finds the contemporary movement's affirmation of free will in a rather mixed, even dubious, condition, with attunement to cosmic forces and destiny threatening to overwhelm the individual in various branches of this worldview grouping.

7. David Tacey, *Jung and the New Age* (New York: Brunner-Routledge, 2001), 11–12.

8. Tacey, x–xi; Wouter Hanegraaff, *New Age Religion and Western Culture: Esotericism in the Mirror of Secular Thought.* SUNY Series in Western Esoteric Traditions (Leiden: E. J. Brill, 1996); Hammer, *Claiming Knowledge;* Michael Schneider, *New Age: Empirische Studien zur New Age Bewegung,* ed. Gerald Eberlein and Anton Maria Kirchdorfer (Vaduz: Bild- und Verlagsanstalt, 1991); Paul Heelas, *The New Age Movement: The Celebration of the Self and the Sacralization of Modernity* (Oxford: Blackwell, 1996); James R. Lewis and J. Gordon Melton, *Perspectives on the New Age,* SUNY Series in Religious Studies (Albany: State University of New York Press, 1992); Mark Woodhouse, *Paradigm Wars: Worldviews for a New Age* (Berkeley, Calif.: Frog Press, 1996); William A. Tiller, *Science and Human Transformation: Subtle Energies, Intentionality and Consciousness* (Walnut Creek, Pa.: Pavior, 1997).

9. Woodhouse, 55, 432–35.

10. *Perspectives on the New Age,* ed. Lewis and Melton; Robert Ellwood, "How New Is the New Age," in Lewis and Melton, 59–67.

11. Catherine Albanese, "The Magical Staff: Quantum Healing in the New Age," in Lewis and Melton, *Perspectives on the New Age,* 68–84; Catherine Albanese, "Mesmer, Swedenborg and Quantum Physics," *Compass* 14:2; cf. Hammer, 271–303.

12. Albanese, in Lewis and Melton, *Perspectives on the New Age,* 73.

13. ———.

14. Bochinger, 498.

15. ———, 387, 477.

16. ———, 510.

17. Broad background in Derek Ager, *The New Catastrophism: The Rare Event in Geological History* (Cambridge: Cambridge University Press, 1995).

18. Bochinger, 103–37.

19. Tacey; Knight, *Conspiracy Culture.*

20. Reinhart Koselleck, *The Practice of Conceptual History: Timing History, Spacing Concepts,* trans. Todd Presner (Stanford: Stanford University Press, 2002); cf. John C. Lyden, *Film as Religion: Myths, Morals, and Rituals* (New York: New York University Press, 2003), 246.

21. David J. Hess, *Science in the New Age: The Paranormal, Its Defenders and Debunkers, and American Culture* (Madison: University of Wisconsin Press, 1993).

22. For example, Ingo Swann.

23. Steve Bruce, *Religion in the Modern World: From Cathedrals to Cults* (New York: Oxford University Press, 1996), 210.

24. Cf. Eduard Schweizer, "Das hellenistische Weltbild als Produkt der Weltangst," in Schweizer, *Neotestamentica* (Zürich: Zwingli Verlag, 1963), 15–28.

25. For the Mars matter, see in Woodhouse, "Appendix. 'Message from Mars': Sacred Geometry and the Evolution of Consciousness by Frederick O. Mills," 535–68. Note the citing on p. 568 of John Michell, *The New View Over Atlantis* (New York: Harper & Row, 1983) as well as R. A. Schwaller de Lubicz, *The Egyptian Miracle: An Introduction to the Wisdom of the Temple* (New York: Inner Traditions International, 1985) and Randolfo Rafael Pozos, *The Face on Mars: Evidence for a Lost Civilization?* (Chicago: Chicago Review Press, 1986).

26. Woodhouse, vii–viii.

27. ———, e.g. 11–12, 177; 154–244.

28. Woodhouse, 244; http://www.deanesmag.com/posts/1147702347.shtml (last accessed July 24, 2007) *God, Creation, and Contemporary Physics.* Bell's Theorem," *Wikipedia,* http://en/wikipedia.org/wiki/Bell%27s_Theorem (last accesssed July 22, 2006); Mark Willima Worthing, *God, Creation, and Contemporary Physics* (Minneapolis: Augsburg-Fortress, 1996), 124–30. See also Woodhouse, 166, 244–49; for the words of Nick Herbert about being "non-local," see Worthing, 128f.; for background, cf. Paul Heelas, *The New Age Movement: The Celebration of the Self and the Sacralization of Modernity* (Oxford: Blackwell, 1996).

29. ———, 164, 190–99, 244, 183–89. On the other hand, more mainstream authorities see the significance of all this quite differently. For example, Heinz Pagels, writing in *The Cosmic Code,* says: "Some recent popularizers of Bell's work when confronted with [Bell's inequality] have gone on to claim that telepathy is verified or the mystical notion that all parts of the universe are instantaneously interconnected is vindicated. Others assert that this implies communication faster than the speed of light. That is rubbish; the quantum theory and Bell's inequality imply nothing of this kind. Individuals who make such claims have substituted a wish-fulfilling fantasy for understanding. If we closely examine Bell's experiment we will see a bit of sleight of hand by the God that plays dice which rules out actual nonlocal influences. Just as we think we have captured a really weird beast—like acausal influences—it slips out of our grasp. The slippery property of quantum reality is again manifested." Quotation according to "Bell's theorem," *Wikipedia* (see n. 28 above).

30. ———, 522, 478, 482–86.
31. Cf. Woodhouse 478, 479–488, 497, 506–9.
32. For example, Woodhouse, 488–519.
33. Woodhouse, 523.
34. For example, Woodhouse, 488, 491, 532.
35. Woodhouse, 513–15.
36. Issues of interpretation surface here; see the preliminary comparison of conspiracy and related thinking in science fiction and *The X-Files* with Christian apocalyptic in Fenster, *Conspiracy Theories,* esp. 14–79. It should be noted that Fenster's typology is somewhat at variance with that of Michael Barkun, who sees a resurgence of overtly dangerous tendencies in adherents of very elaborate contemporary conspiracy theories. See Barkun, *A Culture of Conspiracy.*
37. Jim Marrs, *Rule by Secrecy: The Hidden History That Connects the Trilateral Commission, the Freemasons, and The Great Pyramids* (New York: HarperCollins, 2000), 407.
38. General background: Barkun, *A Culture of Conspiracy;* Barkun, *Religion and the Racist Right: The Origins of the Christian Identity Movement,* 2nd ed. (Chapel Hill: University of North Carolina Press, 1996); Jeffrey Kaplan, *The Cultic Milieu: Oppositional Subcultures in an Age of Globalization: Oppositional Subcultures in an Age of Globalization* (Walnut Creek, Calif.: AltaMira Press, 2002). While some in the radical fringe of the conspiracy culture might, if they had the opportunity, wish to become forces of destabilization, a fair number of those involved in the much larger "commodified" conspiracy culture (cf. Birchall, Fenster, Knight) have, it seems to the present authors, adopted instead a style of thinking that simultaneously explains the hopelessness of conditions and largely dispenses them from the necessity of trying to do much to change things.
39. See Fenster, *Conspiracy Theories*; William Barrett, *Death of the Soul: From Descartes to the Computer* (Garden City, N.Y.: Anchor Books, 1986); Charles Norris Cochrane, *Christianity and Classical Culture: A Study of Thought and Action from Augustus to Augustine* (New York: Oxford University Press, 1957).
40. Fredric Jameson, "Cognitive Mapping," in *Marxism and the Interpretation of Culture,* eds. C. Nelson and L. Grossberg (Urbana and Chicago: University of Illinois Press, 1988), 347–58.
41. Whereas the conspiracist work by Marrs could well fit into a more activist pattern of belief and action than the book by Woodhouse could overtly allow. However, the main reason why in the end one need not worry overmuch about extreme Right-wing conspiracy theories taking substantial shape so as to lead an extreme activist movement against the standing order lies in the parallel possibility rapidly becoming reality to the effect that a more moderate and nonviolent political movement has, as it were, in-flanked the extremists by reshaping the standing order very substantially, moving the media-defined center very much toward the Right, albeit at the cost of polarization that itself brings the possibility of unforeseen consequences in the long run (let the reader understand). Of course, this reshaping of the standing order may eventually evoke

strong counterreactions across the political spectrum, even from the anti-New-World-Order Right.

42. See the works by Barkun and Kaplan. Here we do not pronounce what ultimately scholars like Barkaun and Kaplan might make of Marrs. Nor do we pronounce either on what Marrs's work ultimately means to imply, nor the relation of Marrs in his later phases to less spectacular strands of conspiracy hypotheses in Marrs himself or in other writers. See particularly Michael Barkun, *A Culture of Conspiracy: Apocalyptic Visions in Contemporary America* (Berkeley: University of California Press, 2003), esp. 147 and 181. Note however with care the cautionary words in Paul S. Boyer, "The Strange World of Conspiracy Theories," *The Christian Century,* July 27, 2004, 32–35, online at http://www.religion-online. org/showarticle.asp?title=3075 (last accessed July 27, 2007). Note in particular these observations by Boyer there in his review of Barkun's *Culture of Conspiracy:* "Lest we all too readily dismiss conspiracy theorists, it is well to recall the record of real conspiracies, skullduggery, and deception in real life. . . . Nor does the notion of an all-powerful world system seem unduly bizarre in this era of global corporations, . . . gargantuan media conglomerates and the WTO. Indeed, the worldview of Barkun's cast of characters parallels that of the New Leftists of the 1960s, with their talk of the Establishment, or the contemporary work of Noam Chomsky. According to Amazon.com, buyers of Jim Marrs . . . are also purchasing Chomsky. . . . The conspiratorial-minded, in short, find ample grist in contemporary history." Note as well that while Boyer concludes his review with the warning that some readers of these conspiracy theories might someday imitate Timothy McVeigh, he does so only after seconding Barkun's dictum that this readership is marked by "the absence of formal organization."

Chapter 6

1. Adapting T. S. Eliot's classic term (1919) with a change of directionality of initiative in the process of seeking what corresponds: he intended the poet's act of seeking the appropriate corresponding items in the outside world to call up the emotion in question for his readers; here in seeking "objective correlatives" we play the role of literary biographer, seeking the outside circumstances and ideas that influenced the pessimist's act of writing and, having been located, make more plausible one or more interlocking interpretations of the written document of pessimism.

2. Robert K. Merton, *Social Theory and Social Structure* (Glencoe, Ill.: Free Press, 1957).

3. See Catherine L. Albanese, *America: Religions and Religion,* 2nd ed. (Belmont, Calif.: Wadsworth, 1992), 432–61.

4. Harold Hayes, ed., *Smiling through the Apocalypse: Esquire's History of the Sixties* (New York: McCall, 1970).

5. Meštrović, *Postemotional Society;* Arlie Russell Hochschild, *The Managed Heart: Commercialization of Human Feeling* (Berkeley: University of California Press,

1983); Barbara Ehrenreich, *Bait and Switch: The (Futile) Pursuit of the American Dream* (New York: Metropolitan Books, 2005). On the economic base factor, see Robert Pollin, *Contours of Descent: U.S. Economic Fractures and the Landscape of Global Austerity* (London: Verso, 2003); Jeff Faux, *The Global Class War: How America's Bipartisan Elite Lost Our Future—and What It Will Take to Win It Back* (New York: John Wiley & Sons, 2006).

6. Background: Morris Beatus, "Academic Proletariat: The Problem of Overcrowding in the Learned Professions and Universities during the Weimar Republic, 1918–1933" (Ph.D. dissertation, Department of History, University of Wisconsin, 1975); Fritz K. Ringer, *The Decline of the German Mandarins: The German Academic Community, 1890–1933* (Cambridge Mass.: Harvard University Press, 1969).

7. Paul Craig Roberts, "American Rot: When Opposing Voices Do Not Oppose," *Counterpunch,* April 4, 2005, http://www.counterpunch.org/roberts04042005. html (last accessed June 29, 2006) at various places and also likewise at various places in "Hegemony Lost: The American Economy is Destroying Itself," *Counterpunch,* August 25, 2005, http://www.counterpunch.org/roberts08252005.html (last accessed July 2, 2006). Also Robert Pollin, *Contours of Descent: U.S. Economic Fractures and the Landscape of Global Austerity* (London: Verso, 2003); Byron L. Dorgan, *Take This Job and Ship It: How Corporate Greed and Brain-Dead Politics Are Selling Out America* (New York: Thomas Dunne Books/St. Martin's Press, 2006); Hubert Dreyfus, "Conversation with Hubert L. Dreyfus: The Disembodied Internet," http://globetrotter.berkeley.edu/people5/Dreyfus/dreyfus-con7.html (last accessed July 16, 2006).

8. Phillips, *American Theocracy.*

9. ———, *American Theocracy,* "Preface," ix.

10. Dean, *Aliens in America.* Dean's work sees itself as in many ways inspired by Tom Engelhardt, *The End of Victory Culture: Cold War America and the Disillusioning of a Generation* (New York: Basic Books, 1995).

11. It may be useful to point out that we see no particular correlation between pacifist attitudes and general disaffection with the social, politic, and geopolitical policies of official culture. Younger consumers of cybernoir or *Fight Club* may view the government with skepticism and at the same time be entirely accepting of violence in conflict resolution.

12. Fritz Stern, *The Politics of Cultural Despair: A Study in the Rise of the Germanic Ideology* (Berkeley: University of California Press, 1963); George Mosse, *The Crisis of German Ideology: Intellectual Origins of the Third Reich,* 1st ed. (New York: Grosset & Dunlap, 1964).

13. Oliver Bennett, *Cultural Pessimism: Narratives of Decline in the Postmodern World* (Edinburgh: Edinburgh University Press, 2001).

14. Of course this does not mean we necessarily share all of Bennett's assessments. For Bennett, apparently the most important predictor of a turn toward pessimism or theories of decline in worldview turns out to be a downward turn socioeconomic condition. For recent times, of course, that signifies on Bennett's

terms the transition to a particularly relentless variety of globalizing neocapitalism advanced by government policy, a variety originally developed in the United States but, once exported, posing a serious challenge worldwide to more relaxed varieties of socially concerned capitalistic or mixed economies. Thus with Bennett's recent short monograph on the contemporary resurgence of attitudes of gloom, pessimism, and despair, the reader is brought to the threshold of recent American developments, with a finger pointed at neocapitalism of the recent American type as a prime factor in producing gloom for many and glee for the few. The possibility of converging currents of contemporary cultural pessimism cannot be dismissed out of hand, particularly in the United States, where supernaturalist fundamentalism in religion has enjoyed a blossoming unknown in Europe.

15. Stern, *The Politics of Cultural Despair;* Mosse, *The Crisis of German Ideology.*
16. Deep background in Thomas Molnar, *Twin Powers: Politics and the Sacred* (Grand Rapids: Eerdmans, 1988); Richard Neuhaus, *The Naked Public Square: Religion and Democracy in America,* 2nd ed. (Grand Rapids: Herdmans, 1986); Neuhaus, "Our American Babylon," *First Things* 158 (December 2005): 23–28.
17. On the question of concepts of the self, in particular, here, see Hubert Dreyfus, "Conversation with Hubert L. Dreyfus: The Disembodied Internet," http://globetrotter.berkeley.edu/people5/Dreyfus/dreyfus-con7.html (last accessed April 14, 2006).
18. See, for example, Emilio Gentile, *The Sacralization of Politics in Fascist Italy,* trans. Keith Botsford (Cambridge, Mass.: Harvard University Press, 1996); Emilio Gentile, *Le religioni della politica. Fra democrazie e totalitarismi, collana «Storia e Società»* (Rome: Laterza, 2001); Roger Griffin, "Withstanding the Rush of Time: The Prescience of G. L. Mosse's Anthropological Approach to Fascism," in *What History Tells: George L. Mosse's Study of Modern Europe,* ed. Stanley Payne (Madison: University of Wisconsin Press, 2003); idem., "The Palingenetic Core of Fascist Nationalism," in *Che cos'è il fascismo? Interpretazioni e prospettive di ricerche,* ed. Alessandro Campi (Rome: Ideazione Editrice, 2003), 97–122; idem., "Cloister or Cluster? The Implications of Emilio Gentile's Ecumenical Theory of Political Religion for the Study of Extremism," *Totalitarian Movements & Political Religions* 6:1 (2005): 33–52; idem., ed., *Fascism, Totalitarianism, and Political Religion,* Totalitarian Movements and Political Religion series (Lodon: Routledge, 2005); Vondung and cf. Claes Ryn, *America the Virtuous: the Crisis of Democracy and the Quest for Empire* (New Brunswick, N.J.: Transaction Publishers, 2003).
19. See nn. 20 and 21 below.
20. "Freiheit ist meine Leidenschaft," interview of Fritz Stern by Theo Sommer., *Die Zeit* (January 2, 2006), Nr. 6, http://www.zeit.de/2006/06/Stern?page=all (last accessed July 16, 2006).
21. "Historian Fritz Stern on the Prospects for Fascist Theocracy in America," http://leiterreports.typepad.com/blog/authoritarianism_and_fascism_alerts/index.

html (last accessed May 24, 2006); Chris Hedges, "Warning from a Student of Democracy's Collapse," archived online from the *New York Times* of January 6/7, 2006 by Information Clearing House via Google, http://64.233.179.104/ search?q=cache:T2r80ix_rB4J:www.informationclearinghouse.info/article7643. htm+stern+baeck+fritz+leo+&hl=en&gl=us&ct=clnk&cd=7 (last accessed July 3, 2006); official text of the speech at Fritz Stern, "Acceptance speech delivered by Fritz Stern upon receiving the Leo Baeck Medal at the 10th Annual Dinner of the Leo Baeck Institute," at http://www.lbi.org/fritzstern.html (last accessed July 16, 2006).

22. The present authors do not suggest that these two varieties of determinist self cannot come into public conflict on issues of social policy in some areas, only that they agree and pull in tandem over a wide and significant range of domains.

23. Recalling our heuristic move above, in which we call attention to discussions of rhetorics of sociopolitical legitimacy (civil religion) and their vicissitudes as ways of regarding civil religion rhetorics in America as both an indicator of how Americans respond to the ever-changing mix of real-world conditions affecting their hopes and at the same time as factors in helping shape the sense of political and social participation, the sense of holding a stake in the commonwealth. The simultaneous examination of linguistic categories as both indicators and factors is here taken from the history of concepts (*Begriffsgeschichte*) school founded by Reinhart Koselleck. See Koselleck, *The Practice of Conceptual History: Timing History, Spacing Concepts,* trans. Todd Samuel Presner et al. (Stanford: Stanford University Press, 2002).

24. See in this connection the treatment of Niklas Luhmann in Peter Beyer, *Religion and Globalization* (London: SAGE Publications, 1994), 33–40; Niklas Luhmann, *The Differentiation of Society,* trans. Stephen Holmes and Charles Larmore (New York: Columbia University Press, 1982); also n. 26 below.

25. See Hermann Lübbe, *Säkularisierung. Geschichte eines ideenpolitischen Begriffs,* 3rd ed. (Freiburg i.B.: Alber, 2003).

26. Rolf Schieder, *Civil Religion: Die religiöse Dimension der politischen Kultur* (Gütersloh: Gerd Mohn, 1987), 17f.

27. Here and elsewhere, our discussion closely follows the arguments on Bellah advanced in Albanese and Schieder.

28. See Schieder, 10–279.

29. Albanese, *America,* 457; cf. 456–561.

30. ———, 442.

31. ———, 448.

32. ———, 449.

33. ———, 439–40.

34. Gray, *Enlightenment's Wake,* 155; see also 145.

35. ———, *Enlightenment's Wake.*

36. That is, loss of humanist free will or strong sense of situated identity, or again, loss of the notion of the substantially constituted individual self in a larger political and sociocultural context of multidimensional loss and betrayal, ranging

from loss of shared religious identity to loss of expectations as economic hopes
and as political involvement.

37. On this concept, its participatory and common-good (versus purely acquisitive
or purely Lockean-property-rights reading of the American experience) overtones, and its relation to Hans Baron, Felix Gilbert, Hannah Arendt, Bernard
Bailyn, Gordon Wood, and J. G. A. Pocock, see above all Athanasios Moulakis,
"Civic Humanism," *The Stanford Encyclopedia of Philosophy,* ed. Edward N. Zalta
(Winter 2002), http://plato.stanford.edu/archives/win2002/entries/humanism-
civic/ (last accessed July 16, 2006).

38. See for example Walter Dean Burnham, "The United States: The Politics of
Heterogeneity," in *Electoral Behavior,* ed. Richard Rose (New York: Free Press,
1974), 718, as cited in the suggestive article by Seymour Martin Lipset, "Equality
and the American Creed: Understanding the Affirmative Action Debate,"
http://www.ppionline.org/documents/equality_lipset.pdf (last accessed April
13, 2006); for Berman, see Morris Berman, *Dark Ages America: The Final Phase
of Empire* (New York: W.W. Norton, 2006): 246–47; Chalmers Johnson, *The
Sorrows of Empire: Militarism, Secrecy, and the End of the Republic* (New York:
Metropolitan Books/Henry Holt, 2004). Lipset appears to have exercised a considerable influence on Berman.

39. Gray, *Enlightenment's Wake.* See for example p. 155.

40. C.B. Macpherson, *The Political Theory of Possessive Individualism: Hobbes to
Locke* (Oxford: Clarendon, 1962).

41. Gray, *Enlightenment's Wake,* 155; see also 145. Envisioned here is Gray's presupposition that the uniqueness of the Graeco-Christian heritage derives finally
from its premise that the human is a singularly adequate instrument for getting
hold of a true and adequate ultimate point of view.

42. One wonders whether the scriptwriter had been studying Spengler closely,
since—though Spengler is associated with decline as such—in fact Spengler distinguished carefully between cultural and metaphysical decline (primary) and
ensuing physical and dynamic decline (secondary and gradual).

43. "American Rhetoric: Movie Speech, 'Network' (1976): Howard Beale Declaims
the Death of Democracy," *Movie Speeches: Online Speech Bank: American
Rhetoric Home* (Copyright 2001–2006; transcribed in HTML by Michael E.
Eidenmuller), http://www.americanrhetoric.com/MovieSpeeches/moviespeech-
network5.html (last accessed June 2, 2006).

44. David M. Potter, *People of Plenty* (Chicago: University of Chicago Press, 1954;
rpt. 1958); Gray, *Enlightenment's Wake,* 88, 93, 95.

45. Above all Gray, *Enlightenment's Wake.*

46. Background: Panajotis Kondylis, *Konservativismus: geschichtlicher Gehalt und
Untergang* (Stuttgart: Klett-Cotta, 1986); Gray, *Enlightenment's Wake,* 93–
100. See also Stefan Breuer, *Anatomie der konservativen Revolution,* 2nd ed.
(Darmstadt: Wissenschaftliche Buchgesellschaft, 1995).

47. Oliver Bennett, *Cultural Pessimism: Narratives of Decline in the Postmodern World*
(Edinburgh: Edinburgh University Press, 2001).

48. Michael Vlahos, "Weakness of Empire," *The American Conservative,* May 22, 2006, http://amconmag.com/2006/2006_05_22/feature.html (last accessed May 30, 2006); Andrew J. Bacevich, *The New American Militarism* (Oxford: Oxford University Press, 2005).

49. Phillips, *American Theocracy;* Berman, *Dark Ages America;* Johnson, *The Sorrows of Empire.* See also the impressionistic remarks in Gore Vidal, *Imperial America: Reflections on the United States of Amnesia* (New York: Thunder's Mouth/Nation Books, 2004). Less negative on the American transformation is, of course, Niall Ferguson, *Colossus: The Rise and Fall of the American Empire* (New York: Penguin, 2005).

50. The arguments in these paragraphs represent a carrying forward of hints in Bacevich and Vlahos, heavily indebted at each stage to those writers, yet pressing to conclusions from which those writers might shrink and for which they cannot be held responsible so far as the domestic function of the New Model Army among our New Model Puritans is concerned.

51. The important historical prelude is outlined in Richard M. Gamble, *The War for Righteousness: Progressive Christianity, the Great War, and the Rise of the Messianic Nation* (Wilmington, Del.: ISI Books, 2003).

52. On this especially the reflections of Vlahos require attention: Michael Vlahos, "The Weakness of Empire,"

53. "For Immediate Release Office of the Press Secretary April 18, 2006 President Bush Nominates Rob Portman as OMB Director and Susan Schwab for USTR," http://www.whitehouse.gov/news/releases/2006/04/20060418–1.html (last accessed July 26, 2006).

54. Vlahos, "The Weakness of Empire."

55. Bacevich, 23, citing George Will, "Forrestal Lecture Series," U.S. Naval Academy, January 24, 2001; and Tom Morganthau, "The Military's New Image," *Newsweek,* March 11, 1991.

56. George Steiner, "The Archives of Eden (1981)," in his *No Passion Spent: Essays, 1978–1996* (London: Faber & Faber, 1996): 266–303.

57. Meštrović, *Postemotional Society.*

58. ———, *Postemotional Society,* 2–17, 42–98.

59. ———, *Postemotional Society,* 1.

60. Kevin Phillips, "The American Presidency and the Rise of the Religious Right," in his *American Dynasty: Aristocracy, Fortune, and the Politics of Deceit in the House of Bush* (New York: Viking, 2004), 211–44.

61. See above, nn. 11 and 17–18.

62. Shuck, *Marks of the Beast,* 18; cf. Vondung, *Magie und Manipulation;* Roger Griffin, " 'I Am No Longer Human. I Am A Titan. A God!' The Fascist Quest To Regenerate Time. History Seminar," http://www.history.ac.uk/eseminars/sem22.html (last accessed July 31, 2006).

63. Phillips, *American Theocracy,* xiii–xiv.

64. Thus here and subsequently, we move toward clarifying the nature of the connections between modes of contemporary political involvement and shifting

concepts of political legitimacy (civil religion, America's legitimating ideology or fundamental beliefs, the rather generic set of God-connected and
government- and value-anchoring beliefs that are essential to forging a common identity and setting the nation apart from other nations). For as it turns
out, those premises, in a time of perceived crisis and threatened decay and
decline, tend to vary in ways that are linked consistently with greater or lesser
kinds of political involvement. Specifically, we need to explore the possibility that, far from being a bland and inconsequential set of assumptions, civil
religion in America may contain within it assumptions that, once activated,
turn out to stand in positive association with highly activist or conservative
courses of action: for if one truly regards America as an elect nation, one must
conclude by the same token, that some other nations probably are not and
that in consequence, certain courses of action are prescribed for Americans.
Now, while it might be tempting to ascribe the veering of the political center rightwards to either laziness on the part of the Left or to the more than
two-thousand-year-old organizing and propagandizing experience of Judeo-
Christian organizational structures (churches, temples, professional clergy, and
their followers) basically convinced of their divine right of being implicitly
if not explicitly supported by governments they in turn support, the analysis
takes us beyond these points. It suggests that directions or biases are built in
to American rhetorics of legitimation, as it were activatable built-in steering
devices, mechanisms for emergency use that—in extreme situations—tend to
come into play in such a way as to predispose American policy under certain
kinds of specific stress to move in certain "elect nation" or divinely favored
directions, directions that by this point appear as "conservative" or Rightist,
but that in any case favor a consistent strengthening of state power and inter-
vention at home and abroad. Whether that kind of default course toward a
blatantly religious politics (one in which the religion of "civil religion" implies
more than an occasional mention of God when opening Congress), meaning
the course traversed over the last forty years, must remain as the only way, or
whether a relocating of direction and course is feasible, also deserves eventual
consideration. Background: Robert N. Bellah, "Civil Religion in America,"
Daedalus (Fall 2005), http://www.findarticles.com/p/articles/mi_qa3671/
is_200510/ai_n15744610/print (last accessed July 24, 2007); Rolf Schieder,
Civil Religion: Die religiöse Dimension der politischen Kultur (Gütersloh: Gerd
Mohn 1987); Vondung, *The Apocalypse in Germany;* Ernest Lee Tuveson,
Redeemer Nation: The Idea of America's Millennial Role (Chicago: University
of Chicago Press, 1980); Emilio Gentile, *The Sacralization of Politics in Fascist
Italy,* trans. Keith Botsford (Cambridge, Mass.: Harvard University Press,
1996); idem., *Le religioni della politica. Fra democrazie e totalitarismi, collana
«Storia e Società »* (Rome: Laterza, 2001); Griffin, "Withstanding the Rush of
Time"; idem., "The Palingenetic Core of Fascist Nationalism,'"in *Che cos'è il
fascismo? Interpretazioni e prospettive di ricerche,* ed. Alessandro Campi (Rome:
Ideazione Editrice, 2003), 97–122; idem., "Cloister or Cluster?" 33–52; Robert

Higgs, *Resurgence of the Warfare State: The Crisis Since 9/11* (San Francisco: Independent Institute, 2005); Kevin Phillips, "The American Presidency and the Rise of the Religious Right," in his *American Dynasty: Aristocracy, Fortune, and the Politics of Deceit in the House of Bush* (New York: Viking, 2004): 211–44; and (with caution!) Katherine Yurica with Laurie Hall, "The Despoiling of America: How George W. Bush Became the Head of the New American Dominionist Church/State," *Yurica Report*, February 11, 2004, http://www.yuricareport.com/Dominionism/TheDespoilingOfAmerica.htm (last accessed July 17, 2006); North and DeMar, *Christian Reconstruction;* Claes Ryn, *America the Virtuous: The Crisis of Democracy and the Quest for Empire* (Brunswick, N.J.: Transaction Publishers, 2004); Bacevich, *The New American Militarism.*

Chapter 7

1. For the direction of Gray's development, see his many books, of course; besides *Enlightenment's Wake,* we single out in particular his *Endgames: Questions in Late Modern Political Thought* (Cambridge/Oxford: Polity Press/Blackwell, 1997), esp. his "Foreword," vi–xi, e.g., ix: " . . . the Soviet collapse may in retrospect be seen . . . [as] very nearly the opposite of what Francis Fukuyama read into it when he interpreted it as signifying the universal triumph of the western idea and the end of history. One of the endgames plotted in this book is that of the westernizing universalism that has animated the political projects both of the Left and of the Right." Again, in the same place: "The animating theme of this volume [*Endgames*] is the meltdown, as yet far from complete, of the ideologies that governed the modern period."

2. See esp. Edward Luttwak, "Why Fascism is the Wave of the Future," *London Review of Books* 16, April 7, 1994, 3, 6; cited in Gray, *Enlightenment's Wake,* n. 5, p. 190. See also Luttwak, *Turbo-Capitalism: Winners and Losers in the Global Economy* (New York: HarperCollins, 1999).

3. Gray, *Enlightenment's Wake,* 101.

4. For these and related points see for example Gray, *Enlightenment's Wake,* 88–91, 93, 95, 100–1, 105, 108, 121, 126, 129, 145–55, 179.

5. Edward Luttwak, "Why Fascism is the Wave of the Future," *London Review of Books* 16, April 7, 1994, 3, 6; cited Gray, *Enlightenment's Wake,* n. 5, p. 190. See also Luttwak, *Turbo-Capitalism.*

6. Gray, *Enlightenment's Wake,* 88–108, 110, 179. Gray at several places dwells on the stumbling block that the givenness, nonchosenness, of identity poses for advocates of an infinitely exportable free market version of the Enlightenment self (reduced to mall-walking and online-trading *homo economicus* worldwide).

7. An argument made in several ways by John Gray throughout his *Enlightenment's Wake,* e.g., 95–184.

8. E.g., Gray, *Enlightenment's Wake,* 95–129, 144–55.

9. For Gray's model, see for example Gray, *Enlightenment's Wake,* 95, passim. Whether the model of the difficulties of Thatcherism can be seen to apply to

contemporary American reporting of government-generated statistics remains to be seen. See Darrell Huff, *How to Lie with Statistics* (New York: W. W. Norton, 1993; 1st ed., 1954); Robert Pollin, *Contours of Descent: U.S. Economic Fractures and the Landscape of Global Austerity* (London: Verso, 2003).

10. Edward Luttwak, "Why Fascism is the Wave of the Future," *London Review of Books*, April 7, 1994, 3, 6, cited in Gray, *Enlightenment's Wake*, n. 5, p. 190; Edward Luttwak, *The Endangered American Dream: How to Stop the United States from Becoming a Third World Country and How to Win the Geo-Economic Struggle for Economic Supremacy* (New York: Simon & Schuster, 1993); Richard Rorty, *Achieving Our Country: Leftist Thought in Twentieth-Century America* (Cambridge, Mass.: Harvard University Press, 1999); Luttwak, *Turbo-Capitalism*.

11. Gray, *Enlightenment's Wake*, 155; see also 145.

12. ———, *Enlightenment's Wake*, 155.

13. ———, *Enlightenment's Wake*, 95.

14. The entire set of these dilemmas, we reiterate here in detail, was strikingly foreshadowed over a decade ago by philosopher John Gray in an extremely negative treatment of the prospects of Enlightenment humanism in an age of globalization. Now, in fuller context and looking back on our selection of pessimistic documents in context, we can begin to see the fuller significance of the outlook of Gray sketched above precisely because of the way that scenario of weakening connects with the downs or ups of real-world economic conditions. Gray, we recall, asserts that globalization and liberal economic reduction of Western individualism to universally fungible versions of the economic self tends to be self-defeating. That is, claims Gray, it winds up undoing the structures of lived community that make life worth enduring and defending over time, so that the globalization championed by allies of Reagan and Thatcher ends by depriving Western individualism of the heritage of lived community values that its various embodiments require to maintain plausible hope for survival—and makes sustainable political legitimacy perilously dependent on overt signs of continuing tangible prosperity and abundance. In pointing to the specifically British decline of support for Thatcherism as a paradigm for what is to be expected longterm elsewhere, Gray writes: "The parties will be judged on how they address issues having to do with the quality of life rather than on narrow issues of economic management" (*Enlightenment's Wake*, 95). It is precisely in this connection then that Gray goes on to cite the fateful words of Edward Luttwak in an essay Luttwak entitled "Why Fascism is the Wave of the Future":

> ". . . neither the moderate Right nor the moderate Left even recognizes let alone offers any solution for, the central problem of our days: the completely unprecedented personal economic insecurity of working people, from industrial workers and white-collar clerks to medium-high managers." (Gray, *Enlightenment's Wake*, 96; quoting Luttwak, "Why Fascism is the Wave of the Future," 6)

Again—deliberately reiterating for emphasis—we point to Gray's pithy words from 1995, which here connect the weakening of traditional structures of social legitimacy with the placing of an unprecedented burden on economic indicators:

> The effect of market liberalism has been to run down our common stock of cultural traditions by propagating the absurd view that we do not need a common culture but only common rules, while the patent failings of this . . . view have inspired the vain attempt to recapture a lost cultural unity. Cultural fundamentalism has emerged in a vain attempt to shore up the tottering edifice of market fundamentalism. Neither conservative position answers to our present needs. (Gray, *Enlightenment's Wake*, 110; cf. p. 108)

Now of course Gray's position here involves the view that Christianity and economic individualism and secular humanism are different editions of the same basic text, so that (in millennial American terms) evangelical fundamentalisms as cultural myths and globalizing free market economics are inherently supportive of each other—with, we would suppose, the further corollary that any culture-wide weakening of a sense of powerful individual human agency likely would be reflected across the palette of alternatives. And precisely that weakening, in a situation in which official rhetoric remains assertively individualistic even as governmental and socioeconomic pressures nonetheless render the individual more and more likely to feel hollow and impotent, precisely that multifactorial undermining, and with it the rise of ever more self-regulating modes of social control of the hollowed-out individual, is what we have traced in the work at hand.

15. Thomas Molnar, *Twin Powers: Politics and the Sacred* (Grand Rapids: Eerdmans, 1988); Neuhaus, *The Naked Public Square.* Here one has to do with a highly traditional or paleo view of the necessity of transcendence for adequate political legitimacy. This may be termed a minority self-perception, one that of course thinks it has located a root cause for American fragmentation and crisis. Now our attempts to start a debate on the accuracy of this minority self-perception and the concomitant pessimistic view of the realities of American politics and public life must allow that these minority report religious pessimists have never given up entirely on the possibility that for those who so perceive themselves, the situation could perhaps be improved. That hope has rested on the possibility that idealized American participatory democracy had rested for two hundred years on an unstable and shifting compromise involving forces with debts to Arminian and even predestinarian Christianity in constant tension with Stoic and Enlightenment or Renaissance humanist, even totally secular, outlooks, all operating within some shared and fuzzy-edged common outlook—one inherited from Greece and Rome, but also from Sinai and Jerusalem and for that matter from Paris, London, Wittenberg, and Geneva. As for the present authors, we do not pronounce on whether adequate legitimacy requires transcendence, at least in the Western tradition. However, we definitely have

supposed that the accelerating decay of the conventional American shared outlook of selfhood and moral responsibility in the later decades of the American
twentieth century correlates with both the sense of fragmentation and powerlessness and with the stronger and stronger calls for a highly ideologized religious re-legitimating of American public life along extremely intense lines—a
view not too far from that espoused, for example, by Kevin Phillips when he
writes with regard to the currents leading up to the so-called "American theocracy" under the second President named Bush:

> Such was religion's enduring importance in the United States when it was
> trod upon in the 1960s and thereafter by secular advocates determined
> to push Christianity out of the public square, a mistake that unleashed
> an evangelical, fundamentalist, and Pentecostal counterreformation that
> in some ways is still building. . . . strong theocratic pressures are already
> visible in the Republican national coalition and its leadership, while
> the substantial portion of Christian America committed to theories of
> Armageddon and the inerrancy of the Bible has already made the GOP
> into America's first religious party.

Now hitherto our discussion has not dismissed definitively the possibility
that by serious tinkering and a bit of good luck the trend toward extreme decay
of the classic American paradigm, the idealization of some version of participatory politics resting on interplay between various forces stressing human worth
and moral responsibility, could be stopped—even to a degree rolled back. But
since this is a mapping of territory with an eye on the religious and the transcendent, at the end we have to admit the obvious: the truly alarmed Americans
about whom Phillips is writing, those who have allegedly "already made the
GOP into America's first religious party" are becoming more and more skeptical
about moderate measures, that is, not at all so optimistic.

In point of fact, for the kind of observers Phillips describes, pessimism is
the norm; for their theoreticians and ideologues have long since gone on record
about the empirical and theoretical impossibility of any such retrieval, and that
because in their view it is in principle impossible. This gloomy view rests on the
conviction that the real issue in American politics is religion or foreclosing of it
in modernity, and that in turn because, ultimately, the vision of transcendence
in a society is what determines everything else in public life, like it or not. On
such a view, the move from the Renaissance into the Enlightenment and then
the age of Darwin and Einstein has been a period of increasingly definitive cutting off from effective sources and models of transcendent order that could yield
common values and common agreement on what responsible selves and participatory politics could mean aside from barely suppressed anarchy threatening to
turn into civil war of an extreme variety. Moreover, on such a view the United
States from 1776 to some point in the later twentieth century was as it were
living as an entire society off of capital that Enlightenment modernity ostentatiously refused to renew or even reinvest—a transcendent capital perhaps still
available publicly in the early Enlightenment, but one decisively shut off when,

around 1800, walls of separation were erected (state by state) to separate public life from transcendent religiosity.

On such a view, once the common coherence of American society has exhausted its nonrenewable capital of transcendent order derived from its origins in the Christian faith of the founders of Massachusetts Bay and Virginia and the other original plantations of the colonial East Coast, and decisively moved into the world of rule-governed secularism, that common coherence has embarked upon an entirely untried course, with unforeseeable results, a frightening experiment that almost immediately evoked extreme course correction of the kind described by Kevin Phillips and advocated by readers of *Left Behind* and Reconstructionist volumes.

This view of matters is all the more striking because it is put forth with specific reference to postwar America by any number of conservative writers whose theology has significant differences. For this perspective religion is a largely unmentionable elephant in the room of mainstream liberal analysis, but an elephant that bulks very large for most Americans. It was after all none other than the greatest of all theoreticians of historical atheism and secularization, Karl Marx, who prefaced all his work on the advance of atheistical communism with the admission that he could not go forward before the historical process (embodied in the Left Hegelianism of Feuerbach) had first disposed of otherworldly illusions and the brakes represented by centuries of faith in a transcendent power. The gloomy point of view just mentioned—maintaining that America's coherence as a polity and society has been living off a transcendent capital that, as an order-conferring power, began to give out in the later twentieth century—is one essentially coherent with that of Karl Marx: for such a point of view, if the public order as such decisively moves into a totally secular mode, it has carried out a tremendously important step, one thought irresevisble by liberals, yet one demanding reversal if improvement is to be obtained.

Now mainstream academic American thinking supposes that civil religion and the ceaseless vigor of American churches and sects can endlessly replenish a kind of generic force or religiopolitical *mana* highly desirable for politicians and secular liberals wishing to live in a stable polity undergirded by a shared sense of order yet immune from excessive religious zeal. Precisely that point is denied by the kind of observers who maintain that the society as such must explicitly seek a pattern of order derived from transcendence or automatically make a gradual descent into irretrievable anarchy—the point of view behind activists of many stripes, including those like Tim LaHaye who describe anarchy in literally apocalyptic terms. Likewise, Dominionists and Reconstructionists do not paint the horror of disorder in eschatological terms, yet they devote equal energy to seeking a return to transcendent order at the expense of unbelievers and liberals. This point of view wants to reverse the move to secularity that Marx and secularists thought irreversible, to make visible the invisible elephant of religion in public life.

Obviously this strong transcendence or "no cheap renewal of religious energy in politics" school of thought is very rarely heard from in detail in academic circles: on that account, and because of the ominous and inscrutable signs on the American horizon, we have decided to give the reader a more detailed look at how articulate theorists of Christian conservatism view the unfolding of the American story. We could choose from any number of theoreticians, including some extreme cases from Calvinist Reconstructionism who combine advocacy of stoning (lapidation) for adulterers with written attacks on the separation of church and state. But we have chosen to restrict ourselves here to an advocate of a "strong transcendence" perspective less readily characterized simply as an irrational extremist in order to illustrate for readers the full force of the Christian conservative point of view as a position that will need to be answered in detail and effectively if activists on the moderate Left are to capture undecided voters with worries overlapping those of the Christian Right.

Our example of an analyst making use of a strong transcendence or high Christian position with regard to modern society and the prospects for the post-modern self in a situation of religious pluralism or indifference does amount to something of a minority reporter among intellectuals who have taught at colleges and universities, but there can be no doubt concerning his broad education, profound learning, and incisive analytical powers. He is a European Roman Catholic of conservative persuasion very familiar with the America he has lived in for decades. He can serve here as the most academically respectable articulator of a religious perspective on decline that in fact is paralleled in Protestant circles by writers far more extreme who write from apocalyptic or from Dominionist perspectives. Yet a basic congruence on the importance of transcendence for social order and the necessity of decline in the absence of transcendent order unites all these conservative perspectives.

Let us examine the outline of this view at its most sophisticated. The Hungarian-American Catholic thinker Thomas Molnar is a conservative Roman Catholic with a strong mastery of anthropological and sociological theory, including some of the most sophisticated French thinkers. His 1988 work, *The Twin Powers*, is far too complex to summarize in detail here, but its outline is of interest as a high-level summary of what many Christian conservatives instinctively conclude even though they may have no familiarity with conservative social theory and may have interest in Roman Catholics only as temporary tactical allies in political activism.

The general point of view can be surmised already. For Molnar, traditional societies became ordered bodies only by means of founding visions institutionalized for the purpose of ensuring continuity and organic cooperation. The state in the tradition of the Christian West was, along with the church, the mediator of this transcendent power and authority and thereby derived an authority behind its power resting among other things on the capacity to produce steady cooperation. For Molnar, postEnlightenment modernity in its various regional forms constitutes the conscious denial of this traditional arrangement and the sacralization of the people and their governments or bureaucracies, in the meantime utilizing remnants and memories of the former mediation of transcendence in order to encourage hope in a new beginning and a new future on a new basis. Built in to the new arrangement in various areas of modernity is an institutionalization of constant envy and conflict between competing pressure groups. As to the outcome, according to Molnar it is unknowable, since before the Enlightenment and the revolutions of the eighteenth century no experiments in a society with no institutional mediation of transcendence had been tried; but Molnar is exceedingly skeptical about this experiment, fearing the worst.

For in Molnar's diagnosis, the empirical result (two hundred years on) amounts to an unending envious anarchy and moral chaos, a society in decline and disarray, one unable to count on the stable production of organic social organs and one increasingly in difficulties with mounting crime and accelerating disunity. As for experiments in artificially producing a substitute for transcendence under secularized conditions, they are doomed to failure, as the Soviet example and the Nazi example illustrate. In addition, Molnar explicitly comments on how the traditional and axiomatic public function of religion becomes an unmentionable topic in official discourse after the secularization of society with the triumph of modernity.

Two further points made by Molnar are of considerable interest here. First, Molnar adopts so strong a version of his position that he denies any pluralist-based restoration of some version of transcendence is possible or practicable. Specifically he denies practicality to the proposal of Richard Neuhaus, according to which a propluralistic, mitigated version of traditional Christianity could restore American society to a kind of integrated functioning adequate to preserve it from descent into self-destructive outright anarchy, which in the view of Catholics like Molnar and Neuhaus and their Protestant readers appears as a real and none-too-distant possibility. For Molnar, the sacred pattern is so primal that it appears to him pointless to start with the primacy of political order as something to serve as the end for which religiosity is to be the means: such a view is for Molnar obviously a misunderstanding that can have no lasting good results. The religious perspective is taken as primary.

Second, it is noteworthy that Molnar's diagnosis directly connects the modernist separating of transcendent religiosity from public order with the appearance of what we have summed up as "hollowed out selves." Molnar writes: " . . . such brilliant writers as Aldous Huxley, George Orwell, Evgeny Zamatin, and Alexander Zinoviev suggest that society's desacralization leads to the mechanical efficiency and robotization of humanity. Such literature . . . never existed before—it is a true invention of our century." Thus, far from seeing extreme religious ideology as a source for a "hollowed out" self, Molnar (writing before the political prominence of dispensationalists and extreme Dominonists) tends to focus on Virilio-like or Melley-like factors as the sole cause for the appearance of images of robots and zombies.

This kind of sophisticated statement is not what most Christian conservatives read, nor are they likely to read its nearest analogues amid educated Protestants like Gary North. Nonetheless the thrust of these interconnected points and their coherence as a minority report summing up modernity and postmodernity is grasped intuitively by many on the Right, if one is to judge from the success of cultural activist campaign approaches. Activists and thinkers wishing to check the advance of the Christian Right in the public sphere will need to provide a coherent and credible Leftist alternative analytic vision for social processes if they are serious about capturing swing votes in election campaigns at all levels. In addition, they will need to understand what Marx on the Left did understand in Germany, the fact that purely secular and materialist politics cannot be a topic for limited discussion until religious issues of transcendence have been settled one way or another. Whether America can produce its own Feuerbach, rendering religious questions largely obsolete and preparing the way for a regional Marx on his or her continent, is an open question.

Beyond this, readers who do not at all share Christian conservative views, and who see religious scripting in an eschatological or predestinarian mode as a potential source for fatalistic and deterministic views of the self (a point of view that, in millennial American context we have upheld in this book), need to reflect on the paradoxical claim made by some experts that Augustine's entire outlook did not result in a simple transformation of believers into robots, at least from their point of view. One of the most eminent of experts on late antiquity and early Christianity, Charles Norris Cochrane, in fact contended that classical philosophy had failed to provide a reasoned and sustainable philosophical basis for active engagement in the world based on walking a line between mechanistic determinism and slavish repetition of eternal archetypes. Augustine the Christian philosopher, argued Cochrane, did however provide such a basis, and did so paradoxically while upholding a predestinarian view of religious orientation, doing this (thus Cochrane) without running the danger that one could "rescue mankind from the tyranny of nature only to make him the puppet of God"—which latter outcome Cochrane vehemently and cogently denies specifically with regard to the mature Augustine's overall outlook.

On Cochrane's account (and detailed it is, precluding summary here), Augustine integrated the life of the senses and the life of the body with the individual quest for a rational happiness under divine guidance, thereby foreclosing at once both the notion of human beings as mere "automata" and the burden of national or ethnic secularist politics embodied in a deified government. This Augustine is said to have rejected in favor of an eternal commonwealth of spiritually free individuals illuminated by a rational and defensible quest for happiness in the universally good and beneficent. Cochrane put forward this synthesis (and implicit defense) of Augustine as a kind of philosophical antidote to what he saw in 1939 as the dangers of totalitarian anthropology coming from Hitler and Stalin, moreover presenting Augustine's paradoxical enlisting of predestination in a bigger program of defending divine illumination of individuals as antiquity's final answer to the perennial questions and thus one of interest in his own day.

We cannot investigate in detail whether Cochrane's reading of Augustine has merit on its own. But the perennial appeal of such views to cultural conservatives and pessimists does need to be underlined. That appeal, like the internal consistency of Molnar's kind of pessimistic diagnosis of millennial American society, must be thoroughly understood if defenders of Enlightenment modernity and its political alliances with freewill Christianity and other currents (certain strands in New Age, for example) are to have any success in posing viable alternatives to the high intensity rejuvenation programs advanced by America's religious right.

For all this with regard to documentation, see Kevin Phillips, *American Theocracy*, xiii–xiv; Gary North, *Political Polytheism: The Myth of Pluralism* (Tyler, Tex.: Institute for Christian Economics, 1989) gives a Christian Reconstructionist updating of Charles Beard's view of the composing of the United States Constitution as a plot or conspiracy, not from economic motives, but with the motive of carrying out a Deist-Newtonian-Freemasonic conspiracy to undo the Christian-Trinitarian oaths binding together citizens in twelve of the thirteen existing states, thereby imposing a secularized "Rhode Island" model on the subsequent version of American polity. See further Molnar, *Twin Powers*, 108–19, 128–32, 138ff., and esp. 138, n. 30. In addition, it is equally remarkable how Molnar's analysis furnishes a kind of preliminary theoretical explanation for how contemporary politics and policy, however locked in by elites for elite purposes, curiously seem to favor the appearance of supporting theatrically countercultural positions. According to Molnar, from the outset scripts for reconstituting society on a secularized and "modern" basis amounted to a permanent glorification of outgroups and the values temporarily celebrated by festivals of carnivalistic misrule in order to legitimate the radical and total reversal of values represented by the shutting-out of transcendent order at the triumph of secularist Enlightenment. See Molnar, 114–15. A moment's reflection will suffice to show how Molnar here is in effect providing an explanation for how remembered perception of historic loss can become a major factor in modern policy-formation and political life, a fact usually but not uniformly viewed critically by religious conservatives. See also Charles Norris Cochrane, *Christianity and Classical Culture: A Study of Thought and Action from Augustus to Augustine* (Oxford: Clarendon, 1940, 1944, 1957), 437, 480, 481, 508–13; "puppet," 481; "automata," 508. Cochrane's argument is connected with the way the Augustinian rejection of an automaton-anthropology is represented as bound up with the rejection of notions of the entire cosmos as a giant machine.

16. Cf. Michael Vlahos, "The Weakness of Empire," *American Conservative*, May 22, 2006, http://amconmag.com/2006/2006_05_22/feature.html (last accessed July 16, 2006): "In crisis, a republic can claim all the energy and resources of its citizens because in the end the citizenry and the republic are the same. In empires, however, former republican citizens have given over their political authority to the trust and keeping of empire—and also their deepest responsibility to the nation as well. The emperor now manages; the emperor now defends.

This is the heart of the imperial compact, and it is expressive of a fundamental political transaction: the citizens yield over management powers to the imperial person in exchange for a release from civic responsibility."

17. Cf. Meštrović, *Postemotional Society.* As John Gray himself realized back in 1995, Western political legitimacy has rested most ultimately not on mere economic performance, but on claims to institutionalize a unique vision of accessibility to the knowing self as the locus of ultimate truth and meaning and to make that vision accessible in ways conducive to justice. This vision, leading in the Enlightenment and in Arminian Christianity to the enshrining of individual choice as a desirable and indeed exportable sine qua non, encounters a reality obstacle in the fact that (as Gray pointed out repeatedly) cultural and individual identities are in fact not only unchosen givens in most situations, but as well givens that the players often will die to keep rather than exchanging for a hollowed-out, fungible identity of choice optimized through lack of social and faith content. For Gray, this dilemma signifies that the entire civic humanist and Enlightenment project of truth and institutionalized liberty is but an illusory notion. Yet this entire circumstance itself rests on certain prior assumptions and developments that Gray does not consider in adequate detail.

18. The work of Griffin has certain connections, for example, with the work of Klaus Vondung. See Vondung, *The Apocalypse in Germany,* and above all his earlier work *Magie und Manipulation: Ideologischer Kult und politische Religion des Nationalsozialismus* (Göttingen: Vandenhoeck & Ruprecht, 1971).

19. Emilio Gentile, "Fascism, Totalitarianism and Political Religion: Definitions and Critical Reflections on Criticism of an Interpretation," trans. Natalie Belozentseva, *Totalitarian Movements and Political Religions* 5.3 (2004): 326–75, esp. 337–38, 361, 364, 365, 339, 355–56, 334–35, 349, 352, 345, 346; idem., "The Sacralisation of Politics: Definitions, Interpretations and Reflections on the Question of Secular Religion and Totalitarianism," *Totalitarian Movements and Political Religions* 1.1 (2000): 18–55. See also Alessandro Campi, ed., *Che cos' è il fascismo* (Rome: Ideazione, 2003), xxxix–xliv (cited by Gentile in "Fascism, Totalitarianism and Political Religion," 355–56). See also Gentile, in "Fascism, Totalitarianism and Political Religion," 374, n. 56, who cites Roger Griffin, "The Palingenetic Political Community: Rethinking the Legitimation of Totalitarian Regimes in Inter-War Europe," *Totalitarian Movements and Political Religions* 3.3 (2002): 37.

20. See Gentile, "Fascism, Totalitarianism and Political Religion," 356, citing Campi; also Gentile, "Fascism, Totalitarianism and Political Religion," 352, on revolutionary totalitarianism as a "process" aiming at ongoing change "which by its nature can never be considered 'perfect' or 'completed.'"

21. In the 2004 article referred to in the previous notes, Gentile cites (besides works mentioned immediately above) Roger Griffin, *The Nature of Fascism* (London: Pinter, 1991), as well as Griffin, "Withstanding the Rush of Time," in *What History Tells Us: George L. Mosse and the Culture of Modern Europe* (Madison: University of Wisconsin Press, 2004), 110–33.

22. Gentile, "Fascism, Totalitarianism and Political Religion," 327–29, 337, 339, 342, 352, 356.

23. ———, "Fascism, Totalitarianism and Political Religion," 356, 334, 314.

24. Gore Vidal, "The Erosion of the American Dream," *Prometheus,* Dateline, SBS-TV Australia, interview of March 12, 2003, http://www.meaus.com/gore-vidal-03.htm (last accessed November 13, 2006).

25. Here Fritz Stern obviously means to compare Adolf Hitler's presentation as a savior descending from the clouds in *Triumph of the Will* with George W. Bush's presentation of himself descending from the clouds onto an aircraft carrier. Note how Stern is at pains to insist that ordinarily he resists facile parallels with Nazi-related extremism, but does not do so now. Jordan Mejias, "Amerika unter Bush: Die Leni-Riefenstalisierung," *Frankfurter Allgemeine Zeitung,* January 20, 2005, http://www.faznet/s/Rub117C535CDF414415BB243B18B8B60AE?Doc~E4 42A4421BB514732A8659D451A81D433~ATplnEcommon~Scontent.html (last accessed November 13, 2006).

26. Basic background in John Armitage, ed., *Paul Virilio: From Modernism to Hypermodernism and Beyond* (London: SAGE Publications, 2000), 1–24. See also Hubert L. Dreyfus and Harry Kreisler, "Conversation With History: Hubert Dreyfus: Artificial Intelligence," http://globetrotter.berkeley.edu/people5/Dreyfus/dreyfus-con6.html (last accessed July 2, 2006).

27. Basic: "Paul Virilio," *Wikipedia,* http://en.wikipedia.org/wiki/Paul_Virilio (last accessed July 17, 2006); Steve Redhead and Paul Virilio, *A Theorist for an Accelerated Culture* (Edinburgh: Edinburgh University Press, 2004). See also Georg Christoph Tholen, "Geschwindigkeit als Dispositiv: Zun Horizont der Dromologie im Werk Paul Virilius," in Von Michel Serres bis Julia Kristeva (Freiburg: Rombach Verla, 1999), 135–62. Excerpt online under the same title at http://www.sammelpunkt.philo.at:8080/archive/00000204/01/ 16573.0.thovirilio.pdf (last accessed July 24, 2007).

28. This formulation is a close paraphrase of the summary of Virilio's work in the important study by Jason Adams, "POPULAR DEFENSE IN THE EMPIRE OF SPEED: Paul Virilio and the Phenomenology of the Political Body," M.A. thesis, Political Science, Simon Fraser University, November, 2003, online at http://www.geocities.com/ringfingers/thesis.html (unpaginated) (last accessed June 2, 2006). Adams' careful and multifaceted work is fundamental to a real grasp of Virilio and is relied on heavily throughout this section on account of its clarity and capacity for making important connections. Adams' study is a logical point of departure for any serious study of Virilio's widely dispersed and enigmatic texts. Also of significance is the work of his advisers, i.e., Ian Angus, *Disfigurations: Discourse/Critique/Ethics* (London: Verso, 2000) and Andrew Feenberg, *Transforming Technology* (New York: Oxford University Press, 2002). On Virilio, see for example by Sylvère Lotringer and Virilio *The Accident of Art;* Virilio, *Ground Zero;* Armitage, *Paul Virilio;* Armitage and Graham, "Dromoeconomics," 111–23; Virilio, *Art and Fear;* idem., *The Information Bomb;* Virilio, *The Aesthetics of Disappearance* (New York: Semiotext[e],

1991); idem., *Lost Dimension* (New York: Semiotext[e], 1991); idem., *Strategy of Deception* (London: Verso, 2000); idem., *War and Cinema;* idem., *City of Panic;* Douglas Kellner, "Virilio, War and Technology," in Armitage, ed., *Paul Virilio;* or as Kellner, "Virilio, War and Technology: Some Critical Reflections," in *Illuminations: The Critical Theory Project,* http://www.gseis.ucla.edu/faculty/kellner/Illumina%20Folder/kell29.htm (last accessed July 17, 2006); Douglas Kellner, *Jean Baudrillard: From Marxism to Postmodernism and Beyond* (Stanford: Stanford University Press, 1989); Louise Wilson, "Cyberwar, God and Television: Interview with Paul Virilio. Louise Wilson for CTHEORY," in which Virilio says: " . . . The research on cyberspace is a quest for God. To be God," www.ctheory.net/text_file.asp?pick=62 (last accessed July 17, 2006); cf. on so-called god-games Shawn Miklaucic, "Virtual Real(i)ty: SimCity and the Production of Urban Cyberspace," *Game Research,* http://www.game-research.com/art_simcity.asp (last accessed July 17, 2006).

29. See for example Virilio, *Desert Screen: War at the Speed of Light,* trans. Michael Degener (London: Continuum, 2005).

30. Adams, chap. 1, part 3, http://www.geocities.com/ringfingers/thesis.html, unpaginated (last accessed June 2, 2006).

31. ———, chap. 1, part 3, vital for our view of the matter here and closely followed in our text, http://www.geocities.com/ringfingers/thesis.html, unpaginated (last accessed June 2, 2006).

32. ———, chap. 1, introduction, closely followed here and important for our take on these issues.

33. Here relying on the key discussion of cyborg technology and its implications in Jason Adams, esp. his second chapter.

34. See "Paul Virilio," *Wikipedia,* http://en.wikipedia.org/wiki/Paul_Virilio (last accessed August 1, 2006). Background: Claus Morisch, *Technikphilosophie bei Paul Virilio: Domologie* (Würzburg: Ergon-Verlag, 2002).

35. Here making use of numerous suggestions on the interconnection of Virilio's notions of resistance in Adams, chaps. 2 and 3. Additional documentation in, for example, Redhead, *Reader,* 210ff.

36. Louise Wilson, "Cyberwar, God, And Television: Interview with Paul Virilio," ctheory.net, ed. Arthur and Marililouise Kroker, December 1, 1994, http://www.ctheory.net/articles.aspx?id=62 (last accessed July 17, 2006).

37. Virilio, *Ground Zero:* 39–43.

38. ———, *Ground Zero,* 39–43.

39. Here again we rely on the important synthesis of disparate concepts in Virilio in Adams, chaps. 2 and 3.

40. Redhead, *Reader,* 228.

41. Wilson, "Cyberwar."

42. Cf. for example Der Derian, 29ff.

43. Adams, "Abstract," a key formulation of the issues in this connection. We cannot recommend the analysis and synthesis in Adams highly enough—even though we do not share his basic outlook of so-called postanarchism.

44. Note the use of Bill Joy by Virilio in conjunction with the reading of Genesis as the narrative of a "scientific suicide," in Redhead, *Reader,* 250

45. As Ernst Jünger mythically explained in the 1930s; see the background in Michael E. Zimmerman, *Heidegger's Confrontation with Modernity* (Bloomington: Indiana University Press, 1990); text available as Ernst Jünger, *Der Arbeiter: Herrschaft und Gesellschaft,* Cotta's Bibliothek der Moderne (Stuttgart: Klett-Cotta, 1982; 1st ed., 1932).

46. Redhead, *Reader* 259–61.

47. Paul Virilio, *Speed and Politics: An Essay on Dromology* (New York: Semiotext[e], 1986), 101, 122.

48. ———, *Popular Defenses,* 66

49. ———, *Popular Defense,* 64f. See also Adams, chaps. 2 and 3 in his key discussion. See also David Cook, "Paul Virilio: The Politics of 'Real Time,'" ctheory. net, January 16, 2003, http://www.ctheory.net/articles.aspx?d=360 (last accessed November 29, 2006).

50. The intersection with phenomenology is nicely put into context by Jason Adams in the first chapter of his thesis, a summary of great importance to our presentation here.

51. See also Adams, chaps. 2 and 3.

52. We note the foregrounding of this theme by Adams in his chap. 3. See also Redhead, *Reader,* 34–37.

53. Virilio, *Speed and Politics,* 101, 122.

54. That such is Virilio's basic drift is understood by the best commentators on him. To be sure, Jason Adams in the later part of his seminal study struggles heroically to argue for practicality of Virilian measures of decelerating resistance to this world-historical tendency; yet the dominance of this tendency is urged with compelling power in the commentary by Douglas Kellner, who doubts the practicality of Virilian resistance. See also Carlos Oliveira, "Global Algorithm 1.7: The Silence of the Lambs: Paul Virilio in Conversation," trans. Patrice Riemens, *ctheory.net,* June 12, 1996, http://www.cheroy.net/articles.aspx?id=38 (last accessed December 3, 2006).

55. Virilio, *Speed and Politics,* 101.

56. Here we remind the reader that we distinguish between an early or Anglo-Scottish or moderate Enlightenment tradition not inherently unfriendly to civic humanism, free will varieties of revealed religion not permitted to control the government, and extreme varieties of the Enlightenment tradition tending toward monism and determinism and a heavy control of religion.

57. Gray, *Enlightenment's Wake,* 110; cf. p. 108. See also Graeme Garrard, "The Curious Enlightenment of Professor Rorty," *CIAO: Critical Review* 14.4 (2000), archived online as http://64.233.161.104/search?q=cache:ADkJhjdebqsJ:www. ciaonet.org/olj/cr/cr_v14_4_gag01.pdf+&hl=en&gl=us&ct=clnk&cd=1 (last accessed July 17, 2006); kindly called to my attention by Mr. Ben Saxton; Edward Luttwak, "Why Fascism is the Wave of the Future," *London Review of Books,* April 7, 1994, 3, 6; cited Gray, *Enlightenment's Wake,* n. 5, p. 190; Luttwak,

The Endangered American Dream: How to Stop the United States from Becoming a Third World Country and How to Win the Geo-Economic Struggle for Economic Supremacy (New York: Simon & Schuster, 1993); Richard Rorty, *Achieving Our Country: Leftist Thought in Twentieth-Century America* (Cambridge, Mass.: Harvard University Press, 1999); Luttwak, *Turbo-Capitalism.*

58. Cf. the note immediately above and the words of William Faulkner: "I believe that man will not merely endure: he will prevail. He is immortal, not because he alone among creatures has an inexhaustible voice, but because he has a soul, a spirit capable of compassion and sacrifice and endurance." William Faulkner, "Banquet Speech: William Faulkner's speech at the Nobel Banquet at the City Hall in Stockholm, December 10, 1950," *Nobel Lectures, Literature 1901–1967,* ed. Horst Frenz (Amsterdam: Elsevier Publishing, 1969), http://nobelprize.org/literature/laureates/1949/faulkner-speech.html (last accessed June 2, 2006).

59. Gray, *Enlightenment's Wake,* 108.

60. ——, *Enlightenment's Wake,* 108.

61. See for example Gray, *Enlightenment's Wake,* 122–23, 106, 113, 117, 126, 121, 110–13, 168, 144–45, 162, 155–56, 161–84.

62. Timothy Melley, *Empire of Conspiracy: The Culture of Paranoia in Postwar America* (Ithaca: Cornell University Press, 1999).

63. Melley, *Empire,* 56ff., 154, 159, 163, 171.

64. Melley, *Empire,* 189.

65. In other words, Melley is working on his version of what this study has been investigating in the wake of the work of Riesman and Meštrović and Hochschild. To us, speaking crassly and broadly, all these images and concepts of intensifying impotence appear as different handles on the same phenomenon, in fact, the production of a self habituated to an economics and politics of docility and servitude under the particular conditions of the electronically linked and corporate driven globalizing economy—and the media-driven, corporate-linked transformation of the political process accompanying this entire set of developments. This process of generating a new kind of controlled and calibrated self (whether consumerbot-controlled, zombie-rapturoid, or even cyborgian postwomynist) seems to us to mark a new stage in social and personal evolution, quite along the forward-projected lines of what Riesman meant to signify years ago with his early work in *The Lonely Crowd.* There he looked at images of human isolation and correlated them with the diffusion of selves subject to an unprecedented degree of socially adaptable internalized control based on forward-leaning chameleon capacity, so to speak.

66. As for tracing the results of this spread of hollowed-out selves, selves lacking in backbone and malleably ready for determination by outside forces and the demands of corporate or social chameleonism, those consequences were already readable for the discerning in the Eisenhower years. The premier chronicler of those years, David Halberstam, following Irving Horowitz's lead, carefully notes how the appearance of this phenomenon occupied the research interests of C. Wright Mills, David Riesman, and Nathan Glazer. At the opening of the

decade already, Mills sounded a double note in American society, one pointing to "the growth of ever greater American power externally" as well as "a feeling of a decrease in personal power among its citizens." The fuller elaboration of the theme came with Riesman and Glazer, who chronicled in detail the emergence of a "lonely crowd" of "outer-directed Americans" who, in the words of Halberstam, "wanted to be a part of the larger community so much they would adjust their morality and ethics to those of the community almost unconsciously; in the end they seemed to take on the coloration of their institutions and neighborhoods with frightening ease."

Halberstam here traces the first stages in registering a long-unfolding change of incalculable significance, one of which insomniac Jack in *Fight Club* (hallucinating at the xerox machine and writing hive-haiku in the office e-mail) will be a late and far advanced symptom. For documentation on the early social science background from the period in question, see Melley, *Empire*. See also David Halberstam, *The Fifties* (New York: Villard Books, 1993), 534 and 533.

67. For example, Melley, *Empire,* 48.
68. Here see esp. Melley, *Empire,* 31–32.
69. Virilio, *Speed and Politics,* 101, 122.
70. See for example chapters two and three in Jason Adams. The centrality of Adams's vision of Virilio for our reading of his works should be kept in mind.
71. We note the foregrounding of this theme by Adams in his third chapter.
72. Virilio, *Speed and Politics,* 101, 122.
73. Joseph J. Trento, *Prelude to Terror: The Rogue CIA and the Legacy of America's Private Intelligence Network* (New York: Carroll & Graf, 2005); James Risen, *State of War: The Secret History of the C.I.A. and the Bush Administration* (New York: Simon & Schuster/Free Press, 2006); Robert O'Harrow, *No Place to Hide: Behind the Scenes of Our Emerging Surveillance Society* (New York: Simon & Schuster/Free Press, 2005); James Bamford, *Body of Secrets: Anatomy of the Ultra-Secret National Security Agency* (Garden City, N.Y.: Anchor, 2002); Johnson, *The Sorrows of Empire*. See also Robert Bryce, Cronies (New York: Public Press, 2004).
74. No mainstream sociologist or political scientist can, by definition, give serious consideration to the possibility that American society and political culture may be approaching the point at which integration according to conventional mechanisms and under conventional American ideology threatens to become impossible: to do so is to rule oneself out of court. Certainly the present authors do not represent such a fringe viewpoint. On the other hand, we do here consider the possibility that American political culture at the moment is undergoing a desperate and far-reaching search for new modes and languages of effective reintegration, and that the candidates for inclusivist reintegration are on the whole as unpromising as is the selection of talents in national politics. As a way of saying the unsayable, see the oblique and determinedly

upbeat suggestions in Paul Cantor, *Gilligan Unbound: Pop Culture in the Age of Globalization* (Lanham, Md.: Rowman & Littlefield, 2001). Scholars writing in later decades will need to consider the debates in millennial America about open and closed borders, mono- or multilingualism, religious identity, academic multiculturalism, and the like in the light not only of demographic data, but also of evidence not yet available on the degree to which conventional American politics does or does not succeed in dealing with rather than excluding from view a wide range of potentially explosive political, social, and economic issues. Only once that untold story has been recounted (and it cannot be told while the current generation of Americans is alive) will observers be able to assess how close America as a political and sociocultural system was to approaching fragmentation in the first decade after the turn of the millennium. And here it will be necessary to pay attention not only to policy decisions made, but as well to questions that could and could *not* be put into words for fear of excommunication in millennial America. Implicit argument in favor of dangerous fragmentation and polarization in the American population runs throughout Phillips, *American Theocracy.* See esp. 389: " . . . the Bush coalition is too narrow to govern successfully. . . ." Note as well p. 347 citing the words of Garry Wills, *The New York Review of Books,* 2005: "If religious extremism is only one large set of bodies in this fringe constellation [of Republican interest groups], it is a powerful one." Or Phillips, 393, speaking of the dominant role in Republican electoral politics of "by an array of outsider religious denominations caught up in biblical morality, distrust of science and a global imperative of political and religious evangelicalism. These groups may represent only a quarter to a third of the U.S. population, but they are mobilized."

75. Claes G. Ryn, "Leo Strauss and History: The Philosopher as Conspirator," *HUMANITAS* 18.1–2 (2005), http://www.nhinet.org/ryn18–1.htm (last accessed April 9, 2006). Cf. John Laughland, "Flirting with Fascism," *American Conservative,* June 30, 2003, http://www.amconmag.com/06_30_03/feature. html (last accessed July 19, 2006).

76. See, for example, Michael Ledeen, "Michael Ledeen—a multicultural personal history," *Pajamasmedia,* http://pajamasmedia.com/pages/2006/01/michael_ ledeen_pj_media_editor.php (last accessed July 19, 2006); Jamie Glazov, "FrontPage Interview: Michael Ledeen," *FrontPageMagazine.com,* December 30, 2003, http://www.frontpagemag.com/articles/ReadArticle.asp?ID=11512 (last accessed July 19, 2006); "Michael A. Ledeen," *Benador Associates, Public Relations,* http://www.benadorassociates.com/ledeen.php (last accessed July 19, 2006); "Michael Ledeen," *Wikipedia,* http://en.wikipedia.org/wiki/Michael_ Ledeen (last accessed July 19, 2006); Michael A. Ledeen, "United States Policy toward Iran: Next Steps. Posted: Wednesday, March 8, 2006. TESTIMONY Committee on International Relations (U.S. House of Representatives)," http:// www.aei.org/publications/pubID.24022,filter.all/pub_detail.asp (last accessed July 19, 2006).

77. Concerning the so-called neoconservatives as a whole and in general, the present authors regard them as a crucially and highly ambiguous phenomenon, and that in more than one key regard, a posture that puts them at the center of many contemporary uncertainties. Above all we do not regard them as essentially hostile to religion, a posture that makes it possible for them to work with evangelical leaders behind the scenes and to coordinate moves in ways hitherto impossible in elite policy making. Their complex neoRomantic roots by no means exclude a sympathy for religion, whether it be Jewish or Christian or generic Western; the ancestors sometimes noted (above all, Leo Strauss, more remotely, various Italian Fascists or protoFascists) include conservatives with an interest in rebuilding Europe after the French Revolution and Napoleon. If Machiavelli is indeed a main source, certainly his attitude toward religion was complex enough that we need not rule out some positive appreciation of its utility. As for the "Trotskyite" component so often noted, we think it is only one of many ingredients in the heritage of the neoconservatives whom we ourselves prefer to think of as neoRomantics, the influential policy-shapers in various think tanks and universities with ties to the inner circles of millennial Republican conservatism. With regard to anthropology, we find no one view dominant among them, and indeed sometimes wonder if they may not at times exercise a restraining effect on the tendency toward nonhumanist determinism in millennial conservatism—though their ties to corporate technocracy do not make us especially optimistic in this connection.

78. See Charles Norris Cochrane, *Christianity and Classical Culture: A Study of Thought and Action from Augustus to Augustine* (Oxford: Clarendon, 1940; rpt. 1944, 1957), for a wartime recourse to Augustine as a defense against the deterministic and authoritarian outlook of the totalitarianism—note esp. 437, 480, 481, 508–13.

79. Reasons for pessimism appear in these works, among others: Paul Craig Roberts, "The Death of U.S. Engineering," *Counterpunch,* June 6, 2006, http://www.counterpunch.org/roberts06062006.html (last accessed July 19, 2006); Gabriel Kolko, "Why a Global Economic Deluge Looms," *Counterpunch,* June 15, 2006, http://www.counterpunch.org/kolko06152006.html (last accessed July 19 2006). See also Paul Craig Roberts, "America's Bleak Jobs Future," *Counterpunch,* March 6, 2006, http://www.counterpunch.org/roberts03062006.html (last accessed July 19, 2006). Roberts's comments are supportable by reference to the research of economists with Left-liberal credentials; the dramatic decline in prospects for stable employment and economic advancement for young white males is strikingly documented in the comparison of the relative prospects for white males entering the job market in the 1960s and the 1980s; see Martina Morris, Mark Stephen Handcock, Marc A. Scott, Annette D. Bernhardt, Mark S. Handcock, *Divergent Paths: Economic Mobility in the New American Labor Market* (New York: Russell Sage Foundation, 2001). See also John Yoo, *The Powers of War and Peace: The Constitution and Foreign Affairs after 9/11* (Chicago: University of Chicago Press, 2005); Gene Healy and Timothy Lynch,

Power Surge: The Constitutional Record of George W. Bush (Washington, D.C.: Cato Institute, 2006); Andrew Bard Schmookler, "An Interview With Bruce Fein," *AfterDowningStreet.org,* June 30, 2006, http://www.afterdowningstreet. org/node/12594 (last accessed July 19, 2006).

Here further recalling the lines cited in the introduction from "Rabbi Ben Ezra" by Robert Browning (1812–1889):

> Grow old along with me!
> The best is yet to be,
> The last of life, for which the first was made:
> Our times are in His hand
> Who saith "A whole I planned,
> Youth shows but half; trust God: see all, nor be afraid!"

For the context in futurist literature, see Johnny Pez, "The History of the Positronic Robot and Empire Novels, 1947–58," http://www.asimovonline. com/oldsite/Robot_Empire_history.html (last accessed July 19, 2006).

Epilogue

1. Certainly it gives cause for reflection when the cover of *Harper's* (April 2006) features eminent policy experts and military analysts discussing the possibilities and impossibilities of a military move against the civilian government of the United States: "Forum: AMERICAN COUP D'ETAT: Military thinkers discuss the unthinkable," by Andrew J. Bacevich, Brig. Gen. Charles J. Dunlap, Jr., Richard H. Kohn, and Edward N. Luttwak, *Harper's* (April 2006): 43–52.

2. Much of this philosophy is owed to the work of Mark C. Taylor. We would like to say we could have come at it completely independently, but scholarship does not work that way. Or, as Professor Taylor might put it, originality is overrated.

Index